CENTURIES OF SILENCE

The Story of Latin American Journalism

Leonardo Ferreira

PRAEGER

Westport, Connecticut
London

Library of Congress Cataloging-in-Publication Data

Ferreira, Leonardo, 1957–
    Centuries of silence : the story of Latin American journalism / Leonardo Ferreira.
        p.   cm.
    Includes bibliographical references and index.
    ISBN 0–275–98397–8 (alk. paper)—ISBN 0–275–98410–9 (pbk : alk. paper)
    1. Press—Latin America—History.   2. Journalism—Political aspects—Latin
    America—History.   I. Title.
    PN4930.F47   2006
    079.8–dc22   2006015112

British Library Cataloguing in Publication Data is available

Library of Congress Catalog Card Number: 2006015112
ISBN: 0–275–98397–8 (cloth)
        0–275–98410–9 (pbk)

First published in 2006

Praeger Publishers, 88 Post Road West, Westport, CT 06881
An imprint of Greenwood Publishing Group, Inc.
www.praeger.com

Printed in the United States of America

The paper used in this book complies with the
Permanent Paper Standard issued by the National
Information Standards Organization (Z39.48–1984).

10 9 8 7 6 5 4 3 2 1

To my eternal stars, *mi* Gaby, Taty, Luisita, Sarita, and Juanita. To my inspiring and beloved mom, the courageous *Mary*, and to my precious *Angie*. All determined women, like most others, born to fight for freedom and a sense of harmony in this troubled planet.

Contents

Preface

Once a boy in a bilingual Presbyterian school in Bogotá (to avert the burdens of Catholic education), the author of this book grew up in a virtual *école des Refusés*, the alleged *Colegio Americano*, founded in 1869. I had to live in the Great Lakes to understand that "Americano" did not really mean "of the Americas," as most of us presumed, but of the "United States."

My classmates were Jews (who did not want to go to Hebrew academies), descendants of Arabs (rejected anywhere else), children of middle-class professionals (e.g., small store owners, emerald traders, and broadcasters), Protestant "gringos" (living among adventurous families of preachers), *mestizo* kids (who were lucky to pay the low tuition avoiding rundown public schools), and the occasional offspring of a white and wealthy, though usually immigrant politician or diplomat, willing to mix with these fellows in an exotic environment of no required creed. Later, in North America, I realized with disappointment that Presbyterians were far from the significant openness of their counterparts in the Andes.

Doña Luisa Santiaga Márquez Iguarán, mother of Nobel Literature Award winner Gabriel García Márquez, once called my school a *"cubil de luteranos"* (a lair of Lutherans), forbidding her son to join a branch of such burrow in Barranquilla. "He [my dad] would have preferred [for me to study at] the *Colegio Americano*," wrote the prestigious Colombian journalist in his biography *Vivir Para Contarla* (Living to Tell the Tale), "but my mother discarded [the idea immediately]. Today, in honor of my father, I have to admit that one of my biggest flaws in life as a writer has been not to learn how to speak English," stated Gabo.

So, like the assassinated presidential candidate Luis Carlos Galán, I was lucky to study at this school, and I ended up learning English—although thanks to my wife's coaching more than anything else. I also experienced less parochial ways of life, including the two decades of academia in the United States, tasting the power to freely express my mind, despite numerous and frustrating lessons of censorship in both North and South.

If my graduation took place in the midst of an unprecedented strike (with dozens of my friends having to leave the school), my university education at the *Universidad Nacional* (a so-called nest of Marxists) and the *Universidad Externado* of Colombia (a house of "radical liberals") went on equally unstable, witnessing repeated closures, the clubbing of fellow students on campus, and the arrival of a long list of Latin American exiles, silenced and displaced by neighboring dictators, corrupt local politicians, imposing church authorities, and intolerant and greedy mass media.

In a few years, just by changing schools, I had moved from the epithet of Lutheran to that of a radical. Inspired by college professors, honest priests, and fellow students (some of them reporters and activists subsequently killed in the devastating war against guerrillas and drugtraffickers), I aired some journalistic reports at the *TV Mundo-Channel 7*, telling the story of Brazilian, Chilean, and Bolivian families and individuals, torn apart in their own countries.

Once enroute toward graduate studies in the United States, a miracle in middle-class circles which rarely enjoy such a benefit, I left my loved ones in a country soon to be engulfed in the flames of narcoterrorism. A whole nation, already quiet by human rights abuses, went nearly mute with sheer violence: drugtraffickers, paramilitary, and paid murderers (*sicarios*). Narcotized guerrillas also became addicted to violence and drug proceeds, and the oblivious elite and their mass media, previously profiting from illegal drugs, had little if anything to say about their country's crisis and people's suffering. Still, courageous reporters (many of them killed in the process to this day) plus a handful of news outlets, ultimately destroyed, dismantled, or absorbed by conglomerates (e.g., *El Espectador*), managed to raise the image of Colombian toughness and ethics in journalism, hoping unsuccessfully to give voice to those crying to speak up.

Meanwhile, in the "developed" world, consumers procure narcotics with the same ease as buying a pint of Häagen-Dazs, when millions of Latin Americans are paying a terrible price, often with their own lives. What a painful lesson it is for a decent Latin American to watch for twenty-three years the cynical business, enforcement, and hypocrisy around drugtrafficking in the United States and Europe. My adopted country, convinced that it is second to none in freedom, continues to live in denial of its widespread corruption and self-censorship, unable to effectively guarantee full fundamental rights to African-Americans, Hispanics, and other minorities in most communities. The kingdom of silence clearly reigns here and there, in Anglo-America as much as in Latin America and the Caribbean.

Now that bright U.S. and Latin American critics, including noted communication pioneers, have come to denounce their media and societies as a plutocracy of moguls and enchanters, journalism scholars, practitioners, and audiences may begin using Elisabeth Noelle-Neumann's *spiral of silence* to explain why contemporary societies keep talking about freedom and democracy, when war, poverty, crime, censorship, prejudice, and religious or ideological narrow mindedness dominate our news.

Indeed, it is essential to ask why people do not openly express deviant opinion? Do they truly believe that ours is a free world that only needs to defeat terrorism to live happily ever after, as if we were in a paradise of liberty? What paradise? Whose paradise? Answers are contextual, that is, more complex in geopolitical, socioeconomic, technological, ideological, and cultural terms of what Neumann originally proposed, but her model is worth using as a starting line for improved analysis. Then, let's get serious and try to clarify why the vast majority of people are not free to voice their views, their frustrations, and their discontent in a so-called free world.

I take this opportunity to deeply thank my long-term mentors Professors Bella Mody of the University of Colorado, Joseph D. Straubhaar of the University of Texas–Austin, and Bradley Greenberg, Barry Litman, Thomas Muth, and the late Marilyn Fife of Michigan State University (the latter also with Temple University) for their teaching and support. I also want to thank my original editor, the retired professor Michael H. Prosser of the Rochester Institute of Technology for his extraordinary encouragement and advice. To my dear friends and colleagues Miguel Alvaro Sarmiento of the Associated Press Mexico, Rosental C. Alves of University of Texas–Austin, William Over of St. John's University, Rick Rockwell of American University, Federico Subervi of Texas State University–San Marcos, the late Michael Perkins of Brigham Young University, the late Patricia Anzola of Michigan State University, and Mercedes Lynn de Uriarte of the University of Texas–Austin, my sincere appreciation for recommending this volume.

I also express my gratitude to the extraordinary Bolivian Dr. Luis Ramiro Beltrán Salmón, a Michigan State University giant, who became my earliest inspiration in the field and who kindly stopped in Miami to give me valuable materials, especially his book on our Great Communicator, Simón Bolívar.

My deepest gratitude goes as well to both my Praeger editor Hilary Claggett of the Greenwood Publishing Group, defending and making this project possible, and my copyeditor Vivek Sood, who kindly and patiently tolerated in India repeated additions and delays. I hope to meet and embrace Vivek soon. To my friends Sallie Hughes, Gonzalo Soruco, and Michael Salwen of the University of Miami, thanks for their conversations, ideas, and feedback.

Finally, I also dedicate this book to my best friend and guide.

Dr. Oscar Iván Andia, who persuaded me, during my early years of law school, to also study communication. To my father, Cesar Augusto Ferreira, thank you for all of those touching conversations, with much human insight about our countries. And thank you to my sister Tatiana and my brothers Boris and Omar, for permanently feeding my spirit with their family visits, during my most trying times in Miami.

It goes without saying that this book would have never been completed without the constant love, assurance, and insight of my beloved artist, my wife Angie, and the pride of my life, my daughter Gabriela, playing her soothing piano in the background and flashing her smiles at me in difficult moments. And I also dedicate every page to my exceptional mom, Mary. I know she is proud and satisfied, because this book's impetus has her imprint.

When Good News Is Bad News

The history of Latin American journalism ironically begins in Russia, with the memory of a Soviet veteran championing liberty in both antiquity and modernity. Yuri Valentinovich Knorosov (1922–1999), the Red Army artillery spotter who during the Cold War revived the Mesoamerican scribe, is this unsung hero, a genius that in isolation deciphered the pre-Columbian Maya script misunderstood for centuries. Thanks to this Ukrainian epigrapher, Amerindians are in good position to restore their millenary chronicles and contributions to universal literature. Yet, when our Champollion of the Americas brought back ancestral readings that lessen the centrality of the European word, journalists in the Western Hemisphere barely mentioned him.

No newspaper in the United States, even *The New York Times*, offered Knorosov an obituary, and the Latin American press also skipped his departure.[1] Except for a few notes published in Mexico (including decent profiles in *La Jornada* and *El Universal*), citizens in this continent had little to learn from their headlines about this man's extraordinary accomplishment.[2] In fact, readers can locate far more references about Dr. Knorosov, the Maya, and their writing system in humble Belizean journals than in reputable North, Central, and South American dailies.[3]

Why such hostility against an inspiring linguist who enlightens the true origins of writing and reporting in the New World? The answer lies in the Red Scare of the twentieth century, that sinister mentality that fifteen years after the collapse of the USSR lingers in reinvented labels and clichés.

THE UNWELCOME STORY

Y. V. Knorosov is key to the vitality and identity of Latin American journalism in two respects. First, he reorients the region's attention to homegrown narratives beyond the veil of colonial accounts, and second, he opens a huge entrance door to the genuine beginnings of media civilization in the Americas. Although contemporary reporters like to preach about accuracy, fairness, and objectivity, the disregard for this exceptional scholar shows the fragility of their *Creed*.[4]

Yuri is a forgotten character explains Tiahoga Ruge, producer of the award-winning documentary *The Decipherment of the Mayan Script* (with Eduardo Herrera), because prevailing institutions such as the mass media have had a hard time recognizing a Russian since the Bolsheviks.[5] Unpopular speakers have constantly been censored as radicals in our news media past, but down to his final days, complained Ruge, experts still questioned the validity of Knorosov's discovery despite firm evidence of its accuracy. So, as an act of justice, she said, "we thought important to record his story before he [left] us."[6]

When I realized this gentleman had cracked the Maya code, confessed the late Mexican historian Patricia Rodríguez-Ochoa, editor of the *Compendio Xcaret de la Escritura Jeroglífica Maya* (1999), "I had to do something, it was a matter of justice."[7] She deplored how difficult it was to print this collection so that Hispanic Americans could read, in Spanish, the odyssey of the decoding process from the father of Maya decipherment. Even academic authorities such as the *Consejo Nacional para la Cultura y las Artes* (CONACULTA), the *Universidad Autónoma Nacional de México* (UNAM), and the *Fondo de Cultura Económica* (FCE) rejected her initiative: a strange decision for the Mexican archaeology establishment, wrote Malvido in *La Jornada*.[8] Criticized as tools of political control, CONACULTA and its affiliates, including the *Instituto Nacional de Antropología e Historia* (INAH), finally acknowledged Knorosov in the mid-1990s.[9]

"It caused us great pain," stated Rodríguez-Ochoa, "that [because of lack of resources and support] Dr. Knorosov couldn't live to see the [*Xcaret Compendium*] finished, although he knew we were working on it."[10] In many ways, his personal hardship epitomizes the unfolding of Latin American media and society, an endless drama of poverty, war, obtuse authority, censorship, intolerance, bigotry, jealousy, and other maladies, simply more visible in the developing than the "developed" world. Editor Rodríguez-Ochoa died within a few years of the successful publication of their masterpiece.[11]

This Russian-Latin American saga of reviving the old Maya accounts goes back to May 1945 when Yuri Valentinovich, age 22, entered Berlin with his comrades of the Soviet armed forces. At the German National Library, observed Knorosov, boxes full of books were waiting "to be sent somewhere else. The fascist command had packed them and since they [the Nazis] didn't have time to move them anywhere, they [the books] were simply taken to Moscow."[12] In one of these crates, he found a copy of *Códices Mayas* by the Guatemalan Villacorta brothers, a serviceable work originally printed in a Mexican periodical in 1930, according to the *Sächsische Landesbibliothek*.[13] The *Dresden Codex*, a favorite Maya manuscript preserved to this day, resides in this public library. It is the only pre-Columbian book held in Germany.

That Yuri Knorosov came upon the Maya codices during the Soviet advance in Berlin is surrounded by speculation. "After finding the National Library on fire," recites German epigrapher Nikolai Grube, the young soldier rescued a few books of his interest, the Villacortas and Diego de Landa's *Relación de Las Cosas de Yucatán* (Account of the Things of Yucatan).[14] Yale University archaeologist Michael D. Coe repeats this scene in his revised edition of *Breaking the Maya Code* (1999) as the brave infantryman saved both publications "out of the thousands of books being consumed [by the flames]."[15] But "there simply wasn't any fire in the library, it was a misunderstanding," clarified the Russian scholar.[16] "What newspapers say about the Berlin Library is only a legend. I never saw a library in flames."[17] Besides, he had seen the first Maya glyphs as a child in school, not as a soldier.[18]

Embellishments in journalism or academia are harmless unless they turn into elaborate libels. John Eric Sidney Thompson (1898–1975), a University of Cambridge anthropologist and star researcher at the Carnegie Institution mounted a poetic defamation against Knorosov solely because he considered him a communist, *"por el solo hecho de considerarlo comunista,"* remarked Corzo-Gamboa.[19] As the Englishman cast doubt over the Russian's *"honradez científica,"* that is, upon his scientific integrity and morality, the calumny began to spread in *Español* (purists would say, in *Castellano*), a rare deference to Hispanics since they seldom spark major scholarly debates in Anglo-American circles.[20]

Sir Thompson, once a *gaucho* (cowboy) in Argentina, blocked the decipherment of the Maya code till well beyond his death.[21] In his dogmatism, he told Professor Coe, "I won't live to see the results of the ongoing research about the Maya writing but you will. And then you'll know who was right: the dammed Russian or me."[22] Observers now know that "that blessed Russian won" (*que ganó ese bendito ruso*), even if heavy communist propaganda did frame Knorosov and his groundbreaking essay *Drevniaia Pis'mennost Tsentral'noi Ameriki* (Ancient Writing of Central America, October 1952).[23] This is the stormy scenery of the revival of the pre-Columbian Maya chronicle and, consequently, of the new early history of journalism in the Americas.

In 1954, the *Partido Comunista Mexicano* (PCM) published a Spanish translation of this paper with a hard-line introduction by comrade S. P.

Tolstov, editor of *Sovietskaya Etnografiya*. It is the historic *Number 5* of the *Biblioteca Obrera* (Worker's Library) series reproduced at the *Fondo de Cultura Popular*, a small editorial house established in 1937 during Lázaro Cárdenas' presidency under the auspices of Hernán Laborde, secretary general of the Communist Party.[24] Mr. Laborde, a union leader, had also been editor of the PCM's *El Machete*, the socialist weekly muralists David Alfaro Siqueiros, Diego Rivera, and Javier Guerrero started in the mid-1920s. As the voice of Soviet communism, General Plutarco Elías Calles closed it down and persecuted its collaborators between 1929 and 1934.[25]

Beyond the *Pecesitos* (the communists), no one seemed interested in Knorosov's work.[26] His research emerged during a most sensitive time, the year when the Eisenhower administration activated a 3-million-dollar operation (*PBSUCCESS*) to overthrow the democratically elected Colonel Jacobo Arbenz Guzmán, president of Guatemala. With in-site support of Nicaraguan dictator Anastasio Somoza García ("Tacho"), the CIA launched this covert operation in June 1954, its first in a chain of dark intrusions in Latin America and the Caribbean. Born at President Harry S. Truman's desk (as *Operation PBFORTUNE*, 1952), the plan called for Guatemalan communists to be disposed of through "executive action" (murder), imprisonment, and exile. This conspiracy resulted in a deadly aftermath, "a massive counter insurgency campaign that left tens of thousands [of people] massacred, maimed, or missing" throughout the Mayan motherland.[27]

In the name of liberty, press freedom, and stability, the Organization of American States (OAS) declared Arbenz head of a communist infiltration during a meeting General Marcos Pérez Jiménez hosted in Venezuela, another dictator accused of presiding over a political system based on "a security force that silenced opposition leaders by jailing and torturing."[28] This book carries the title "Centuries of Silence" partly because communication in this region, since antiquity, has been plagued with episodes where power-hungry rulers and the elite (often with outside support) repressed their people for personal gain, manipulating media while silencing dissenting voices. Intrepidly, Costa Rica declined the invitation to Caracas "because of her disapproval of the Venezuelan regime."[29]

In 1959, the University of Yucatan lauded J. Eric S. Thompson with a Doctor of Law degree. Later, he took home from Spain the Order of Isabel La Católica (1964), and from Mexico both the Order of the Aztec Eagle (1965) and the Sahagún Prize (1971). Tulane University's LL.D. and the University of Cambridge's doctorate in literature also thickened his portfolio in 1972. But the proudest moment arrived when her majesty the Queen of England conferred upon him the knighthood of the Order of the British Empire (1975) to celebrate his seventy-sixth birthday. All this time, however, Knorosov had been right and Thompson arrogantly and notably wrong on the mystery of the Mayan hieroglyphs.

It is silly to undermine the latter just because the former was correct on the issue of Mayan phonetic writing, warns the Mexican professor Miguel León-Portilla. Yet, as he agrees, "we owe Knorosov to have initiated, on firm ground, the reading of Maya inscriptions."[30] Study the criticism of unorthodox Mayanists throughout the Cold War, especially against Tor Ulving, David H. Kelley, Floyd Lounsbury, and Michael Coe, and you will see how intolerant academia can be when idolized figures are permitted to rule methods, issues, or authors as scholarly unsound. In the politics of knowledge, said the Russian linguist, the establishment may be "like with Marx: you c[an't] oppose. [One person] dominate[s] and nobody object[s]."[31] The same occurs in the world of news. After publishing their opinions, Thompson and his fans "d[idn't] care what other people d[id] or wr[ote]. [S]o how is it going to be in the future [when] nobody admits what other people have accomplished."[32]

Not until late 1990 did Yuri Valentinovich begin to receive adequate recognition for his contribution. Before leaving office, President Marco Vinicio Cerezo honored him with the *Order of the Quetzal*, the highest Guatemalan distinction for outstanding service to the nation. A local daily welcomed the Soviet veteran with the headline: "Russian epigrapher breaks the [Berlin] Wall and lands in Guatemala."[33] Regrettably, when touring *Tikal* and *Uaxactún*, right-wing death squads threatened Knorosov and forced him out of the country. In fact, Guatemalans had to endure five more years of abuse to end thirty-six years of civil war since Arbenz, a conflict that killed over 200,000 fellow citizens and injured about 50,000 people mostly Maya Indians—including 626 massacres in Maya villages with senior security officials supervising the carnage.[34] Yuri made it safely back to Russia, wrote Coe, but "the man who had allowed the ancient Maya scribes to speak with their own voice was still unable to walk freely among the cities in which they had lived."[35]

In 1995, Mexico asked him to return. As preamble, the Mexican Embassy in Moscow awarded him the *Order of the Aztec Eagle* (1994), a tribute Thompson had received twenty-nine years earlier.[36] Linda Schele, the late and noted Mayanist of the University of Texas at Austin, greeted him in Yucatan although Knorosov, touched and appreciative, stated that "not even out of courtesy he could agree with U.S. scholarly interpretations"— they have been "barely rigorous" and far from "a truly comprehensible readings of texts," he said.[37] Indeed, lack of context is a typical problem in studies from the United States. Notwithstanding, the UT Office of Public Affairs honored both scholars in an obituary claiming that "the decipher[ment] begun by Knorosov and continued by Dr. Schele is the biggest linguistic discovery since the Rosetta Stone helped scholars un-lock the mysteries of Egyptian hieroglyphs."[38]

In 1997, short before death, Yuri Valentinovich paid a final visit to the New Continent. With a health so fragile that hardly let him walk small corners of *Chichén Itzá*, he traveled across the Yucatan peninsula to the ar-chaeological zone of *Dzibilchaltún* where his dictionary of ancient Maya signs was formally handed out to President Ernesto Zedillo Ponce de León.[39] He then flew to the United States of America, the once unthinkable voyage. In the southwest, Yuri searched for the *Siete Cuevas* (Seven Caves or wombs) in today's *Mesa Verde National Park*, a place where he thought the Mesoamerican protopatria or ancestral homeland had probably been born.

On March 30, 1999 (some say March 31st or even April 1st), Yuri Valenti-novich Knorosov died penniless and abandoned. He was 76, the same age as Thompson when the Englishman passed away. Dead of a stroke and pneumonia (after being left unattended in the freezing hallways of a crowded hospital), relatives had to bury him in an old dumpsite of his beloved St. Petersburg, the former Leningrad.[40] The only institution to do-nate money for his funeral was the Mexican Embassy in Moscow.[41] This kind man, grieved Ruge, who gave us the gift of reading the ancient Maya, "was dying without the world noticing it [...] and leaving a legacy that has still not been fully recognized."[42]

This unpopular story is "a triumph of spirit and intellect over almost in-superable odds," concluded Coe. From fighting the Nazis at the German front, entering Berlin victoriously, to defeating the isolation, absurdities, and censorship of both Soviet communism and Western capitalism bring-ing back the ancient Maya script, there is little else one can ask of a lifetime.[43] Still, newsmakers find him uninteresting. Corzo-Gamboa is rather mundane with his moral. This Russian scientist, he says, shows at the very least how incredibly possible it is to learn about unknown cultures and languages from thousands of years and miles away, just by working quietly and in the company of a cat, a cigarette, and a bottle of vodka.[44]

In 1999, Harvard University decided to honor the aging linguist with a *Tatiana Proskouriakoff Award* for "his contribution to Maya decipher-ment," but the recognition came too late.[45] Knorosov died within weeks of this academic consecration. Fortunately, generous Guatemalans had al-ready thanked him almost a decade before the venerable Harvard col-lege, and for much more than a contribution to reading the ancestral Maya. On September 27, 2004, family, scientists, and diplomats joined Sergey M. Mironov, chairman of the Federal Assembly's Council of the Russian Federation, and dedicated a monument to the great savior of the Maya scribe.[46] At least, he would have now a decent place to rest at the Kovalevsky Cemetery in St. Petersburg.

TIME FOR A REWRITE

During the late 1760s in Bologna, Italy, Spanish Americans in exile, dreaming of freedom from monarchs, made a wise recommendation: review the continent's history so that "erroneous beliefs" and "misinformed impressions" about America in Europe are forever corrected.[47] Two and a half centuries later, Latin Americans had accomplished little in this regard. In other words, oppressive assumptions in dominant countries and their social memory persist to this day. Thus, this book is an invitation for everyone to work harder on identifying such stereotypes and helping remove them.

For example, the roots of ancient reporting, if not the entire history of information in the Americas, require a careful rethinking and revision. Trace the origins of news and realize that the dawn of communications media in the Western Hemisphere, which journalism experts virtually ignored, began long before the arrival of the printing press. Gutenberg's reinvention is obviously a milestone in the evolution of modern society, but early breakthroughs in the New World's reporting of events began with Native Americans, not Iberians and other Europeans. This is when Knorosov's discovery comes in, "shed[ding] light on the indecipherable," wrote Altamirano, so that ordinary people, not just specialists, can learn about the existence and implications of a pre-Columbian media culture and their writings.[48]

Because of its continuing biases and omissions, readers are encouraged to reexamine this hemispheric media history as a whole. Obviously, a complete appraisal cannot be expected from one author in one publication, but this book will revisit centuries of media antiquity, colonialism, and republicanism basically to highlight episodes that need critical thinking and interpretation.

Was there a nascent or proto-journalism in pre-Columbian America? Chapter 1 brings up the issue of whether news information reached audiences in the New World before the Spanish conquistadors. Until recently, naturalists, archaeologists, and historians have avoided the study of pre-Cortesian inscriptions as a media phenomenon, so news researchers should further investigate the "reporting" and chronicling functions of the Mesoamerican codex, the Andean quipus, and other ancient narratives. After all, they are the genuine antecedent, the true roots of "the press" in the Western Hemisphere. In this detailed chapter, the author explains the imposition of a structural censorship during colonial times, a lasting system based on racial and sex discrimination, official despotism, technological elitism, and both religious and ideological intolerance.

Chapter 2 gives us an overview of the patriots' ideals about the liberty of the press when liberating Latin America from Spain, including experiences and perspectives on their use of the printing presses while fighting for independence and building the new nations. Chapters 3 and 4 take the reader into the continent's plunge into the pools of war, censorship, and media propaganda of the nineteenth century, while technology and modernization come to service governments, the military, and if peace allows, social projects. Chapters 5 and 6 explain how the war agenda increases with even more powerful actors and implications, that is, when revolutionary news media technologies, new journalism trends and practices, and new country dynamics with new forms of silencing the majority immersed the continent into a Cold War.

This book concludes with Chapters 7 and 8 discussing the conflicting reality of globalization and the dream of a fair and humane world, where extraordinary steps toward democratization have been overshadowed by a seemingly endless fight against terrorism, illegal drugs, and corruption. Poverty and inequality, the slow pace of the digital democratization, sophisticated forms of news control and public and private censorship, plus continued levels of violence against reporters and civil society remain, in the meantime, unresolved. In a positive note, since there is little to celebrate in the long history of Latin American journalism, the author concludes with recent media and political developments, opening possible new roads for an effective democracy in this region, especially for the poor. As with Knorosov's story, new Latin American social movements should not be prejudged as bad news, unless they defy the rights to both dissent and communicate.

Chapter 1

Whose Truth on *True Street*

El Zócalo, that smoggy square in the Historic Center of Mexico City, is an ideal place to start the writing of a fresh history about journalism in Latin America. Stand at the corner of *Moneda* and *Licenciado Verdad* streets where *The House of the First Printing Press of America* miraculously survives, and echoes of a long human suffering will come to greet you. Social inequity, individual hardship, and racial prejudice permeate this downtown intersection as do religious fanaticism and official vanity, but this museum house at *Primo Verdad No. 10* symbolizes an old particular imbalance: the cultural gap between largely neglected pre-Columbian records and overly celebrated colonial publications. Why do news historians in *América*, from Alaska to Patagonia, underestimate the fascinating story of indigenous communication?

Indifference toward native chronicles has revolved around the once favorite *New York Times'* assumption that American Indians whether Aztec, Hopi, or Inca were incapable of interacting in languages as natural as those of Europe—meaning English, French, and Spanish.[1] In practice, however, "*los inca-paces*," jokes screenwriter José Rivera in *The Motorcycle Diaries*, the truly incapable ones judging cultural achievements of ancient civilizations in the Americas have been the colonizers, their children, and great grandchildren.

No one should question now that Native Indians, prior to Columbus, built an information environment as vibrant as the overseas literary centers of the Middle Ages. By the time Leif Ericksson landed in today's L'Anse aux Meadows at the northern tip of Newfoundland (Canada, c. 1000 CE), the Mayas and the Zapotecs of Oaxaca already had stelae and other means to register life stories and big social events—in other words, their "news." Apparently, these writings helped the Mayas exert considerable intellectual and religious influence all over Middle America.[2] This is a rare lesson in schools of journalism beyond Mexico and Central America, and oftentimes, even in these lands.

Pre-Hispanic Maya scribes knew how to put ideas in writing with remarkable fluidity. After adequate training, anyone can read pre-Columbian Maya accounts in their own words, although missing much of their historical context. In fact, "a rough-and-ready reading knowledge of the script may be gained by relative neophytes within the space of a single week!" This does not mean that the Maya writing system is a simple one.[3] People "can now hear ancient Maya glyphs as the scribes wrote them and not merely interpret them as soundless visual patterns," cheers Professor Coe.[4] In other words, "a ruler or scribe who lived over a thousand years ago can speak to us across the gulf of time and space, and be understood."[5]

Serious sources including Coe's *Reading the Maya Glyphs* (with calligrapher Mark Van Stone, 2001) offer amateur audiences a step-by-step guide on how to interpret relatively easy pre-Cortesian texts. The *ts'ib* glyph, for example, means both writing and painting. Once this symbol interacts with the pronoun *u*, it reads "he writes it/he paints it," or "his writing/his painting" (*uts'ib*). This is also a reminder to contemporary journalism researchers that reporting events is an activity intertwined with the arts. In Mesoamerica, communication combined text, science, and art, free from the artificial boundaries and specialization of modern times. With ancient grammar rules articulating verbal forms like *uti* ("it happens"), *utiy* ("it happened"), *utom* ("it will happen"), and *iut* ("and then it happens"), the information possibilities of the pre-Columbian Maya chroniclers were infinite.[6]

ANCIENT SCRIBES AND REPORTS

Centuries before the landing of any Viking or Spanish ship, indigenous inscriptions with details of major social and political occurrences proliferated in urban centers of Classic Mesoamerica and beyond, just as in Sumerian and other Mesopotamian cities.[7] Many pre-Hispanic literary expressions announced an array of socially relevant information, abundant and worthy Maya stories in stone stelae, lintels, panels, tombs, and murals, or in paper codices, pottery, bones, jewelry, wood, textiles, and seashells. Writing, through either painting, carving, engraving, inscribing, or incising, "sprang up early *to celebrate great events in the life of the elite*."[8] This is a biased and "official" chronicle of rulers and aristocrats, legitimizing their power over commoners and captives from other places.[9]

Journalism historians should stop introducing the history of news in the Western Hemisphere with Spanish chroniclers and the printing press, as if there was no spread of information in the New Continent. "Before Columbus dreamed of sailing west, the peoples of America were already writing and recording the world," underscores Brotherston from the British Museum.[10] Written accounts emerged well before the Lucky's landing in North America and clearly among "Maya scribes that began to record deeds of their rulers some two thousand years ago."[11] One-fourth of the lowland Mayans may have been educated and "if the Classic Maya kings had felt it necessary that everyone in the society be literate, more than 90 percent would have been so," because it was easier to read than write.[12] The disregard for the pre-Hispanic contribution to the realm of information diffusion, especially in Mesoamerica with its intercultural communication, is a flaw that needs to be promptly corrected.

Professor Linda Schele, an art historian, and David Freidel, an archaeologist, believe that, in a modern sense, the ancient Maya had no mass communication. Their populations, they said, mostly illiterate, had no paperbacks or weekly journals. But this limited definition of mass communication conflicts with observations made by late journalism professor Mary A. Gardner, who showed how the Spaniards actually relied on journalists without journals to grasp and conceptualize their conquest.

At Michigan State University, when international communication dragged as a timid field some thirty-five years ago, Dr. Gardner realized that the practice of journalism in the Americas should be traced back to the *cronistas* who accompanied the Spanish conquistadors. Their mission, she wrote, "was to report the New World, its conquest, and its peoples. Indeed, they [the chroniclers] were the precursors of America journalism, even though journalists without journals."[13] Still, reporting in this continent effectively began with the Mesoamerican scribe, not with the Spanish chronicler. Aztec codices, to name a fine example, "were used to carry *news* from one part of the empire to another."[14] It is puzzling why such an eminent news scholar, familiar with both Mexico and Guatemala, paid no attention to the history of the Maya scribes and their writings.

Although probably not mass communication, and surely not in a "modern" sense, Schele and Freidel admit that the pre-Hispanic writings had the capacity to *inform history*. Unlike ongoing information consumers centered on new tools, the Mayas invented a flow of "ideas" harnessing social energy. Only then, "the writing and pictorial imagery used to interpret and record the[se conceptions] comprised a particular type of technology—*similar in nature to what in our time we call the media.*"[15]

A pre-Columbian scribe had the skill to chronicle an array of events, from information on wars and victories, laws, legends, and prominent people or places to transcendental rites and ceremonies, such as childbirths, marriages, sacrifices, and funerals. Genealogies, scientific knowledge, agricultural data, teaching practices, tributes, contracts, mythologies, personal thoughts, ambitions, dreams, and views of the world are all part of the literary diet of high-ranking ancient citizens.[16] Even the habits of their lords, the deeds of kings and ancestors, the activities of priests, and the routines of artisans, merchants, and farmers found their way in the glyphs and pictures of pre-Cortesian times.[17] There is also exciting evidence to show how public information flowed within and between communities in Mesoamerica and the Andes.

In *Lenguaje de las Piedras*, the late Román Piña-Chan highlighted Stela 14 of Monte Albán (Phase II, c. 200 BCE–100 CE), a simple but telling chronicle. Its likely translation reads: *On the year that 6 Turquoise began, this place was conquered. The day was 11 Arrow of the month 5 Fortress.*[18] This Zapotec inscription is worth discussing in a basic newswriting course of any journalism program. In our times, wrote Professor Piña-Chan, "the decipherment of Mexico's ancient iconography and writing is of great importance, because, when doing so, we rescue the voice and memory of our ancestors, deepening the roots of our own citizenship."[19] Entries like Stela 14 abound in Middle America, announcing interesting dates and facts. Our job, as journalism historians, especially in the Maya world, is to read, interpret, and classify them whenever possible.

Unusual, notes epigrapher David Stuart of the Peabody Museum at Harvard University, is the small group of Maya texts carrying "a pivotal event" on Stelae 31 in Tikal and both 5 and 22 in Uaxactun.[20] It is one of those few historical dates posted at different sites and referring to the same event: the intriguing *11 Eb Episode* of the Early Classic period (Long Count date 8.17.1.4.12 11 Eb 15 Mac or January 16, 378 CE). As Stuart explains, these inscriptions tell the story of a newly appointed king of Tikal, a foreigner named Nun Yax Ayin (Curl Nose or Curl Snout), son of the probably Teotihuacan monarch Atlatl Cauac or "Spearthrower Owl." The plot involves another stranger, Siyah K'ak' ("Smoking" or "Smoke Frog," also translated as "Fire is Born"), the character who shows up at the lowland Maya city two days before and immediately instigates, perhaps under Spearthrower's orders, the rising of *Curl Nose* to power. Smoke Frog's presence in this urban capital coincides with *Great Paw*'s death (aka *Jaguar Paw*), ending a local reign of six decades according to an older engraving.

Altogether, these writings seem to indicate that aliens from the Mexica highlands came to Tikal, killed its king, and installed a new ruler totally unrelated to the last dynasty. Stuart believes that these accounts document "the single most important political or military episode of Early Classic Maya history, when Teotihuacan established itself as a dominant force in the politics and elite culture of the central Peten."[21] This story reiterates Tatiana Proskouriakoff's revolutionary findings, a discovery that the Russian American artist and archaeologist made four decades ago. Maya inscriptions had, in fact, the power to inform history, "opening up a world of dynastic rivalry, royal marriages, taking of captives, and all other elite doings" typical of our social existence.[22]

At its simplest, argues Professor Elizabeth Hill Boone of Tulane University, "a history is a story about the past. To the Aztecs, as to [other Mesoamericans and] us, histories are created by the combination of four elements: participant, event, location, and time. These are the *who, what, where,* and *when* familiar to us from journalistic accounts. [A]ll four elements are required by a story."[23] More than describing a situation, however, a mix of dates, facts, places, and actors had a primary purpose in ancient America: to guarantee that certain historical episodes were not forgotten, offering readers, interpreters, and performers clues to enhance their memory when telling a story. The assumption is that the speaker should have been "somewhat familiar" with the general scope of the incident.[24] Because scribes and scripts registered primarily events, the *why* seemed absent in antiquity.

In *Stories in Red and Black*, Boone illustrates how the Mexica had historians writing purposeful accounts to reconfigure their past, including stories of genealogy, migration, conquest, and the consolidation of power.[25] Back and forth, reports traveled through an efficient network of messengers informing Aztecs and Incas that strange bearded men of very white skin and long hair had invaded their coasts. "Bold" and "imposing" gods, said the news, had arrived in floating "towers" to land and then ride a sort of enormous "deer without horns" (horses), accompanied by huge dogs of intense yellow eyes that spilled fire. In *Primeras Noticias de la Llegada de los Españoles* (first news of the Spaniards' arrival), León-Portilla details how verbal reports of these terrifying images reached Mexico-Tenochtitlan long before Hernán Cortés entered the Aztec capital on November 8, 1519.[26] Indeed, it is extraordinary how reported information could have traveled at that time, even as far north as the Great Lakes, wrote the Mexican historian Jaime Montell.[27]

The same happened in the Andes when Francisco Pizarro and his men advanced on the Inca empire in November 1532. Quick and specific news of their arrival was made available to *Atahualpa* since the time the Spaniards appeared in the northern shores of the Pacific.[28] If the Mexicas put in codices and other written documents the trauma of the conquest at contact and afterward (as the "important news" of native informants suggest in the codices *Ramírez* and *Florentino*), it would be reasonable to expect that the Incas somehow recorded this drama in their quipus and related media.[29] After all, textiles, including their mostly undeciphered system of knotted and dyed cords (also known as khipu), had been an old Andean practice of securing religious, political, and administrative traditions through weaving, their "primary medium of expression."[30] As Middle Americans must have felt, Andeans also needed to make sense of the conquest by consulting their history and tradition.

Europeans used chronicles, news, and *relaciones* (accounts) to learn about the discovery and the conquest and so did Mesoamericans with their *cantares* (poems), chronicles, testimonies, and pictures, narrating the horrors of the Spanish invasion. In South America, where decipherment of the quipu should be a priority, the challenge is to prove whether the Inca and neighboring cultures employed their abstract media to "know" and "remember" occurrences and other information.[31] Since pre-Hispanic media "were fashioned as signal references to an oral story," an Inca quipu may not have been essentially different from an Aztec pictorial chronicle.[32] These literature, pre-Columbian, on the one hand, and European, on the other, are "the two distinct faces of the historical mirror in which the Conquest is reflected."[33]

One definition of news, without imposing modern notions on ancient realities, speaks of significant events reported in the form of dramatic stories.[34] And there was plenty of drama in the pre-Cortesian literature. There is no universal definition of news, cautions Professor Barbie Zelizer of the University of Pennsylvania's Annenberg School for Communication, because the concept of journalism "is not in fact consensual. [Thus, critics] need to remember the difficulty, if not impossibility, of producing a whole and complete picture of journalism."[35] While some intellectuals see news as a social science, others regard it as art or an ideology.[36] Yet, a baseline agrees that news is at least new information about recent happenings, that is, reports on issues of some perceived public interest. Consequently, Zelizer claims that "news is no more than an account, chronicle, or story about an event," with "newsbooks" carrying new information "roughly [...] in the same way *for at least 500 years.*"[37]

It is evident that ancient stelae, codices, and other media provided Middle Americans with vital public information. While definitions of news remain broad to this day, it seems essential to recognize that there is a significant news value in many pre-Columbian writings. In the end, writing and news cannot be so narrowly defined as to perpetuate the exclusion of non-Western discourses. But it is also important not to glamorize the pre-Hispanic media production. Information in ancient America, based on what we know today, is clearly biased. Scribes wrote mostly the story of their monarchs, priests, and nobles.

Ancient Maya history, a prime example, is "the privilege of the elite and powerful. [A]t best it gives *an accurate reflection* of *their views on what happened,* [but] it is mute about the life of the ordinary people."[38] Those chronicles are an "official" history, concludes Northern Illinois University professor William Fash, Director of the Copán Acropolis Archaeological Project, except for the far more mundane and equally fascinating themes of domestic pottery.[39] Let's keep in mind, adds Professor Sharer, curator of the University of Pennsylvania Museum, that the "Maya kings were very interested in advertising their achievements. Like early Old World histories, these accounts must be critically evaluated because they probably contained *propaganda intended to boost the prestige of their royal sponsors.*"[40]

The Toltecs, Mixtecs, and Aztecs also cherished this tradition of publicizing events through their media, just as the Otomis, Tarascans, Tezcocans, and Tlaxcalans relied on manuscripts to preserve and circulate their actuality, wisdom, and heritage.[41] The New World is simply not as immature mediawise as Euro-centered historians made it sound like all this time. On the contrary, Middle America, an eloquent universe in the art of communicating since antiquity, gives humanity a splendid body of information postmodern societies are only beginning to truly understand.[42] A most interesting case today is the Incan *quipus* of the Andes and its promising research, an art form where colored knots seem to "tell stories of their world."[43]

Experts know now that a fundamental function of indigenous writings is to record history. In ancient America, both literate and illiterate people, with proper guidance, could go back a few weeks or hundreds of years to revisit information on ancestral events, myths, and prophecies, chronicling episodes with precision. And they could share this information with their peers. That reporters ultimately build archives with posted information is a fact journalists should never forget, as we are reminded by Ed Wasserman, a Knight professor of journalism ethics at Washington and Lee University in Virginia.[44] Urban sociologist Robert E. Park, a news research pioneer, once wrote, "it is obvious that news is not physical knowledge like that of the physical sciences. It is rather, insofar as it is concerned with events, like history. Events [are] invariably fixed in time and located in space."[45] Thus, neither history nor journalism admits rigid definitions, alerts journalism historian Margaret Blanchard.[46]

History, education, and information are all structural elements in books and other writings of pre-Hispanic America. As a matter of fact, they are all about both cultural history as Amerindians lived it and the world as they saw it.[47] Mexican archaeologists often classify the precolonial codices as ritual-calendrical or historical, with the colorful Mixtec bibliography heading the list as the most devoted to recounting the past. Whereas the Maya, Aztec, and Mixtec-Puebla books of the Borgia Group are all considered ritual-calendrical, the six surviving pure Mixtec manuscripts are essentially regarded as historical. The *Codex Colombino*, a history of Tututepec in Oaxaca, is the only pre-Columbian screenfold in full care of the National Museum of Anthropology in Mexico City. The rest are in Europe.[48]

Ancient scribes used skillful techniques to fabricate paper. Called *amate* or *amatl* in Nahua lands (*kopo'* in Maya communities), native paper came mostly "from the inner bark of one or more species of *ficus*, a wild fig [or *higuera*] of the order Moraceae."[49] In ceremonial festivities, it helped dress priests, dancers, and sacrifice victims, while during times of war, strips of *amate* wet the warriors' dry throats or wrapped their wounds.[50] Paper on bowls also served as collector of dripping blood in private and public sacrifices. When scarce or unavailable, rags, deerskin, and fibers of maguey came to the rescue, replacing the ficus-based medium. In any case, like preparing a canvas for a painting, scribes smoothed out the surface with a thin layer of plaster for better writing results. After folding the codex in pagelike intervals, wooden boards framed it at both ends, though not always.

It is amazing to say that fine brushes traced texts so delicate in pre-Columbian times that modern pens could hardly replicate their lines. With green as the center of their worldview, especially among the Maya, the handful of sacred colors is complete with the cardinal points, the four divine directions: yellow signifies the south; white, the north; black, the west; and red, the east. Hieroglyphic texts in the codices are always painted in black and red, the land of wisdom and writing.[51] Before Columbus, artisans from the Valley of Mexico and the Maya lowlands reached the highest level of mastery when fabricating paper.[52] Even the colonists used native paper in New Spain whenever theirs had been lost or depleted. Authorities in Tlaxcala, for example, a labor center, ordered the manufacturing of indigenous paper for their municipality despite colonial prohibitions against this production for fears of paganism.[53] Paper manuscripts blossomed as a communication activity throughout the Classic and post-Classic periods, so the apparently paperless Olmecs and Zapotecs of the pre-Classic period used ceramics and stone as writing surfaces, primarily basalt and jade.[54]

More than a screenfold, a pre-Columbian codex is a true book: elaborate, thorough, and in some instances as coherent as the Bible. A 1,000-year-old practice in pre-Contact times, writing codices was already an art, merging text with mathematics and playing essential roles in the evolution of Mesoamerican society. Ancient *tlahcuilolli*, meaning what is painted or written, is a place to see this media symbiosis at work. In antiquity, an artificial separation between art and science was downright inconceivable.

Archaeologists and epigraphers believe that the Maya texts are the most sophisticated books of Mesoamerica, carrying a full range of cultivated contents. But the *Tonalamatl de Aubin*, a divinatory codex of fates and days, proves, among others, that sacred written books were also refined and fundamental among Nahuatl audiences.[55] In fact, a genuine history of pre-Hispanic Tlaxcala, notes local historian Elia Salas de León, could not be written without relying on their old maps and codices, the pure or nearly pure pre-Columbian forms of Tlaxcalan expression.[56]

Knowledge and information in pre-Hispanic America and the early conquest spread through paper codices and other communications, recreating stories of "commemorative events, annals, and epic passages written in elegant and careful language."[57] At least, this is what most, if not all, Mesoamericanists are ready to accept. As León-Portilla states, citing chronicler Chimalpahin Cuauhtlehuanitzin (a sixteenth-century trainee of the Franciscan College of the Holy Cross in Tlatelolco), "for hundreds of years, the ancient Mexicans had the custom of recording in their inscriptions on stone and in their books of *amate* paper or deer-skin *events which were particularly meaningful to them.*"[58]

Presumably, carving signs in stone, shells, bones, and jewellike jade or obsidian came earlier than writing with brushes.[59] In the Mayan case, however, this assumption is flawed. There is every reason to believe, affirm Coe and Kerr, "that all Maya monumental texts were first painted on the prepared stone surfaces, before the carver or carvers took over. The most compelling evidence is the nature of the writing itself, which clearly mimics in stone the movement of flexible brush tips."[60] Looking at the incised panels of Palenque, "there can be little doubt that the writing was both painted and then cut by one and the same master," they say.[61] Even so, poems in both Nahua and Maya polities perhaps arrived ahead of the painted book.[62]

Anthropologist Bruce Love agrees that the advent of the elegant and decorative Maya calligraphy derives from a style born in brush strokes rather than chisel and other carving instruments. From the beginning of Maya writing, "scribes probably composed texts on paper or skins. [S]everal [Classic]Maya pottery vessels [also] bear images of scribes with codices."[63] In fact, Maya ceramics is a challenging source of "information about the origins and development of the *early Maya*, their trade networks, kingship relationships, social and occupational differences, diet, rituals and religious beliefs, funeral practices, and lives of both elite and commoner," he says.[64] Unlike manuscripts in monumental stones and a few surviving codices, painted ceramics might be the source we need to rescue the ancient life of ordinary Mayans.

The use of books in ancient Middle America is elusive. As an art of the word, this type of manuscript boiled in an environment of media influence and authority. According to the Codex Mendoza, books and other long papers, including stories about memorable war and victories, famines, plagues, and either prosperous or adverse times, "were used in a variety of ways and contexts."[65] Family, schools, temples, courts, farmlands, markets, and government houses predominated as habitual settings. Trying to reenact the likely social scenario of a Mayan codex, Dr. Love imagines that priests "took out their books and spread them out on the fresh boughs which they had for their purpose, invok[ing] with prayers and devotions an idol named *Kinich Ahau Itzamna*. [He] was the first priest, the most learned. They looked at the book and read the prognostic of that year, manifest[ing] prophecies] to those who were present. And they preached to them a little, recommending the remedies for their ills."[66] Solemnly, the codices announced the forecasts.

Since rulers, notes León-Portilla, "realized it was impossible for most people in the community to have their own books, they insisted on systematic memorizing as a means of preserving tradition and knowledge."[67] Native kings and nobles feared stagnation, a world of ignorance absent of enlightened poems, eloquent speakers, and sacred books. As with early new media in modern times, the role of the pre-Columbian codex is in the first place to educate. Teaching the official story of society was also a principal goal. Explaining the importance to communicate, one verse in the *Colección de Cantares Mexicanos* reads: *I sing the pictures of the book and see them spread out ... for I make the codices speak within the house of pictures. [Y]our songs are written, but you spread them out beside the kettle drums*, urges the text.[68]

In pre-Columbian schools such as the Aztec *Calmécac*, "codices or painted books were always the basis of teaching."[69] Encouraging children to learn to read the manuscripts, teachers urged their pupils to accurately memorize written texts or oral lessons with the assistance of a codex. Traditions, knowledge, and events passed generation to generation as songs, poems, and speeches written in the codices. Using books, both revered speakers and priests taught, often to smaller groups, the doctrines, achievements, and prospects of their deities, kings, and communities.[70] This is not to say that Mesoamerican rulers did not aptly utilize mere "pictography for political and social ends [...], creating a broadly understood corpus of visual conventions that communicated effectively across ethnic and linguistic boundaries."[71]

Ancient Americans distinguished good writing from bad writing, and good speaking from bad speaking. Mayan scribes could persuasively write every feeling, sound, meaning, and grammatical structure they wanted. Good writing for them meant the creation of innovative sentences and harmonious sequences of times, actions, and actors. As Schele and Freidel put it, "in the Maya inscriptions, the standard sentence normally began with the time of the action, followed by the action itself, the thing acted upon, and finally the actor. [To] the Maya, it was not only what the text said that counted, but also how the scribe chose to say it: and not only how it was said, but also where and on what it was said."[72] Journalistically, there is much to do research on. As Boone suitably concludes, the pre-Columbian literature "offers food for thought to scholars in a variety of disciplines who think comparatively about histories and/or graphic systems of communication."[73]

It is hard to identify the media model of pre-Hispanic America, since not only speakers and audiences but also social settings should be determined before defining what type of communication actually governs. Here is when one needs to study the "context" of the texts, as Professor Sue Carry Jansen proposes.[74] During medieval times, aristocrats, namely kings and priests, had full and direct access to literature, but, unlike the Middle Ages, the clergy, the nobility, and other wise people in ancient Mesoamerica wished to spread rather than guard information. Was there no censorship in Middle America? Finding "official restraints" in pre-Columbian societies is a usual concept, but Aztec emperor Itzcoatl (c. 1427–1440) allegedly ordered books burned and rewritten to accommodate his needs. "Their history was preserved," recites the *Códice Matritense de la Real Academia de la Historia*, "but then it was burned, when Itzcoatl reigned in Mexico."[75] Again, codices and history appear as ancient instruments of political control.

Journalism historians ought to analyze how Itzcoatl ran a process of Mexica glorification through the power of writing.[76] For the Aztecs, books meant knowledge, so this king decided to expunge embarrassing episodes from historical records, burning a number of existing screenfolds. Seeking to renew their cultural past and, essentially, to redefine and rewrite Mexica history, Izcoatl "ordered the destruction of the old chronicles."[77] He "erased the collective memory of his people," inventing a new official version of Aztec history.[78] Such manipulation of the media deserves a close scrutiny, exploring how royal scribes helped this emperor consolidate a Triple Alliance in c. 1428, the mightiest military, economic, and cultural expansion ever organized in the Valley of Mexico (Tenochtitlan with Texcoco and Tlacopan).

This is a provocative story to investigate, separating myth from fact and asking not if "there was censorship" but rather "what kind of censorship."[79] If societies in the age of the scribe had censored written symbols, including early Sumeria and Egypt, why should Mesoamerica be the exception? There is a scanty literature on the roles and uses of ancient American media, but increased documentation and information is inspiring observers to raise new and interesting questions.

As true masters of calligraphy, native scribes enjoyed a preeminent position in American antiquity. Books in Mesoamerica flourished with the priestly class, an elite dedicated to write down happenings, sciences, and myths in the hope of spreading knowledge across towns and provinces. Functioning as priests of the ritual arts, royal scribes became experts in the dynamics of gods and unseen forces, gaining great respect for it.[80] Without being rulers, they belonged to an elevated circle of specialists, which also included ball players, shell and metal workers, and other skilled people.[81]

Pre-Columbian scribes dealt with the everyday worries and activities of their chiefs. They were often nobles but rarely, if ever, kings, although some were children of rulers as the middle-aged man found in *Copán's Chorcha* structure in Honduras (the famous Tomb of the Royal Scribe). Because of this remarkable discovery, Copán gained status in history as "the Athens of the New World," that is, if we accept that the Mayas resemble the Greeks, and the Aztecs, the Romans. With Sylvanus Morley, the archaeologist-spy who worked for the U.S. Office of Naval Intelligence in Central America (Agent no. 53), Emeritus Professor John A. Crow of UCLA (University of California, Los Angeles) trumpeted the Mayas' reputation as the Greeks of the New World in *The Epic of Latin America* (1946).[82] This is another example of the marked Eurocentrism prevalent among Mesoamericanists until recently.

Burial XXXVII-4, a tomb chamber of a scribe close to the Copanecan king, indicates that the deceased could have been the second son of either Smoke Imix God K or 18 Rabbit. With the highest honors, this royal scribe carried into the *Otherworld*, accompanied by red-colored and painted pots, a spondylus shell, a painted wooden bowl, numerous residues of coated and painted plaster, and a very large codex, unfortunately reduced to flakes by time.[83] Ancient American scribes enjoyed great social esteem, serving as members of an elite who could escape the *Underworld*. This *ts'ib* at Copán went buried with a low-class twelve-year-old assistant to help him conduct his duties in the afterlife. Copán, an urban center that may have reached at its peak 20,000–25,000 inhabitants, is crucial to reconstruct our memory of the Maya writing system. Many Mesoamericanists believe "no other city of aboriginal America ever attained so high a level of cultural achievement."[84]

Were there females scribes in pre-Hispanic America? Apparently, at least in the Maya and Aztec worlds where a number of *"ah k'u huns* [keepers of the holy books or *tlacuilos*, from the Nahuatl verb *tlacuiloa*] could have been women. [E]pigraphers observed that [this] title is appended to several women's names on the monuments, notably at Yaxchilán."[85] Uniqueness, skill, and wisdom secured both male and female scribes a place in the upper echelon of society, especially in Copán, a remarkable literary capital where patriarchs, specialized in the arts of writing, received full recognition of their royal house.[86] A deeply philosophical affair, written communication and other forms of expression worked with devotion here and elsewhere in Middle America.

Also ball courts, the equivalent of Spanish colonial plazas, functioned as points of transcendental encounters, arenas of "confrontation and communication [...] in which life and death, victory and defeat, rebirth and triumph played out their consequences."[87] But the most symbolic means of intimate connection with their gods transpired in blood flows from human sacrifices. Blood scrolls were speech scrolls. The act of bloodletting, publicly and privately, among nobles or commoners, helped them "communicate with their ancestors."[88]

According to literary editor Andrew Robinson, the Mayas were obsessed with blood and war. One of the principal goals of a lineage-proud king was to capture the ruler of a rival city-state in battle, torture him, and humiliate him, sometimes for years. Then, the prisoner would be subjected to decapitation following a ball game that he was always destined to lose.[89] Bloodletting, nevertheless, was an act of piety as much as of communication, a vital ritual in Mayan life. To effectively understand it, as to explain their wars, trade, economic system, and environmental pressures, contemporary minds need to go beyond the veil of Spanish and other European accounts and find their reasons.

In sum, the pre-Columbian literature, particularly the codices, a collection of ancestral rules, memoirs, and speeches, is a key source when trying to explain thoughts and actions in ancient American societies. Religion and philosophy and communication and politics are simply aspects of the same concrete reality. As Schele and Freidel advised introducing *A Forest of Kings*, "[ancient] chronicles speak in the language of a great philosophical, scientific, and religious vision—a charter for power as eternal and as flexible as the American Constitution."[90]

DEEPER ROOTS

Before the Zapotecs and the Mayas, ancient Olmecs might have been the first to register events in ceramic and stone works inscribed with dates and other hieroglyphs. Florida State University professor Mary E. D. Pohl recently announced that "a cylinder seal and carved greenstone plaque bearing glyphs dating to ca. 650 BC have been uncovered near the Olmec center of La Venta in Tabasco, Mexico. These artifacts, which predate others containing writing, reveal [a connection between writing, the calendar, and kingship] in Olmec writing. They [also] imply that Mesoamerican writing [and its earliest use for political purposes] originated in the La Venta polity."[91]

Archaeologists are unable to fully translate the signs of the plaque fragments found in *San Andrés*, five-kilometers northeast of La Venta, but they are persuaded that the speech scrolls in the cylinder seal utter the words "king" and "3 Ajaw." Together, they read as "King 3 Ajaw," a calendar-based title of a ruler who probably ordered the use of the ceramic seal to imprint clothing, the human body, and perhaps bark paper in his honor.[92] Because the carving of monumental and precious stones had been "one of the principal means by which high-status individuals conveyed the message of kingship [and military conquest,] the San Andrés seal can be interpreted as *a tool for printing a royal message.*"[93]

Prudence is recommended however, suggests Professor Gary Haynes, chairman of the University of Nevada's Anthropology Department at Reno, where ceramist Von Nagy, one of the Olmec seal discoverers, resides. We, educators, declares Haynes in the *Reno Gazette-Journal*, "will be waiting to see if [the assertions] hold up. If they do, it will be a fairly important discovery. That would make it something remarkable because scientists are always looking for the biggest, the fastest, the best and the earliest."[94] Unfortunately, researchers (and reporters) often look for the fashionable and profitable as well, a big threat to quality science in all fields.

In La Venta, an Olmec capital of the Middle Pre-Classic period (1200–400 BCE), with influence from Central Mexico to El Salvador and from the Isthmus of Tehuantepec to early Mayan and Oaxacan city-states, writing and its use for politics might have emerged as transcending legacies. "It was odd that writing had been attributed to other groups [after] the Olmec [had] initiated many of Mesoamerica's cultural traditions including urban settlements and monumental architecture," commented Dr. Pohl. Since "the Olmecs were the first to put together a political state, and writing is closely connected with rulers in terms of *publicizing their power*, it makes sense that they would be the first to use [this practice]," concludes the Florida State University professor.[95] Fascinating! Olmec rulers were interested in inscribing messages to "publicize" their power. If confirmed, the role of political communication has not radically changed over two and a half millennia.

Illustrating this ancestral gift, an Aztec passage recites how ancient people, across the Gulf of Mexico and beyond, mainly wise men and priests who possessed the knowledge of measuring time, "carried with them the black and red ink, the manuscripts and painted books, the wisdom. They brought everything—they said—the annals, the books of song, and their flutes."[96] Also, Olmec literati are said to have invented the Long Count, the reliable registration of time previously attributed to the Mayas. A virtual "Mesopotamia of the Americas," the Olmec area is the likely birthplace of our native literature, around the times of Pericles and Athens' Golden Age. The American chronicle emerged long before Christ, Columbus, and the Pilgrims. Sadly, from childhood on, lamented Schele and Freidel, "we have been taught in our schools that the Mediterranean is the only 'cradle of civilization,' when, in fact, human beings developed the civilized state also in northern India, China, Middle America, and Peru."[97]

It is mind blowing to contemplate these findings, views, and subsequent social implications against the imposed assumptions of past decades and centuries. Communicators should also research the role of Olmec stamps as an early form of elitist, political, and printing activity in the literary heritage of pre-Columbian Americans.[98]

ISTHMIAN ACCOUNTS

One intriguing treasure of post-Olmec times is the six-inch-tall *Tuxtla Statuette*, found near *San Andrés Tuxtla* in southeastern Veracruz, Mexico, in 1902. Carved in jade between the Classic Olmec period and the Mayan Golden Age, this green figurine displays bar-and-dot numbers corresponding to a Long Count date of March 14, 162 CE. The inscriptions allegedly bear a pre-proto-Zoquean language, believed to be an ancestor of current Mixe-Zoquean tongues of the Isthmus of Tehuantepec. They contain a total of seventy (others say, sixty-four) characters.[99] What does this writing say? Nobody really knows, but a decipherment in progress

purports that the statuette appears to narrate events related to the performance and "representation of a shaman in his animal alter ego."[100] This
statuette has "significant apparent implications for ruleship and shaman-
ism in the late Formative period."[101]

Some epigraphers also claim to have identified epi-Olmec morphemes
in *La Mojarra Stela 1*, another extraordinary post-Olmec relic. Arguably,
this stela, the Tuxtla statuette, and shorter recovered samples in the
Isthmian style (less than ten objects) convey full or partial words such
as "who," "king," "lord," "priest," "day," "year," "to appear," "to sing,"
"throne," "holy," "sacrifice," "blood," "now," and "and then," all useful
terms for an incipient practice of chronicling. Even with controversial interpretations, the existence of writing in these pieces is undisputed.[102]

The four-ton *La Mojarra* surfaced from the waters of the Acula River in
November 1986, next to San Lorenzo in the lowlands of Veracruz. This
beautiful manuscript on basalt, with twenty-two written columns, holds
about 535 incised glyphs. Because of its two Long Count dates, May 21,
143 CE, and July 13, 156 CE, it is "one of Mesoamerica's oldest known
texts."[103] Named after the place where it was found (within forty miles
of the Tuxtla Statuette), *La Mojarra* supposedly tells the story of a warrior
called *Harvester Mountain Lord* and his accession to the throne. Epigraphers John S. Justeson of the State University of New York and Terrence
Kaufman of the University of Pittsburgh believe that this personal title is only an epithet of the protagonist, not a real name. The narrative refers "to his success over time in ensuring good harvests for his
people."[104]

Monica Stapley, citing Stuart and critic Angela Schuster of *Archaeology*
magazine, aptly summarizes the content of this piece as "*essentially a political poster* recording the endeavors of a warrior-king named Harvester
Mountain Lord. The monument alludes to 'his accession to the throne and
rituals of sacrifice celebrated in his new rise to power.' There is mention
that th[is] ruler held a 'yet-to-be-deciphered title for twelve or thirteen
years and that he was able to transform himself into an animal.' Witnesses
are [also] mentioned [in this poster], specifically, 'a shaman instrumental
for rituals associated with his accession.' The 'commentary' ends with the
king crushing a coup led by his brother in law."[105]

In 1995, closer reexamination of this unusual document revealed a faded
and probably last column (the twenty-second). The passage describes the
gruesome execution of the protagonist's brother-in-law, which goes as
follows: "Behold, he was for twelve years a [Harvester Mountain Lord].
And then a garment got folded. He [utter]ed: the stones that he (had)
set in order were thus symbols, [?] kingly ones. What I chopped has
been planted and harvested well. (A) shape-shifter appear divinely in
his body." Although the previous sentence could also be interpreted as:
"What I chopped is a planting and a good harvest," or even "What I
chopped has been planted; the latter was well harvested."[106]

This is the record of a deadly battle for power between relatives where the executioner appears to have gained some kind of local or regional control as a result of the victim's beheading. It is also a bloody account connected to a recent happening, taking place shortly before the likely erection of the stela (October 169 CE). The wording "set [the stones] in order" implies separate events in time, while the expression "and then" denotes an effort to chronicle the episode. The apparent use of the verb "to utter" or "to speak" (the -*wu* sign group) seems an explicit attempt to publicize the chopping, burying, and so-called harvesting of the enemy's head and blood, insofar as human sacrifices were believed to promote good crops in the Olmec and post-Olmec mythology. This would be a remarkable written description on a relevant issue among pre-proto-Sokean speakers. If the decoding is correct, it is also a fabulous early evidence of the instrumental role of the media at the service of powerful people in ancient America.

Not everyone agrees. Robinson sums up the dissenters' perspective noting that "reconstruction of the grammar of the pre-proto-Zoquean language is highly speculative. There is no solid internal evidence for what [Justeson and Kaufman] think these particular sign sequences represent [e.g. verbs]. There is doubtfulness in their contribution."[107] Still, he and others, including Professor Stephen D. Houston of Brown University, also unconvinced, admitted that it was hard to dispute those findings because of Justeson and Kaufman's reputation as competent epigraphers. Nevertheless, a text as complete, coherent, and grammatically structured as their translation raises a great deal of suspicion.

In January 2004, Houston and Coe revisited this issue. "We have just found another [Isthmian] inscription, which allows us to plug in some of the supposed readings, and it comes up with a nonsensical pattern," announced Houston.[108] They evaluated earlier interpretations and found them "wanting." Their conclusion is based on a previously unknown ancient mask from a private collection with assumed Isthmian signs, but there is no exact information as to where the object was found nor about its context. Dr. Houston is confident that this Teotihuacan-styled mask with some 101 glyphs, 25 of them totally new to the Istmian "alphabet," dates back to between 300 and 500 CE. We subjected "the claimed decoding" of the epi-Olmec writing to "rigid standards of proof" and it showed "that this script remains undeciphered," concluded Coe.[109] If this is the case, Justeson and Kaufman's reading of *La Mojarra* would be pure fiction. The debate continues.

Either way, the incredibly detailed *La Mojarra Stela* is one of the longest manuscripts discovered in Mesoamerica thus far. Its length is precisely the reason why some museum curators and scholars mistrust its originality, arguing that it "is a modern forgery added to an authentic pre-Hispanic monument."[110] The majority, however, believe that the stela is genuine.

PAINTED TALES

In the cosmopolitan center of Teotihuacan, the sixth largest city of the world at 600 CE, murals with speech scrolls displayed colorful voices and lively verbal activity. Tantalizing examples are the volute coming from the mouth of a coyote in the White Patio in Atetelco and the jaguar-man addressing a temple in Tetitla (mural 7, room 12). In Middle America, the jaguar is a complex duality, another self that evokes power and government, intelligence, beauty, strength, courage, danger, victory, war, magic, and sacrifice, especially among kings and priests. This icon is repeatedly expressed in sculpture, architecture, ceramics, painting, and paper. Modern visitors often missed both Tetitla and Atetelco when touring Teotihuacan.[111]

Painting, particularly mural painting, is an indispensable communication medium that spread throughout Mesoamerica. Unlike universal traditional arts, which try to create a virtual reality, the pre-Columbian murals reproduce plain and direct conceptual representations of what people believed of themselves, their environment, and the cosmos. Ancient mural themes were rich and diverse, explains historian Beatriz de la Fuente, professor of pre-Hispanic painting at UNAM (Mexico's National University). These murals can be classified as *"conceptual* in Teotihuacan, *narrative* in the Mayan area (with inscriptions included, as in Bonampak and Mulchic), *illustrative* in the Gulf Coast, and *mythical* and *historical* as in the Mexican highlands (Cacaxtla)."[112] Although less frequently, murals also dealt with quotidian affairs. In Cacaxtla, state of Tlaxcala, they narrate the social and political instability following the collapse of Teotihuacan.[113] This art form is the ancient equivalent of the present-day poster, billboard, or magazine cover.

Its respected iconography helped Teotihuacan transcend as a place of dynamic communication between rulers, gods, and people of diverse backgrounds, possibly up to 200,000 dwellers including post-Olmecs, Zapotecs, Mayans, and other pre-Hispanic residents and travelers. The Zapotecs, for instance, had a wall painting tradition heavily influenced by this urban center, resulting in a so-called *Oaxacan codex-styled muralism* during the late Classic period.[114] More importantly, states Jorge Angulo, archaeologist of the ENAH (the National School of Anthropology and History in Mexico City), these murals of Teotihuacan "make up a plastic language with contents that generate multiple readings, many of them still undeciphered to us. This pictographic or pre-alphabetic writing *describes events, stories, historical passages and mythical facts*. The pre-Hispanic painting grows in the ambiguous realm of the metaphor, in a kingdom where realist representations mix with symbolic or abstract ones."[115]

Generally, the premise has been that the *Teotihuacanos* lacked a true writing system, rendering inscriptions that represent a mere and sporadic iconography.[116] But that is wrong, replied anthropologist Karl A. Taube of the University of California–Riverside. As he points out, "Teotihuacan had a very developed hieroglyphic writing system. It is very probable that most of those texts were written in books of deer skin or paper, materials that disappeared long ago. Many other texts are preserved in murals, ceramics, and carved monuments that still have a lot to tell us about the Teotihuacan writing."[117]

There must have been scribes within the crowd of traders, artisans, and other skilled workers in Teotihuacan. Coe believes that "although no books have survived from the Classic [period] into our day, we have every reason to believe that many peoples possessed them."[118] In his view, books functioned for both ritual and administrative purposes, although, if writing existed, it was only in rudimentary form. In fact, there are a few isolated glyphs that have been identified on the pottery and the frescoes, states Coe. In this last sentence, Professor Taube disagrees. He thinks that the writing system of Teotihuacan included inscriptions more regularly than initially thought of. Tied to their iconography, the Teotihuacan glyphs formed a rich collection of calendrical and speech signs, places, and personal emblems or names.[119]

Commercial networks, with Teotihuacan as a focal point, brought active transactions across Mesoamerica, including tours of messengers sharing costumes, rituals, and ideas in the lands of the Maya, their neighbors, and probably distant territories. Schele and Freidel explain this intercultural exchange as "the establishment of an international network of trade [transferring] material goods and ideas. This interaction between the peoples of Mesoamerica resulted—they say—in a florescence of civilized life, a cultural brilliance and intensity that exceeded even the accomplishments of the Olmec."[120] Like modern times, communication and both cultural and political power were all pieces of the same puzzle of ancient American trade.

Before discovering the Olmec plaque and seal of *San Andrés*, Zapotecs of the middle to late pre-Classic periods appeared to have been the likely first scribes and chroniclers of the *Oneworld* (Mesoamerica), carving stones around the year 500 BCE. No pre-Classic Zapotec books have been found yet.[121] The Zapotec registered memorable facts such as historic scenes in stelae, palaces, sanctuaries, and tombs, chronicling royal and divine conversations as well as other events including the birth of princes. Decipherment of the Zapotec writing is far from the code-breaking process of the Maya script, but the late and prominent archaeologist Alfonso Caso interpreted many of the Zapotec symbols as "records of town conquests."[122] Others believe, that instead of conquests, what the stelae really depict are ceremonies in honor of the city's founders.[123]

Logophonetic in nature, the Zapotec script deals with places and individual names, weather conditions, calendrical data, and sacrificial clauses, many of them sculpted in the chests of the *Danzantes*. Verbs such as "slain," "capture," "defeat," and "sacrifice" are common in Monte Albán, making short sentences such as "Face Striker was slain" or "Were-jaguar was captured [and] sacrificed to the Wind."[124] Mexican scholar Javier Urcid, a specialist of Mesoamerican scriptures, estimates the total unearthed written legacy of this civilization in nearly 570 glyphs considered definite writing.[125]

These records carry both calendrical names and the relation scripture–power which seems explicit of the political competition of the times. Informed speculation suggests that the Zapotec rulers also used writing for propaganda purposes, a refined script portraying the nobility in elegant forms while visuals of commoners are sloppy and confusing. With the increasing cultural influence of Teotihuacan, the idea of iconography as a universally interpretable medium gained popularity, leading to a reassessment of "the propaganda value of a language specific system of writing whose message was accessible only to a local Oaxacan elite."[126] This discussion about the actual character of the Zapotec writing is an exciting area in the study of ancient American communication and its roles.

Other creators, such as the epi-Olmec and the Maya, could not be easily ruled out as book pioneers. In *The Art of the Maya Scribe*, Coe and Kerr also speak of an "intriguing" Olmec white-ware ceramic bowl kept at the University of Notre Dame's Snite Museum, where incised representations appear to show "side views of codices, each bound with a ribbon or cord. If so, the screenfold codex made from *amate* bark coated with gesso may already have been in Mesoamerican culture as early as 1200 BC."[127] Regardless of who was the pioneer, native codices and their stories, whether Olmec, Zapotec, Mayan, or Teotihuacan, became a "pan-Mesoamerican phenomenon" during the Classic period.

This discussion about the dawn of historical reporting overlaps with the origins of writing in Middle America. The reason is that writing and information go hand in hand as archaeologist Piña-Chan suggested several years ago, working for the Center of Historical and Social Studies at the National Autonomous University of Campeche. Based on Hanns J. Prem, he wrote: "writing is not only a visual registration of spoken language [but] also a system of signs, a semiotics that represents information, that is, a graphic expression used with the purpose of transmitting information."[128]

REMAINS OF A PROLIFIC BIBLIOGRAPHY

After so many codices served the One World, what we have today is "a pitiful remnant of the thousands of books that once formed the basis of [Mesoamerican] knowledge" and they are mostly in Europe under alien names.[129] This massive annihilation of screenfolds and libraries took place during the conquest because of the "stupid zeal" of fanatical priests and soldiers, wrote Father José de Acosta in 1590.[130] As works of the devil, Spanish chroniclers and missionaries documented the burning of numerous pre-Hispanic codices, a destruction that brought untold humiliation and affliction to native people.

Four hundred years later, studying a pre-Hispanic codex was still a taboo, the exclusive privilege of a small group of Mesoamerican archaeologists, linguists, and historians. What scientists discovered about American antiquities, only scientists knew, complained Manuel Galich, the noted Guatemalan author and politician, working for the Arbenz administration until the CIA orchestrated a coup to overthrow their national government. Alternative indigenous perspectives were then politically incorrect, even subversive, especially when a Soviet scholar (Yuri Knorosov) had the upper hand deciphering the Maya texts. The collapse of the Berlin Wall brought at last the flexibility needed to let Knorosov, Coe, and a few others publicize the decipherment of the Maya script, fertilizing the ground for a redefinition of the emergence of communications in the Western Hemisphere, including the dawn of journalism.

The Maya finally speak, "releasing a written language no one had read since the sixteenth century," wrote David Stuart, Associate Director of the corpus of Maya hieroglyphs at Harvard University's Peabody Museum.[131] Common wisdom held that the glyphs were nothing more than a cumbersome pictographic system in which each image represented a specific word or idea, but that view was utterly wrong, he said. Maya writing was, in fact, a robust phonetic script that used a combination of signs, each representing consonant-and-vowel syllables to spell words including dates followed by life stories. Now that the ancient Mayas can tell us their narrative, doors are flung open on the history of this great Mesoamerican civilization.[132] Today, about 80 percent of Maya inscriptions are readable and the writing system is essentially deciphered.

Only four books, others say three known Maya codices (with the authenticity of the *Grolier Codex* recently challenged), lived through the rage of the European conquest and colonization. Archaeology studies tend to show that both Zapotecan-speaking people in the mountains and Maya communities in the lowlands of the Great Constriction (the Isthmus of Tehuantepec) planted and spread the use of books in Mesoamerica. But, as mentioned earlier, the debate continues as there are no pre-Hispanic Zapotec codices to confirm their existence, leaving modern Americans with a tiny sample of a presumably large Maya library.[133]

Foreign names *Dresden*, *Paris*, and *Madrid* identify the surviving pre-Hispanic Maya codices, endorsing the sophistication of the ancient bark-paper book culture. Non-Maya pre-Columbian manuscripts also carry tags in Latin and other European languages, oblivious to the ethnic origins and colonialism that decimated their authors. Five of them are the codices *Borgianus* (Codex Borgia), *Vaticanus B, Cospianus* (Codex Cospi), *Liber Hieroglyphicorum Aegyptorum* (Codex Laud), and the *Codex Fejérváry Mayer* of the so-called *Borgia Group,* all presumably written in the *Mixteca-Puebla* region between northwest Oaxaca and the south of Puebla. The first two books are in the Vatican City, the *Cospi* is in Bologna (Italy), and the remaining ones are in Oxford and Liverpool, respectively.[134]

These screenfolds, "principally used for religious purposes, were vehicles of communication between humans and divinity, a pictographic system as ingenious and precise as it was harmonious and full of color."[135] Such a body of attractive literature could have been produced only by a civilization of artists, wrote historian María de los Angeles Ojeda Díaz, curator of the Collection of Mexican Codices of the National Library of Anthropology and History in Mexico City. Indeed, the *Codex Colombino,* one of six surviving Mixtec manuscripts on skin, is "the only pre-Hispanic" book "legally" owned by Mexico through a public institution.[136] The rest are in England and Austria. Two of them, the *Codex Bodley* and the *Codex Selden,* are in Oxford, and *the Codex Zouche-Nuttall* is in the British Museum of London. The last two Mixtec books, the codices *Becker I* and *Vindobonensis,* are in Vienna. There are no known pre-Cortesian codices in private hands anywhere at this time.

Finally, only two Aztec books escaped the rampant Spanish destruction of pre-Columbian codices: the *Codex Borbonicus* or *Codex du Corps Legislatif* of the French National Assembly's Library and the *Tonalamatl de Aubin,* taken by a Mexican journalist from The Bibliotheque Nationale de France (BnF) and now in "temporary shelter" at the National Museum of Anthropology and History in Mexico City.

Exquisite in form and content, the *Dresden Codex* is perhaps the most complete and best regarded of all existing pre-Hispanic manuscripts. It miraculously endured the brutality of both colonialism and modern war, including World War II (although badly damaged) when Churchill ordered the bombing of Dresden on February 13, 1945.[137] Avoiding the hatred and the infamous burnings of Spanish invaders and their clergy, Hernán Cortés allegedly shipped the screenfold to the Iberian peninsula as a Royal Fifth or tribute to his King Charles I, also monarch of Austria during the conquest.[138]

Thirty-nine folios (78 pages, 4 of them blank) portray the deeply cosmic and philosophical life of the Mayas in this codex. Texts of authority, profound scientific meaning, and terrifying images of human sacrifice tell the story of the harsh life of ancient Americans. Nature, divinity, and society blend with complex ancestral rites and transcendental beliefs.[139] Three and a half meters long (exactly 356 centimeters, with pages 9 centimeters wide and 18.2 centimeters tall), the Dresden Codex recreates the sacred reality, time, and universe of pre-Columbian America. In this book, according to the memorable Mexican historian, archeologist, and art critic

Salvador Toscano, we find the "faithful representati[on] of the precocity and elegance of the Ancient Maya."[140]

On page 8, *Itzamná*, the inventor of writing, divinity of the night, the moon, and the sky, allegedly debates with the End-of-the-Year deity on how to remake humanity.[141] Next page, the former god is found in active conversation with the divinity of maize and agriculture discussing over the creation of human life. The codex concludes with *Itzamna* (at page 53 in Knorosov's and 74 in Ernst Forstemann's enumeration), turning himself into a celestial caiman and releasing floods that destroy the world forever.[142] Calendrical computations based on these writings prophesy a cataclysmic destruction of our existence on December 21, 2012.[143] Others, with different motives, speak of June 5, December 22, or December 23 as the day of the final judgment or collapse. Massive flooding will supposedly consume our planet, ending the fifth era in the Maya mythology.[144] "We can only feel apprehension for the future of the earth" as the year 2012 approaches, speculate Gilbert and Cotterell.[145]

Speech volutes, that is, upward curls flowering from a speaker's mouth, appear throughout this *Códice Dresde* with various actors. They help gods inform humankind about their sacred commands.[146] Still, interpretation beyond translation of the pre-Columbian codices, ceramics, canvasses, stone panels, and other written media is in its infancy despite remarkable recent progress, including Maya readings. At this point, observes Elizabeth H. Boone, we continue to ignore what many ancient Amerindian writings really meant, how they functioned in society, how and what kind of information they conveyed, and who or how audiences actually received their messages.[147]

The *Dresdensis*, on the other hand, was the first Mayan codex publicly recognized. Sixty-six years after acquisition of this priceless document by the Royal Library of the Court of Saxony in Dresden (from a private Vienna collection in 1744), geographer and naturalist Alexander von Humboldt published five pages of the relic in his famous Atlas of 1810 (*Vues des cordillères et monuments des peuples indigènes de l'Amérique*). Basic motifs of this luminous pre-Columbian manuscript had also appeared in an interior decoration album entitled *Depiction and history of the taste of superior peoples*, printed in Leipzig in 1796.[148] Somewhere, somehow, the notion that ancient Andeans and Mesoamericans reached high levels of cultures capable of producing impressive books faded away in Europe, leaving behind an insulting paternalism or neglect of native people and Creoles that eventually spilled over Anglo-America.[149] As the codex sits in Dresden's *Sächsische Landesbibliothek* (the Saxon State Library in Germany), manuscript lovers held their breadth once again when rising waters, nine meters high, flooded Dresden, threatening historic places full of masterpieces in the summer of 2002.

From Johann Christian Goetze, the Royal Library director who first cataloged this screenfold as "a strange Mexican book" in 1744 to Constantine Samuel Rafinesque who identified it as a Mayan manuscript in 1829, the *Dresden Codex* had been a silent link between media modernity and the New World's literary antiquity. Edward King, the Irish Viscount Kingsborough, had everyone confused with his assertion that the *Dresdensis* was an Aztec artwork. But specialists later confirmed the data and narration as definitely Maya, including its invocations to history and genealogy, trade, education, and mythology. This marvelous codex, however, does contain an "Aztec-influenced iconography," and thanks to Von Racknitz (1796), von Humboldt (1810), John L. Stephens, Frederick Catherwood, and Ernst Forstemann, it finally received serious attention in scholarly circles.[150]

Once accepted as a Maya codex, debates focused on its geographic origins. Cholan more than Yucatec roots led experts to believe that the *Dresde* came from the late Classic period in today's *Departamento del Petén* in Guatemala, probably Tikal or a neighboring city-state. Mexico's Palenque and the erudite center of Copán in Honduras also emerged as possible birthplaces.[151] But, today, the *Dresdensis* appears more closely connected to Yucatan, possibly the Maya of Chichén Itzá. This "very late pre-Conquest" document, perhaps copied from a previous original by five to eight different scribes with their own personal writing styles, was presumably in use when the conquistadors landed on Cozumel in 1519.[152]

Two additional Maya books, the *Paris* and the *Madrid* (initially, just the *Codex Troano*), reappeared in 1859 and 1866, respectively. News of a second part of the *Madrid*, the *Codex Cortesianus*, broke out in 1875.[153] In time, the *Madrid Codex* became technically known as the *Codex Tro-Cortesianus*. A fourth book, the *Grolier*, really a fragment and a partial view of the Venus almanac, is the only ancient manuscript "rescued" during the twentieth century. It first appeared at a New York book collectors' exhibition (the Grolier Club) in April 1971. Its authenticity "is seriously questioned" as a modern fabrication, considering that a few days in a modern library—with pieces of genuine native paper—is all professional counterfeiters need to come up with a persuasive forgery.[154] Unlike the *Grolier*, the *Paris* is a better preserved manuscript, offering with "veritable graphic clarity" various thirteenth-century Maya astronomical observations.[155]

The story of the *Paris Codex* or *Peresianus* (currently in the National Library of France) is evocative of Latin America's image abroad. One day in Paris, Professor Léon Louis Lucien Prunol de Rosny ran across this manuscript looking into "a basket among some old papers in a dingy and neglected chimney corner of the library."[156] The twenty-two-page Maya book, bearing the name "Pérez" (a library staff member who apparently worked on two reviews about this codex in 1859), had twice disappeared before Mr. José Pérez found it. Then, Léon de Rosny came along, publishing a colorful and historic study entitled *Codex Peresianus, Manuscrit hièratique des anciens indiens de l'Amerique centrale conservé à la Bibliothèque Nationale de Paris*.[157] Ironic to say the least, both the front and back covers of the codex clearly display library stamp marks reading "Bibliothèque Imperiale."[158]

Scholars prefer to use the name *Paris* instead of *Peresianus* to avoid any confusion with a codex known as *Códice Pérez* (*The Book of Chilam Balam* of Maní).[159] Obliterated in the margins and in need of deeper and interdisciplinary analyses and interpretations, the *Paris Codex* remains as a book of calendric predictions, making references to rituals, prophecies, and historical events. Contents in two pages are now "lost through deterioration of the original."[160]

Like the *Paris*, the *Madrid* or *Tro-Cortesianus* also has an intriguing past. Charles Etienne Brasseur de Bourbourg, the French cleric who uncovered two famous books, the *Popol Vuh* (the sacred book of the Quiché Maya) and the known copy—from the lost original—of De Landa's *Account of the Affairs of Yucatan*, also rescued this third treasure. Thanks to Don Juan de Tro y Ortolano, a descendant of Hernán Cortés, Brasseur obtained the first part of the *Madrid Codex* in 1866. He named it the *Codex Troano* in his friend's honor, with blessings from Napoleon III. A second part, the *Cortesianus*, held by Don Juan Ignacio Miró and defined by Leon the Rosny as "one and the same [Madrid] codex," surfaced nine years later, making this entire *biombo* the longest pre-Columbian Maya book ever found (56 leaves or 112 pages).[161] The two *Don Juanes* came from Extremadura, the region where Cortés had been born.

For now, the Tro-Cortesianus rests in the *Museo de América* in Spain and should not be confused with Leonardo Da Vinci's *Madrid codices*, also the historic notebooks of the maestro's mechanical inventions and physical theories, new musical instruments, and lessons for would-be painters. Early criticism viewed the Madrid Codex as a work of crude and careless craftsmanship. Yet, this manuscript, a mixture of Yucatecan and Cholan Maya, contains valuable information on agricultural practices, diseases, and hunting, as well as important descriptions about gods and rituals related to the sacred 260-day and 365-day calendars.

Even more interesting is the discussion on whether this codex is truly pre-Hispanic or not. According to Professor Coe, the Madrid Codex could have been assembled in the mid- to late 1600s, perhaps near the fall of *Tayasal* in 1697. Over 200 years since Columbus the Spaniards struggled to finally defeat the Itza in the Central *Petén* region of today's Guatemala, ending with the last independent Maya kingdom since the discovery. Characters in Latin, including what appears to be the word *prefatorum* and the incomplete name "... *ríquez*," are "sandwiched between two layers of bark paper, evidence that [this text had been] incorporated into the codex during its manufacture."[162] With as many as nine scribes involved, this codex allegedly incorporated Fray Juan Enríquez's signature. Enríquez had died in this area during a failed Spanish attempt to take over the Petén in 1624. Almost four centuries later, experts were requesting permission from the *Museo de América* in Madrid to conduct infrared, ultraviolet, and X-ray tests on the reverse of folio 56, hoping to establish how alien were those marks.

The existence of a fourth pre-Columbian Maya book has also been hotly debated. During the mid-1970s, a so-called *Códice Porrúa*, in honor of librarian Don Manuel Porrúa in Mexico City, hung around as a possible new pre-Hispanic Maya manuscript. But the 105 pieces of cured manatee skin with no unity, uniformity, or consistency made the veracity of this codex extremely unlikely.[163] Following Spanish theosophist Mario Roso de Luna (1872–1931) and its early twentieth-century writings, a few authors believe that the *Porrúa* codex is a Maya book from the late pre-Classic or early Classic periods. Indeed, Roso de Luna claimed that ancient Mayas had also written on animal skins and not only bark paper, and that "their libraries contained very old books."[164] To this day, however, no reputable Mayanists support these assertions.

Then, the *Grolier* came up as a real possibility.[165] It appeared during an exhibit on ancient Mayan calligraphy at the *Grolier Club* in New York (April 20–July 5, 1971), and unlike the mostly unknown *Codex Porrúa*, the press immediately announced it as a pre-Columbian book shedding light on the religion and astrological philosophy of the Maya. "Dr. Michael Coe, who attests to the authenticity of the codex, says that [its survival] is a miracle," reported *The New York Times*.[166] Sir Eric Thompson immediately and strongly disagreed, arguing that the confusing mix of astronomical calculations and iconography in the Grolier was not the product of Maya acculturation but of a skillful falsifier.[167]

The story on this screenfold is as perplexing as the others. Found in poor condition inside a wooden box of a cave in *Tabasco*, the manuscript, one-fourth of a twenty-page table about the movements of the planet Venus, was initially ruled a fraud. After Coe insisted on its authenticity, based on his exhibition review *The Maya Scribe and His World*, scholars began to accept it. "Mystery of the Maya," a film presented at the Canadian Museum of Civilization in Quebec, coproduced by the Mexican Institute of Cinematography and the National Film Board of Canada, in association with the Natural Science Museum of Houston, agreed with Coe. The *Grolier* is genuine, they say, dating it back to approximately the year 1230 AD. News welcomed the piece as the oldest book among the Maya codices.[168]

In a jungle of merchants, forgers, and speculators, this conclusion has been consistently rejected in various circles. Significant scholarly publications exclude the *Grolier*—sometimes called *The Mexico City Codex*—because the circumstances of its appearance, its supposed role, and its iconography do not make sense, wrote author Claude-François Baudez.[169]

Although critics are becoming more vocal, those who believe this codex is a forgery simply choose not to mention it among the trilogy of uncontested ones. For example, a 1997 chart in *Arqueología Mexicana* (no. 23, on *Prehispanic Codices*) including an article entitled *Códices Mayas* by Professor Laura Elena Sotelo-Santos of the UNAM, completely ignored the *Grolier*.[170]

When experts think of a fake codex, archaeologist José Luis Franco usually comes to mind, warning that there are blank sheets of genuine pre-Hispanic paper in caves with no humidity waiting to be forged. After studying a facsimile of this codex, concludes Baudez, "I quickly became convinced that the manuscript made no sense in part or as a whole. Thus, I wish to share my deep conviction that the ten or eleven pages of this supposedly Maya and pre-Hispanic codex are a modern fabrication."[171] Whether these critics are today's Thompsons of the world criticizing another Knorosov (Coe) remains to be seen.

There is much to study and clarify with regards to the workings of these ancient books and other written media. According to interpretations of Fray Diego de Landa, priests and kings made good use of the codices, although not necessarily in public. In contrast, other views recognized that the codices did contribute to create a robust culture of communication without turning into a sort of pre-Columbian mass media. A third group of observers argue that along with or beyond the codices, lintels and stelae played predominantly a "mass function" just as a communication medium could possibly do it at the time and in the circumstances in which they operated. In other words, insofar as people could presumably and freely see these inscriptions in their towns, even if not completely understood, basic glyphs and ideas could flow nurturing a public media environment where it was easier to read than write.[172]

STOLEN TREASURES

On June 19, 1982, a thirty-six-year-old Mexican editor of a small newspaper in Cancun, the Yucatan Peninsula, entered the Bibliotheque Nationale de France (BnF) in Paris and walked out with an Aztec codex, the *Tonalamatl Aubin*. The intruder took it to Mexico and ultimately handed it over to the federal authorities after being located and identified by the Interpol. All codices, our heritage, must be returned to their homeland and people, their rightful owners, claimed Jose Luis Castañeda de Valle, a student of pre-Hispanic culture, as he was reportedly set free. The French Embassy in Mexico City demanded both the codex and Castañeda, but the public, including newspapers, defended his fellow countryman as a quixotic hero.

Following centuries of smuggled treasures worldwide, Mexican audiences and the mass media believed that "the extradition of such a patriot was surely out of the question."[173] In fact, weeks before the scandal, the Mexican delegation at UNESCO had demanded former colonial powers to return valuable objects in their possession to the countries of origin. Should historic milestones such as the Mesoamerican codices be sent back to Mexico and Central America? In the early 1970s, the United States tentatively agreed to restore all pre-Hispanic and colonial objects brought to this country without permission from Mexican authorities.[174]

Not long ago, a top Guatemalan official sobbed with joy on television news after the U.S. government returned thirty pre-Hispanic Maya pieces smuggled through Miami.[175] Still, the French government argues that giving up the codices would be as unthinkable as sending the Mona Lisa from the Louvre back to Italy. Overcoming the greatest obstacles, however, *Guernica* returned to Spain in September 1981. It took six years for the Museum of Modern Art in New York to finally surrender the masterpiece to Madrid's *El Prado* after dictator Francisco Franco died in 1975, but the United States did send it back.[176] Of course, ownership and historical circumstances between these two paintings are very different.

Since before the Romans, stated Riding, "art [has been] treated as war booty. Throughout Europe's turbulent history, art works have regularly changed hands through armed conflict or political domination. And from the 19th century, Europeans began bringing Asian, African, and Latin American treasures into their museums to save them—it was claimed—from destruction. Increasingly, however, victim countries are refusing to view history as a closed book. Greece has long demanded the return of the Elgin Marbles, [which amounts to] 253 sculptures from the Parthenon in the British Museum."[177] Clearly, Mexicans would love to have the *Dresden Codex* or the *Penacho* (feathered headdress) of Aztec emperor Motecuhzoma now in a Vienna museum back in their country.[178] But, if returned, would they forward the codex to Guatemala if the *"Dresden"* proves to be from the Petén region instead of Yucatan's city of Chichén-Itzá? Admittedly, this is a speculative and difficult question to answer, but it would be a Mesoamerican issue for Mesoamericans to resolve.[179]

When asked whether his country would return all the pre-Cortesian codices in its possession, Mr. Alberto Aza, Ambassador of Spain to Mexico, replied: "difficult it is to think that museums and governments of countries will be disposed to come up with good will acts and return the art works. Cultures are shared. In all countries, there should be art expressions of the others and nationalism today is giving way to a universality we should take advantage of."[180] It is a skillful answer which does little to limit the thousands of dollars a Mexican (a Central or a South American) citizen needs to travel across the Atlantic and personally enjoy a pre-Columbian Maya codex—although, once in Europe, except Spain, they may not be asked to show the academic credentials, recommendations, and permits Mexico requires to observe a genuine pre-Hispanic codex.

This is something, for instance, anyone can do for free at the British Museum's Mexico Room No. 27 in London (see the Codex Zouche-Nuttall).[181]

Stories of Discovery and Colonialism

For centuries, "the world had been trembling on the verge of mass media," wrote the late Steven Chaffee and Everett Rogers in *The Beginnings of Communication Study in America*, and so our age of information is in many ways the result of antiquity.[182] One fundamental gift of ancient times, they say, is the brilliance of the Greek philosophy, art, and rhetoric. Other legacies are the armies of scribes since the Romans, the established libraries and publishing houses of the classical era, and the paper and movable-type printing of the Chinese and Koreans well before Gutenberg. And this is not to mention the literary marvels of Mesopotamia, notably Sumeria, or of Egypt, India, and Phoenicia. Again, the ancient Middle American scribe is nowhere to be found in this vignette.

The Press and America, an interpretive history published since 1954, barely speaks of a Mesoamerican contribution. The closest to the New World is a brief recognition about the role of seals, engravings, pictographs, and ideographs in "what is now Mexico"—basically, the drawings of animals, objects, and humans turned into hieroglyphs.[183] Even journalism professor Nancy L. Roberts of the University of Minnesota dropped this brief reference in her revised (ninth) edition of 2000. The deletion came after the decipherment of the Maya script and its groundbreaking reinterpretation of pre-Hispanic Maya codices and other writings in the early 1990s.[184] One should not entirely blame Roberts as it became fashionable among publishers in the heat of globalization to avoid historical nuances in favor of a simple, standardized, and open-market view of the world.

Skipping the importance of indigenous communication and perpetuating the notion that colonialism brought all media civilization to the Western Hemisphere, Gardner made the fundamental point that a nascent journalism appeared in the New World before Gutenberg's mechanical printing press. She raised the issue that news reporting in America predates the Spanish colony and its printing houses. If bells could not toll in churches and marketplaces, then town criers, horns, or military bands gathered people before announcing major accounts, such as royal decrees. House-to-house *recados* (private messages) and gossip hardly ever failed in early Spanish America, while serenades "served more than a romantic role: they also were subtle vehicles for criticizing and transmitting information about unpopular persons, particularly the authorities," she wrote.[185]

But what about the aboriginal *sonajeros* (noise-markers) of pre-Contact tribes nicely portrayed in the film *Cabeza de Vaca*, recreating the odyssey of conquistador Alvar Nuñez in Tampa Bay, Florida, beginning in 1527?[186]

Before paintings or graphs in caves, walls, and stone monuments, commented Chivelet, early societies had gestures, artifacts, and other forms of announcing when they wished to make important episodes public. These were the *avisos*, she says, the news or *novedades* of their time. They are "the vestiges of a distant communication we practice today, only [less] evolved and [with obviously less] sophisticated media."[187]

In *Naufragios*, originally known as *Relación* (1542), Alvar Nuñez Cabeza de Vaca tells stories about his nearly ten years living with ancestors of the Seminoles, the *Criks*, and the Chichimec *Susolas* and *Avavares*. The conquistador-chronicler shows in these absorbing adventures how unsophisticated natives already had "news" of both the Spaniards' presence and Núñez's presumed abilities to cure.[188] For centuries, these kinds of accounts traveled in pre-Hispanic America through messengers, runners like the Inca *Chasquis* informing kings and high officials of the latest occurrences in battlefields, commercial markets, and other social events. Strictly speaking, a *Chasqui*, from the verb *chasquiy* in Quechua, exchanged, delivered, or received things, especially, announcements.[189]

In her monograph *The Press of Guatemala* (1971), Gardner failed to realize the importance of Mesoamerican stelae and codices as a source of study and inspiration, although admitting that the Spaniards relied on the *Chasquis* to effectively deliver news over large distances. In the end, this dedicated scholar, intrigued with the Hispanic roots of American journalism and the European influence, never passed through the veil of the Spanish chronicle to investigate the gifts of pre-Columbian communication.[190]

Too often, journalism authors glamorized the role of Gutenberg's printing press in detriment of this continent's precolonial media. This is a flaw that news historians like Gardner understood and intended to correct, focusing on the peculiar importance of news during the early years of the conquest from Mexico down to neighboring Guatelama as departure points. Unfortunately, only 58 of 27,835 studies indexed from top English-language media journals between 1979 and 1999, a mere one-fifth of 1 percent, dealt with Mexico, the cradle of written communication in the Western Hemisphere so far.[191] One noted exception, *Rebellion in Chiapas: Insurrection by Internet and Public Relations*, examined the use of new media in the heart of Mesoamerica without a single reference to its ancient literary history.[192] Attention to other Latin American countries, regions, and civilizations, including the Andes and its clever recording and delivery of messages, has also been negligible.[193]

Volume after volume, media publications tend to neglect or underestimate the pre-Hispanic times. Not surprisingly, communication students graduate believing that literary masterpieces or paper manuscripts originated in this continent along with the Spanish or the British printing press. At times, there is hope when lovely adventures such as Wendi Silvano's

The Inca Chasqui, published by the *Cricket Magazine Group* in Peru, Illinois, reach the classroom showing children a different face of our native ancestors.[194] If only similar stories helped educate uninformed adults, many of them journalists, images of oppressed people in this hemisphere would likely be very different.

VIKING REPORTING BEFORE COLUMBUS?

Could a news historian argue—as done with the Spaniards—that the Old Norse were the first "foreign reporters" of the Americas? Anonymous Viking tales before *Colón* such as the *Icelandic Sagas*, namely *Eirik the Red's*, *The Greenlanders'*, and *The Saga of Bjarni Herjolfsson*, spoke of encounters with aborigines in new lands whom they called *Skraelings* (savages). These chronicles, also known as the *Vinland* Sagas and published in the early thirteenth century, described the enigmatic rendezvous between two worlds when Norse sailors attempted to settle, timber, and trade in the Canadian Arctic. Nevertheless, the fascinating Viking experience remains little known across the Americas, especially in Latin America, unable to break the hegemonic tradition of the Spanish discovery of the New Continent.[195]

The sagas had also reported how the Vikings colonized the Shetland, the Hebrides, and the Faeroe Islands (860 CE), advancing toward Iceland (870 CE) and Greenland (982 CE) prior to the Norse westward exploration of the Land of Wine or Vinland in today's Canada. Popular nineteenth-century translations of these accounts even depicted a grassy terrace called *Leif's Camp*, but everything remained pure fantasy. This story of a *Leifsburdir* or *Leifsbodarna*, sometimes called *Strömsfjord* or *Straumord*, appeared speculative simply because landings of Viking mariners in North America 1,000 years ago seemed far-fetched.[196] As the prolific Colombian journalist-historian Germán Arciniegas pointed out, voyages over the Atlantic before Columbus, "like those of the Vikings, were written on water and lost in the infinite silence of the shackled ages," the medieval times.[197]

The skepticism ended in the 1960s when Norwegian writer Helge Ingstad and his wife, archaeologist Anne Stine, finished a remarkable eight-year excavation (1961–1968) that proved the irrefutable presence of the Old Norse in eastern North America. In L'Anse aux Meadows, Newfoundland, they unearthed clear evidence of the Viking's brief stay, rescuing authentic artifacts, such as an eleventh-century ringed pin of bronze, a soapstone spindle whorl, a stone oil lamp, and iron nails and rivets that could have come from medieval Europeans only. Woodcuts and other pieces of bronze, stone, iron, clay, charcoal, and bone were also found at this site. Turf foundations of eight carefully dated and identified Norse-styled buildings also showed signs of living quarters, fireplaces, and the earliest smelting of bog ore or brown iron in the Americas. Ingstad, Stine, and their team publicly declared, "in our opinion, [t]he settlement is of Norse origin, and ... it appears to date from the first part of the eleventh century AD."[198] There were no vestiges of writing, however.

L'Anse aux Meadows, Canada, the earliest known location of European structures in the New World, of iron working, and of encounters between Native Americas and Europeans, officially became a National Historic Park in 1977. On September 8, 1978, UNESCO proclaimed this Viking landmark a *World Heritage Site*, the globe's first historic monument to receive such a title on behalf of the international community. The sagas helped the Ingstads limit their search to the coastline north of New England, defying enthusiasts who argued that the Norse traveled well inside the continent or deep south into the states of Georgia and Florida. In fact, there are baseless claims that the Vikings explored the jungle in Brazil as well, sailing through the Amazon River.

We now know there were specialized craftsmen in Vinland, predominantly smiths, carpenters, and shipbuilders. But, were there scribes in Leif's or subsequent voyages? In a novel funded by the Scottish Arts, the Canada Council, and the Newfoundland and Labrador Arts, Joan Clark envisions the presence of Viking scribes such as servant Ulfar, taking notes and reporting on North American expeditions like *Eiriksdottir's* (c. 1015 AD). Following Leif's advice, *Freydis*, his half-sister, supposedly relies on Ulfar's dexterity, a man who skillfully turns wood into trade goods, repairs a ship, and keeps written records of long excursions run by rustic seafarers. In this story, Ulfar from the Hebrides, a Christian raised by Culdee monks, wraps his writing materials in oiled sheepskin to carefully carry them inside a sleeping bag. As the *Vinland* sails away, he stows his sack in the prow of the ship, hard against the bow and between the strakes and the planks where careless hands could reach neither his vellums nor his woodworking tools.[199]

This scene may be historical fiction, but trips such as Eiriksdottir's went on for at least 200 years in the America's North Atlantic, around the times of the *written* sagas. Today, the *Icelandic Sagas* are recognized as truly useful documents of Viking voyages, chronicling expeditions by Bjarni Herjolfsson's (985–986 AD), Leif Eiriksson's (c. 1000 AD), Thorfinn Karselfni's, Thorvald Eiriksson's, and Freydis Eiriksdottir's.[200] Novelist Jane Smiley thinks that "the Vinland Sagas, like almost all other sagas of the Icelanders, contains memories of real characters and events, recounted in a literary medium. [These] celebrated [narratives] began a new chapter in world history," she says, offering *"the oldest descriptions of [both] the North American continent and ... the first contact between Europeans and Native Americans."*[201] Author Milan Kundera agrees, arguing that the glory of the sagas is clearly indisputable.

In their journeys, the Vikings had mostly violent but also peaceful relations with the natives, like Karselfni's and his trading of milk for fur with the aborigines among several other goods.[202] According to the *Saga of the Greenlanders*, "clashes between the two players often ended with death."[203] Norse explorers probably spent several winters in Vinland celebrating Christmas and telling stories about their pursuits in the new lands. After freely wandering around Newfoundland, the St. Lawrence River, New Brunswick, and adjacent places, their adventures appeared recorded in Icelandic vellums.[204] Although there are no more written narratives about colonization beyond the Icelandic Sagas, subsequent settlements of Scandinavians "may have existed. In 1121, Erik Gnuppson, a Greenlander bishop, went to Vinland probably to visit a congregation in need of pastoral care. It is [also] logical that the Greenlanders visited Vinland and *Markland* [the Land of Forest] to find their vital timber, for the distance to Norway was much greater."[205] Archaeologists in Canada think that "Norse contacts with the New World continued and [that] knowledge of the new lands likely remained among European sailors, facilitating the re-opening of the Atlantic sea lanes in the 1490s."[206]

In the United States, from Maine, Rhode Island, and Massachusetts to as far West as Oklahoma, Arkansas, and Minnesota, people claim to own runic inscriptions made by medieval Vikings. Of a *Futhark* type (an ancient Greek lettering system meant to be carved on wood or stone), most if not all of these writings have been ruled hoaxes.[207] And no one should be surprised of hearing about Viking inscriptions in the Amazon Basin.[208] They are in surfaces too soft to survive seven to ten centuries and many are not written in proper Old Norse or confused with Native Indian carvings. A *G Nomesdal* runic character in Le Flore County, Oklahoma, for instance, had probably been written for fun by a Scandinavian member of a French expedition between 1718 and 1720.[209] The same is said of an apparent rune stone found in the Great or Grave Creek Mound in Moundsville, West Virginia.

Still, a heated discussion revolves around the legitimacy of Minnesota's *Kensington Rune Stone* or *KRS*, a manuscript "discovered" by Olaf Ohman in his Douglas County farm in the fall of 1898. The marker reports the tragic fortune of thirty Viking explorers in the Great Lakes. Translated it reads: "(We are) 8 Goths [Goter people from Vastergotland] and 22 Norwegians on (an) exploration-journey from Vinland over the West. We had camp by 2 skerries [shelters], one days-journey north from this stone. We were (out) and fished one day. After we come home (we) found 10 of (our men) red with blood and dead. AV(e) M(aria) Save us from evil. (We) have 10 of our party by the sea to look after our ship(s?) 14 days-journey from this island. *Year 1362.*"[210]

Scholars have clashed over the authenticity of this stone, notably Hjalmar R. Holand, Erik Wahlgren, Theodore C. Blegen, Ole G. Landsverk, and Robert A. Hall, which is a sort of pre-Columbian "crime news."[211] Holand, a graduate of the University of Wisconsin, called it "the oldest

Native document of American history," while Blegen, a historian, pronounced it a complete fraud in a monograph of the Minnesota Historical Society.[212] Most critics agree with Blegen, particularly because people living in the area at the time could have fabricated the relic.

Historian Erik Walhren lists the objections as follows. To begin with, the Kensington slab was found in a Scandinavian immigrant community with a style, spelling, grammar, numeral system, and content that forbid us to think of it as medieval. Also, important evidence to assess the inscription's antiquity has been suppressed or ignored, and the research of the early 1900s is *dominated by private [and] promotional interests*. In fact, the rune stone may have been carved in the 1890s in time for celebrations of the Quadricentennial Columbian Exposition at Chicago (1892), including the sailing of a replica Viking ship from Norway in 1893.[213] In sum, like all other alleged Viking writings in the New World, the KRS issue is deeply affected by deceit, pride, localism, political manipulation, greed, misinformation, and censorship.

Curators of the 2000 Smithsonian *Vikings* exhibition also question the validity of the Kensington Rune Stone, noting that previous endorsements of this piece had resulted from strong political pressures in Washington, DC. In 1948, the Minnesota Congressional delegation had successfully lobbied the Smithsonian Institution for recognition of the KRS in time for the commemoration of the stone's fiftieth anniversary, but five years later, the institution removed it from public display.[214] Then, linguist Robert Hall of Cornell University restated in two books that the rune stone was both "authentic and important," prompting scholars again to adopt a more cautious approach toward the slab.[215]

In 2004, an exhibition of the KRS at the Museum of National Antiquities in Stockholm, Sweden, finally settled on a significant though transitory consensus. Richard Nielsen, a runologist from Houston, Texas, and Henrik Williams, professor of Scandinavian Languages at Uppsala University, agreed that further study of fourteenth- and nineteenth-century linguistic discrepancies on the stone is necessary before reaching "a secure conclusion."[216]

Four outcomes are possible from this controversy. First, that the KRS is indeed a serious forgery that failed to make money or trigger the intended political effect. Second, that it is a joke written by someone knowledgeable of obscure medieval runes, unfamiliar to professional linguists in the twentieth century. Third, that it is a pre-Columbian record, reporting a tragic message left by fourteenth-century Viking explorers in the heart of North America. Or fourth, and less likely, that the KRS is a medieval stone created by Vikings who later moved it to Minnesota for some reason.[217] The majority believes that this monument is a fake because there are too many runes in doubt and too many inconsistencies. No text can be so unique and so unexpected and be genuine, critics say, although Nielsen and Williams warn that "even certified genuine text display discrepancies."[218]

If the majority prevails, states Professor Iver Kjaer, once with the University of California–Berkeley and more recently with the University of Copenhagen and the Society of Danish Language and Literature, the Kensington Rune Stone "is not an unimportant fake but a central identity-bearing symbol in the history of Nordic-American immigration."[219]

COLONIALISM AND STRUCTURAL CENSORSHIP

During the quincentennial celebration of Columbus' first voyage to America, King Juan Carlos of Spain invited the Old and the New Worlds to look at each other and rediscover themselves. In his view, "the discovery is a historical concept" where both Spaniards and indigenous people understood reality in its entirety as protagonists. Yet, today, there is a need for a different reencounter, he says, a dialog among equals where everyone finds "the path of our enormous possibilities of doing great things together."[220] Don Juan Carlos is persuaded that Iberian America's new goal shall be to recognize cultures more than markets.

Although a thoughtful expression of Hispanic brotherhood, this "reencounter" is meaningless without correcting the unjust and painful outcome of Iberian–Latin American relations. Modernity can be traced back to the Spanish caravels opening commercial routes across the Atlantic, but after five centuries of trade with Iberian, Anglo-Saxon, and other European centers, both Latin America and the Caribbean are still undeservedly poor and disadvantaged, with markets failing their population in the name of democracy, freedom, and progress. Part of this frustration comes from a weak access to global economic, political, and technological benefits including the media. Since the conquest, systemic forms of censorship have done much to block the free flow of information and knowledge needed for Hispanic Americans to advance.

In censored societies, with "socially structured silences," Church and Crown (government) have traditionally held "exclusive monopolies over public channels for the distribution of knowledge," namely politics, pulpits, press, and pedagogy.[221] Add markets dominated by wealthy families, their businesses, and big foreign capitals and corporations and Latin America's persistent inequality and repression is more easily explained. From Europe, Latin America inherited a structural colonial censorship built on at least four pillars: racism, official intimidation, technological elitism, and ideological intolerance.[222]

It is difficult and sensitive, as noted earlier, to study whether restraints reigned in ancient American societies. Mesoamericanists largely dismiss the subject of censorship as an inapplicable research theme, although there are a good number of investigations on pre-Columbian politics, power, and writing. The assumption is that, in antiquity, freedom of speech or *"individual independence of action must still have been a virtually unknown concept."*[223] In pre-Hispanic polities, they say, communication functioned as an integral part of a mystic-visionary view of destiny and life.[224]

Still, Itzcoatl's order to burn and rewrite the ancient codices, glamorizing his kingdom in a new official chronicle that made him appear as the chosen monarch of the gods, seems an obvious example of the abusive power of sacred rulers and priests for social control in American antiquity. The *Códice Matritense* also speaks of Aztec leaders promoting the idea that it was unsuitable for people to know the paintings, and that minds could be corrupted or go astray because of the many lies preserved in the books.[225] Regardless of a conscious individual right to speak or not, Professor Jansen shows how ruling classes at various times in history use censorship as a tool to supervise public morals, including the duty to control media and insure they carry nothing offensive against the government.[226]

Between totems and taboos, all societies, either modern, colonial, or pre-Columbian, including ancient civilizations as old as Mesopotamia, the Mediterranean, India, China, Egypt, Middle America, and the Andes, "exercised controls over words, symbols, and ideas." The question is how structured were those constraints. The institutionalized and normative censorship of colonial America seems incomparable to the rules imposed by pre-Columbian societies, primarily because of the "malice," that distinctive predatory intent or desire colonialists used to manipulate, harm, and exploit their own people, let alone foreigners.

RACIAL AND SEX DISCRIMINATION

The conquistadors and other conquerors silenced the Native American civilization by extermination, and their heirs also censored Indians and other ethnic groups by selective killings during colonial and republican times. Besides the hundreds of thousands murdered as imported slaves (between one and two million Africans killed just in the so-called middle passage, that is, crossing the Atlantic), most of the native population before the conquest lost their lives in colonial America, probably no less than twenty million men, women, and children: *a demographic catastrophe*—that is, if we accept that the New World was not sparsely populated as originally presumed and that "there were probably more people living in the Americas than in Europe."[227]

Critics of the "Genocide of the Americas," notably Professor David E. Stannard of the University of Hawaii, claimed that "sixty [to] eighty million people from the Indies to the Amazon had perished as a result of the European invasion even before the dawning of the seventeenth century. Although much of that ghastly population collapse was caused by the spread of European diseases to which native peoples had no immunity, an enormous amount of it was the result of mass murder—a good deal derived from simply working the enslaved native laborers to death."[228] Others, both in the New and the Old World, especially those in former colonialist nations, think these numbers are "*una enormización*," that is, an exaggerated calculation of casualties, which is in fact irritating.[229]

The conquest had tragic but "unintended consequences," accidental effects such as the spread of deadly diseases and warfare for population-production reasons, observed the late anthropologist Marvin Harris of the University of Florida. "The conquistadors never intended to indiscriminately kill large groups of Indians," concludes as well the epidemics historian Alfred Cosby. But, "this is a comforting lie," replied Dr. Stannard.[230] That the conquerors meant to murder is well documented in most area histories of the Americas, from Hispaniola, Meso and Central America to the Andes and Brazil. The invaders' testing of their swords and manly strength on captured Indians, the mutilation of women's breasts for sport, the decapitation of pleading victims, the feeding of babies to their wolfhounds and mastiffs, among other atrocities, are no accident, said Stannard, author of the *American Holocaust: Columbus and the Conquest of the New World*.[231]

In detail, this book argues that from the 1490s to the 1890s (up to the U.S. Army's massacre of Sioux Indians at Wounded Knee), "the native population of the Western Hemisphere declined by as many as 100 million people."[232] Even if this figure is inaccurate, the aboriginal history of the Americas is plagued with massacres, from Cholula, Mexico, to *Caxamalca* (Cajamarca), Peru, and beyond. In Cajamarca, November 15, 1532, wrote scholar William Sullivan, Francisco Pizarro's men killed "an estimated . . . seven thousand men and seriously wounded as many as ten thousand more," taking the Inca *Atahualpa* captive.[233]

Commenting on Stannard's book, a *Los Angeles Times* review points out, this work is "a much needed counterbalance to centuries of romantic confabulation. [It is] an impassioned examination of the religious and cultural roots of Euro-American racism and genocidal behavior. [Sadly, the] destruction that lasted for more than four centuries . . . continues in many places even today."[234] In *Hurakán*, journalist Germán Castro Caycedo also shocks the Latin American reader with a book-length reportage on the bloodshed of the conquest, the roots of today's violence in the region and especially against Native Indians. "I didn't know it was bad to kill Indians. [They may be] Christians but they are missing something we have: civilization," declared the convicted murderers of sixteen Cuiva natives in *La Rubiera*, a farm in the Orinoco region at the Colombian–Venezuelan border. And this tragedy occurred roughly "five hundred years after Columbus."[235]

Professor León-Portilla recommends not to persist in unnecessary recriminations, since the past is "inalterable." For him, it is more appropriate and fruitful to open doors and look for new ways of building multilateral bridges and friendships. Nevertheless, an Indian association from Paraguay asked in Madrid's *Cambio 16* magazine, "why can't Spain [and other colonizers] simply apologize for all the harm caused to our people in this continent?"[236] If the United States for much less recently apologized in Rwanda on behalf of the international community, why can't Spain and others do it? As President Clinton said on March 25, 1998: "We cannot change the past, but we can and must do everything in our power to help [victims of a genocide] build a future without fear and full of hope."[237]

The Spanish carnage subsided when the conquest ended and the colonial period began around 1550, the year when the best of Spanish theologians, jurists, and politicians met in Valladolid to discuss the treatment of Indians. This *junta* is the famous meeting where the self-appointed protector of the natives, Fray Bartolomé de las Casas, confronted Juan Ginés de Sepúlveda, a priest and chronicler of King Charles I of Spain. The Crown ultimately favored Las Casas's view.

Despite efforts from Spain to stop the abuses of noblemen and prelates, colonial authorities and institutions did much to degrade the American Indian and other commoners, particularly women. People in Latin America and the Caribbean still use the word *indio* or *negro* to denote backwardness and ignorance. The worst treated were Indian and black females, lower-class individuals assumed to be prostitutes and who had no honor to protect. Ordinarily, their children and families carried the victim's shame well beyond her death.

Although admired as a strong and virtuous queen, Isabel of Castile and her image did little to improve the status of womankind. Church, law, and tradition negatively "affected the role of women in the Iberian peninsula and by extension in the American colonies," observed Professor Susan M. Socolow of Emory University.[238] Regarded as intellectually inferior, prone to error, and evil or uncontrolled carnal appetites and temptation, "women were admonished to keep silent."[239] Indeed, voices of early modern women and the poor are often absent from the printed pages of colonial America, but many women and their stories, "deviated significantly from the ideals of silence and obedience," challenging the structurally imposed seclusion and anonymity of their gender.[240] One good, if not the best, example of female resistance to dominant behavioral constraints is Sor Juana Inés de la Cruz in New Spain.

Even if regarded as overly emotional, inconsistent, gossipy, irrational, changeable, weak, deceitful, and profligate, notes Socolow, the legal status of women at that time seemed far more favorable in Iberia and Spanish America than the rest of Europe.[241] In Spain and her colonies, unmarried daughters and widows could at least own, buy, sell, exchange, and donate property, as when colonial women inherited their father's or husbands' printing houses and business.[242]

Misogynist, racist, and socially discriminatory, the deeply Catholic Spanish conquistador treated brutally the native servant and mixed-blood slave. The tragedy is that these feelings remained in the conscience of Hispanic American males during republican times, just as occurred with English and French men in the north.[243] Unsurprisingly, contemporary Latin American newspapers reported with special emphasis the election of Chilean President Michelle Bachelet, a victim of hatred during Pinochet's dictatorship who, as she said, has committed four major sins: being a woman, divorced (with one child outside her marriage), agnostic, and socialist. In one of the most formally religious, socially conservative, and male-dominated countries of Latin America, her election symbolizes the end of an old era, a firm step toward effectively overcoming gender inequality as well as religious and political intolerance, if not in the Americas, at least in Chile.[244]

OFFICIAL DESPOTISM AND CONTROL

In the New World, Europeans tasted the true flavor of freedom, becoming increasingly aware of their personal liberties and restrictions. Chronicler Pietro Martire d'Anghiera (Pedro Mártir de Anglería) is one historian who noted how the conquistador believed that the new continent enjoyed "a golden world where people lived innocently without laws, judges, or libels."[245] At any rate, modern censorship began to rule once Columbus and his mariners disembarked, with their racism, sexism, greed, religious and military authority, technological power, and sense of cultural superiority.

Fray Diego de Landa (1524?–1579), Custodian of *Yucatán*, is a classical example of the contradictions of a Spanish censor. A learned friar on Indian arts and sciences, his religious fanaticism made him burn all the native codices he diligently collected. This Franciscan prelate, like others of his stature, mirrored the ironies of their time. After launching his career as an assistant and guardian at the convent of *Izamal*, De Landa, tried in Madrid for his bloody methods of Christianity, and published his famous compilation *Accounts of the Things of Yucatan*, detailing ancient Mayan customs and beliefs.[246] It is not coincidental that to convert the natives to Catholicism, he and the Church had decided to build a large convent (*San Antonio de Padua*) at Izamal, the pre-Hispanic town formerly devoted to venerate *Itzamná*, the Mayan god of writing.

Colonial life diligently nurtured both the state and the Church, the oldest powers of this continent, often at odds with each other. Replacing the monastic (1522–1533) and episcopal (1535–1571) inquisitions, three cities in Spanish America saw the *Santo Oficio* formally established in central quarters. Lima (1570), Mexico City (1571), and Cartagena *de Indias* (1610) set up palaces of inquisition, although Buenos Aires also came to consider a site for a Holy Office during the unification of the Spanish and Portuguese crowns between 1580 and 1640. At the River of La Plata, Spaniards showed an especial concern with the regular entrance of Judaizers and banned books.

In the Viceroyalty of Peru, social tensions run high, so much as to justify the launching of an inquisition tribunal even before New Spain. During the late 1500s to mid-1600s, explains Professor Kathleen Myers of Indiana University, the dangers of earthquakes and pirates, of deep political and religious rifts, and of struggles over Indian labor fused with imminent signs of native rebellion, civil war, fractions within religious orders, and unrest due to the extirpation of native religions in the Andes that threatened particularly Lima, then a city of nearly 26,000 people. The wealth of the elite, she wrote, sharply contrasted "with the increasing number of American-born vagabonds, displaced indigenous people, and African slaves."[247]

British editor Derek Jones narrates the story of chronicler José de Acosta to illustrate the kind of censorship oppressing not only colonial Lima and the entire Viceroyalty of Peru but also Spanish America and Mother Spain. In *De Procuranda Indorum Salute* (On Procuring the Salvation of the Indians, 1576), this Jesuit missionary, Provincial-General in New Castile (Peru), reported that the introduction of Christianity had deleterious effects upon the native inhabitants of the Caribbean and South America. Criticizing the violence and hypocrisy of the Christians, Acosta writes, "not only have we *failed to bring them the news of Christ with sincerity and honest faith, but we have betrayed in our deeds what we professed in our words*."[248] King Philip II of Spain immediately suppressed this work at the insistence of members of the Spanish academia, Acosta's superiors at Toledo, and the Jesuit order's hierarchy in the peninsula. The report will remain censored for 410 years until its reappearance in the University of Salamanca in 1985.

A similar censorship took place against Rosa de Santa María, America's first saint during the mid-1600s in Peru, when the Inquisition confiscated her writings soon after her death because of concerns about the rise of excessively devoted lay religious movements in Lima, prosecuting several of her followers. Living a life of prayer and penance at home, she was finally canonized in 1671 after fifty-four years of inquiries by the Inquisition. Only then, bells rang to announce the Papal Bull honoring *Santa Rosa de Lima*, as the city "had received God's favor" wrote Dominican chronicler Juan de Meléndez.[249]

In New Spain, the prolific chronicler Fray Bernardino de Sahagún practically inaugurated the Inquisition denouncing a Franciscan brother, the also reputable chronicler Fray Toribio de Benavente Motolinía, "el pobre" (the poor). This particular charge came after Motolinía's death, accusing him of publishing devilish and misleading lies, such as defending and justifying the native calendar as free from idolatry or superstition.[250] Inquisition proceedings against libelers and scandalous speakers, sexual deviants, and heretics or witches, and rumors of its terrible trials abound in colonial centers, contributing to enforce the climate of silence and obedience, although bureaucratic inertia, cost, and corruption made this institution far less effective than initially claimed, even in its golden times of the seventeenth century.[251]

Without a *Tribunal da Inquisiçao*, Brazil also endured secret inquiries. Since the late 1500s, Lisbon orchestrated inquisitorial *pesquisas* to punish Jews, sorcerers, and sodomites under heavy influence from Spain. Starting in 1702, Rio de Janeiro gained the reputation of a main port in the shipping of *Marranos* (pigs or "forbidden things" as Jews were called) back to the metropolis. Bishop Francisco da San Jeronimo of Evora championed these persecutions as soon as he became governor. In the end, both Portugal and Spain officially operated the Inquisition until the nineteenth century, that is, 1821 and 1834 respectively, even if Spanish sources complain it had effectively disappeared in 1820.[252] No one should underestimate or sanitize the strength and impact of this institution, but exaggerations are also an obstacle to grasp the extent and dimension of colonial censorship in the Western Hemisphere.[253]

The Inquisition, a practice that goes back to post-Constantine Roman emperors and medieval Popes Alexander III and Innocent III, fighting heresy and blasphemy in Central Europe, formally emerged with Pope Gregory IX and his Bull *Excommunicamus* in 1231. Others find its roots in the councils of Reims, Oxford, or Verona, or in the synods of Avignon (1209) and Toulouse (1229). Anyhow, Innocent III stepped up the inquisitive zeal of the Vatican at the Fourth Lateran Council in 1215, the year when King John granted the historic Magna Carta under threat of civil war. By then, burning people at the stake alive was an accepted punishment, especially for unrepentant heretics. In 1252, Pope Innocent IV endorsed torture as a prime mechanism to obtain confessions (Bull *Ad Extirpanda*).[254]

Spain, through the Kingdom of Aragón, experienced the Inquisition as early as 1232, while the English had their own in the memorable Court of Star Chamber in the mid-fourteenth century, beginning to repress dissenting voices under Henry VIII in 1542. The House of Tudor and Stuart, notably King Charles I, abused it as a political weapon, expropriating, jailing, and torturing victims with corporal punishments such as whipping, pillorying, branding, and mutilation.[255]

After a transitory decline, the Catholic kings, with due Papal approval (Sixtus IV's), revived the Inquisition in 1478. Promising to unify Spain while controlling the nobility, Queen Isabella and King Ferdinand spread the Catholic orthodoxy with the infamous Council of the General and Supreme Inquisition established in Seville: the *Consejo de la Suprema y General Inquisición*, better known as *La Suprema* (1483).

As with the genocide of Native Indians, debates are furious about how many suspects lost their lives in the Inquisition. Numbers range from thousands of European *relajados* (victims burned in person or in effigy) to less than one hundred of such deaths in Spanish America. A recent book on the Spanish Inquisition by historian Joseph Pérez, Emeritus Professor at the University of Bordeaux and Honorary Director of the Velázquez Museum in Madrid, claims that "nearly 32,000 people were publicly burned at the stake, with the 'fortunate' ones being merely flogged, fined or imprisoned."[256] Yet, Spanish America, at least New Spain, appears to show a much lower inquisitorial activity, especially against "groups of dissidents or intellectuals," concludes Alberro.[257]

Although the Spanish-American Inquisition is not incomparable to its headquarters in the metropolis, the mission of this institution was to spread fear and rancor across colonial towns, a structural symbolism and machinery organized to destroy heresy and pagan practices, irreligious behavior, sexual immorality, and slave's complaints and sorcery. Silently and secretly, inquisitors and their assistants ushered and preceded numerous repressive actions against individuals during the colony, particularly in the mid-1600s. Both the Church and the Crown worked as best allies in maintaining order and discouraging change in the Americas, accompanied by the settler class as in the youngest Viceroyalty of the Río de La Plata.[258]

In his translation of the seventeenth-century diary of a military officer in Perú, historian Robert R. Miller, Professor Emeritus at California State University–Hayward, describes yesterday's (and today's) Ibero-American capital: "fronting on Lima's large main square, called *Plaza de Armas*, were offices and residences of the powerful men of church and state. On the west was the viceroy's palace, where [the viceroyal guard] was stationed. The cathedral and archbishop's palace were on the north; the *cabildo* or city hall on the south; and adjacent were the jail, post office, courts, and important administrative agencies."[259] In spite of multiple revolutions and liberal reforms, Latin America continues to display a centralized and vertical communication structure.

In Lima, as in other prominent colonial centers, military parades, official ceremonies, executions, tribal dances, and bullfights took place in front of the highest authorities: ecclesiastics and aristocrats. During *Carlos I*'s rule (1517–1558), novels of fiction and chivalry, indecent drawings, and subversive books and manuscripts were expressly forbidden. Even without priests on board, sailors and travelers crossed the Atlantic censored in their ships. Meanwhile, corruption and double standards made possible the traffic of illegal literature to the New World, smuggling banned works inside wine caskets, chests, barrels, cracks, and other hideouts. After all, the law was to be respected though not obeyed, read an old adage in Hispaniola.[260]

Next to the orderly conversion of the Indians, the Catholic kings vowed to curve all kinds of abuses, including illegal activities and publications. Orthodoxy plunged the Inquisition into a crusade against idolatry, polygamy, sacrifices, and other pagan rituals. Devoted clerics and the *patronato real*, an alliance of civil, military, and religious authorities, erected a regime of intimidation that lasted well beyond the independence.[261] Indeed, until today, fear of isolation and punishment has been an element oppressors have effectively used in Latin America to impose a spiral of silence upon society and its media.[262]

A person charged with heresy and Judaizing could be sentenced to the stake. Sentences for blasphemy, sexual immorality, murder, and political crimes (through speech or action, especially treason, subversion, and rebellion) could also mean the ultimate penalty, namely burning, hanging, or being clubbed or stabbed to death. Felonies in Spain and its colonies were not different from those in England, particularly the lethal seditious, blasphemy, and obscenity libels. Private defamation, especially slander, was somewhat "less serious," although convicts could have their tongues perforated with nails or needles and end up in the public places pricked, kicked, and stoned.[263] Under "normal" circumstances, torture was an interrogation method in order to obtain a confession, not a final punishment, and such confession might even be declared invalid in court. The more fortunate were simply exiled, whipped, or fined.

Autos de Fe such as those the Holy Office pompously conducted in Mexico City on April 11, 1649, and in Lima, the City of the Kings, between January 22 and January 23, 1664, did take place in the Spanish colonies. In fact, 30,000 people attended the one in New Spain, and the *limeños* commented for years how city authorities made of French Mateo Salado and Fray Francisco de la Cruz the first *relajados* (burned in person): the former for Lutheran, on November 15, 1573, and the latter for subversion on April 13, 1578.[264] In two and a half centuries, the Lima tribunal reported thirty-two convicts sentenced to capital punishment, half of them burned alive and the others clubbed to death. In Mexico, perhaps no more than thirty-seven offenders faced *la hoguera* alive.[265]

Meanwhile, in Cartagena, the *Santa Inquisición*, with its collection of gruesome instruments, built a reputation of torture and autos de fe against heretics and sorcerers (mainly black slaves), but there was no burning of victims throughout the seventeenth century. In 1622, inquisitors and *comisarios* conducted an auto de fe in the *Plaza de la Inquisición* forcing Leonor Zape, on the one hand, to wear a *San Benito* for life, and the other, sentencing Guiomar Bran for witchcraft. African slaves had in the spoken word a sacred link between the dead and the alive, helping them to endure slavery, but the Inquisition simply saw their rituals and socialization as devilish speech. The Santo Oficio made great efforts to persecute and eradicate those *"brujos,"* rebels, and *"demons."*[266]

For financial and internal political reasons, burning heretics at the stake in *autos de fe* was a rare episode in Spanish America. However, they were "big" news when organized, as some of them convicted up to forty suspects in one session (Lima, 1605). At five in the afternoon of Tuesday, January 22, 1664, wrote the Spanish Sargent Josephe de Mugaburu y Hontón, "a procession led by Father Barbarán, provincial of the Dominican monastery, left from the Holy Office for the platform of the Holy Cross. [A]ll the religious orders took part, [including] the Fathers of the Society [of Jesus]. [T]hen the convicted were brought out. One [the Portuguese Manuel Henríquez] was burned [at the stake], two were burned in effigy, and three were wearing *sanbenitos* [yellow tunics or penitent *sacos benditos*, with huge red crosses back and front]. There were four friars, and others that had been witches. In all, twenty one were sentenced."[267] The reading of punishments took twenty-four hours but the investigation of Henríquez lasted thirty years. Neither the viceroy nor the inquisitors or the oydors took time out to eat during the entire day, observed Mugaburu.

Killings and abuses were no different between Spanish and Portuguese colonists, except for the more aggressive emphasis on the trade and exploitation of blacks among the Lusitanians. Not until it lost its influence in Africa, India, China, and Indonesia, Portugal paid a more benevolent attention to the Brazilian enclaves.[268] But not everything was intimidation, repression, and abuse of authority by clerics and bureaucrats. Some of them firmly rejected the ongoing evangelizing methods. Critical of the conquistador, though loyal to the Catholic faith and the concept of a fair state, Fray Bartolomé de Las Casas (1474?–1566), Bishop of Chiapas, condemned the legitimacy of any regime imposed by force.

Denouncing the inequality of men, Dominicans such as De las Casas, Gil González de San Nicolás, and Francisco de Vitoria (pioneer of international law), defended the Indians as rational individuals deserving of rights and a humane treatment. De las Casas and De Vitoria vigorously opposed Juan Ginés de Sepúlveda (1490?–1573), chaplain of Charles I, posing the thesis of "pure evangelism," a theory where Crown and Church had the privilege to preach, not force the act of faith, unless the infidel resisted the Christian action.[269] Actually, the visionary theologian Fray Francisco de la Cruz, mentioned earlier, was burned at the stake in Lima (1578) for spreading a subversive doctrine contrary not only to official Catholicism but also to the Spanish monarch Philip II, inviting Peruvians to rise against him and appoint their own viceroy.[270]

Their beliefs fueled a spirit of emancipation two centuries later. Inspired in their teachings, Chilean friar Camilo Henríquez (1769–1825) founded and edited the first newspaper of his homeland, confronting the Inquisition while supporting the independence in his *La Aurora de Chile*, 1812–1813. Two more heroes are the priests Miguel Hidalgo y Costilla and José María Morelos y Pavón, leaders of the Mexican independence in 1810. Pupils of the same seminary in Valladolid, now Morelia (Michoacán), Morelos and Hidalgo were executed by firing squads with the complicity of the Church.[271]

Along with the Inquisition and to repress social turmoil, the monarchy established both the *Royal and Supreme Council of the Indias*, top executive authority of the Americas, and the *House of Trade*. This last entity imposed major restrictions on the press, commerce, and the shipment of values from the New World. With their corregidors (magistrates) and oydors (judges), provincial authorities such as the viceroys and the captain generals (military governors) controlled political, administrative, and disciplinary local matters. Royal tribunals, city halls, and an army of mayors, public notaries, and alguazils completed the costly imperial payroll. Each and every one of these offices had the capacity to censure individual speakers and printing presses.

Based on the *Fuero Juzgo* (an adaptation of the old Roman–Visigothic law) and the *Fuero Real* (a collection of principles produced by King Alfonse X, The Wise), better known as the *Siete Partidas* (Seven Chapters), the Spanish Crown dominated Hispanic America. All these laws erected a system of privileges that increased the resentment between *criollos* and peninsulars. By the mid-seventeenth century, colonial cities were centers prone to popular revolts. Fearing bloody clashes such as the endless war against the Araucanian Indians in Chile, town authorities prohibited blacks, zambos, and mulattoes from carrying weapons, even if accompanied by their owners. Penalties ranged from dozens of lashes to years of imprisonment, and in the case of rabbles or escapes, death or mutilation of genitals and limbs were in order.

As in all English, Portuguese, and French colonies (e.g., in Saint Domingue, now Haiti), blacks in Spanish America were forbidden to learn, particularly read or write. Agitators, primarily opinion leaders, rebel speakers, and printers, also faced swift and severe punishments in colonial times. The United States had this inhumane policy against blacks and other minorities for decades after 1776. "Communication among [blacks]" wrote author Jerome R. Adams, once a Peace Corp volunteer in the Andes, "was kept difficult as a method of control. [S]tudents of Indian or mixed blood were never, until after independence, allowed to matriculate at the University of San Marcos in Lima."[272] As the *Telegrafo Mercantil* put it in the River Plate in 1801, the colored classes, "debased simply by their status and birth, are denied admission to the primary schools, in order to prevent their associating with children of Spaniards."[273]

Every colonial town seemed potentially explosive. Yet, one thing was the coast and another the cordillera. The port of Buenos Aires, capital of the Viceroyalty of La Plata (1776), envied the famous Potosí (now Bolivia), a wealthy Andean city in the Spanish colony with more than 160,000 inhabitants in 1650. Lima, near the Pacific and capital of the Viceroyalty of Peru (New Castile, 1542), had little in common with Cuzco, the capital of the Incas in the Andes. The same happened in the Caribbean *Cartagena de Indias* and the totally different Santafé de Bogotá, capital of New Granada (1718) in the mountain range. Caracas was not a Coro. And if Quito competed with Guayaquil in Ecuador, Mexico City did the same with Veracruz in the gulf. Latin America inherited a profound rivalry between the littoral and the *sierra* (the mountains). Provincial animosities also framed the media.

Over the years, Latin American censorship came to reflect this complex and enduring mix of localism, social tension, state repression, and religious mysticism. Class differences, racial discrimination, and parochial quarrels among cities and provinces framed speech and other individual rights in the Americas then and now. Control, however, differed depending on how isolated towns operated from the centers of power. Ursurprisingly, the independence revolt emerged in peripheral areas first, such as Caracas and Buenos Aires. A breakdown in communication between Spain and the Viceroyalty of La Plata, observed Emeritus Professor John Lynch of the University of London, facilitated the outright independence of the Creoles in the future Argentine Republic (May 1810).[274]

TECHNOLOGICAL ELITISM

Spanish news moved slowly before the printing press, far less reliably than the Incan messengers or *Chasquis* of the *Tawantinsuyu*. Thus, an anxious and tedious routine for the colonists was to wait for the dispatch ship. From time to time, travelers and sailors from the Old and New Spain, the Caribbean, Peru, or Panama (*Tierra Firme*) arrived with gossip and documents. Some dramatic reports informed people of relatives lost to pirates, sudden battles, hurricanes, earthquakes, and other tragedies, including shipwrecks loaded with gold, silver, and precious stones. In fact, the May Revolution in the *Rio de la Plata* began soon after an English vessel docked in Montevideo with news about the French Army taking over Seville in Spain.[275]

Little is said in our news media literature about those Indian runners, carrying mail and quipus and delivering them to every corner of the kingdom in a matter of days. According to the *Orejones* (big-ear quechua nobles), Incas like *Pachacuti* (1438–1471) organized a network of posts (*o'kla-cuna*) capable of covering a distance of 240 miles in twenty-four hours. Nobody could then make such a trip as skillfully as a Chasqui, crossing with exceptional ability thorny terrains, deserts, and snow peaks. Every five kilometers there was a small wooded station with two runners, water, food, and a place to rest, a responsibility of nearby villages. Mile after mile, accurate information flowed up and down the Andes and neither pleas nor threats, goes the story, could make a Chasqui reveal his message before or after delivery.

Fascinated with the *Camino Real* or Inca highway system, and after seventeen years of trips and censorship, Spanish soldier Pedro de Cieza de León wrote: "one of the things that most took my attention [...] was how and in what way the great, splendid highways we see throughout could be built. [I]f the emperor were to desire another highway built like the one from Quito to Cuzco, or that which goes from Cuzco to Chile, truly I do not believe he could do it, with all the power and the men at his disposal, unless he followed the method the Incas employed."[276]

For Cieza, the *Chasquis* and their highways represented one of the highest levels of Inca civilization, government, and political organization. Was the "Prince of Chroniclers" exaggerating? Not really. "Against the Winds," an online exhibition set up by Harvard University's Peabody Museum of Archeology and Ethnology, recently confirmed the efficiency of native runners, especially among the Incas—by far, the greatest couriers with roughly 16,000 kilometers of trails covering 2,500 miles from northern Ecuador to southern Chile. The Aztecs and the Iroquois, to name a few more cultures, also delivered news and goods quite effectively.[277]

In 1553, the Holy Office finally gave Cieza permission and royal privilege to publish Part One of his *Crónica del Perú*: [*description, landmarks*], *rites and customs of the Indians and other strange things worth knowing*. In time, the press will come to drive far more attention than rumors and the mail.

The first Spanish printing press, with approval of Viceroy Antonio de Mendoza, arrived in Latin America about a 100 years before New England's Harvard College press (Cambridge, Massachusetts, 1638). Many sources claim that Mexico's importation of the revolutionary technology took place in 1539 but Professor Jacques Lafaye, director of the Sorbonne's Institute of Iberian and Iberian American Studies, highlights that the foundations of the future Royal and Pontifical University of Mexico and the introduction of New Spain's first printing press may have occurred almost simultaneously in 1538.[278] The following year, Franciscan Fray Juan de Zumárraga, Mexico's first bishop and former inquisitor (charged with hunting witches in his native Vizcaya), hired Lombard printer Giovanni Paoli or Juan Pablos, pupil of the prestigious *Casa de Juan Cromberger* of Seville, son of the deceased and noted printer Jácome or Jakob Kronberger.

Official sources in the Federal District prefer however to say that the first printing press arrived in Mexico City sometime during 1534 and 1539, leaving open the possibility that in this segment an earlier printer, Esteban Martín or Etienne Martin, may have published in the colonial capital the popular San Juan Clímaco's *Escala Espiritual*, probably in 1536.[279] But there is no original to confirm it. In any case, the viceroy's and the bishop's intentions were to produce as many religious books as possible, teaching materials to carry out the Christianizing of infidels first in Mexico, then in Peru, and finally in the Philippines.

On Fray Zumárraga's orders, Pablos printed the bishop's *La Breve y mas Compendiosa Doctrina Cristiana en Lengua Mexicana y Castellana* (1539), the first book of New Spain and the Americas, sadly lost now. In Nahuatl and Spanish, this bilingual doctrine or catechism launched a series of publications at Juan Cromberger's shop, releasing thirteen titles between 1539 and 1544.[280]

Turned archbishop of Mexico in 1547, Zumárraga kept at least four of these volumes in his forty-one-book personal library, including his own *Dotrina Breve Muy Provechosa de las Cosas que Pertenecen a la Fe Catholica y a Nuestra Cristiandad* (Very Brief and Beneficial Doctrine of the Things That Belong to the Catholic Faith and Our Christianity, 1543). The other three were Fray Pedro de Córdoba's *Dotrina Christiana para Instrucion e Informacion de los Indios: por manera de Hystoria* (Christian Doctrine for the Teaching and Information of Indians: In a History Fashion, 1544), Dionisio Richel's *Este es un Compendio Breve que Tracta de la Manera de Como se han de Hazer las Procesiones* (This Is a Brief Compendium That Deals with How Processions Should Be Conducted, 1544), and the French theologian Joannis or Juan Gerson's *Tripartito* (*a qualquiera muy provechosa*, Very Beneficial for Anyone, 1544).[281] As with the pre-Columbian codices, Cordoba's and Zumarraga's precious books, including his *Doctrina Cristiana* (1545), are not in Latin America; they are part of the Benson Library's Mexican Colonial Collection at the University of Texas in Austin.

Bishop Zumárraga's selective and exclusive library, the first of the Americas, had also books printed in Europe's most reputable publishing centers, such as Venice, Lyon, Paris, Colonia, Basel, Amberes, Salamanca, Sevilla, and Alcalá de Henares, including Pedro Martyr de Anglería's *De Orbe Novo* (1530). To have been an inquisitor and a zealot burner of codices, this appointed "Protector of the Indians" promoted humanist Erasmus of Rotterdam's ideas including criticism of the immoral behavior of Catholic authorities. He also "supported the unlimited diffusion of the bible" and ancient philosophers like Plato and Pythagoras.[282] Fray Pedro de Córdoba is another interesting and contradictory case. This first inquisitor, sent to the Americas in 1510, became a true and respected protector of the Indians, persuading Las Casas of renouncing his plantation in the Caribbean, joining the Dominican Order, and dedicating his life to protect the natives. As all books in the New Spain, Córdoba's *Dotrina Christina* was revised and examined by an inquisitor prior to publication.[283]

Viceroy Mendoza also charged Juan Pablos with printing legal volumes such as the historic *Ordenanzas y Compilación de Leyes*, edited in 1548. Seven years earlier, the Italian had also published the famous *Relacion del espantable terremoto que agora nuevamente ha acontecido en las yndias en una ciudad llamada Guatimala*, the first news report of the Americas (1541).[284] It had been written by Juan Rodríguez, resident of Almolonga, today *Ciudad Vieja* (Old City), near Antigua, a chronicle that became *"the oldest [modern] antecedent of journalistic information in the Americas which can be classified as a reportage"*—according to Carlos Alfredo Chamier, discoverer of the *Relación* en Mexico.[285] With extraordinary skill and accuracy (or should we say, "objectivity"), Rodríguez not only described the events but also researched and interviewed the survivors of that tragic and *"memorabilísimo"* September 11, 1541, the unforgettable 9/11 of colonial times. At least 600 people lost their lives in this landslide, confused with an earthquake at that time.[286] Simply put, Rodríguez and Pablos revolutionized America.

Fearing their use, printing presses would be even more tightly controlled. Religious and civilian authorities made printing progressed extremely cautiously in Spanish America. Other reasons for the delay were the lack and poor quality of paper, the extreme protection of the Iberian editor, and the trade restrictions with foreign nations. Following the Valladolid debates on Indian rights (1550), which launched the colonial era, the printing press began its slow process of diffusion in the Americas. Mexico City and Lima, capitals of the original viceroyalties, secured their center positions.

Editorial competition emerged with Antonio de Espinosa, from Jaén, Andalucia, who printed Fray Maturino Gilberti's *Gramática* (1559) and the voluminous *Missale Romanum Ordinarium* (448 pages in 1561). Literary and scientific texts came to furnish the University of Mexico and the University of San Marcos in Lima, both established in 1551. And Father Alonso de la Veracruz's *Physica Speculatio* and the *Sumario Compendioso* (1554), printed at Pablos' shop, emerged as the continent's first books on mathematics. Yet, the aristotelic and thomistic escolasticism, more than Erasmus's humanism, eventually took over the classrooms, retarding the colonial academia by at least an entire century from the new science of Copernicus, Galileo, and Newton.[287]

In 1580, another Italian, Antonio Ricardo (Ricciardi), moved from México to Peru to inaugurate Lima's printing press. *Pragmática de los Diez Dias del Año*, a Gregorian calendar proclaimed by King Phillip II, had to wait four years for its publication until civil authorities lifted a ban on all

Peruvian printing. Unlike Mexico, where a handful of widows came forward to manage their husbands' printing shops keeping contracts with both Church and government, the extreme male dominance of colonial Lima did not allow women to perform the role of printers.[288]

The same year that New England published her first text for Harvard College (*Bay Psalm Book*, 1640), the *Heróica Puebla de Zaragoza* or *Puebla de los Angeles*, now simply Puebla, Mexico, became Latin America's third printing capital. After the *Imprenta Poblana* at the *Palafoxiano* seminary, entrusted to Bishop Juan de Palafox y Mendoza, came those of Antigua or *Santiago de los Caballeros de Guatemala* in July 1660; Paraguay in 1705 (some say, 1700); La Habana in 1707 (others say, 1720); and Oaxaca, Mexico, also in 1720. "It has not been determined with precision the beginning of the printing press in Cuba," declares the José Martí National Library in Havanna, but most Cuban researchers believed that the Belgian Carlos Habré probably started to operate his shop in 1720, publishing with permission the nation's first printed book three years later (*La Tarifa General de Precios de Medicina*, 1723).[289]

Both introduce by priests of the *Compañia de Jesús*, the printing presses of Santafe de Bogotá, now Colombia, and Ambato, today Ecuador, in the former Viceroyalty of New Granada, arrived in 1737 and 1750, respectively. *Septenario al corazón doloroso de María Santísima* (Santafé, 1738) and the *Piissima erga Dei Genitricem devotio ad impetrandam gratiam pro artículo mortis* (Hambati, 1755) emerged as their first publications. Ironically, Bogotá, a cultural niche of yesterday and today, lived almost 200 years without a printing press.[290]

Argentina and Chile are two of the most convoluted stories on how the printing press appeared in their countries. The press came to Buenos Aires in 1780 not without previous important steps in *Loreto*, Province of Misiones (where probably the first Argentine book *Martirologio Romano* was printed in 1700), and Córdoba, with its press at the Colegio de Monserrat (1764–1765) shortly before the creation of the Viceroyalty of La Plata (1776). In a printing shop known as the *Taller de los Niños Expósitos* at the corner of San Carlos and San José streets (today, Alsina and Perú), José de Silva y Aguiar signed a ten-year contract requiring him to hand 60 percent of the profits to the local orphanage.[291] In most colonial communities, the mission of the press was to publish religious books, obituaries, and governmental proclamations.

Three significant laggards of the new technology were the cities of New Orleans, Rio de Janeiro, and Caracas. Founded by the French in 1718, New Orleans did not see a printing press until 1764. Nearly half a century later (May 13, 1808), Rio de Janeiro, capital-in-exile of the regent court of then Portuguese prince *Dom Joao VI*, inaugurated the first Imprensa Régia of Brazil after war minister Francisco Antônio de Araújo e Azevedo, count of Barca, brought it up to criticize the invasion of his homeland by Napoleon, along with Portugal's Royal Library "of approximately 60,000 items, including books, manuscripts, prints, maps, coins, and medals."[292]

Brazilian historians have much to tell about previous failed attempts at establishing a permanent printing press in their country, such as the experiences of Portuguese printer Antônio Isidoro da Fonseca in the mid-1740s and Dutch settlers during their early seventeenth-century occupation of the Brazilian northeast. As King João V stated in a royal order or Provisão on July 5, 1747:

> "Whereas, it is said, that from this kingdom a quantity of typographic letters have gone to Brazil, and whereas it is considered that there is no advantage for the printers to work now in Brazil where expenses are heavier than in the Kingdom [of Portugal], books and papers can be printed here in the Kingdom and sent to to the colony. [A]nd whereas the authorization to print, both on the part of the Inquisition and on the part of my Overseas Council, must come from the Kingdom, these authorizations have to accompany all printed papers. Without said authorization it is forbidden to print or sell any work. [N]ow therefore, I ordered them to be confiscated and remitted to my Kingdom, at the expense of their proprietors. [T]he breaking of this order will be punished by sending the culprit or culprits to my Kingdom to appear before the Overseas Council which will pass sentence on them, in accordance with the crime committed."[293]

Da Fonseca was then silenced forever. As a matter of fact, in 1747, *com licenças do senhor bispo*, in other words, under ecclesiastical license, Mr. Fonseca (spelled "Fonceca" in what is considered the first book published by the Portuguese in the Americas) printed his memorable *Relaçao da Entrada*, account of the arrival made by the venerable excellency D. F. Antônio do Desterro Malheyro, Bishop of Rio de Janeiro and former Bishop of the Kingdom of Angola. Uneasy with this operation, somehow regarded as rebellious, the court in Lisbon issued a decree closing down Fonseca's *officina* (printing shop). The Dutch, on the other hand, had tried to introduce a printing press in Pernambuco under Count Mauritz of Nassau's initiative (c. 1630), but printer Pieter Janszoon who went to work on the typography supposedly sent from Holland "died soon after getting there."[294]

Later, as in Brazil, Caracas, birthplace of liberator Simón Bolivar, had to entrust its first printing press to two British men, the Irish Matthew Gallagher and his partner James Lamb, who set it up in 1808.[295] Some historians argue that the 1789 press in Trinidad, then part of the Captaincy of Venezuela, is the earliest one in this South American nation. But the English invaded Trinidad in 1797 before any printing press appeared in Venezuela. Most of the Caribbean archipelago, with the exception of

Cuba (1707 or 1720), Jamaica (1717), and Martinique (1725), acquired their presses after the mid-1700s. Popular islands such as Puerto Rico (1806) had a printing press as late as Venezuela and Brazil; a striking case is Anguila that did not have this technology until 1967.[296]

When, how, and why was the press introduced is key to understand its character and performance. The rush of Spaniards, British, and criollos for establishing a printing press in Venezuela, for instance, responds to the role that Caracas played in the emancipation process. With the same editors, the *Gazeta de Caracas* went through three different stages. A first stage, from 1808 to 1810, backed the metropolis against Napoleon. The second one, from 1810 to 1811, acted as the voice of the local *junta*, loyal to his rebel son not the king. And the final one, from 1811 to 1812, turned the newspaper into the organ of the Independent Government of Venezuela, under the command of the revolutionary hero Francisco de Miranda.

Four years before its call to support the revolution as "a virtuous action," these pages promised its readers "that nothing would come out without prior inspection by the people appointed for such a purpose by the government. [A]nd that nothing that were to be published would offend the Holy Catholic Religion, the laws governing the country, the good customs, or the peace and reputation of individuals."[297] Following the independence, these principles helped the state to restrict freedom of expression in every young Latin American republic, giving way to the so-called *press crimes* as a normal exception in their legal systems.

GACETAS BY AUTHORITY

The earliest Latin American gazettes also appeared in Mexico City and Lima three decades after the emergence of *Publick Occurrences, Both Foreign and Domestick* (Boston, 1690). Its editor, the astute printer Benjamin Harris, accused in London for seditious libel, published the single edition of his paper with a blank page so that readers could write and share their views. Scandalizing the local competition (seven more stores), his *coffee shop* welcomed men and women.[298]

Harris and his *Publick Occurrences* had little in common with the *Gaceta de México y Noticias de Nueva España*, the first Spanish-American newspaper. Born with the viceroy's permission and the blessings of the Church, its first editor was the subsequent bishop of Yucatan, Juan Ignacio María de Castorena Urzúa y Goyeneche (from January to June 1722).[299] This prelate had been an Inquisition evaluator or *calificador*. A second series (145 issues), also by authority and under the supervision of Father Juan Francisco Sahagún de Arévalo, circulated between 1728 and 1739. Although the origins of the Hispanic American press appear sometimes connected to Lima (because of the reprinting of the Gaceta de Madrid in 1715), the *Gaceta de Lima*, the first newspaper of South America, did not emerge until 1733–1744.

In Peru, journalist Richard Rodríguez-Revollar proudly proclaims that Lima's 1715 Gazette, seven years prior to the Gaceta de México, is the first newspaper of Spanish America. The University Library of Notre Dame in Indiana endorses this view, although mistakenly arguing that the *Gaceta de Lima* is "the oldest newspaper in Latin America," starting around 1744, which is absurd, since most scholars agree that the Mexican Gazette began in 1722.[300] Evidently, the spread of the colonial newspaper followed the same patterns of the printing machine.

From *La Gaceta de México* and the *Gazeta de Goatemala* (often written as Goahtemala, or even Goathemala, 1729–1731), the paper wave reached Peru, with its autochthonous the *Gaceta de Lima*, a publication that reported through the late 1770s. These pioneers were followed by the short-lived *Gaceta de la Habana* and *El Pensador in Cuba* (1764), the *Papel Periódico de la Ciudad de Santa Fé de Bogotá* (1791), *Primicias de la Cultura de Quito* (1792), The *Telégrafo mercantil, rural, político, económico e Historiográfico del Río de la Plata* (1801), and the *Río de Janeiro* and *Caracas* gazettes (1808).[301] Curious cases of the time are the bilingual *The Southern Star*, Uruguay's first newspaper, founded in Montevideo during a brief occupation of the British, and the *Telégrafo Constitucional de Santo Domingo* (1821), launched in the continent's oldest city 325 years after Bartolomeo Colón settled in to rule Hispanola.[302]

Mexico, Peru, and Colombia have managed to maintain since colonial times their reputation as centers of literary, publishing, and journalistic production. On the contrary, events of the republican era made the press in countries such as Guatemala, Cuba, Ecuador, and Bolivia fall to levels inferior to their colonial relevance. The journalistic leadership of nations such as Brazil, Argentina, and Chile is more the result of the modernization imposed by Europeans and North Americans in the mid-1900s, than its peripheral colonial relationship with Portugal or Spain. In the end, the Latin American press ended up revolving around the U.S. magnet.

In short, colonial gazettes in Spanish America, either weekly, monthly, or bimonthly, dedicated their existence to publish brief notes, accounts of major events, news from the metropolis (Spain), and economic or literary commentaries. "Pro-governmental in their spirit," wrote Professor José Villamarín-Carrascal of the Ecuadorian University of the Americas, early Latin American newspapers helped to maintain the colonizers' grip on the general population using two old techniques: informing only what it was convenient to their interests and hiding whatever it opposes them. They all consciously engaged in propaganda as a way to efficiently fulfill the role of ideological arm of the [Crown]."[303] Usually, four categories made up the news: official or administrative, religious or ecclesiastical, sociopolitical, and commercial affairs including maritime information. A distinguished exception will be most of those scientific, cultural, and literary newspapers promoted during the reign of Charles III, particularly in the Andes.

IDEOLOGICAL INTOLERANCE

Despite many legal and religious obstacles, the colonies knew prestigious authors and publications. Challenging the *status quo* in Mexico, the prolific Carlos de Siguenza y Góngora and Sor Juana Inés de la Cruz stood out with scientific works such as their respective *Libra Astronómica y filosófica* (1690) and *Neptuno Alegórico* (1680). Poet, linguist, and historian, Sor Juana Inés De la Cruz (1651–1695) became one of the icons of the struggle for Latin American freedom and equality.

Becoming a nun to pursue her studies, she amassed a personal library of at least four thousand books, the most complete of the viceroyalty at the time. Before her death and rejecting accusations of being a religious woman with secular inclinations (made by the bishop of Puebla), Sor Juana Inés gave up not only her books but also her writing. "Who has forbidden women to engage in private and individual studies?" she once asked in her defense, "[h]ave they not a rational soul as men do?"[304] Facing the Codex Madrid at the *Museo de América* in Spain, one of her famous portraits reads: "Sor Juana Inés de la Cruz, tenth muse, admirable woman of sciences, skills, arts and several languages … wrote most refined Latin, Castillian, and Mexican poems." A similar portrait at the Philadelphia Museum of Arts reiterates this assertation: "R. M. Juana Ynés de la Cruz, Phoenix of America, glorious performer of her sex, is honor of the nation and the New World, reason of praise and admiration of old time."[305]

In contrast, Sor Francisca Josefa del Castillo y Guevara (1671–1742), a neogranadine writer of immense sensibility, chose to obey her superiors, searching for redemption until her death. Sor Francisca Josefa wrote *Vida* (Life, 1724), locked in a cloister.[306] In times when women were severely undermined, there were nonetheless figures such as María de Sansoric, Pedro de Ocharte's wife, who bravely took over the family press defying charges of having Lutheran leanings.

Two other colonial authors were the *Inca Gacilaso de la Vega* (1539–1616) and the also Peruvian Juan de Espinosa Medrano (1632–1688?), better known as *El Lunarejo*. The *Inca*, born to *Huayna Cápac Inca*'s niece and the famous conquistador Sebastián Garcilaso de la Vega, who never recognized him as his, wrote a unique chronicle about her mother's ancestors (*Comentarios Reales*, 1609). The *Lunarejo* (spotty-face), scholar and preacher, produced as well various literary and theatrical works in Quechua, Spanish, and Latin, including the famous *Apologético en Favor de Don Luis de Góngora* (1662). One mestizo and the other Creole, both symbolized the self-improvement of the Latin American citizen in extraordinarily difficult circumstances.

In fact, to publish during the Spanish colony was an odyssey. Besides the favoritism for Iberian works, the inaccessibility to a printing press, and the scarce number of readers, the high cost of publishing made the task nearly impossible. The bureaucratic process was also tedious and dangerous. An impassable requirement was the censorship of doctrinal character stemming from the Inquisition. Even worse, writings on Native Indian themes required a special printing and circulation license from the Council of the Indies.

Any indulgence represented years of waiting, whereby several works remained unpublished and forgotten. Nevertheless, one cannot say that there was an absolute obscurantism in the colonies. The best of the *Siglo de Oro* (Golden Century) and its extraordinary authors, including Cervantes, Tirso de Molina, Lope de Vega, Quevedo, and Garcilaso (the one born in Toledo, not the Inca), were very well known among educated Americans. What the Inquisition did not allow, because of its obscenity or rebelliousness, came in through smuggling. According to official import records, 103 copies of *El Quijote* arrived in Cartagena the same year of its publication (1605).

LIBERATION THROUGH SCIENCE

The cultural event of the upper colonization in Spanish America is the proliferation of scientific expeditions authorized by the Bourbon kings Ferdinand VI (1746–1759) and Charles III (1759–1788), both moderate friends of the Enlightenment. Although with censorship, missions such as the geodetic of Charles Marie LaCodamine (1735–1744), geographical of José de Iturriaga (1753), and botanical of José Celestino Mutis planted in South America the interest for an autonomous thinking and innovation. Botanical, hydrological, and medical excursions such as those of Martín de Sessé, Alessandro Malaspina, and Francisco Javier de Balmis also promoted a spirit of renovation in Mexico and its surroundings. Studies, discussions, and private gatherings or *tertulias* encourage intellectuals to demand a greater flexibility and openness of the press.

In an atmosphere of enlightened despotism, the Crown only intended to energize the metropolis and its colonies. In the end, the expeditions turned against the Spanish monarchy, fueling a criticism and science that favored France and England. Once again, smuggling played a fundamental role in the transfer of French works. Lima, Mexico, and Santafe de Bogotá became centers of intellectual progress and revolutionary ideas. According to Alexander Von Humboldt, "only Joseph Banks, Director of the *Kew Gardens* in London, had a better botanical library than Celestino Mutis' in the New Granada."[307]

Once King Charles III reluctantly joined the French Enlightenment and the insurgency in North America, the Spanish-American colonies saw the proliferation of *Sociedades de Amigos o Amantes del País*: academic clubs where secular experts of geography, science, and literature, regularly called *sabios* (the wise), gather to advance education, liberty, and democracy in the Kingdom, especially after the expulsion of the Jesuits in 1765. They were, affirmed Villamarín-Carrascal, "the journalists of the time, [authors] whose tentacles reached public opinion with newssheets of patriotic character."[308] With little room for criticism and tightly controlled by colonial authorities, printers had in this unique period an opportunity to plant various sentiments of independence.

Both the *Diario de México* and *The Mercurio Volante* (The Flying Mercury), a name probably derived from a series of newsbooks published by Don Carlos de Siguenza y Góngora in 1693, appeared as early Hispanic American journals with encyclopedic tendencies. Then, around the times of the First Amendment, innovative Spanish-American gazettes, notably the *Mercurio Peruano* (January 2, 1791), the *Papel Periódico de la Ciudad de Santafé de Bogotá* (February 9, 1791), and *Primicias de la Cultura de Quito* (January 5, 1792), published pieces by celebrated South American thinkers, including physician José Hipólito Unánue (aka "Aristo"), jurist Juan Egaña, poet José Baquíjano y Carrillo, and writer Francisco Antonio Ulloa, among others. There is contradictory information as to when and how these illustrated papers circulated, beginning with the very *Mercurio Peruano*. Indeed, Jean-Pierre Clément, professor of historic and comparative literature at the University of Poitier in France, argues that this Peruvian paper operated between 1790 and 1795, not 1791 to 1794 as numerous historians say.[309]

It is little surprising that major heroes of the Colombian independence had worked with José Celestino Mutis (1732–1808). Two of the most prestigious ones were the naturalist Francisco Antonio Zea, first vice president of the *Gran Colombia* (1819–1830), and Francisco José de Caldas, an editor and patriot leader executed on General Pablo Morillo's orders during the Spanish reconquest in 1816. Caldas, the Wise, launched the weekly *Semanario del Nuevo Reyno de Granada* in 1808, a newspaper known for its devotion to change, literature, and science.[310]

Arraigned by the Inquisition, Mutis courageously defended a scientist's right to a free opinion governed by reason.[311] His expedition was generously assisted by the Cuban Manuel del Socorro Rodríguez's printing shop, where the father of Colombian journalism edited the *Papel Periódico de Santa Fé de Bogotá*. This weekly was also born printing the best of the New Granada's enlightenment.

On Rodriguez's and Mutis' example, another printer Antonio Nariño an admirer of Benjamin Franklin, organized an influential circle of intellectuals that held secret meetings to promote the political criticism of the colonial regime. From the *Arcano Sublime de la Filantropía*, his *tertulia* in Santa Fé, emerged patriots such as the physician and lawyer Francisco Javier Eugenio de Santa Cruz y Espejo (1747–1795), who published the pro-independence *Primicias de la Cultura de Quito*. Banned because of his "bloody satire," authorities in Quito declared Espejo a *persona non-grata*, a dangerous man dedicated, according to the authorities, to destroy the reputation of honorable people. Soon after his arrest, he died in 1795.

Something similar occurred to his mentor. Convicted to ten years in prison for publishing the seventeen articles of the French Declaration of the Rights of Man and the Citizen in his *Patriotic Press* (December 13, 1793), Nariño purged two-thirds of his sentence in both Spain and the New Granada. As Espejo, he died soon after his liberation. Saturated with oppression, persecution, and sacrifice, the Gran Colombia, as the rest of Latin America, engaged in a full-scale war for independence.

It is good to speculate what could have happened if Europe had not discovered the New World, as colonization took much away leaving behind lasting and important double-edged marks that affect Latin American society today, notably a single language (Spanish), one dominant religion (the Holy Roman Catholic Church), class-based bigotry, male domination, and a broad sense of cultural identity (Hispanic Americanism). Through ancient and colonial records, Latin Americans can also realize that their media history did not begin in Europe, that communication is not pure technology but also art and mythology, and that censorship is an elaborate machinery set up to destroy aboriginal traditions and restraints.

Latin Americans still dream with a truly democratic society and communication, free from poverty, foreign intervention, and political systems of force. Thus, to grasp the problems of the press in this region is to know about the roots and long history of its censorship and limitations. The intolerance with the right to communicate, the monopolization of culture and the media, and the absence of respect to popular opinions and sentiments are all distortions of centuries of abuse and domination.

Two of the most negative factors against freedom of expression in Latin America come from colonial times: the state authoritarianism and the ecclesiastical hierarchy. Indeed, little can be said in the Latin American countries without the approval of the Church and the state. Censorship of the press, nonetheless, is the result of not only impositions by old bureaucratic powers but also various forms of social discrimination, technological divides, and ideological intolerance.

Thus, standing by The House of the First Printing Press of America on *True Street*, one should make an effort to visualize the deep roots of Latin American and Caribbean journalism, branching out in all directions, not just the north.

Chapter 2

A Taste of Freedom

We, the people of this continent, could reach beyond the U.S. Bill of Rights and the Declaration of Independence for significant concepts of liberty, free expression, and other human rights in this continent. West to the New England colonies and before the U.S. Constitution was amended, the Iroquois Confederacy of Seneca, Onondaga, Oneida, Mohawk, and Cayuga Indians developed a Great Law of Peace or *Kaianerekowa*. It mandated rulers to mentor their communities and be prepared for both angry and offensive action and criticism.[1] Although modern communication eventually distinguished between "speech" and "action," the spirit of this Native Indian precedent is something Latin Americans ought to study more deeply.[2]

This chapter highlights important notions of liberty and press freedom introduced by barely known liberators in non-Latin American circles, heroes who defied European monarchs and confessional forms of government, hoping to eradicate colonialism forever. Based on their revolutionary ideals and during independence, the new republics drafted and adopted constitutional principles such as a "responsible" *libertad de imprenta* (freedom of the press), framing Latin American society until today. Indeed, these early and memorable dreams of free speech, free press, and free communication are an adequate and fruitful road to explain past and present-day realities in the Hispanic world.

SEEDS OF LIBERTY DOWN SOUTH

Francisco de Miranda (1750–1816), the renowned Venezuelan *Precursor of Independence*, may not have known the great talents of the Iroquois

Confederacy (although he genuinely admired Native Indians, coming to propose an Inca king for his dreamed Colombia), but he came to the United States to learn about liberty and personal freedom.[3] In the end, he would be more fascinated with the life of ordinary U.S. Americans than the snobbery and reverence surrounding many of their great men, including George Washington, a man who had warned against "the dangers of *otherness* in the American hemisphere" such as "the threat posed by Spanish Americans."[4] Despite their mutual military interests and deference, the two men never moved into a level of friendship. Fame, power, culture, and age separated them a great deal, just as their homelands had been divided for similar reasons.

Traveling the United States, Miranda became more nationalistic, cognizant of both her Puritanism and her tendency to prefer the French people and culture to Spaniards and Spanish Americans. Commenting on the "silly" religious traits of the Union, he wrote, "crass superstition is present in all people of the earth, even the most civilized."[5] Still, he praised highly the order and cleanliness of the U.S. cities and markets, especially Philadelphia, as well as the humility and fairness of their people, their concern for freedom and happiness, and the informality of their unmarried women.

In June 1783, after repeated libels and discrimination, Miranda disembarked in the coast of North Carolina six months before authorities in Madrid issued a warrant for his arrest. Already a lieutenant colonel of the Spanish Army, he was sentenced *in absentia* to ten years in prison for the high crime of betraying the monarchy.[6] This libelous accusation, like others throughout his career, was the tip of a lifetime of bigotry against the Creole Miranda family.

Back in his native Caracas, Venezuela, Francisco de Miranda grew up enduring the insults of the Spanish aristocrats. His father, Don Sebastián Miranda de Ravelo, a native of the Canary Islands struggling to gain a status for his lineage, had also been the target of racial harassment. Degrading his character, *mantuanos* or local nobles used to call Don Sebastián a "mulatto," an "adventurer," and a *mercachifle* (low-class trader), to which he replied with the purchase of nobility titles as part of Spain's corruptive practice of selling social credentials. Depending on the size of the bribery, such accreditation might even include the signature of the Spanish king.[7] Government corruption has been proverbial in Hispanic America, or should we say, in the Americas since colonial times.

Boosting his family name, Sebastián Miranda's son, the intelligent Francisco, went to study in the peninsula. Quickly, he became the center of rumors and slanders among young Iberian nobles, particularly in the Spanish Army that he joined in 1773. Spain had a great mistrust for *criollos* (American-born descendants) inasmuch as they could one day gain enough power to challenge the authority of the Catholic empire. If well educated, the suspicion and animosity ran higher, especially if the Creole was an alien and "spurious" freethinker like Francisco de Miranda.

Thus, the charge of *alta traición* (treason) seemed simply another scheme of jealous Spanish officers who wanted to see the Creole convicted and incarcerated, as he had been denied promotion commensurate to his services despite evident military and diplomatic accomplishments in the United States and the Caribbean. Working with Spanish military officers in Iberia and North Africa, the proud and ambitious Precursor had learned much about the Spaniards' imperial arrogance and disdain for people different than their own.[8] In these circumstances, the United States became a sanctuary for him, although he feared that the North Americans could turn him in as a gesture of gratitude for the Spaniards' support in the Revolutionary War. Indeed, Miranda had fought against the British in the Battle of Pensacola and negotiated their surrender in mid-1781.[9] Yet, because of his many charms and abilities, including valuable information he could eventually provide about Spain, prominent U.S. citizens embraced Miranda with noted hospitality. Few figures, however, became real friends. One letter of recommendation, the unrelenting protocol of closed circles, introduced him as "a gentleman who loves freedom so passionately that he would honor the world's freest country."[10]

The Precursor's ideals were not particularly innovative to influential Anglo-Americans. As Robertson explains, "many people of various nationalities long before Miranda [had] presented full-fledged schemes [for independence of Spanish America] to the consideration of the English government."[11] He visited John Adams, for example, then representing the Union in England, because Adams knew about several plots to "free" these lands for the commercial advantage and exploitation of the British. The Spanish colonies offered a good business potential and their ports and markets meant likely new profits and riches.[12] Consequently, some historians have questioned Miranda's commitment to liberate Spanish America. But few, if anyone, deny that no other Hispanic American besides him "had done so much to lay the groundwork for revolution prior to the final outbreak of the movement in 1810."[13]

Facing financial difficulties, biographers generally admire the hero's resistance to easy comfort (under the protection of Empress Catherine the Great in Russia) and bribery or other forms of corruption, since the liberator knew too well the manipulative power of governments interested in using him. On several occasions, the British government tried to make Miranda work for obscure purposes. Unsurprisingly, many Latin Americans, mixing history with religiosity, still regard the patriot as a messenger of true freedom, as the "Apostle" of the Spanish-American independence.[14]

Yet, Francisco de Miranda was not a typically religious man. Although tolerant of various creeds, he thought religious hierarchies should be under the control of constitutional and political powers. His encyclopedic influences led him to advocate the popular election of ecclesiastical posts, and with the Inquisition in mind, he firmly rejected the intrusion of the Church in public life while deploring and criticizing all kinds of religious fundamentalism. Even so, Miranda greatly sympathized with Jesuits living in exile in Italy, after their expulsion by King Charles III in 1767. In fact, the eventual *generalísimo* trusted these clerics as potential allies in the revolutionary process against Spanish injustice and colonialism.

Intellectually, conventional religion was a fraud for him. Still, politically, faiths were to be respected and tolerated. During his expedition to free Venezuela, aboard the *Leander* (1806), soldiers privately criticized their commander for accepting but not attending religious services. Hours before his death in the prison of *La Carraca* in Cádiz, he dispatched his Catholic confessor with the words: "let me die in peace."[15] Admiring Voltaire, the Precursor became an antiecclesiastical ideologue, condemning tyranny and despotism as forcefully as corruption, abuse, and fanaticism.[16] It is erroneous and an oversimplification to say that enlightened individuals at that time despised the Catholic faith, but they greatly mistrusted the Church, especially the Inquisition, a clearly hated institution. These episodes are significant for the scope of freedom of the press in Latin America, because future *próceres ilustrados* (enlightened leaders), like Miranda, will have a similar perspective, influencing the region for generations to come.

Latin American liberators embodied renovation and activism of the late 1700s, a spirit of reform ranging from a modern reinvention of the economy and a disgust for absolute monarchs to a new political conscience, including secular changes in schools and universities, colonial reading practices, the circulation of books, new concepts of writing and creativity, and a cultural progress marked with new Borbonic ideas, new wise men, and new audiences. Journalist Manuel del Socorro Rodriguez, however, a librarian, feared that the ongoing enlightenment or *Siglo de las Luces* (a Century of Lights) seemed dominated by both ideas of sedition and independence in New Granada. In his view, the advantages of the Spanish discovery of America and its contributions to humanity, religion, the sciences, and the arts had been diluted by the excesses of freedom, poverty, and an immoderate patriotism. For him, the abuses of the press had become a great and pernicious danger, a craft in which scholars had forgotten that there were sovereign kings, laws, and religion.[17]

At one point, modern thinkers such as José Luis de Azuola, a priest, and his cousin Jorge Tadeo Lozano, a member of the Botanical Expedition, dared to request an exemption from censorship to freely publish information in their *Correo Curioso, Erudito, Económico y Mercantil de la ciudad de Santafé de Bogotá* (1801), the second paper in this capital city of approximately 12,000 people. Royal prosecutor Manuel Antonio Blaya instantly rejected their petition, citing "extremely grave inconveniences that could arise from the difficulty to send reinforcement troops into these [Neogranadine] lands."[18]

Years earlier, during the so-called "trials of 1794," also known as "El Complot de los Pasquinistas" (The Complot of the Lampoonists), the Spaniard citizen Francisco Carrasco had denounced before the Viceroy José de Espeleta fourteen young men for posting seditious printings in places of public view, notably Sinforoso Mutis (J. C. Mutis's nephew), Francisco Antonio Zea (José Celestino's disciple at the *Expedición Botánica*), Don Miguel Cabal, and Don Antonio Nariño and his printer Don Diego Espinosa de los Monteros. Upon their arrest, the majority received stiff prison sentences to be served in Spain or Africa, beginning with a temporary detention in *Cartagena de Indias* and then a perilous voyage to Cadiz via Havana.

News of the revolt did travel all the way to the metropolis, if anything, because Antonio Nariño and Diego Espinosa had printed a clandestine translation of the French Declaration of the Rights of Man and the Citizen shortly before, shaking the viceroyalty's public opinion. Activities involving publications of any French revolutionary literature or seditious printings and manuscripts were indeed strictly prohibited, although *pasquines*, "a constant form of colonial communication," tended to merely accuse local bureaucrats and personalities of criminal wrongdoing more than criticizing judges, the Church, or the Crown.[19] Notwithstanding, who had given these youngsters the impression that Spanish America has to accept "the pretentious freedom some people think the French enjoy?" asked Rodríguez. The Cuban journalist dedicated considerable time and space to the French Revolution and ideals in his *Papel Periódico* in Santafe.[20]

Prior restraint is commonplace in the colony, lamented Francisco José de Caldas, the Wise, in the very first issue of his *Semanario del Nuevo Reyno de Granada* (1808). My new paper, he wrote, "has started badly" because this "beautiful prospect, [well] composed and introduced, [has been] ruined ... as you have seen (by the censor?). [L]iterary freedom will expire if the magistrate gives himself the hidden authority to correct works of men of letters [and the sciences]. How can a kingdom prosper with these barriers."[21] By the late 1700s and early 1800s, censorship and intimidation felt so strongly in New Granada that academic societies, though encouraged by enlightened Spanish despots as innovative forms of circulating ideas, exchanges, and communication, had to request permission to meet, many times unsuccessfully.[22]

Likewise, gazettes operated as vital *"papeles públicos,"* that is to say, public papers seen as indispensable instruments in the process of education and modernization, both scientifically and politically. Besides the liberty to write, local newspapers pushed for greater freedom to inform and circulate. But readers already had a significant suspicion for the reliability of their content, a reason why J. C. Mutis used the term "noticias gazetales" (gazette news) to separate passionate notes from serious scientific information. Interestingly, European printings came with a delay of only three months to New Granada in the early nineteenth century, albeit subscribers read the news from time to time instead of daily. At first the *gacetas* came from Madrid, Berlin, Paris, Havana, and Lima (e.g., *La Gaceta de la Habana* and El Mercurio *Peruano*), but, gradually and increasingly, gazettes began to arrive in significant numbers from the United States.

Despite the proliferation of printed matter, both the media and the political environment of the "enlightened" Spanish-American colonies transpired an atmosphere of "fear and repression," with public papers under constant threat of confiscation for seditious operations. Unsurprisingly, and regardless of the dangers of overseas travel, well-to-do Creoles went to Europe and North America to gain experience, knowledge, and social connections.

Touring the United States soon after the triumphant signing of the Treaty of Paris, Francisco de Miranda studied the young nation's laws, political institutions, churches, schools, military barracks, and commercial establishments including printing houses and newspapers. In Philadelphia, a capital controlled by Quakers who regarded entertainment as sinful and artists as lawbreakers, Lieutenant Colonel Miranda, the flute player and nonconformist, had mixed feelings about the country's civil liberties before the First Amendment. He found reasons for admiration as well as for concern, especially after dining with George Washington and fellow heroes.[23]

Miranda thought ordinary citizens excessively worshipped Washington, "as if the Savior had entered Jerusalem!" he wrote.[24] For him, the glory of independence also belonged to humble Americans and the many foreigners who had fought along their side, including U.S. and Haitian blacks, Frenchmen, and Spanish and Creole soldiers. It worried him a great deal the way in which the general and other North American leaders were talking about Florida, Louisiana, Texas, and California, territories that they already believed to be a natural extension of the United States.[25] Still, he generally liked what he saw in Philadelphia and other cities of the United States.

As with Washington, he had a "cordial detachment" with both Thomas Jefferson and James Madison. In the early 1800s, he requested their support, but the two giants of the U.S. independence, uninterested in any active assistance to the liberation of South America, paid marginal attention to him.[26] For Central America and the Caribbean, they had other plans. When referring to Cuba, Jefferson once wrote: "Do we wish to acquire to our own Confederacy any one or more of the Spanish provinces?" Answering his own question, he replied: "I candidly confess, that I have ever looked on Cuba as the most interesting addition which could ever be made to our system of states. The control which [...] this island would give us over the Gulf of Mexico, and the countries and isthmus bordering on it, as well as all those whose waters flow into it, would fill up the measure of our political well-being. Yet, as I am sensible that this can never be obtained, even with her own consent, but by war."[27]

Evidently, these extraordinary Anglo-American leaders had no intention of carrying their ideals of liberty beyond their borders. In fact, regarding Latin America, their mentality seemed little different from those of England, France, and Spain. Consequently, the United States, as a powerful archetype, became the focus of big internal disputes in the future Latin American republics, including constitutional issues such as freedom of speech and of the press. This enriching but also conflicting political ambivalence would be distinctively noticeable in Mexico, the Central American Federation, the New Granada, and the United Provinces of the River Plate, fueling internal tensions between Latin American patriots such as Simón Bolívar and Francisco de Paula Santander in the *Gran Colombia* (Greater Colombia).

Jefferson, for instance, supported the Monroe Doctrine, although not necessarily as a strategy to acquire Spanish possessions in Latin America. He embraced this policy as a mechanism to oppose the forcible attempt of any European power to reconquest, transfer, or acquire emancipated lands in the Americas. But the suspicion Jefferson had against Europeans for their historic and voracious ambitions, Latin American patriots such as Miranda and Bolívar had against the United States for her increasing territorial appetites.[28]

Interestingly, Alexander Hamilton, a statesman amply recognized in his time for his principled politics, became an enthusiastic defender of Miranda's plans of independence, helping the South American liberator to spread his ideas in various political circles of the North. One of his most loyal friends, the prestigious revolutionary and English pamphleteer Thomas Paine also helped and saved Miranda from the guillotine in another charge of treason before the French Revolutionary Tribunal in 1793.

Gossip about his treason charges in Cuba spoiled Miranda's reputation since his first visit to the United States. Generous acquaintances quickly became foes, and only those fully committed against despotism and ideas of freedom and enlightenment anywhere in the continent continued to support the lieutenant colonel, such as Tom Paine. In New York and Boston, he managed to secure a few good friends, especially the prestigious Sam and John Adams, as well as General Henry Knox and Colonel William S. Smith.

In Miranda's opinion, the United States should be admired for her effective participation of constituencies at local levels, her near absence of state barriers, and her devotion to education. But, he noticed and deplored the already existing presumptuousness of wealth, the hypocrisy of religion, and the cult of profits and business. In conversations with Sam Adams, he questioned contradictions such as promising a democracy by the laws of virtue, when, in reality, the supreme rule was wealth and private property. Miranda could not understand how the right to freedom of religion translated into a dominant order of Christians who were the only ones eligible for government and legislative posts. Because of his frankness, Sam Adams learned to appreciate this *criollo*, becoming a good and trusted friend.[29]

Eight of thirteen states had a Bill of Rights that included *free press* guarantees in their constitutional systems, but only three states added freedom of *speech*.[30] Unlike France, freedom of neither *communication* nor *expression* was explicitly protected in the U.S. Constitution.[31] A devotee of the fine arts, Miranda must have looked with suspicion on the Federal Charter. The arts, a suitable criterion to measure degrees of freedom in a society, had been narrowly defined in this document as merely "useful arts." In the commercial spirit of the new nation, applied arts had little to do with the more creative and intellectual fine arts (or should we say, "useless" and even "inappropriate" arts like music), which Miranda treasured throughout his life.[32]

For a long time, up to World War I and beyond, the First Amendment did not protect most people's *free expression* in the United States, primarily those of women and minorities. Thus, during his last visit in 1805–1806, James Madison, father of the U.S. Constitution and champion of the American Bill of Rights, courteously rejected Francisco de Miranda's request to support the cause of freedom and independence in South America. Understandably, as secretary of state of the Jefferson administration, Madison conveyed the unwillingness of the U.S. government to break her peace with major European powers. Yet, in the course of his own presidency (1809–1817), a military buildup took place after a short war with England (1812–1814), paving the way for the imperialistic doctrines of his friend and successor President James Monroe.[33]

Still, people in the Spanish colonies greatly admired the first American Revolution and continue to do so to this day. Hispanic thinkers not only studied the U.S. Constitution but also cherished the free speech and press provisions of the Virginia and Pennsylvania constitutions.[34] In practice, Spanish-American Creoles were probably more acquainted with the Declaration of Independence and the Federal Constitution than the Bill of Rights. Both the U.S. and French declarations of independence had been amply commented and criticized in Spanish gazettes, so intellectuals in Spanish-American colonies had access to and knowledge of them. On December 15, 1793, within months of Miranda escaping the guillotine in France, Antonio Nariño (1765–1823) printed in New Granada the seventeen articles of *Rights of Man and the Citizen*. His translation came from a book entitled *Histoire de la Révolution, imprimé par les amis de la liberté*, owned and borrowed from the viceroy himself, though not directly by Nariño.[35]

For this patriot, as he wrote in his *Bagatela* (A Petty Gazette), newspapers seemed essential. They appeared to propagate liberty, justice, and equality, and to promote public opinion. An agenda setter, Nariño, introduced Spanish America to the world of political journalism, contributing to bring down with his pen the government of the illustrious Don Jorge Tadeo Lozano while becoming President of Cundinamarca in 1811. Like Simón Bolívar and other Latin American liberators and patriots, he opposed the federalism of the United States. Fray Servando Teresa de Mier, for example, a translator of Rousseau's *Social Contract*, persecuted by the Inquisition for almost thirty years in Mexico, had this advice in 1813: even if allied with them, mistrust the example of Anglo-America. Imitating the United States is not the right course to follow.[36] In 1823, in Villa de Leyva, Colombia, Antonio Nariño y Álvarez died within hours of the historic December 15 of his French Declaration in Spanish, battling decades of persecution, humiliation, and disease in the quest for freedom.[37]

Spanish Americans seemed less versed on subtle differences and implications among the various definitions of press freedom in North America. They probably ignored that a motion declaring that "the liberty of the press should be inviolably observed" had been defeated at the constitutional convention.[38] Only fairly few patriots would have been able to recite differences between the First Amendment and Pennsylvania's constitution, proclaiming that the people have a right to freedom of speech, and of writing and publishing their sentiments, instead of the now famous Congress making no law abridging the freedom of speech, or of the press. Few, if anyone, would have then guessed that the First Amendment would be manipulated to mean little effective freedom for millions of Americans for the rest of the eighteenth, the entire nineteenth, and most of the twentieth centuries. Would the United States have been different if a Pennsylvanian or Virginian type of clause had been adopted as the First Amendment? Probably not, for over a century the U.S. Supreme Court used the distorted word "Congress" to condone both state and private restrictions of the freedom of speech, or of the press.[39]

After visiting Russia, Eastern Europe, and Scandinavia, where his ideas, knowledge, and character were greatly expanded and admired, Francisco de Miranda returned to England the year of the French Revolution, hoping for British support of Latin American independence. The Spaniards in London, including envoys of the Inquisition, continued to defame the Venezuelan officer with charges of treason, smuggling, fraud, and other crimes. Allegedly, they even tried to trap and kidnap him.[40] In an interview with the British prime minister, the then Colonel Miranda of the Russian Army (after the *Nootka Sound Dispute*, 1789) formally proposed a liberation campaign of the Spanish-American colonies to the English government. It would be a venture based on mutual interest and respect.

Miranda handed in ten documents to Prime Minister William Pitt, the Younger (1759–1806), which included a *freedom and independency* proposal based on open foreign trade, territorial integrity and sovereignty, and a cooperative, not a colonial or monopolistic, relationship with Latin America. Just as his friend the honorable Hamilton did in the United States, he also put forward a homegrown constitutional monarchy, combining elements of British parliamentarism, U.S. federalism, and indigenous hegemony.[41]

For him, an emperor, like the South American Inca, should rule the new republics. Also, a senate of *caciques*, chosen for life by the Inca, would work in consonance with a chamber of communes elected by the people for one or more five-year terms. And there was a reason for this format: the 1780 uprising led by the Cacique José Gabriel Condorcanqui or *Tupac Amaru* (1740?–1781) in Peru greatly encouraged the Precursor. In politics, education, and conceivably press and speech matters, censors, appointed by the citizens but confirmed by the emperor, would watch over the morals of society. Purely ecclesiastical affairs were to be reserved to the clergy, "but the Inquisition, having become unnecessary, was to be forever abolished."[42]

Undeniably, it was an awkward combination of criteria, illogical and unpalatable to many leaders in Europe and the United States. Francisco de Miranda had proposed an unusual but eclectic mixture of political systems where freedom of the press would be seriously undermined, if not impaired. Although his admiration for Native Indian institutions was remarkable and sincere, an imperial power, even if rooted in the indigenous history of the continent, runs opposite to the advancing liberal thinking and revolutions of the time, which, he decidedly espoused.

Through Miranda's experience, one could identify the challenges, concerns, and aspirations of the unfolding Latin American republics. Ultimately, the goal was to defeat Spain with a triple alliance of English, Anglo-American, and Spanish-American revolutionaries, opening the new nations to the freedom of ideas and commerce that Great Britain and the United States had come to embrace.[43] France was excluded, due to its strategic alliance with Spain through the Bourbon dynasty.

To neutralize the Catholic Church and abolish its Inquisition were also central objectives, ending the long Spanish history of licenses, abuses, and restrictions. Persuading the United States not to invade and expand in Latin America turned into another major goal. But the most important aspiration was building an integrated, democratic, and just "Colombian" continent, a giant Hispanic American nation that he wished to call one day the newly liberated *Colombeia*, including Florida to the southernmost banks of the Mississippi River. Its foundations would be the British, French, and American ideals of liberty, good government, justice, and reciprocity. People who dream about freedom, he liked to say, have no use for blind militiamen and inefficient civilians; what they need is thinkers and philosophers that struggle for nothing but the achievement and defense of their liberties.[44]

In the midst of all his parliamentarian liberalism, anticlericalism, and monarchism, Francisco de Miranda actively defended the importance of patriotic presses and the need for journals to communicate truthful news to the people. As discussed below, he attempted to introduce the first printing press in his homeland and edited a newspaper in London, *El Colombiano* (1810), following a failed expedition to liberate Venezuela between February and August 1806.

OTHER PATRIOTS, PRESSES, AND IDEALS

In 1793, as mentioned above, the Neogranadine Antonio Nariño published in his *Imprenta Patriotica* (Patriotic Press) a Spanish translation of the *Déclaration des Droits de L'homme et du Citoyen*, the famous human rights proclamation adopted by the French Constitutional Assembly on August 26, 1789.[45] For doing so, he was convicted to ten years in an African prison, a permanent ban from living in the Indies, and the confiscation of his property—the same sentence imparted to Miranda a decade later.

Authorities also prosecuted and convicted Nariño's printer, Don Diego Espinosa de los Monteros, to three years of hard labor in the factories of Cartagena and both a perpetual eviction from Santafe and a lifetime interdiction to work in the business of printing. Unlike Zenger's trial and its happy ending, in this case even the defense attorneys were sentenced. Nariño's lawyer, Don Jose Antonio Ricaurte, a relative who bravely agreed to defend the patriot, was captured and sent to purge an eight-year prison term where he ultimately died. Likewise, Don Manuel García, the printer's defender, ended up executed for his professional services in 1816.[46]

Nevertheless, with King Charles III (1759–1788) imitating Paris and Madrid, notably during the 1870s, a series of private intellectual gatherings or *tertulias* bloomed across Spanish America. In New Granada, Santafe de Bogotá became well known for the erudition of its literary circles. Organized by Doña Manuela Sanz Santamaría de Manrique and dedicated to literature, history, and natural science, the *Tertulia del Buen Gusto* (The Circle of Good Taste) was a most prominent one. Others include the classical *Tertulia Eutropélica* led by the father of Colombian journalism Manuel del Socorro Rodriguez and the *Círculo Literario* (Literary Circle, 1789–1794), sponsored by Antonio Nariño, the most political and philosophical of the social gatherings of the time.[47] At the *Eutropélica*, the Cuban journalist, resident of Bogotá, taught literature in addition to collecting contributions for his *Papel Periódico*. Inviting "Creoles with a neogranadine spirit," the *Circle* often disguised itself as a society of agrarian and artistic interests.[48]

In this atmosphere of enlightened despotism, the Spanish monarchy not only tolerated but also promoted an intellectual movement of administrative, political, and educational reform, seeking a revitalization and modernization of both the state and the economy. In the end, as occurred with the scientific expeditions of José Celestino Mutis and other naturalists, the *tertulias* went beyond the Crown's wishes and turned against it, demanding improved levels of intellectual progress, social development, and freedom.

Again, the smuggling and importation of foreign publications played a fundamental role in the spread of encyclopedic works such as those of Voltaire, Rousseau, Montesquieu, and others. Like Sor Juana Inés de la Cruz 100 years before, Antonio Nariño, a book trader, had a library that caused envy among his peers. His political collection was comparable to Mutis' botanical repository, which was in turn praised by Alexander Humboldt as only less complete than that of Joseph Banks in London.[49] Mutis had also helped constitute a tertulia in Bogotá, the *Sociedad Económica*, an idea originally proposed by Jorge Tadeo Lozano in his *Correo Curioso, Erudito, Económico y Mercantil*, New Granada's first private newspaper, founded in 1801.[50]

Obviously, pupils of the Colombian independence came to both Mutis and Nariño. As written earlier, two of the most prestigious were the naturalist Francisco Antonio Zea, and the astronomer Francisco José de Caldas. Caldas, *El Sabio*, drew great respect for him in his *Semanario del Nuevo Reyno de Granada* in 1808.

On Celestino Mutis' steps, Nariño formed his secret *Arcano Sublime de la Filantropía* (The Sublime Arcane of Philanthropy), hoping to encourage the criticism of the colonial regime. From this *tertulia* emerged key patriotic leaders such as the prominent and already mentioned Dr. Eugenio de Santa Cruz y Espejo (born in Luis Chuzhing, 1747–1795), the man who published the noted and pro-independent *Primicias de la Cultura de Quito* (1792). This insurgent newspaper derived from the activities of the *Sociedad Patriótica* (Patriotic Society), where Espejo had been its secretary.[51]

For the Ecuadorian leader, voices of autonomy and liberty and of economic progress and political transformation could not be heard without newspapers shaking public opinion. As a typical ideologue of the encyclopedia movement, knowledge and talent came from six major sources: science, art, agriculture, commerce, economics, and politics. In his view, Quito and the Andes needed to wake up. Believing in the power of news and journalism, Espejo turned into a harsh and passionate social critic: "we live in the most insulting ignorance and the most deplorable misery," he wrote.[52]

A convincing anticlerical activist (even though he wrote sermons for his brother who was a priest), Espejo flourished as a journalist uninterested in mystical stories and explanations. He preferred mundane events such as the news, the languages, the arts, and the socioeconomic, medical, and cultural debates. Progress, human dignity, freedom, and justice were also paramount for him.

In his time, Quito faced a deep social decadence, but the patriot was not ready to accept the mediocrity of his hometown's *status quo*. Determined to be a frontal, controversial, and daring critic, Espejo charged against the laziness and incapacity of the Church, and the corruption and immorality of secular authorities. Naturally, some of his worse enemies were public servants, such as the mayor of Riobamba (south of Quito) who accused the editor of libelous, rude, defiant, and malignant writings (e.g., uncovering the major's extramarital affairs). Also, he was accused of authoring a satire against King Charles III. After three years trying to prove his innocence in Bogotá, he returned to Quito convinced that independence was the only course possible. Arrested, and at forty-eight years of age, Espejo died after a few months in prison.

As with his disciple, *oydors* also arrested Antonio Nariño and threw him in jail. He purged altogether two-thirds of his prison sentences for sedition that added up to nearly ten years. A revolutionary "publicist," Nariño inspired important patriots such as José Antonio Ricaurte, Francisco Antonio Zea, Joaquín Camacho, José Luis de Azuola, and many others. "It just occurred to me," he once wrote, "[we could] establish in this city [Santafe] a circle of literati ... to order samples of the best dailies and foreign gazettes, encyclopedic papers, and materials of that nature. In a couple of hours, the[se] papers can be read and the authors criticized so that we could have fun and useful time."[53]

Called from prison by the revolutionaries, Nariño reappeared in Bogotá in 1810 and opened the following year his famous Sunday newspaper *La Bagatela*. In a special issue, he cried: "For God's sake, let's open our eyes! The time has come, our ruin is without remedy if we don't get together ... if we don't break with this apathy [and] with this inactivity in times so critical. [W]e need nothing more than one sentiment, one goal: we need no distinctions of motherland or of professions to defend our freedom. What we need to hear is only one voice: to save our motherland or die."[54]

In subsequent editions, the human rights precursor denounced the provincial government of *Cundinamarca* for attempting to censor the press through higher taxes. In a column entitled "the press," after the *Cundinamarca* Constitution had proclaimed its freedom as a "sacred" right (1811), Nariño wrote: "It is well known that when someone wants to indirectly prohibit a [publication] the simplest method is to burden it with taxes."[55] How could an author, he asked, in a miserable newspaper, survive by paying outrageously expensive contributions every time it prints? "The Government, only the government can do it," he concluded.[56] In 1811, Nariño and his weekly carried out the first "Watergate" type of coup of Spanish America, forcing President Jorge Tadeo Lozano to resign, and taking his place after a popular election. The ardent *Bagatela* finally closed down in 1812.

In the early 1780s, Francisco de Miranda also wrote in Havana some very critical statements against the unstable and pro-governmental press. In a message to the director of the *Gaceta de la Habana*, Miranda reproached the gazette as a work of minor *fuste* (importance). "But, they (gazettes) are very useful papers to the educated peoples," he said, "for, through the news, [newspapers] contribute to improve civilization. It is said that your [newspaper] is a bundle of things without beginning or end, without neither method nor order. But, I'll just say that you made it with extreme rush. [B]efore telling us about the news of Europe in a confusing tour, wouldn't be easier, since your eminence lives in America, to evacuate first everything that concerns her? The same I should say about the spelling errors, which are plenty. And there is no reason to always blame the bookseller."[57]

In 1806, Francisco de Miranda tried to introduce the printing press in Venezuela. Aware of its power, since he had been both commended and criticized by prominent European papers and authors, he included as a weapon aboard the *Leander*, his liberating ship, six printers, and a press bought in New York City.[58] Between February 21 and March 27, General Miranda ordered 2,000 copies of his independence proclamation, *To the People and Inhabitants of the Colombian-American Continent*, printed.

In the Bay of Jacmel, Haiti, Francisco Miranda and his assistants printed a historical declaration for all Latin and Anglo-Americans. These are some of its most relevant paragraphs:

> [A]ll people in this army are your friends or fellow countrymen; we are all *Americans* and we are all determined to give our lives for your freedom and independence if necessary. [T]he day has come in which our [Latin] America recovers its sovereign independence, where our children will be able *to freely express the whole universe of its generous sentiments* ... [and our people] could peacefully establish its necessary civil order. The good and innocent Indians as well as the gallant dark-skins and free mulattoes should firmly believe that we are all fellow citizens, and that awards are to be granted exclusively by merit and virtue, without distinctions of castes nor colors.

If the Dutch and Portuguese, he reasoned, managed in other times to throw off the oppressive yoke of Spain, just as the Swiss and Americans did, obtaining their freedom and independence, why cannot this most fertile, rich, and indefatigable continent do it? The American and the Swiss were no more than three or four million people, why can't we do the same with a population of at least sixteen million souls, he asked. Here, his motto was that "unity will insure our permanence and perpetual happiness. [T]his proclamation shall be affixed by priests and magistrates to the doors of parochial churches and city halls, so that *all people quickly receive the news*," he urged.[59]

His advance and dreamed insurrection failed tragically. After the disaster, Miranda sold his press to Mateo Gallagher, the Irishman who, with Jaime Lamb and under orders of the Spanish captain general Don Juan de Casas, established the first printing shop and the first *Gazeta* of Caracas on October 24, 1808. In 1796, Gallagher had also produced one of the most popular and historic Caribbean newspapers, the *Trinidad Weekly Courant*.

The rush of Spaniards, British, and Creoles for establishing a printing press in Venezuela responded to the extremely active role Caracas played in the emancipation of Latin America. Curiously, with the same two editors, the *Gazeta de Caracas* showed three radically different faces. First, from 1808 to 1810, it backed the metropolis against Napoleon on behalf of the Spanish military authorities. Then, from 1810 to 1811, it became the voice of the local *junta*, loyal not to the king but to his rebel son (Ferdinand VII). And finally, from 1811 to 1812, it turned into the organ of the independent government of Venezuela, under the command of the revolutionary hero Francisco de Miranda. After his arrest, the *Gazeta* returned to its former loyalist views, including six more years (1815–1821) of "insipid lies and affronts" under the direction of Venezuelan renegade José Domingo Díaz, a man known at the time for seeking "to harm the revolution by mutilating, disfiguring, and inventing news."[60] From Angostura, today's Ciudad Bolivar, the libertarian *Correo del Orinoco* took on its next-door enemy, subsequently renamed *"Gaceta"* de Caracas. The scarcity of printers should be the principal explanation for this remarkable journalistic metamorphosis and survival of the Caracas gazette.

Ironically, four years before its enthusiastic support for the revolution as a "virtuous action," the *Gazeta* had assured its readers "that nothing would ever come out without prior inspection by the people appointed for such a purpose in the government. And that nothing that were to be published would offend the Holy Catholic Religion, the laws governing the country, the good customs, or the peace and reputation of individuals." Following the independence war, these same principles helped to restrict freedom of expression in the young Latin American republics, giving way to the so-called *delitos de prensa* (press crimes) in their constitutional systems.

Back in London, Miranda launched his newspaper *El Colombiano*, hoping to spark a renewed interest in the independence of the Spanish-American colonies. It published five numbers between March 10 and March 15, 1810. Referring to the importance of news, he wrote, "considering the critical circumstances in which the Spanish American possessions must be as a result of the unfortunate events recently occurred in the peninsula, the inhabitants of the New World should be in *need to know* the state of affairs in Spain. Out of the will to be useful to those countries, we feel compelled to tell the people of the Colombian American continent the news we think are both interesting and helpful for their understanding of [Spain's] intricate situation. In communicating these affairs, we'll put the greatest care so that news is truthful and free of any doubt. But, since they are translations of original Spanish works, it is possible that some words may differ, but the meaning will always be the same. If there is in fact any difference between our news and those directly delivered to America from Spain, we ask our readers not to think we have altered them."[61]

In a note to Arthur Wellesley, Duke of Wellington, Miranda complained how Venezuela still lived condemned to have one printing press only (most probably, the machine he had sold in Trinidad after his failed expedition). But, on April 19, 1810, Venezuela ousted Captain General Vicente Emparán, appointing a *Junta Suprema* while giving Miranda the chance to fulfill his dream. Six months later, the Precursor sailed to Caracas in order to participate and eventually lead his native country's political revolution.

Before leaving, the much older Francisco de Miranda met in London the Andean liberator Simón Bolívar (1783–1830) and the educator Andrés Bello (1781–1865). They discussed the future of the revolt. All three agreed that the printing press was essential to achieve the continent's independence, informing, educating, and persuading the public. In fact, when Bolívar and Bello arrived in London as delegates of the autonomous Republic of Venezuela, one of the episodes that caught their attention was the publicity in the English press about their visit. Articles appeared in the *Morning Chronicle*, *The Examiner*, the *Morning Herald*, and both the *Correio Brasiliense* and the *El Español*. In their minds, there was little doubt that spreading the news and winning public opinion would turn the press into a tool of the highest value.[62]

The patriots, most of whom were already or nearly to become journalists and editors, believed in the utilitarian function of newspapers, an approach much in vogue, especially in England, and heavily influenced by the writings of British philosopher Jeremy Bentham (1748–1832). Also, several of the most important leaders, including Bolívar and José de San Martín, affiliated themselves to the *Liberty Lodge* founded by Miranda. The Precursor organized a lodge in America called *Lautaro*, similar to the ones Nariño and other intellectuals founded in Santafé, Mexico

City, Buenos Aires, and other colonial cities.[63] Although there is an absorbing debate about the *masonería* or secret lodges, with their mysterious pledges and rituals, these societies grew more popular among the revolutionaries as a recruitment, propaganda, and discussion device. Moreover, in these meetings, the masons advocated an end to the religious and ethnic hatred confronting Catholic fanatics in the colonies and their imposed values.[64]

Bolívar's press views, for instance, were typical of a liberal, encyclopedic, and pragmatical man. In spite of the differences and even tensions between Francisco Miranda and the Andean liberator, both heroes have similar ideas about the role of the press. For Bolívar, a newspaper represented a fundamental instrument to diffuse the ideals of freedom, independence, and revolution. Freedom of the press was then a sublime political right equivalent to the freedom of conscience and other civil rights in a democratic society.[65] Not surprisingly, looking for support during the liberation campaign, he ordered the creation of two revolutionary newspapers: the *Correo del Orinoco* (1818) in Angostura, Venezuela, under the direction of Francisco Antonio Zea, and the *Gazeta de Santafé de Bogotá* (1819), in the capital of the viceroyalty. The latter carried the slogan "freedom or death," while the former announced in its first issue that it intended to inform, not mislead, the public.[66] "We cannot be responsible for Official [royal] News we print," warned the paper, "so once we announce them as such, it is for the reader to decide what level of trust they deserve. An enlightened public soon learns to read any type of gazette, just as they have learned to read the *Gazeta de Caracas*, which by trying hard to deceive everybody, it has misled no one."[67]

Founded by the Andean liberator in association with reputable patriots, namely, Francisco Antonio Zea, Juan Germán Roscio, Carlos Soublette, Manuel Palacio Fajardo, and Rafael Revenga, the *Correo* reprinted news from over 120 periodicals published in continental Europe, usually Spain and France, England (e.g., London's *El Español* and the *Correio Brasilense*), the United States (*El Americano de Baltimore* and *La Aurora de Filadelfia*), and the Antilles, particularly the Trinidad and Jamaica gazettes.

Browsing through the *Correo del Orinoco*, one can read engaging subjects, such as the criticism of both Iberian and pro-colonial American newspapers with their "fábulas gazetales" (gazette fables), as revolutionaries called colonialist news, including stories about the Inquisition and its catechism, scaffolds, dungeons, and expatriations. King Ferdinand VII of Spain is often referred as *La Criatura* (the Creature), a hideous and royal tyrannical inquisitor. "With equal ease on October 27, 1821, five months after his actual death, the *Correo* informed the passing of the once 'extraordinary' Emperor Napoleon Bonaparte simply as *Muerte de Napoleón Bonaparte*, a soldier for whom deliberation and debate, plus the freedom to speak, act, or give opinions, were privileges that could lead any individual to confusion and destruction," stated the Bolivarian gazette based on a report from *The Times* of London.[68]

This *Correo* also celebrated and reported on the military success of the *"Estados Unidos Angloamericanos"* (The Anglo-American United States) in Florida, once General Andrew Jackson took over *Panzacola*, today's Pensacola. Yet, a few months later, the Bolivarians openly criticized the U.S. government in their paper for the "inexcusable scandal" of expelling and bringing up criminal charges against Spanish-American patriots who had contributed to liberate the Floridian island of *Amelia* from Spanish monarchical control. They had acted on behalf of the Republic of Mexico, observed the paper, so the patriots denounced the United States for having other plans for the peninsula, far from the brotherhood South American liberators expected.

The *Correo* compared President James Monroe to the Spanish monarch, rejecting the notion that God had entrusted the Anglo-Americans with bringing order to Amelia by punishing "all criminals." Mr. *Jaime* (James) *Monroe* has simply lost his use of natural reason, frustrating the liberty and independence of Floridians in this island, cried the "Colombian" gazette (i.e., in Miranda's idea of a "Colombia" or Hispanic American motherland). "We cannot be silent with these excesses," concludes the *Correo del Orinoco*, "because it dishonors the people of that republic and the principles contained in their declaration of independence and constitution."[69]

As most publications of the Spanish-American enlightenment, this newspaper defended both freedom of the press and the revolutionary example of native revolts and their leaders, such as *Don Josef Gabriel Tupac-Amaro* (Tupac Amaru) and his brother *Juan*, *Montézuma* (Motehcuzoma), *Guatimotzin*, *Ataliba*, *Huascar*, and *Henriquilla*. Under the heading *libertad de la prensa* (freedom of the press), the *Correo* defended the proposed Venezuelan Constitution, guaranteeing "everyone's perpetual right to communicate their sentiments through any possible media ... although with just limits, and making people responsible for their printings, words, and writings." Measured penalties should be imposed on those who abuse this freedom. Patriots believed in a pure, healthy, and popular press. Thus, and whenever possible, they enthusiastically informed about any sale or printing of books, primarily those on historical, indigenous, and libertarian subjects. One good example is the sale announcement of Jean François Marmontel's *Historia de la Destrucción de los Incas* in the *Correo del Orinoco* (History about the Destruction of the Incas).[70]

In Bolívar's view, leaders could not overlook the state of public opinion if they hoped to influence it. Battling libelous reports about his alleged desire to control the Argentines, printed in Cuzco's *El Sol* and the Buenos Aires' *Argos* and *El Nacional*, he instructed *La Gaceta del Gobierno* to publish a strong reply, though "with moderation and grace."[71] The liberator often used this and other newspapers to defend himself from vicious attacks, even those coming from Anglo-Saxon papers (e.g., Joseph Lancaster's slurs).[72] His *Correo del Orinoco* also helped him to reply to Jose Domingo Díaz and his diatribes published in the *Gaceta de Caracas*.[73]

Aware of the influential role of gazettes and bulletins, he often advised friendly newspapers to strive for the highest quality of journalism. "I am sending back *El Centinela*, which is badly edited," he wrote to the prefect of Trujillo in Peru, "so that you can both correct it and deliver it for its reprinting, only then we will have a decent and accurate [paper]. Please destroy this infamous version of the gazette to have it improved. The heading is badly placed, the notes [to the editor] should be in capital letters, and the punctuation must be corrected with the inadequacies erased. [In other words], redo everything."[74] On another occasion, he commented about the *Correo de Bogotá*: "It has admirable things, which I endlessly enjoyed, but its defect is the monotonous use of letters which looks like an interrupted correspondence. It matters a lot that this paper of such a fine editors gives regularly the news a journalistic treatment."[75]

Inspired by his fellow leaders and cause, Simón Bolívar often acted as a dedicated editor. Proofreading the patriotic newspaper *El Observador*, he wrote: "It is not good to have this paper in a little format, it would look much better in a full-page. Issue no. 2 lacks of variety and news, which is what matters. Legislative affairs ought to be *communicated* and the columns should follow this order. [First,] *foreign news*. [Second,] *News from the country*, [including] *political and legislative affairs*. [And afterwards,] *varieties*, etc. etc., and things of literary and business nature of major interest that do not belong to the previous items. Then, we can have these other articles: *the curious, the fantastic, the noted, the funny, the scandalous*, and other titles which like these call the public's attention. The whole newspaper should be divided, say, by provinces. If it deals with *taxes*, [title the column] *taxes* and if it deals with rents call it *taxes* [as well]. If it deals with Ferdinand VII put it under *tyranny* or *fanatism*, depending on the issue. If it is about a rare or an unknown event: call it *an amazing, curious, or scandalous anecdote*, according to the case. All columns should be short, spicy, pleasant, and robust. When the government is the subject, do deal with respect; when it is about the legislation, do it with wisdom and poignancy. I wish the newspaper is protected ... but make others or the government appear as responsible; yet, make sure that the [gazette] is elegant, appropriate, and of good taste. Remember, we need to protect the types."[76]

In a charming book, Bolivian scholar Dr. Luis Ramiro Beltrán, one of Latin America's most prominent communication research pioneers, concluded that the great liberator was(is) also a "Great Communicator." Eloquently and with noted journalistic skill, Bolívar and his fellow revolutionaries criticized every loyalist publication, especially when they defended the religious and political despotism of the Iberian monarchs while attacking patriotic movements, such as the Peruvian (1781), the *Comuneros* (1781), or the Pernambuco (1817) revolutions. Both the *Gaceta de Caracas* and the *Correo Brasilense* (printed in London) went down in history as prime targets of the liberator and his associates.

Interested in the arts, particularly rhetorical writings, literature, and journalism, most leading revolutionaries, Miranda, Bolívar, Pedro Fermín de Vargas, José de San Martín, Bernardo O'Higgins, and many others, were writers, thinkers, military strategists, and editors. O'Higgins once told Bolívar through his *Correo*, "Chile's struggle for independence is the same and as committed as those of Buenos Ayres, Nueva Granada, Mexico, and Venezuela, or better said, the whole Colombian continent. [Liberty] would have come earlier to Chile had it not been because of the distance and communication hardships between our nations that impeded it."

Thus, when possible, Latin American liberators traveled to Europe, particularly England, and knew the meaning of solidarity through financial troubles, if not poverty, to the point that it was not unusual to see some of these leaders facing prison because of private debts. Britain became a hard but interesting experience of culture, political learning, deprivation, and exclusion. In a moment of despair, Bolívar confessed: "Always the same lifestyle, always the same annoyance ... I am going to look for another way of life; I am tired of Europe and its old societies."[77] Even so, Bolívar died admiring the European powers, primarily Britain, and whenever they showed respect for the people's sovereignty, the separation and balance of powers, and the civil rights such as the freedom of conscience and of the press. For him, these concepts were among the most sublime in politics.[78]

Another Venezuelan, the educator Andrés Bello (1781–1865), was an especially important and influential thinker and editor. In three journalistic stages, first in his native Caracas, then in London, and finally in Santiago, Chile, he continuously intended to educate his readers not only in political but also scientific, artistic, and ethical matters. His first newspaper *El Lucero*, for instance, included articles on civil morality, history, linguistics, social statistics, physical and natural sciences, poetry, women's issues, and theater. His *Biblioteca Americana* and *Repertorio Americano*, two periodicals published in London, also specialized in the arts and the humanities, mathematics, physical and political sciences, history, and ideology.

An enthusiast in every cause for freedom, he declared in the *Repertorio*: "Years ago, lovers of the American civilization longed for the publication of a periodical work that defended the independence and liberty of the newly emerging states of the New World on its own terms. [T]hrough original essays and historical documents, we intend to illustrate some of the most interesting facts of our revolution, unknown to most people of the world and even the Americans themselves."[79] Miranda, Nariño, Santa

Cruz y Espejo, Bolívar, O'Higgins, and Bello are followed by an endless list of Latin American heroes of the time who fought the independence of Latin America both in the battlefields and in the presses.

REVOLTING FOR FREEDOM

Asking Hispanic nations which independence movement bloomed first in Latin America is both fruitless and pointless. After all, the second revolution of this continent took place not in Spanish America but in Haiti. In 1804, Jean Jacques Dessalines (1758–1806), one of Louverture's "cleverest and also most ruthless" lieutenants, "brought the revolution to its triumphant conclusion, [declaring] Saint-Domingue an independent nation under the old Indian name of Haiti."[80] Today, in this hemisphere, Haiti is rarely remembered for such an achievement, especially when the colonial emperor was the powerful Napoleon I who had been acclaimed by the French Senate that same year.[81]

After Emperor Dessalines's murder, Henry Christophe or Henry I (1767–1820), a little educated and autocratic black king who as a young soldier had been wounded in the siege of Savannah, Georgia, helping the American revolutionaries, ruled the divided country. He governed in open conflict with the mulatto leader Alexandre Sabès Pétion (1770–1818), the president of the South. Both Haitian revolutionaries realized the power of news and of the press, promoting its use but not its freedoms in times when many Spanish-American and Portuguese colonies, like Caracas and Rio de Janeiro, did not even have a press. In 1815, Pétion granted Simón Bolívar political shelter, arms, and a printing press to initiate his liberation campaign.

Thanking Pétion for his help and commenting on the complexities of power, freedom, and politics, Bolívar wrote a letter that partially reads:

> Writing is the best instrument to transmit with freedom the sincere feelings that admiration inspires in me. [T]wenty-five years of sacrifice, glory, and virtue have invested in you the unanimous suffrage of your compatriots. In fact, power is not what constitutes the most glorious attribute of authority a free country has confided in you; it is charity. You, Our Excellency, are destined to make us forget the memory of the Great Washington ... the hero of the North who only found enemy soldiers to defeat and whose major triumph was his own ambition. You, Mr. President, have overcome everything: enemies and friends, foreigners and nationals, the founding fathers and even the virtuous of your brothers.[82]

Although popular revolts had also broken in Bolivia (Alejo Calatayud, 1730), Peru (Tupac Amaru, 1780), and New Granada (the Comuneros of

Socorro, 1781), the first *Juntas de Gobierno Americanas* (provisional Latin American governments) erupted not until the Napoleonic invasion of Spain in 1808.[83] These *juntas* or ruling bodies may be classified in three types. Between 1808 and 1809, they were all of a royalist character, following the requests of the *Supreme Central Junta* of Aranjuez (September 25, 1808) and calling for the defense of the Spanish throne and possessions on behalf of King Ferdinand VII. Such loyalist councils popped up in Mexico, Montevideo, Buenos Aires, Santafe, Chuquisaca, La Paz, and Quito.[84]

Only the last three transpired *autonomist* tendencies, advocating the replacement of peninsular authorities with Spanish-American Creoles on behalf of the king of Spain. In 1809, Charcas (May 25) and La Paz (July 16), in today's Bolivia, and Quito in Ecuador (August 10) saw popular insurrections promptly crushed and kept away from the public opinion. By then, and looking for support, Spain's *Supreme Central Junta* began making announcements about Spanish Americans and the Indies not as colonial pawns anymore but as free subjects deserving of equal treatment, dignity, and education.[85]

Dismissing such promises, most colonies rapidly advanced into the autonomous trend set by the presidencies of Charcas and Quito. In what is known as the *Political Revolution of 1810,* from Mexico to Rio de la Plata, the colonies signed numerous declarations of independence, although expressing loyalty for Ferdinand VII rather than the provincial authorities.[86] Especially relevant for its subsequent role in the process of Latin American independence were the belligerent juntas of Caracas (April 19), Cartagena (May 22), Buenos Aires (May 25), Socorro (July 10), Santafe (July 20), Mexico (September 15), and Santiago (September 18). Unlike the more urban and Creole movements of all other provinces, the famous *Grito de Dolores* (Dolores proclamation) in Mexico, commanded by Father Miguel Hidalgo, was both a rural and Indian revolution. Cities not experiencing an autonomist revolt were Lima, Montevideo, Cuzco, La Habana, Panama, and Guatemala, among others.[87]

A last and definite stage came with a series of declarations of *absolute independence* beginning in 1811. Indeed, absolute independence is what our lands demand, trumpeted Fray Servando in Mexico in 1812, arguing for "an America for Americans," completely different from the eventual Monroe doctrine.[88] On July 5, based on principles of liberty, human dignity, self-determination, love for the motherland, and national unity and integration, the United Provinces of Venezuela stated: "The Supreme Congress of Venezuela has agreed this day upon the absolute independence. This is it, people of Caracas, we do not recognize, we do not depend on any other superior being on earth beyond our Eternal God. But, this sublime idea, this elevated enterprise can only be conceived and carried out by men inspired with liberty."[89]

Three days later, the full text of the Independencia de Venezuela circulated in print. Like the U.S. Declaration of Independence, the Venezuelan
proclamation observed the importance of respecting all opinions of the
human race, calling for the regard, friendship, and "communication" with
other nations.[90] Francisco de Miranda signed as a delegate of the province
of Barcelona. In fact, these and other concepts of absolute independence
were published a week before in the *Mercurio Venezolano*, a newspaper
edited by the Italian-born encyclopedist Francisco Isnardy (1750–1814).
Evidently, the purpose of the press was to guide and educate in political
and cultural matters.[91]

On November 11, 1811, the province of Cartagena in New Granada also
declared that Cartagena of Indies was a sovereign and independent state,
"absolutely free to do everything all free and independent nations can
and might do."[92] Other independentist *juntas* followed suit by 1813, starting with the provinces of Cundinamarca (July 16), Antioquia (August 11),
and Tunja (December 10). The slogan "God, Motherland, and King" had
been replaced in less than five years with the theme of "Liberty, Equality,
Fraternity, and Popular Sovereignty."[93]

HOW MUCH FREEDOM

Without much elaboration on freedom of the press as a key right, the
Precursor proposed four different constitutions between 1790 and 1808.
The first three were officially delivered to the British government, specifically to Prime Minister William Pitt Jr., who barely responded to his proposals. Explaining his views to Pitt in 1790, Miranda deplored the lack of
freedom of movement in Spanish America, where natives had to request
licenses in order to travel. Worse yet, as he noted, people had their minds
oppressed "by the infamous Tribunal of Inquisition, [forbidding] the reading of any useful books or publications."[94] According to the Venezuelan
hero, what the authorities pretended was simply to degrade, to make people prisoners of superstition, and to condemn all Spanish America to ignorance. Not surprisingly, his constitutional proposal of 1801 called for the
abolition of the Inquisition as well as for the freedom of commerce and
religion.

The U.S. Constitution, despite the amendments, was not the role model.
Although fond of the American Revolution, the Latin American liberators
and constitutional framers looked first at England, then France. As Bolívar
once recommended to the Angostura congressmen, which launched the
Greater Colombia in 1819: "[T]here is no liberty without solid foundations. Therefore, I recommend you, delegates, to study the British
constitution destined to work on the greatest benefit of the people who
adopt it. Still, no matter how perfect it is, I am far from asking you its
slavish imitation."[95]

Other heroes had similar persuasions about the scope of liberty, independence, and freedom of expression as fundamental rights. On January 12, 1812, Bernardo O'Higgins, the Chilean liberator, on behalf of the Junta of Santiago, declared (along with Don Manuel Fernández Vásquez de Novoa, a representative of Concepción) that "freedom of the press shall be protected according to the rules and principles adopted by free and well-educated nations, countries where the whip of despotism, mystery and tyranny no longer governs."[96] Within a few months, the Chilean provisional government decreed that the only means to preserve liberty, form and guide public opinion, and diffuse enlightened ideas was to guarantee "a full and absolute freedom of the press."[97] This concept of absolute liberty reflected the encyclopedic belief that press freedom served the people as the strongest weapon against tyranny and arbitrary government and as an indispensable tool to secure the natural right to communicate ideas and express opinions.

Nevertheless, in 1819, revising his principle of absolute freedom, O'Higgins championed the adoption of significant rules limiting the press, particularly when it involved matters of decore and honesty, law and public tranquility, the Catholic religion, and government officials' and the people's right to an individual reputation. The same occurred with most liberators, including Simón Bolívar. In fact, as part of his proposal for a Bolivian Constitution and in order to protect the freedom of expression, Bolívar recommended the creation of a "Chamber of Censors," that is, legislators with the moral and political authority to oversee how people observed the constitution and public treaties, as well as the rules of education, the sciences, the arts, and the press.[98] Everyone should be able to communicate his or her thoughts and opinions verbally or in print and without prior censorship, posed the ethical Bolivarian sentiment, but under the responsibility prescribed by law.

With O'Higgins' support, Camilo Henríquez (1769–1825), the heroic Chilean priest and revolutionary, journalistically known as Quirino Lemachez, edited *La Aurora de Chile* (1812), the country's first newspaper. He had three goals in mind with his paper: to freely diffuse ideas, to defend the people's right to form an independent government, and to fight for the right to a free press without prior restraint. During the government of José Miguel Carrera, authorities set up a press censorship commission expecting the *Aurora* to inform the public about its creation, but Henríquez refused to publish the official news, printing instead an English text which defended the freedom of opinion.

His paper eventually evolved into the *Monitor Araucano*, and after years of exile in Argentina where he collaborated with *El Censor* and the *Gaceta de Buenos Aires*, he returned to Chile on O'Higgins' invitation to be in charge of la *Gaceta Ministerial*, the National Library, and other public bulletins ending up in *El Mercurio de Chile*. Like Bolívar and others in the

Correo del Orinoco, Henríquez also exalted the native heritage of glorious Araucanian warriors who had fought with great "valor, intrepidity, and skill" against their colonizers.[99] They all believed that the press played a fundamental role as a propaganda tool in the diffusion of revolutionary voices and sentiments, or as the Venezuelan hero once said, in war, "the press is as useful as the armament. [Our cause is protected] not only by an effective force but also by the first of all forces, public opinion."[100]

As a matter of fact, according to Dr. Beltrán, Simón Bolívar ascribed five major roles to the press: fostering a sentiment of independentist nationalism, spreading civic education, strengthening regional unity, encouraging international support, and promoting good government.[101] Another giant liberator, General José de San Martín, "Protector of Peru" and editor of *La Gaceta* in Chile, not only freed Lima from the Spanish domination but also introduced its people to a free press and free education through a public library since 1821. He knew too well, as the *Telégrafo Mercantil* had reported back in his native River Plate that ordinary locals, "debased simply by their status and birth, [were] denied admission to the primary schools, in order to prevent their associating with children of Spaniards."[102]

Since San Martín could not bear that because of lack of resources and caste differences there were no available books, he donated his personal collection to what later became the *Biblioteca Nacional del Perú*. In this respect, he shined as a Thomas Jefferson for the Andean society, persuaded that it was "one of the most effective means to circulate intellectual values."[103] Another national hero, the Uruguayan José Gervasio Artigas once wrote to his intermediary, priest Dámaso Antonio Larrañaga, "I will never stop putting my seal of approval on any work which has as its clear objective the prosperity of the public. I know how important public libraries are and I hope you will use your efforts to help me improve them."[104]

In early 1812, the *Generalísimo* San Martín launched a new political movement around a *Sociedad Patriótica,* that is, a Patriotic Society organized with independentists Carlos María de Alvear and Bernardo de Monteagudo, all affiliated to the Masonic *Logia Lautaro.* This society trumpeted the slogan "independence, constitution, and democracy," and Monteagudo, the protector's closest political associate and ardent editor, founded a paper named *Mártir o Libre* (Martyr or Free), following the steps of Mariano Moreno's the *Gazeta de Buenos-Ayres* who the former had helped to turn "into an organ of radical views."[105]

Like Bernardo O'Higgins, who as Chile's first president or supreme director also edited a newspaper in 1817, each of them believed in the importance of the press as a vehicle to fight against the "ignorance, pride, and fanaticism of the Spaniards [as much as] the[ir] Inquisition, its spies, its dungeons and its tortures."[106] The Precursor Francisco de Miranda had taught them that lesson years before, particularly and personally to

O'Higgins back in London. Similarly, the priest José María Morelos, a victim of the Inquisition, which charged him as a heretic, atheist, renegade of the holy faith, materialist, libertine, evil seductor, and traitor, used the printing press to oppose the European clergy and the Spanish crown. He only wanted to free Mexico from the political, social, and economic oppression of the Europeans who usurped the rights of his people, noted Professor Emeritus Wilbert H. Timmons of the University of Texas at El Paso.[107]

In his quest, a secret society of patriots called *Los Guadalupes*, a militant group of journalists, authors, and lawyers, helped Morelos to procure both confidential government information and a printing press, thanks to the courageous action of patriot women who smuggled it by horse out of Mexico City. With this machine, the insurgents made several publications, including *El Ilustrador Americano* (1812) and *El Correo del Sur*, which Morelos entrusted to printer José Rebelo and editors José María Cos, José Manuel de Herrera, and Carlos María Bustamente. The viceroy, Francisco Javier Venegas de Saavedra, tried to neutralize the rebel printings by granting a freedom of the press supervised by royal censors in case of sedition, but he voided such a liberty when the criticism became unacceptable—one of those "false Spanish freedoms," replied José María Morelos.[108]

Professor Villamarín-Carrascal explains how, during the wars of independence, the "press was an extension of the army," in other words, journalists were also soldiers and politicians, or vice versa. Bolívar invested much time at war, commenting and correcting papers, including his own *Gaceta de Bogotá*. He sometimes lost patience criticizing *Libertad o Muerte*, *El Centinela*, and *El Correo de Bogotá*, while praising *El Paisano*, *La Indicación*, and *El Insurgente*. The Great Marshall of Ayacucho, Antonio José de Sucre, Bolivar's most trusted friend, also published *El Monitor* (1823) in Ecuador, Argentinean Manuel Belgrano disseminated new knowledge with his *Correo del Comercio* (1810) in Buenos Aires, and patriot General Juan José Castelli introduced the first printing press and the first newspaper in Bolivia, *El Telégrafo* (1811).

Yet, in time, liberators grew increasingly weary with the powers of the press, as when José San Martín commented at the end of his career:

> "Liberty! Give a child of two years a box of razors to play with and see what will happen. Liberty! So that all honest men shall see themselves attacked by a licentious press, without laws to protect them, or, if there laws, they become illusory. [I] prefer the voluntary ostracism that I have imposed on myself to the joys of that kind of 'liberty.' "[109]

Despite their differences, Bolívar echoed San Martín on this feeling a year before his death. "There is no good faith in America. [T]reaties are papers; constitutions are books; elections are fights; freedom, anarchy; and life, a torment."[110]

Does this mean, asked recently a contemporary journalist, that these independence heroes, once extraordinary democrats, turned into dictators? Professor José Ignacio García Hamilton of the University of Buenos Aires responds by saying: "all of them were democrats in their youth. They were republicans, followers of the principles of the French Revolution, and most of them were Franc Masons, who believed in science, philanthropy, tolerance and progress. But, later, after they liberated their countries, [the liberators] became dictators (e.g. San Martín, O'Higgins, and Bolívar)."[111] Perhaps, as most founding fathers in North America, if not all, they never had in mind an absolute or unconditional freedom of the press.

For example, the first South American constitutions emerged during the times of Nueva Granada's *Patria Boba* (Silly Fatherland), in the midst of clashes between centralists and federalists (1810–1816)—a process also known as the Patria Vieja (Old Motherland) in both Chile and Argentina. One of the first charters regulating freedom of the press as an independent state was the *Cundinamarca* Constitution of 1811 in New Granada. Adopted on March 30 and promulgated five days later, this historic document prescribed in Title I that "the government guarantees all citizens the sacred rights of Religion, property, and individual liberty, [including] the freedom to print, being the authors, not the printers, the ones responsible for their productions. [O]bscene writings and those which offend the Dogma [were] excepted from these general rules. And even then, if they look[ed] like carrying such contents, these materials could be neither withdrawn nor condemned without hearing the author. Freedom of the press does not extend to the sacred books, whose printing depends on [the Council of Trento]," commanded this supreme law.[112]

In Title XII, under *Rights of Man and the Citizen*, the Cundinamarca Constitution prescribed: "when using their liberty and legal power, [individuals] cannot be proscribed from expressing their opinions either through the printing press or any other lawful means."[113]

As Febres-Cordero emphasized, the founding fathers of the Colombian continent feared a drastic departure from the previous monarchical controls. The French Revolution was still fresh in the minds of most policy makers and prominent leaders like Miranda warned against the radicalism of the Jacobins, which he found both anarchical and excessive. What many wanted was a mediated, regulated, or even a "censored" freedom if at all possible.[114] In December 27, 1811, the general congress of the provinces of Mérida, Cumaná, Barinas, Barcelona, Trujillo, and Caracas enacted the *Constitución Federal para los Estados de Venezuela*. Published on February 7, 1812, article 181 of the first Venezuelan Constitution reads: "The right to express thoughts by means of the press will be free. But anyone who exercises this right will be held responsible if with his opinions attack and disrupt the public peace, Dogma, Christian morality, property, and the honor or esteem of any citizen."[115]

As constitutions proliferated throughout Latin America so did an increasing number of exceptions to freedom of the press. Historic but unclear exclusions in countries with a substantial contemporary tradition of press freedom, such as France, England, the Netherlands, and Sweden, had then seditious, obscene, heretical, and treasonous speech proscribed. Convicted speakers and printers could even be sentenced to the death penalty.[116] In the United States, where the constitutional framers omitted freedom of speech, the Bill of Rights emerged as a marvelous improvement. Nevertheless, not until the civil rights movement of the 1960s and beyond, did most U.S. Americans including women, minorities, and critics of the *status quo* begin to enjoy meaningful rights of freedom of expression.[117] And they still confront, in the United States and most nations, significant hidden perils in the early twenty-first century.

It would have been remarkable if Latin America had become the exception to prior restraint and Blackstonian views of subsequent punishment of speech. But, it did not. One by one, national constitutions in the Americas started to erect rules to restrict rather than protect the press. In New Granada, for example, publications deemed subversive because of their proclivity against good customs, Christian morality, and national security were added to the already existing press crimes.[118] The latter condemned all threats to religion, decency, individual honor, the public peace, and private property, as well as state sovereignty and constitutional government.[119] Many of these abuses came to be known as crimes of *lesa patria* or high treason.

On the other hand, a number of constitutions were more interested in the duties of citizens than in their civil rights, in the rights to a free commerce, free navigation, and free right of way more than in the freedoms of speech or of the press.[120] Still, some of these documents carried provocative clauses, such as article 7 of the *Tunja Constitution* that reads: "the law should protect individual and public freedom against the oppression of those who govern" (although the term "guarantee" is preferable to "protect"). In 1815, a less popular document, the *Constitución del Estado Libre de Neiva* (The Constitution of the Free State of Neiva), came up with a wise statement defining freedom of expression as follows: "Title I, Rights of Man in Society, article 3. The right to express our freedom of opinions and thought, by either the press or any other means, and to peaceably assemble cannot be prohibited."[121]

Omitting the right to a free exercise of religion, the Neiva Constitution transcribed almost verbatim a clause proposed by Mariano Picornell in 1797, days before La Guaira conspiracy led by Manuel Gual and José María España in Venezuela. This paragraph had been mistakenly attributed to Juan Germán Roscio and even Tom Paine. Besides "the free exercise of creeds," stated right after the freedom to peaceably assemble, Picornell added this sentence: "The need to make the rights of man known supposes either the presence or the recent memory of despotism."[122]

In turn, Picornell's clauses of the Neiva Constitution and other constitutional charters throughout the Americas seem probably inspired in the Marques of Lafayette's proposal to the French National Assembly, which states that "every man comes to this world with inalienable and inviolable rights." They include the freedom of thought, the protection of honor and life, and the right of property. These prerogatives also involve "the freedom to govern his own person, his work, and his aptitude, the expression of ideas through any means possible, and the tendency towards both his well-being and his resistance to oppression."[123]

In the end, the French revolutionaries, as did many other national proclamations and constitutions of independence, settled for article 11 of the Declaration of the Rights of Man and the Citizen, "the true paper basis of all paper constitutions" as Carlyle called it.[124] Some provinces simply copied the French Declaration on their respective charters (e.g., *La Constitution de Barcelona* [1811] in Venezuela). Years later, the Spaniards, either on their own initiatives or under the influence of the French, adopted two major constitutions which have a considerable impact in Spanish America: the liberal *Constitution of Cadiz* (1812) and the French-oriented (or *afrancesada*) *Constitution of Bayona*. Both of them tried to attract the interest of the colonies, promising deep social reforms including freedom of the press with few restrictions.[125] Obviously, the Inquisition was being legally suppressed.

Yet, the newly independent colonies barely listened to these proclamations, as they wanted freedom autonomously defined from Europe and their laws. The France of Napoleon and oppressive Spanish rule were especially hated. In colonies under heavy control of Spaniards, such as Mexico, Peru, and Cuba, the *Constitution of Cadiz* meant, however, two things: more energy to publish but also more repression and tighter controls. In Cuba, the Captain General Miguel Tacón became famous for his ruthless persecution of journalists. The viceroy in Mexico City, fearing the criticism and abuses of the press, also delayed all announcements of the Cadiz Constitution. Forced from Spain to apply the new law Don Francisco Javier Venegas, viceroy of New Spain (1810–1813), managed to restrict and even suspend activities of rebel presses and editors.[126]

One of the first victims of his repression was the prestigious Mexican journalist Joaquín Fernández de Lizardi, accused and convicted of seditious libel. Lizardi used irony to criticize the viceroy, bringing up issues rarely touched by late colonial newspapers such as slavery, the control of clerics by civilian authorities, and the brutality of bullfights. Carlos María de Bustamante, a colleague in the *Diario de México*, also took asylum in Oaxaca in order to avoid an arrest warrant. With the revolutionaries, and under the effective support of Commander Morelos y Pavón, Bustamante launched the pro-independence *Correo del Sur*, a newspaper that filled its columns with articles censored in the capital of New Spain.[127]

Repealed by King Ferdinand VII once the French left Spain in 1814, the Cádiz Constitution gave way to the Spanish reconquest (1815–1819), known in some American quarters as the *Regime of Terror*. To orchestrate the persecution, General Pablo Morillo erected in Santafe three major institutions: The Tribunal of Purification, the Board of Kidnapping, and the permanent War Council.[128] During Morillo's "*Pacification*," 25,000 to 30,000 *criollos* were charged with insurrection. At least 200 intellectuals were shot or hanged, including the Granadine heroes Francisco José de Caldas, editor of the popular *Semanario del Nuevo Reyno de Granada* (1808–1809), and Camilo Torres, author of the eminent *Memorial de Agravios* (Brief of Grievances, November 20, 1809). As expected in a capital colonial enclave, royalist newspapers in Mexico City readily published the list of those accused of insurrection.[129] Luckily, one of the few men to survive this carnage was the future liberator Simón Bolívar.

In search of Bolívar and other "traitors," the archbishop of Caracas circulated a letter in August 1812. In it, he ordered all priests "to report without delay, though quietly, people with posters, illustrations, books, or prohibited papers. They should specify their full names, places of residence as well as the titles of the books or documents, the number of volumes, their location, and the place where posters or illustrations have been affixed. The use and the handling of any books or communications of such pestilent doctrine [of independence, must be reported as well]. In the same manner, you will inform me of any public sins, especially of clerics and the impious, of the seducers and apostle of incredulity, of the procrastinators of communion and annual confessions, and of those who have resisted the nuptial blessings."[130]

It would be a lengthy and tortuous road before Latin American nations had the opportunity to draft national constitutions on their own, including legal principles on basic civil rights such as freedom of speech and of the press. With Miranda's quest, both England's political organization and the French Enlightenment stood high as primary sources of inspiration for the Latin American framers. The United States, cause of fondness and respect for its revolution, increasingly generated feelings of mistrust, anxiety, and disappointment among Latin Americans. Yes, the U.S. federalism and intellectuals, notably Benjamin Franklin and Sam Adams, remain loved and influential in Hispanic America. But, because of the prominence and prestige of the French Declaration, the First Amendment practically played no role in the early Latin American deliberations about a free press.

Beginning with the scientific expeditions of the late 1700s, the Latin American patriots developed a keen interest in the printing press. As editors or writers, and often both, most liberators and heroes had something to do with the press. They regarded the printed page as the best means of diffusion of their revolutionary ideas. Few revolutionaries, however, were willing to accept a right to freedom of the press without certain limitations and legal responsibilities. In the end, all that enthusiasm for a robust, if not an irrestricted liberty to think, speak, write, or print during the early days of the revolutionary war would become, with a few exceptions in later times, an exquisite but momentary taste of freedom, an immortal but unfinished revolution.

Chapter 3

Taken by War and Censorship

For most, if not all, Latin Americans, effective freedom and independence have been elusive, frustrating, and unfulfilled. The final collapse of the Spanish garrisons in the nineteenth century did not translate into new and independent nations with liberty to think, act, and communicate without fear. Even contemporary Latin Americans, enjoying the relative democratic progress of recent times, cannot genuinely say that they live in open societies, with basic human rights guaranteed for everyone including freedom of expression.

Violence, overt or subtle, continue to physically and mentally impair millions of lives in a region where people face unrelenting levels of poverty and social injustice, war and crime, human rights abuses, and environmental degradation in every nation of the Latin American and Caribbean geography. The freedom Latin American heroes tasted and dreamed about during the independence was quickly frustrated by dynamics of war, greed, religious and political intolerance, corruption, and censorship imposed by governments and the private elite.

In this chapter, and practically to the end of this book, the author examines the constant social tragedy of the Latin American and Caribbean continent: a series of internal and external armed conflicts where dominant media usually play the role of cheerleader, with utmost disregard for ordinary people. Alternative or popular presses and periodicals are then swiftly and repeatedly reduced to prostration, if not crushed in most countries. Long before Walter Lippmann or Edward L. Bernays and prior to the German National Socialist Party and its propaganda minister Paul Joseph Goebbels, the continent's journalism began serving war purposes, advocating either liberation or oppressive messages and hoping to manipulate public opinion.[1]

If Bolívar thought that the first of all liberating forces against colonialism should be the public opinion, with the press pushing readers toward the cause of freedom, presidents James Madison, James Monroe, John Quincy Adams, and other U.S. heads of state ended up believing that "the divine providence had chosen them [...] to develop the highest level of freedom and civilization no other country had achieved," through both electrical machinery like the telegraph and the use of the printing press.[2] Editor John L. O'Sullivan, the journalist who allegedly coined the expression "Our Manifest Destiny" in 1845, claimed that the United States, as the most equitable and admirable federative republic, ought to spread all over North America, thanks to its sturdy skeleton of railroads and its nervous system of magnetic telegraphs integrating the empire.[3]

Like Thomas Jefferson, U.S. politicians saw their country as an "empire for liberty," predestined to rule all Mexico, Central America, and the Caribbean while preaching canons of hard work, liberty, and security in the name of fundamental human values. In this context, newspapers and magazines functioned as vehicles of propaganda, actively spreading the U.S. missionary sentiment beyond its borders and fueling the Union's ambition to take the whole hemisphere. From the savage icelands of the North to the more welcoming and abundant regions of the South, *America* (The United States) would be one nation, one language, and one culture, a system where the horizon would not be limited to the frontiers of the original federation nor U.S. citizens had to look at the world from below. Now, civilization and the emancipation of humanity had to largely depend on *Americans*. These kinds of statements came from a *New York Herald* article published on September 15, 1845.[4]

By the time Simón Bolívar called up his famous Anfictionic Congress to unify the Latin American countries in Panama City (June 22, 1826), President Monroe had already pronounced his suspicious state of the Union address of 1823, declaring all European attempts to "extend their systems to any portion of this [American] hemisphere as dangerous to our [U.S.] peace and safety."[5] If there was any doubt about the U.S. aim and the Bolivarian apprehension, President James K. Polk confirmed both of them twenty-five years later, celebrating on December 5, 1848, that "the amicable relations between the [United States and Mexico], which had been suspended [because of the "Mexican War"], ha[d] been happily restored, and [were] destined, [he] trust[ed], to be long preserved."[6] Naturally, most Mexicans, if not all, have a radically different perception about this catastrophic conflict where they lost "half of their national territory."[7]

Why have we, Mexicans, talked so little about the war of 1846 against the United States? asked journalist Francisco Martín Moreno in his recent novel *México Mutilado* (Mexico Mutilated). Why have our people conveniently hidden the reality of their past instead of exposing, once and for all, the true enemies of Mexico? This historic book, announce the publishers, reveals how top authorities of the Church, distinguished generals, presidents of the republic, legislators, journalists, entrepreneurs, and aristocrats conspired against their own country. Typical of war times, newspapers disappeared while others contributed to justify, enhance, tear down, or revive political and private reputations for petty interests.[8]

Still, a number of Mexican publications, like *El Republicano*, denounced the war as follows: "No one has any doubts about the intentions the Washington cabinet has had for some time now with respect to Mexico. [O]ne fights in the name of usurpation; the other defends justice. [T]he war has begun and the nation has a great deal at stake, since even if justice is on its side, that is unfortunately not enough to triumph and hold back the excesses of a powerful enemy." More concise and direct, *El Tiempo* simply commented: "The American government acted like a bandit who came upon a traveler."[9] Defenders and invaders use news propaganda as an "electric fire" during times of war, implied the *Correo del Orinoco* in the early nineteenth century, so psychological warfare through the mass media in the Americas has been an old "tool in the toolbox of the military strategist, and more specifically, strategists based in the United States."[10]

ENDLESS WAR AND PROPAGANDA

On January 13, 1846, Miranda, Bolívar, San Martín, and other Latin American founding fathers' greatest fear materialized when President James K. Polk (1795–1849) ordered General Zachary Taylor to move "about half the U.S. Army (nearly 3,500 troops)" to a position bordering the Rio Grande.[11] Nearly three months later, this so-called Army of Observation advanced into Mexican territory, building outposts such as Fort Texas. On May 11, based on news a week old from the actual events, President Polk read a war statement to the U.S. Congress: "[The Mexicans] have shed American blood upon the American soil; [t]he war exists ... by the act of Mexico herself."[12] A 50,000 corps of volunteers and 10 million dollars were readily approved to "save" the Union's national defense.[13]

As every armed conflict, the Mexican-American War plagued the papers with misinformation. Scandalous, exaggerated, and manipulated news quickly defeated accuracy and sound stories. As a groundbreaking operation for the U.S. military in several respects, that is, first and successful offensive in a foreign country, first occupation of a foreign capital city, and first application of U.S. martial law in a foreign soil, this war launched as well the era of modern news and international correspondents in the Americas.[14] One of its principal exponents was George Wilkins Kendall, editor-publisher of the *New Orleans Picayune*, a journalist who made history bringing forth a breed of "special correspondents" who, from Mexico, reported on the U.S. victories with a mix "of pride, jingoism, and business sense."[15]

Because of the fresh and revolutionary start of the telegraph, civilian news about the conflict often traveled faster than military reports and mailed messages. The telegraph worked in unison with the flourishing and more efficient operation of newspapers and private railroads. A report in the *New York Herald* celebrated how newsboys were as good or better than the troops in their own battle: charging upon the public with their extras.[16] Thanks to the combination of ambitious reporters, improved common carriers (steamers, railroads, mail, and telegraph lines), and newsgathering alliances such as the emerging *Telegraphic and General News Association* (1851), newspapers showed great effectiveness. Eventually, this last organization would evolve into the Associated Press (AP).

Media history often highlights how President Polk received the news of the victory at *Veracruz* not from his military command but from the *Baltimore Sun* (on April 12, 1947). After all, by the mid-1840s, speed and persuasion were already essential elements in the newspaper business. For almost an entire decade, public opinion in the United States had been fed with accounts of General Santa Anna's abuses in Mexico, including news of bloody assaults where Texans had been either slaughtered or burned alive. As one report vividly pointed out: "[in this country] there is a pronounced predilection for revolt, a Spanish inheritance highly refined in Mexican experiences."[17] Thus, for Anglo-America, Mexico was nothing but a surge of lawlessness and instability, following the failed Emperor Agustín de Iturbide's constitutional Mexican monarchy (Agustín I, 1822–1823, although he came to power with support of the revolutionaries in 1821). He had risen to power demanding the supremacy of Roman Catholicism and a ban on all other religions, while obligated to guarantee an immediate independence from Spain and equality for Creoles and Spanish (Plan de Iguala).[18] In many respects, however, U.S. news was not always war propaganda or far from the truth of the frustrating Mexican politics in (d)evolution.

General Antonio López de Santa Anna, an influential and equally opportunist Mexican president, ruled his country with a merciless fist. Abusing the civil rights of its citizens, including Texans, the latter responded by declaring their independence and writing a constitution on March 2, 1836. A massacre of 487 soldiers in two attacks, Alamo (February 23) and Goliad (March 27), radicalized the conflict to such a level that Santa Anna himself fell prisoner to Texan general Sam Houston in the Battle of *San Jacinto* (April 21, 1836). Determined to legalize slavery, however, Texas demanded either annexation to the United States or recognition for its republic. Despite the Texan request for annexation, Washington waited, trying to cool off increasing tensions over the issue of slavery between northern and southern states. Eventually, the *Lone Star Republic of Texas* was officially recognized as an independent state on March 3, 1837.

Originally, Mexico refused to grant such recognition. Eventually and gradually, however, it changed its mind, pressured by England and France. The Mexicans realized that it was preferable to have an independent rather than annexed Texas, as the new nation could serve as firm political limit to the continuous expansion of the United States. After the election of Texan president Mirabeau B. Lamar, who advocated a line of independence from the United States, such a possibility seemed plausible. But, Mexico's offer to recognize the independence of Texas came too late (March 1845). Using a formula entered by President-elect Polk, and voting on a resolution that bypassed the normal two-thirds senate majority required by law, the United States formally approved the annexation of Texas on February 28, 1845.

The roots of the Mexican-American War (1846–1848) have even deeper roots. Back to the late 1700s when the liberated United States targeted the west with their views of a "Manifest Destiny," the belief was that not only neighboring territories but also Latin American countries were fated to belong to the Anglo-American Union. In fact, Robert C. Winthrop, a U.S. representative from Massachusetts, once referred to it as "the right to spread all over this whole [American] continent."[19] Instead of politicians, journalists, mainly from New York, coined and orchestrated the ill-conceived theory. Apparently, columnists of the *U.S. Magazine and Democratic Review*, such as John N. O'Sullivan, used the term Manifest Destiny for the first time in articles published in July-August 1845. Also, George Sanders, a leader of the Democratic Party's *Young America* movement, introduced it as a desirable policy. Both of these men and others justified the U.S. drive toward territorial expansionism as a fortune predetermined by Providence, a destiny for the free, commercial, and monetary exploitation of neighboring lands under white Anglo-American and Protestant rule.[20]

Over the years, the Manifest Destiny grew hand in hand with the Monroe Doctrine, a strategy officially introduced on December 2, 1823. Warning the European powers that the Americas would no longer be subject to transatlantic colonization, the United States announced that any future European intervention in the political systems of the Western Hemisphere was a direct threat against the Union. As President James Monroe (1758–1831) made this policy official, the U.S. government paved the way for future military interventions in Mexico and other countries of the Americas.

Mimicking the invasion and spirit of Spanish conquistador Hernán Cortes, the U.S. Army stormed the city of Veracruz with 11,000 soldiers. After forty-eight hours of implacable battering, buildings smashed, and innocent civilians killed or wounded, foreign diplomats asked General Winfield Scott to grant a cease-fire that allowed the women and children evacuate the city. The U.S. commander not only refused but also stepped up the bombardment. Advice of the U.S. Secretary of War William L. Marcy, about treating the Mexicans as enemies while guaranteeing their civil rights and emphasizing the U.S. government's "friendly intentions," had been totally forgotten.[21]

Victorious in Veracruz, General Scott advanced to the capital, blocking elementary Mexican communications such as roads, pigeons, and couriers on horseback or mules. On September 8, 1847, four months after landing in the Mexican gulf shore, the U.S. forces marched into Mexico City, confiscating public buildings though this time scrupulously protecting private property. The humiliation of the Mexicans was simply indescribable: the "insulting gringos," as they named their invaders, had finally taken the main city streets.[22] Seven thousand Mexican soldiers were killed defending its capital and nearly 4,000 more were taken prisoners. For the U.S. government, it was the most memorable operation, praised even by prestigious European officers like the Duke of Wellington who applauded it as an able military maneuver.

On February 2, 1848, Mexico signed the painful Treaty of *Guadalupe Hidalgo*. In addition to Texas, the central reason for this war, the United States received 500,000 square miles of new territory, including the current states of California, Nevada, Utah, most of New Mexico and Arizona, and parts of Wyoming and Colorado. As compensation, the U.S. government paid 18.2 million dollars: up from the 3 million dollars Mr. Polk had planned to pay on the treaty's ratification but less than the 30 million dollars the Mexican negotiators ultimately requested. Actually, the price tag was 15 million dollars plus 3.2 million dollars in connected claims involving the Rio Grande. Besides the thousands of lives on both sides, the war cost the United States 58 million dollars in military expenses and 64 million dollars in long-term veteran pensions.[23] Deep down for every Mexican until today, the cost of this war has been simply unthinkable and unforgettable.

In skillful settlements and for innocuous prices, the United States had previously purchased other territories such as Louisiana from France (1803) and Florida from Spain (1827). Even a world power like France chose to make a bad deal, selling 828,000 square miles between the Mississippi River and the Rocky Mountains. Napoleon considered it unwise to enter a distant and expensive war with the United States. Arguably, part of the story with the French is that an influential reason for their sour decision to settle on Louisiana has been the high costs associated with François-Dominique Toussaint Louverture's rebellion in Haiti.[24] The purchase of the Louisiana territory meant thirteen additional states for the Anglo-American Union.

By the end of the U.S. aggression in Mexico, other Latin Americans and Caribbeans knew that this was only the beginning in a series of imperialistic moves of the United States against fellow nations in the continent. Even prominent members of the "American" public opinion believed that the Mexican War was totally unjustified. As the famous journalist Horace Greely of the *New York Tribune* stated when the combat broke out "[the Mexican-American war] is one in which Heaven must take part against us [the United States]."[25]

NEW WARS, NEW MEDIA

Two years before the initiation of the Mexican-American War, Samuel Morse had completed the Baltimore to Washington telegraph line (May 24, 1844). Similarly and rapidly spreading, the railroad emerged as a new and crucial technology. In 1846, the U.S. military began its use of the telegraph for official business. Although with limited reliability, the recent electric telegraph did permit rapid transmission of orders between Washington and New York. Railroads and steamboats then were also and to "a degree [...] unknown, but both had seen earlier military use."[26] Still, these new technologies, railroads and telegraphy, greatly contributed to transform the newspaper business, from a politicized and family based operation to an increasingly massive and commercial enterprise. The *Penny Press* Revolution also dominated North America at the time, matching notions of popular democracy with a market society of growing cities, sales, and advertising.

In contrast, Mexico lacked both telegraph and railroad lines. Only after the war did the Mexican government move to grant an exclusive concession for a telegraph system. On May 10, 1849, a consortium of two immigrants, Juan de la Granja and William G. Stewart, received a license to build the first telegraph line between Mexico City and Puebla, which they put into service in 1851.[27] With the leadership of President Benito Juárez, an orphan Zapotec who became congressman during the Mexican War, both the telegraph and the railroad received major attention.

Juárez symbolized the early spirit of reform, progress, and modernization that a fellow Oaxacan disciple, Porfirio Díaz, inherited and developed a few years later. Up to 1876, there were 400 miles of railways built in Mexico; with Diaz in power, the railroad system expanded to over 11,000 miles in 1910.[28] By then, the national telegraph network also included nearly 400 offices.[29] With the combination of telegraph wires and railroads, both presidencies intended to achieve greater levels of infrastructure development, economic modernization, centralized communications, and national security and sovereignty. For these purposes, a Secretariat of Communications and Public Works was established on July 1, 1891.

Because of the lack of money, peace, and administrative skills, effective communications following the independence lagged throughout Latin America. In Mexico, like everywhere else in the region, political factions wondered, mostly in times of war and dictatorship, what to do with their relative freedom, their future, and their countries. Except for the last two decades, and only in a few countries, Latin America remained a collection of "isolated [and] militarized zones where the exercise of power was a local phenomenon" during the nineteenth century.[30]

With the Mexican-American War, emerging Latin American nations began to learn that communication infrastructures, including the press, had to serve fundamental government interests, such as state security and national sovereignty. Not only was the Mexican War the prelude of a series of U.S. military actions in the region but also was the basis of a permanent suspicion against foreign governments including close neighbors. Mexico's invasion by the French in the early 1860s simply confirmed the rule. Thus, communication in times of war, primarily though not exclusively point to point services, turned out to be regulated with lasting policies of preferred government access, national security, sedition laws, and emergency regulation.

A key principle in public policy, state intervention grew more prominent in the mid-1800s, including regular expropriations of private property, military restrictions, and operation controls of telecommunications. State priorities rather than a public service emerged as a rule of thumb for new and traditional communication technologies. In this respect Baur wrote, "whether in anticipation of local uprisings, civil wars, or foreign invasions, Latin American states extended telegraph lines along routes they considered strategically important. Moreover, the role of the military as a central political actor heightened the belief that state management of telecommunication was vital to *national security*."[31] When Archduke and Emperor Maximilian of Hapsburg (1832–1867) assumed the throne in Mexico with the support of the French, both European invaders and resistance forces applied much of their war efforts to building better telegraphic lines. By the end of the war, the victorious liberals consolidated all telecommunications in a single entity: *the Líneas Telegráficas del Supremo Gobierno* (Telegraph Lines of the Supreme Government).[32]

Similar uses and policies on post offices, railroads, and telegraph wires emerged in subsequent armed clashes throughout Latin America. The best examples are the *War of the Triple Alliance* (1864–1870) and *War of the Pacific* (1879–1883) in South America. In the Triple Alliance War, a conflict bringing Argentina, Brazil, and Uruguay together against Paraguay, network telegraph expansions and tighter rules of both content (seditious messages) and technology (network exclusivity) proliferated. During the Pacific War, where Peru and Bolivia confronted Chile, a sudden wave of new and reconstructed military wires and telegraph stations also took place on both sides.[33]

Yet, repercussions of this conflict were especially devastating for Bolivia, as this country lost its entire coastline in the Pacific. The once

Bolivian *Atacama* Desert and littoral became Chile's Antofagasta province. As compensation for making Bolivia the second landlocked nation of the continent (with Paraguay), the Chilean government promised to build a railroad from La Paz to Arica, a city also surrendered to the Chileans by Peru.[34] In more than 100 years since this war, neither Peru nor Bolivia have grown accustomed to this painful loss of territory. In 1987, for instance, right after negotiations with Chile for a path to the Pacific had once again failed, Bolivia formally announced its full participation in a cooperative satellite program with Peru and other Andean partners except Chile (then *Project Cóndor*, now *Project Simón Bolívar*).[35] Repeatedly and whenever possible, the Bolivian diplomacy, media, and society have openly denounced their status as landlocked nation and their discontent with their geographic isolation.[36] Similarly, in the early 1900s, Colombia ran the risk of becoming the third territorially enclosed nation of South America, after international news talked about a possible secession of the country's Atlantic and Pacific provinces prior to Panama's independence and the United States' takeover of the Panama canal zone.

In the midst of all these external and internal tensions, the Latin American press played a central role, resulting and seriously affected by war discourses and dynamics. The U.S. military propaganda, for instance, arrived with their own newspapers to the very streets of Mexico City. The triweekly *American Star*, edited by John H. Warland, an infantry sergeant and Harvard graduate, turned into "a mouthpiece" for the invading forces. On October 13, 1847, one of his columns foolishly celebrated the opening of a U.S. Army lounge baptized as the "Aztec Club."[37] Calling the Mexican War "an excellent opportunity to demonstrate news enterprise," professors Emery and Emery noted how U.S. citizens established twenty-five "war newspapers" in Mexican locations before the fighting ended, "including two dailies in Mexico City."[38]

Mexicans and their press abhorred the U.S. presence. Yet, the domestic infighting of conservatives versus liberals generated incredible proposals such as seeking the protection of Spain and other European powers. "To save Mexico from the claws of the North American republic," noted *El Universal* (1848–1855, articulated voice of the Mexican conservative elite), following the invasion, "we say, without hesitation, that we ask for the protectorate of Spain, if not Russia or even Turkey."[39] Otherwise, they warned, this country, "now using the pretext of Texas, tomorrow of *La Mesilla*, and the next day of Tehuantepec, is going to absorb our nationality and exterminate our race." The liberal daily *Siglo XIX*, under the direction of Francisco Zarco, firmly rejected this idea, arguing that Mexico and only Mexico could solve her problems, whether it be the threat of a foreign invasion or any other. Once Benito Juárez's liberal administration took office and the outspoken editor of *El Universal*, Lucas Alemán, died (1853), the conservatives gave up this claim.

After the war, two types of Mexican newspapers dominated the news landscape. The first one was a pro-governmental press publicizing new policies to alleviate the humiliating Mexican defeat, the other a group of commercially oriented periodicals such as *El Eco del Comercio* (The Commerce's Echo), edited by the liberal Manuel Payno and focused on revitalizing the business class.[40] Paradoxically, critics in the United States, primarily in the northern states, continued to call the war "a cynical [and] calculated despoiling of the Mexican state: a greedy land-grab from a neighbor too weak to defend herself."[41] Certainly, a divided public opinion in the United States sharply condemned President Polk and "his" war machine. Some of the most poignant were giant writers such as Walt Whitman, Henry David Thoreau, James Russell Lowell, and the abolitionists Reverend Theodore Parker, congressman Joshua Giddings of Ohio, and the editor of *The Liberator*, William Lloyd Garrison.

Echoing many Americans, Giddings thought that the war was simply a way of extending slavery. Whereas Reverend Parker called for a boycott of recruitment offices and weapon manufacturers, Garrison openly wished for a U.S. military defeat. Inspiring in this conflict for his famous essay "Civil Disobedience" (1849) is David Thoreau, who preferred to spend a night in jail rather than contributing to the invasion. For six years, he refused to pay the so-called Massachusetts poll tax. In defiance, he wrote: "Witness the present Mexican war, the work of comparatively a few individuals using the standing government as a tool; for, in the outset, the people would not have consented to this measure. [The U.S. government and its merchants] are more interested in commerce and agriculture than they are in humanity, and not prepared to do justice to the slave and to Mexico, *cost what it may*. [T]his people must cease to hold slaves, and to make war in Mexico."[42]

According to Whitman, the Mexican War was the time to see that "America knows how to crush, as well as how to expand."[43] But, as he hoped in *Leaves of Grass* (1855), Americans of all nations would one day realize that they are made of *the fullest poetical nature*. "The United States are essentially the greatest poem," he wrote. Still, "the genius of the [U.S.] is not best or most in its executives or legislatures, nor in its ambassadors or authors or colleges or churches or parlors, or even in its newspapers or inventors . . . but always most in the common people."[44]

Although much happened mediawise during the bloody Mexican, Triple Alliance, and Pacific wars, they remain largely unknown in modern Anglo-American and even Latin American circles. The Mexican-American War, for instance, has received the least attention in the history of U.S. political and/or media analyses. Perhaps, as Singletary noted, the American public still feels a sense of guilt about such a crusade of anything but expansionism.[45]

After the U.S. invasion came the French occupation (1862–1867), another European attempt at colonization this time by Napoleon III. In his chess game, he expected to create a colonial enclave and supposedly neutralize U.S. expansionism, taking advantage of the civil war that had recently broke out in North America. Skillfully, French generals, the Mexican church, and conservative politicians and newspapers misled Maximilian about his popularity and people's support.[46] During his reign, Mexican journalism entered into a period of serious decadence, showing signs of economic deprivation, political manipulation, and war exhaustion. One of the few newspapers to rescue from this period is *La Chinaca* (1862), a sarcastic and antioccupation paper.[47]

Following Maximilian's execution (1867) that marked the end of the foreign intrusions in Mexico, a close and influential Caribbean neighbor, Cuba, embarked on a ten-year war of independence from Spain, also known as the *Guerra Grande* (Big War). It failed, once the rebels had to accept the Pact of *Zanjón* in 1878, but even under Spanish rule, Cuba had enjoyed the reputation of a prolific, poignant, and high-quality journalism. The 1868 Revolution brought not only more repression but also more dynamism. After the assault in *Bayamo* (October 10), the revolutionaries created *El Cubano Libre*, a newspaper edited by the poet José Joaquín Palma and published in the jungle until the printing press was captured by the Spanish forces (1871).[48]

El Boletín de la Guerra, which replaced *El Cubano Libre*, *La Estrella Solitaria*, and *El Mambí*, a name given to Cuban insurrectionists fighting against the Spanish domination, continued the resistance. All of these newspapers built upon prior experiences of José Quintín Suzarte's *El Siglo* (1862), a reformist periodical that bravely confronted *El Diario de la Marina* and *La Prensa*, two of the most conservative Cuban newspapers, defending the absolutist Spanish regime. As opposition journalists and editors had to flee into exile, they actively created a tradition of Cuban newspapers in foreign lands, primarily the United States. One of the most prominent was *La Revolución de Cuba*, or simply, *La Revolución* of Enrique Piñeyro, who also edited the popular *El Nuevo Mundo* and *La América Ilustrada*.

Enroute toward becoming a vital Latin American power, economically, politically, and journalistically, Argentina also experienced an explosive growth of newspapers during the 1860s and in the following decades. Two centenary dailies, José Camilo Paz's *La Prensa* (1869) and Ex-President Bartolomé Mitre's *La Nación* (1870), historically, one of the most prestigious in Latin American, were created during the *War of the Triple Alliance*. Also known as the *Paraguayan War*, this period witnessed the establishment of many foreign language and provincial newspapers, including *Le Courier de la Plata* (1865), a French publication that remarkably ran until 1946, and *La Razón Española*, edited by Alfageme de la Oliva for the

Argentine Spanish community. In Rosario, during this war, emerged the Argentine Republic's oldest newspaper, *La Capital* (1867), hoping to see this city some day as the nation's capital. Significant wartime developments are also Rosario's and the country's first student periodical, *El Colegial*, launched in 1869, the *Revista de Agricultura* (1866), and the prestigious *Revista de Legislación and Jurisprudencia* (1869).[49]

The Brazilians, who until now had been apparently contented with a tolerant and enlightened king, Emperor Pedro II (*Dom Pedro De Alcántara*), featured a mix of satirical, multilingual, and commercial periodicals. There was freedom of the press although in paternalistic and supervised terms, and he enjoyed prestige and respect for guarding the country's sovereignty in disputes with Great Britain and the United States while gaining new territory from Paraguay. A reign dominated by land oligarchs, Brazil imported as many as 50,000 slaves in 1850 against the king's wishes. During the demanding War of the Triple Alliance, critics at publications such as the *Revista dos Dois Mundos* compelled the Brazilian-born monarch to abolish slavery, which he officially decreed as late as 1888. Sarcastic newspapers such as *O Mosquito* (1869), with the celebrated cartoonist Bordalo Pinheiro, were especially critical. Still, even in the most difficult times of the conflict, the so-called Philosopher King maintained his ideological openness, political balance, and increasing expansion and development of the press.[50]

In 1889, soon after the abolition of slavery, the military forced his abdication. For the next 100 years, this South American giant displayed a rocky history of social conflict and inequality, elitism, war and military intrusions, censorship, discrimination, and self-serving governments, with a conventional press acting as mouthpiece of wealthy minorities versus alternative media and courageous critics trying to speak for the impoverished majority in both rural and urban areas. Actually, Brazil throughout the twentieth century may well be an eloquent reflection of the sad and conflicting reality of the Latin American media and society, with worthy but only transitory freedom here and there.

In Uruguay, the above war inflamed an already explosive political environment. Two major newspapers emerged in the early years of the conflict. One was José Cándido Bustamantes's *La Tribuna* (1865), one of the "most vibrant" Uruguayan publications of the time, dominated by the *Partido Blanco* (White Party) and which lasted until 1875. The other was *El Nacional*, the opposing *Colorado Party*'s newspaper that criticized the war, the economy, and the presidency of General Venancio Flores (1865–1868), later assassinated in the middle of the Paraguayan War.[51] In contrast, the *Triple Alliance* was tragic for Paraguay. One of the few Latin American presidents to die in the battlefield, Francisco Solano López (1826–1870), a hero for many Paraguayans but a failed "South American Napoleon" for most historians, responded to a Brazilian invasion of Uruguay in 1864. With half of his country's population dead over a period of six years, the incipient Paraguayan press defended his leader.

Edited by the poet Tristán Rosa, *El Centinela* (1867) appeared first in Asunción and then moved with the president as the circumstances imposed it. Two other papers, the bilingual and sardonic *Cabichui* (Wasp, a Spanish-Guaraní paper between 1867 and 1868), and *La Estrella* (1869), directed by Manuel Trifón Rojas, also became casualties of war. By the end of the conflict in 1870, and further humiliating the Paraguayans, the Brazilian and Argentinean armies published their triumphal newspapers: the Portuguese-language *Saudade* and *El Chaco*. Reactions to the occupation such as *El Paraguay*, produced by Juan José Brizuela, and *La Opinión* barely survived the year. In fact, the most stable Paraguayan newspaper, Juan Andrés Kelly's *El Semanario de Avisos y Conocimientos Utiles* (The Weekly of Useful Knowledge and Announcement), founded in 1853 with governmental support, disappeared as well in 1868.[52]

Less critically, though painfully, Peru and Bolivia also suffered serious human, territorial, and media losses during the *War of the Pacific*. In Lima, the *Revista Peruana* of the Soldán Brothers lived only two years (1879–1880) and Manuel Gonzáles-Prada's *El Correo del Peru*, an eight-year-old newspaper, closed down at the beginning of the war. More importantly, on a government order, the historical *El Comercio*, dating back to 1839, had to close its doors for three years beginning in 1879. Lima kept going with its remaining five dailies. *La Opinión Nacional* (1873), founded by Avelino Aramburu, Reynaldo Chacaltana, and Manuel María Rivas, filled in the vacuum criticizing the Peruvian government for joining the war. Soon after, on a nationalistic tone, this paper closed ranks as soon as the troops entered a full-scale battle. Whereas *La Opinión Nacional* accepted the onerous terms of the *Ancón* peace treaty, other dailies openly rejected it, namely *La Patria*, *El Nacional*, and *La Sociedad*.

The war with Chile brought immediate consequences to the Peruvian press. First, newspapers and the public sharply split into supporters and adversaries of the Peruvian involvement. During the occupation of Lima by the Chileans, all presses suspended operations until October 1883, once the capital was freed. The struggle for power between Miguel Iglesias (1822–1901) and General Andrés Avelino Cáceres (1833–1923) also translated into a fierce battle inside the press. Both rulers applied strong prior restraints against newspapers during their administrations. Because of its [antiwar] campaign, *El Comercio* closed down in 1879.[53]

In Bolivia, government authorities and newspapers also clashed, generating deep public opinion and press disputes. Once the Chilean troops invaded Bolivia in 1879, editors and journalists sided *en masse* against the aggression. The prominent *La Tribuna* and *El Civilista* in La Paz joined forces with *La Patria*, a newspaper created by Emeterio Cano and Luis de Salinas Vega in 1881. But, when defeat became inevitable, the press split into a pacificist–conservative position, such as Tarija's *El Trabajo* and *La Patria*'s, controlled by the then Bolivian vice president Aniceto Arce (1824–1906), and the positivist and combative position of liberals such as the bimonthly *Las Verdades* in La Paz. Yet, other periodicals such as *La Confederation* and *El Club Patriótico* recommended patience and pragmatic attitudes.[54]

Conversely, Chile experienced a significant media stability and even progress during this particular war. Valparaiso, for example, then a city of nearly 100,000 inhabitants, came to have seven printing presses and three dailies (*El Mercurio*, *La Patria*, and *El Deber*) during the conflict. The English-language newspaper *West Coast Mail* also made history then. In 1880, *La Epoca* emerged as a prominent literary newspaper including correspondents as prestigious as the Nicaraguan poet Rubén Darío. Soon after acquired by the financier and industrial mogul Augustin Edwards Ross, *La Epoca* joined the *El Mercurio* Group, with editions in Valparaiso (going back to 1841), Santiago (since 1900), and Antofagasta (1906), the former Bolivian port in the Pacific.

STATE EMERGENCY RULES THE PRESS

During the 1810 Revolution in Mexico, liberators and printers suffered the deadly consequences of their colonial censorship and repression. Miguel Hidalgo y Costilla, for instance, defied New Spain's press law by founding *El Despertador Americano* on December 20. Advancing the slogan "freedom and independence," this and other revolutionaries published radical newspapers that, like Hidalgo's, had not only editors but also readers threatened and persecuted. Remarkably, one issue of *El Despertador Americano* released up to 2,000 copies, an "absolutely exceptional" media achievement in those days.[55] And also, hoping to persuade the Mexican public about the justice of his revolt, this publication produced seven regular numbers and two extras in only one month. The paper stopped when Hidalgo fell prisoner. He was shot and decapitated on July 30, 1811.

In the town of *Sultepec*, José María Morelos y Pavón edited the weekly *El Ilustrador Nacional*, soon after called *El Ilustrador Americano* (April/May, 1811, respectively). In these papers and *El Semanario Patriótico* wrote major insurgent leaders such as Andrés Quintana Roo and Ignacio López Rayón, printing both political editorials and revolutionary war news. The local authorities, in the meantime, responded with both censorship rules and an equally forceful propaganda campaign in state-sponsored newspapers, principally *La Gaceta del Gobierno de México*, *El Telégrafo de Guadalajara*, *El Centinela contra los Seductores*, and *El Español*.[56]

With the liberal Constitution of Cadiz (1812), local authorities found increasingly difficult to carry out their agenda of restraints. Article 4 of this charter ordered that officials were "obligated to keep and protect through just and wise laws the civil liberties, property, and other legitimate rights of all individuals that comprised [Spain and the Indies]." Article 131 specifically commanded "the political freedom of the press."[57] This legislation gave breathing space to innumerable publications throughout Latin America. Some of them included the strongest bastion of New Spain such as the critical *El Pensador Mexicano*, *El Juguetillo*, Oaxaca's *Sud*, and both *El Misceláneo* and *Clamores de la Fidelidad Americana contra la Opresión*, from Yucatan, charging against the colonial authorities and their proverbial corruption. Quintana Roo's father printed *Clamores* (Clamors of the American Loyalty against Oppression).

In March 1821, Agustín de Iturbide (1783–1824), a manipulative colonel appointed as Agustin I, proclaimed the Pact of Iguala. The globe's greatest nations, he stated, "were dominated by others, and until their lights did not let them settle their own opinion, they did not emancipate. It has been three hundred years that [Spanish] America has been under the tutelage of the most Catholic, merciful, heroic, and magnanimous nation. [Then] the town of Dolores in 1810, that year that brought so many misfortunes to our then beautiful country, set the public belief that a general union of Europeans and Americans, Indians and natives, was the only solid base our happiness may rest on."[58] Unlike Venezuela and the New Granada, Mexico had not entirely broken away from Fernando VII, expressing either admiration or loyalty for the Spanish monarch even in her revolutionary gazettes.

With this native-grown emperor and his confusing allegiances, Mexico secured its independence. A Spanish royalist, Iturbide had fought against both Morelos and Hidalgo, and once in power his conservative reign of censorship and political persecution propelled a number of progovernment newspapers such as *La Gaceta del Gobierno de Guadalajara* and *El Diario Político Militar Mexicano*. After a short exile in Italy, Iturbide was arrested and summarily executed on July 19, 1824.

Describing the situation of Latin America, right before his famous Unity Congress of 1826 in Panama, Bolívar wrote: "brothers make war to brothers. [E]verything is blood, everything is terror in [Spanish] America. [E]ither we build a strong government to oppress ambition and protect freedom or we will be the laugh of the world and our own victim."[59] Still, by the end of the Greater Colombia (1819–1830), after the failed Ocaña Convention (April 1828), the liberator turned his presidency into a military dictatorship which restricted civil liberties such as freedom of the press, religion, and commerce.

At the 1819 Congress of Angostura in Venezuela, establishing the *Gran Colombia*, freedom of the press was guaranteed. Notwithstanding, it was subject "to proportionate penalties against those who licentiously exercised it in detriment of the public peace, good customs, life, honor, and individual property and reputation."[60] Two years later, the Constitution of *Cúcuta* ratified the Union of Venezuela, Quito, and New Granada, defining freedom of the press in similar terms. "All Colombians," it stated, "have the freedom to freely write, print, and publish their thoughts and opinions, without any examination, review, or censorship prior to its publication. But, those who abuse this precious right will suffer the punishments they deserve according to the law."[61] Obviously, the Inquisition was abolished.

In September 1821, number 6 of the *Gazeta the Colombia* devoted its pages to a press statute (law 17) where not only freedom to publish but also press crimes and abuses are both classified and regulated.[62] Still, during the early years of the *Gran Colombia*, critical newspapers proliferated, targeting top government authorities such as the Vice President Francisco de Paula Santander. Simón Bolívar, the president, was at the time campaigning against the Spaniards in the south. *El Fosforo de Popayán* (the Match of Popayan), *La* Miscelánea, and Nariño's *Los Toros de Fucha* worked as the most poignant periodicals to which Santander responded with the creation of his own journal, *El Patriota*. A tense but free press, nevertheless, reigned in the Gran Colombian Republic throughout the early and mid-1920s.

Once Bolívar declared himself a dictator, shortly before an assassination attempt on June 13, 1928, the liberator launched a silent but furious crackdown against government critics. Some of the conspirators were sentenced to death including Santander but his sentence later changed into exile. Gradually, the criticism gained adepts. Unwelcomed nationalist newspapers, such as *La Revista*, *El Argos de Caracas*, *La Aurora de Apure*, *El Argos Republicano de Cumaná*, and *El Pensador Quiteño*, called for the separation of the Union in Venezuela and Quito.

Because of big disputes between Bolivarian and Santanderists, centralists and federalists, pro-integration and separatist groups, Bolívar felt that press restraints were indispensable, especially when divergent threats and ambitions from Europe's Holy Alliance, England and the United States also contributed to aggravate the Gran Colombia's crisis. For Bolivia, the liberator proposed a constitution (the *Constitution Boliviana*), taken from the Haitian experience and combining elements of the British, U.S., and Roman legal systems.[63]

Introducing this document, Bolívar declared:

> Legislators, duty calls upon you to resist the clash between two enemy monsters that reciprocally struggle against each other, and that together will attack you. Tyranny and anarchy form an immense ocean of oppression around a small island of freedom, perpetually subjected to the violent charges of waves and hurricanes.

[A Chamber of Censors] shall exercise a political and moral power similar to those of the Areopagus of Athens and the censors of Rome. [T]hey will protect the morality, the sciences, the arts, the education, and the printing press. The most terrible but also most noble function belongs to these prosecutors. [They shall] maintain intact the law of laws: equality. Without it (equality), all liberties, all rights will perish.[64]

In spite of its structural and potential threats to the press, the Bolivian newspapers enjoyed a significant freedom after the 1826 Constitution, particularly during the presidency of Andrés de Santa Cruz. He used the press to promote its political and social reforms, encouraging the growth of newspapers such as *El Iris de la Paz* (1828), *El Boliviano* (1829), and *El Eco del Protectorado* (1838). Following the end of the Peru–Bolivia Confederation (1836–1839) and the relative peace and protectionism of the Santa Cruz years, the press initiated a long period of anarchy, war, and repression.[65]

Something similar occurred in Bolívar's homeland. Disintegrating the Gran Colombia, the Republic of Colombia returned to its former colonial name of New Granada, adopting four different constitutions in only two and a half decades (1830, 1832, 1843, and 1853). The charters between 1830 and 1850 defined freedom of the press along the same lines of the Gran Colombia's *Constitución de Cúcuta* (1821), but they introduced an increasing number of unwritten exceptions. Without prior restraint, freedom to express or print thoughts and opinions had to operate in accordance with the law. Importing a foreign judicial practice, the 1843 *Constitution of the Republic of the New Granada* required juries in all trials dealing with press crimes and abuses (art. 163).

By 1853, liberal clauses defining freedom of the press as a right without limits began to emerge: only publications clearly deemed illegal were to be excluded. In fact, law 2100 of 1851 in New Granada proclaimed "an absolute freedom of the press," a principle which revolutionized Colombia in the second half of the nineteenth century.[66] On the contrary, Venezuela maintained an unrelenting grip on the media following Bolívar's death. Between 1830 and 1858, also known as the conservative-oligarchy era, the Venezuelan Congress passed two press laws (1847 and 1855) which opened the door to a complete state intervention, terminating with any possible influence of the Gran Colombian years while facilitating the *caudillo* regime of the Monagas brothers. The number of Venezuelan papers sharply decreased in those years. One important survivor was *El Venezolano*, a newspaper founded by the influential journalist Antonio Leocadio Guzmán and the strongest voice of the emerging Liberal Party.[67]

Besides the Gran Colombia, significant integrated republics in Latin America such as the Central American Federation (1824–1838) and the

Peruvian–Bolivian Confederation represent in many respects a golden time and opportunity for these regions. Like the Gran Colombia, these two "might have led [their peoples] to become greater nations before many decades have passed."[68] Unfortunately, all of them failed. During the presidency of Francisco Morazán (1792–1842), "father of Central America", a decree reminded all authorities "to protect the freedom of speech, writing, and of the press of those who make a legitimate use of this right. This prerogative cannot authorize any public official to persecute a speaker."[69] Trying to enforce the existing Federal Constitution, Morazán responded to numerous complaints involving violations of individual guarantees by government offices and authorities.

In 1824, the *Constitución Federal de Centroamérica* had explicitly ordered "not to restrict in any case and under any pretext the freedoms of thought, speech, writing, and printing."[70] This already revolutionary writing was further complemented with one of the most liberal press laws ever adopted in Latin America: the *Federal Decree of May 17, 1832*. Aware of the importance of people's rights, particularly the right to communicate thoughts free from the intrusions of power, this statute regulates "freedom of the speech, of writing, and of the press as the freedom to give opinions on legislative, religious, and administrative matters including abstract, material, and moral issues." This liberty protects the freedom to examine and condemn every official action of the supreme powers and their officials. It involves as well the right to inspect "private conduct or private flaws clearly and directly connected with public behavior, or with the performance of duties of every public official or employee."[71]

And there is a lot more in this historic decree. Distinguishing between conceptual (pure speech) and expressive (speech plus) press freedoms, article 2 claimed that freedom of expression is "so absolute that no prior censorship, no rule, and no special or regular tribunal could restrict it. Not even a commotion to the constitutional order, an armed rebellion, or a civil war will be a valid reason to restrict the press. On the contrary, depending on the circumstances, such situations will make these liberties rather necessary to know the opinions of the people, and the necessary decisions to restore peace and the law."[72]

The Central American Republic in 1832 had a press law that regarded freedom of expression as a protector of all other civil rights, making every effort to save it from either public or private threats and attacks. Although it professes a near absolute constitutional freedom of speech, thought, and press, there are some narrow restrictions to these guarantees: basically, defamation, copyright, and privacy (family peace). Public order could not be an excuse to censure the press. If a Penal Code needed to refer to this right, freedom of speech should come out enhanced rather than affected by criminal clauses. According to articles 6 and 7, to openly persuade someone of committing a crime, using force, or employing an illegal or violent method against the legitimate authorities or the law may be a reason for criminal prosecution. Yet, the decree also emphasized that imputations against the government did not constitute an unlawful incitement against established rules and institutions.

This press statute dedicated almost half of its entire text to sanctioning government officials who breached basic civil rights such as the publication of any written or printed work (arts. 8 and 10). To avoid prior restraint, any public authority who under any excuse, such as libel or sedition, and whether it was true or false, blocked, restricted, or seized any publication, received a fine and a penalty of up to four years in prison. In cases of demonstrated violence against an individual to obstruct his constitutional rights, including freedom of the press, the perpetrator was subject to a fine and ten months in prison. If the convict were a lawmaker, a judge, or a government official, the penalty would also carry a suspension of all political rights for four years.[73]

Member states, namely Guatemala, El Salvador, Costa Rica, Honduras, and Nicaragua, also adopted internal constitutions in the same tenor. On April 18, 1826, for example, the *Constitution of the State of Nicaragua* stated: "The rights of the Nicaraguans are liberty, equality, security, and property. [F]reedom of speech, of writing, and of the press is one of the first and most sacred rights of Nicaraguans." The law can neither prohibit it nor bound it to a prior restraint under any cause or pretext whatsoever.[74] Thanks to the above protection, many newspapers flourished throughout Central America, including *La Tribuna* (1924), *El Redactor General de Guatemala* (1824), *El Centro-Americano* (1826), *La Tertulia Patriótica* (1826), *El Indicador* (1824), *El Liberal*, and *La Gaceta del Gobierno Federal*.[75]

In 1838, with the end of the federation, the *Political Constitution of the Sovereign, Free, and Independent State of Nicaragua* went back to the conventional formula of a free press. No prior censorship, but authorities expected a press "responsible before the law for the abuses committed with this freedom."[76] Public order and decency, morality, and damages to third parties were reinstated as broad exceptions. The second half of the nineteenth century in this country is characterized by constitutional shifts between the two regulatory philosophies: freedom of the press as a mostly absolute right or as a guarantee full of unwritten exceptions, primarily in governmental affairs.

Unlike the Central American Federation and its remarkable notions of the time, most of Latin America was governed by restrictive, conservative, and defensive laws of the press during the first half of the nineteenth century. In Mexico, following Iturbide's empire, society and the press were in the hands of whom Bolívar called the "new Dessalines" of Latin America: General Antonio López de Santa Anna.[77] In his eleven times in the Mexican presidency, General Santa Anna imposed a tight censorship, forcing newspapers to avoid politics as the only way to survive. De-nounced as seditious by *El Diario del Gobierno*, federalist dailies such as *El Voto*, *El Censor*, *La Reforma*, and *El Siglo XIX* became prime targets of gov-ernment actors loyal to the centralist constitution of 1835. The U.S.-styled *Siglo XIX* (1841) excelled as a truly independent newspaper, displaying higher levels of technology (a press imported from the United States), business organization, and longevity (fifty-five years of operation).[78]

During the Mexican War, Santa Anna repeatedly suspended freedom of the press, closing newspapers and banning reports on political and military news. The U.S. invading forces also contributed to censorship, founding newspapers for propaganda purposes throughout the occupied Mexican territories. The most prominent titles included the already men-tioned *The American Star* in Mexico City (1847–1848), *The American Eagle* in Veracruz, *The Californian Star* in San Francisco, and both *The República de Río Grande* and the *Diana de Matamoros* in the northeastern border.

After securing the control of Mexico City, U.S. authorities issued decrees such as the already infamous *General Order no. 20* imposed in Veracruz, proscribing activities likely to threaten the public "peace" including news and other publications. Not only Mexicans but also U.S. Americans could be severely tried for murder, rape, robbery, theft, written works on U.S. military operations for publication, desecration of churches, and destruc-tion of private property.[79]

In the Southern Cone, the regulatory pillars are found primarily in Argentina and Uruguay. After a decade of political and military confronta-tions, following the independence, the Argentines, particularly the liberal opposition, endured the dictatorship of Juan Manuel Rosas (1793–1877). In the mid-1830s, Rosas implemented the deadly *Mazorca*, a political po-lice created to persecute and destroy any government resistance, forcing hundreds of dissidents into exile. Those who managed to stay defied the authorities, publishing papers such as *El Clasificador* (1830), *El Mercurio Bonaerense* (1832), the *Diario de la Tarde* (1831), *El Cometa Argentino* (1831), *El Defensor de los Derechos del Pueblo* (1833), and *El Iris* (1833), among a few others. *El Clasificador*, for instance, edited by Pedro Feliciano Cavia, was officially suspended in 1832. By 1835, both the Mazorca and the legal bans threatened Argentina's political press with virtual extinction. Only literary and commercial journals had some space to operate, such as the case of *El Telégrafo del Comercio*, *El Almanaque Astronómico*, and the *Guía de Forasteros*.[80]

From this generation of expatriates, living in neighboring countries such as Uruguay, Bolivia, Peru, and Chile, came two of the most promi-nent leaders against Rosas, the subsequent presidents Bartolomé Mitre (1862–1868) and Domingo Faustino Sarmiento (1868–1874). Criticizing the abuses and lack of freedom in his native Argentina, Mitre, an accomplished journalist, writer, and orator, contributed frequent essays in foreign newspapers such as the Bolivian *La Epoca* and the Chilean *El Progreso*. It was in these papers where Sarmiento, a distinguished journalist as well, published the eloquent anti-Rosas and anti-caudillo manifesto: *"Facundo, Civilización o Barbarie"* (1845). Sarmiento himself in 1842 had founded *El Progreso*, a daily owned by the Vial family. It eventually lost the government's subsidy, something common at that time in Chile and elsewhere, after Mitre published an article favoring the opposition. Attacking the political anachronism of Argentina, Domingo Faustino Sarmiento repeatedly denounced his home country's violence and backwardness not only in *El Progreso* but also in *El Mercurio*.[81]

In Uruguay, Rosas forced President Manuel Oribe (1792–1857) to censor the Uruguayan newspapers, precluding them from discussing the internal situation of Argentina. Oribe, founder of the Blanco Party, often used his presidential power to silence the opposition press, temporarily closing newspapers such as *El Nacional* in which the noted writer Juan Bautista Alberdi collaborated. Born in 1835, this publication was out of circulation between 1836 and 1838. It is also worth noting that during the second occupation of the Portuguese (1816–1820), Uruguay was subjected to a strong period of censorship that ended with a press law dictated by King Joao VI on July 12, 1821, forced by liberal revolts in Brazil and Portugal.

For the next seven years, this small nation was known as the Cisplatina Province, part of the Brazilian empire of Pedro I.[82] In 1824, this monarch, son of the king of Portugal and a so-called Perpetual Defender of Brazil, adopted a liberal constitution known for its civil rights including freedom of the press. Critics, however, complained that the king never observed his own constitution, showing on the contrary proclivities to impose authoritarian styles of government.

As in the United States with its antebellum abuses and civil war, Latin American countries also had to undergo bloody and costly periods of political and military fighting before they saw any serious signs of media and social modernization in their homelands. This is one reason why Simón Bolívar and other liberators, such as Bernardo O'Higgins, decided to rely on "censors" in order to avert the imminent anarchy of their recently freed nations.[83] Modernization would be a painstaking process led by unusual and innovative Mexican, Central American, and South American statesmen and entrepreneurs, increasingly inspired in Anglo-American models.

Argentina, for instance, commented Professor José I. García-Hamilton, would demonstrate between 1853 and 1930 "that it could be a wealthy and democratic nation."[84] And so did Costa Rica and Brazil, laying the foundations of a "modernist" and fairly respected freedom of the press even under dictators like General Tomás Guardia (1870–1881) and King Dom Pedro II de Alcântara (1831–1889), "a long reign characterized by social change, material progress, and wars with neighboring nations."[85] For the most part, however, Latin America and the Caribbean, particularly

Mesoamerica and the Andes, would remain marked by the "media" manipulation, hostility, and elitism of their ancestral times. Let us remember here that, while significantly cultured and advanced, the Mayas, Aztecs, and Incas also experienced censorship and propaganda, suppressing texts or using writing to exalt rulers and humiliate rivals.[86]

Chapter 4

Modernization and the Press

Concepts of modernity emerged in Latin America since the 1850s, even in brutal dictatorships such as the one commanded by the Paraguayan López family, but firm models of social progress based on the introduction of new technologies, commercial ventures, and open trade were most visible in Mexico and Southern South America especially in the late nineteenth century. Unevenly, and with the noted dominance of Great Britain, Latin America entered an intercontinental order where new republics supplied raw materials for manufactured goods. In the exploitative trade of the mid- to late 1800s, a handful of countries managed to attract both modern media and innovative techniques based on foreign loans.

Early construction of railroads and telegraph lines in Argentina, Brazil, and Mexico illustrates this phenomenon. Long distance and speedy communications became a priority in the operation of new and juicy markets overseas. Consortia in Europe and North America were then ready to spend millions of dollars to build indispensable communication infrastructures in the underdeveloped world. And a few clever rulers in Latin America, understanding the postindependence environment, tried to capitalize on the potential mobility and flexibility of their nations, combining government incentives with natural resources as a magnet to bring in foreign capital and technology.[1]

In the historic expansion of the half-century before 1914, industrialized Europe, wrote Robinson, cast its imperial influence over the most agrarian world, laying down railways in other people's countries. The locomotive had already proved its remarkable capacity to connect local and national economies, and once the trunk lines had been completed with sizable profits at home, the railway mania spread abroad. The power of railroads to swallow weak states into their empires fascinated Europe's geostrategists.

Railroad and telegraph imperialism led to the submarine telegraph, telephone, radiotelegraph, and broadcast dominance of the north, not to mention their ultimate control of other communication means during and beyond this remarkably profitable, greedy, and competitive period of our history. Naturally, the Latin American newspapers, though originated in Spanish America in the early 1700s, could not escape the impetus of the modernity, foreign influence, and dependence imposed primarily by the Europeans. The United States, temporarily distracted by a secession war and internal industry urgencies, could not show her renewed hemispheric ambitiousness until the end of the nineteenth century. Let us try to understand how the modernization thinking arrived and shaped the press in Latin America.

THE MODERNIZATION IDEAL

The roots of Latin America's public modernization can be found in the journalistic activities of Argentine leader Manuel Belgrano (1770–1820). Two months before the May Revolution of 1810, Belgrano launched the *Correo del Comercio*. His goal was to promote the progress of agriculture, science, industry, and education for commercial purposes.[2] With Hipólito Vieytes in Buenos Aires, Belgrano also worked in setting up the pioneering *Semanario de Agricultura, Industria, y Comercio* (the Agriculture, Industry, and Commerce Weekly). Beginning on September 1, 1802, the *Semanario* promised to spread lessons and initiatives of practical importance to people dedicated to economic, agricultural, and industrial activities. On February 11, 1807, this historical publication, which was truly the first Argentinean newspaper, disappeared because of the second British invasion.[3]

Exploring the role of the press, Vieytes and Belgrano planted a standard of quality journalism based on experimentation with different reporting styles, such as mixing the arts with trade, politics, and economics.[4] Intellectual leadership and service to different publics constituted a central focus as well. A lover of books, Manuel Belgrano had studied these subjects under the direction of Jesuit priest Luis José de Chorroarín at the Colegio Real de San Carlos, subsequent member of the *Junta Conservadora de la Libertad de Imprenta* (Freedom of the Press Guarding Board, 1812) and the second director of the *Biblioteca Pública de Buenos Aires*, now Argentina's National Library. In turn, this institution had been founded by Mariano Moreno, a leading patriot and forefather of the new government's *La Gaceta de Buenos Aires* (1810–1821), showing the intimate connection between books, newspapers, merchants, and the freedom to express ideas. Actually, the *Correo del Comercio* was the immediate antecedent of the

Gaceta in Buenos Aires, a newspaper where the Chilean revolutionary journalist Camilo Henríquez once worked as an editor.[5]

To better understand the nature of Belgrano's *Correo del Comercio* is key to remember that the first newspaper in today's Argentina was the *Telégrafo Mercantil, Rural, Político-Económico, e Historiográfico del Rio de la Plata.* Born on April 1, 1801, under the direction of the Spanish Francisco Antonio Cabello y Mesa, this biweekly published, in addition to political news and literary works, trade news, food prices, civil contracts as well as lost or stolen goods, and job opportunities. With *Supreme License* of the Royal and Supreme Council of Castile, the *Telégrafo* operated out of the Royal House of Orphan Children for eighteen months until it was permanently suspended by the local authorities.

Trade and commerce had always been an aspect of fascinating interest for the Argentines, particularly the *Porteños* (those from Buenos Aires). After all, Spanish restraints were loose in the Viceroyalty of La Plata, facilitating a business mentality fueled by constant pressures of British invaders who played a major role in shaping the social character of the area. Unsurprisingly, nearly seventy years later, the Argentine Republic was among the first in Latin America to enter the sphere of the assuming cosmopolitan, trading-oriented, and modernizing states.[6]

Similar actors, situations, and press orientations surfaced in Mexico, Brazil, and a few other states, where important ports offered the mix of significant commerce, government offices, and new products and practices. Nurturing economic circles in commercial centers such as Veracruz, La Habana, Cartagena, Rio de Janeiro, and Caracas, dailies such as Lima's *El Comercio* (1839), one of the oldest in Latin America, announced their operation as a business for commercial exploitation, not for simply political purposes. In Havana, *La Lonja Mercantil* (c. 1810) may have been the first strictly commercial newspaper of all Spanish America. Also, in Veracruz, the *Jornal Económico Mercantil* (1805) emerged as Mexico's first provincial newspaper, followed by the equally specialized *Diario Mercantil* (1807–1808). The *Semanario Económico* (1808–1809) had published as well agricultural and naturalist works in Mexico City. Even memorable revolutionary papers such as *El Despertador Americano* (1810), inspired by Miguel Hidalgo y Costilla and edited by Francisco Severo Maldonado in Guadalara, called itself a "political and economic mail."[7]

During the reign of Pedro I, Rio de Janeiro also inaugurated the noted *Jornal Do Comercio,* often called "Dean of the Brazilian Press" and one of the few Latin American newspapers to last over a century in competition with the *Diario de Pernambuco* (1825) among Brazilians.[8] The prestigious house of Emile Seignot Plancher, Rio's and the country's principal printing shop, published this *Jornal.*[9] Born the same year of the renowned Chilean daily *El Mercurio* (1827), the *Jornal Do Comercio* replaced the *Folha Mercantil* established in 1824, initiating the tradition of the centenary dailies baptized as "The Commerce" papers such as Lima's *El Comercio* (1839), Cuzco's *El Comercio* (1896), and Quito's *El Comercio* (1906).

This Latin American commercial press, with the relative exception of Brazil, owed its format and inspiration to the Spanish *El Correo Mercantil de España y sus Indias*. This Iberian newspaper circulated in Málaga, Sevilla, Cádiz, and in the principal ports and interior cities of the Americas, as well as in manufacturing capitals of the metropolis such as Valladolid and Murcia.[10] The connection between commerce, law, and freedom of expression is one of the most enduring in the history of journalism, even in the closed and defensive monarchies of Spain, a symbiosis that blossomed with the exacerbating British dominance and mercantilism of the nineteenth century.

BENTHAM ON LATIN AMERICA

During the preindependence years and well into the early republican era, English philosopher, economist, and jurist Jeremy Bentham established close relationships with different Latin American leaders. Among the most prominent are those with the Precursor Francisco de Miranda; the liberators Bernardo O'Higgins, Simón Bolívar, and José de San Martín; the Brazilian king Pedro I; and statesmen such as the Haitian Alexandre Pétion, the Central American José Cecilio Del Valle, the Gran Colombian Francisco de Paula Santander, and the Argentinean Bernardino Rivadavia. He also befriended the reputable Venezuelan jurist, journalist, and educator Andrés Bello. In other words, Bentham advised and influenced some of the most powerful and capable rulemakers of Latin America during the first half of the nineteenth century. Both the English philosopher and the Latin American revolutionaries knew well that the young republics needed serious social reforms, constitutions, and laws, including those relating to freedom of the press, and Bentham's innovative ideas were extremely attractive to the patriots.[11]

The British thinker believed in a utilitarian utopia, a principle of utility whereby correct actions provide the greatest happiness for the greatest number of people. For him, happiness could be measured through a moral-mathematical calculation, a basic formula of units of pleasure minus units of pain.[12] The total efficacy of institutions and lifestyles in society, he said, depended upon the application of proper and systematic rules contained in an all-comprehensive code of laws. Visionary, eccentric, and unorthodox Bentham assisted the United States in writing her Federal Constitution, maintaining a fruitful and active correspondence with Alexander Hamilton and James Madison.[13] Combining concepts of liberalism with rationalism, Bentham opposed the theory of natural rights, "in which human beings are believed to possess certain inherent and unalterable social [rights] and requirements."[14]

For half his life, this British philosopher dreamed of going to Latin America and applying his knowledge and ideals. Disillusioned with his country's common law system where the lack of written codes went against his goal of a universal manual of utilitarian legal morality, Bentham looked at Latin America as the ideal laboratory for a systematic collection of laws. "The good which I could do to mankind if I were in the House of Commons, or even if I were minister," he wrote, "is inconsiderable in comparison to that which I may hope to do if I go there [Spanish America]."[15] Before and during the Latin American independence, the English jurist sketched and proposed plans for constitutional charters and codes of criminal law in the Americas, suggesting educational reforms and an interoceanic canal or *Junctiana Canal*. He believed that the liberty of the press played a prominent role, and during the French Revolution, Bentham produced a series of essays entitled *Principles of International Law* where press freedom became one of the six measures of happiness in an international order without war.

Thinking of going to Mexico first, he looked for information about Veracruz and Mexico City on the *Almanaque Mercantil y Guia de Comerciantes para el Año 1806*, a commercial guide published in Spain. Bentham was so detailed that he looked for information on Mexico's availability of paper, candles, tea, printers and engravers, sculptors and architects, and botanical gardens and libraries including French and English books. He also asked his friends for an *Index of Expugatorius*, the Spanish Inquisition's blacklisting of authors and publications, trying not to violate travel laws when moving to Mexico. He asked for maps as he once confused Acapulco in the Pacific with Veracruz in the Gulf of Mexico. In fact, General Miranda also gave him a map of Colombia.

When the Spaniards blocked his trip to Mexico delaying the travel permit, Bentham switched his attention to the "still more charming province of Venezuela, alias the Caracas," as he called it. Writing to his acquaintances, he affirmed: "Whatever I give them for laws, they [the Venezuelans] will be prepared to receive as oracles."[16] Weeks before sailing to Caracas as the revolution's spearhead, Miranda provided Bentham with a draft of his law for the liberty of the press. That Spanish America should be made strong was his advice to Miranda, for any functioning utilitarian state should have a written, systematized, and all-comprehensive complete code for an adequate development. Along with the law of the liberty of the press, he gave the Precursor the *Caracas Necessity of an Entire New Body of Law for Venezuela*. Obviously, Bentham was thinking not only of Venezuela but also of the whole Spanish-American world.

Although admired across the Latin American political spectrum, his ideas were not always warmly received. Looking often too eager to experiment, the British philosopher generated certain suspicion in the Americas.

The fact that he was a foreigner and perhaps even "incompetent," according to some detractors, increased the mistrust to giving him the task of writing out a constitution for a new nation. Although respecting his abilities, Bolívar, for example, had cooler connections with Bentham, particularly after the liberator announced his dictatorship in 1828. They first met in Bentham's garden in London in 1810 but he paid no attention to Bolívar. Then, Bentham began writing to him in 1822. Apparently, the liberator returned the discourtesy by not inviting him to the Gran Colombia as a legal advisor. More than the British jurist, Bolívar's admiration turned to Mr. Bentham's editor, James Mill, father of John Stuart Mill.

In the end, the English author never set foot in Latin America. In 1826, Bentham received a formal invitation from Guatemalan leader José del Valle in order to advise him and the Central American Federation in writing their constitution and other laws. But, the British jurist was already seventy-eight years old, with little physical energy to endure a trip to Central America. Still, he enthusiastically sent various materials including his *Traité de Legislation* and over 400 pages of his constitutional code, the majority written in Spanish.[17] He warned Del Valle that merchants would gladly praise any advance of their metallic interests but that the interests of knowledge were far more important. Del Valle showed his appreciation by proclaiming Bentham "Legislator of the World."

Besides the exchanges with Miranda, Del Valle, and Bolívar, Jeremy Bentham also had a fluid correspondence with the Argentinean patriots José de San Martin and Bernardino Rivadavia, the Chilean Bernardo O'Higgins, and the Venezuelan Andrés Bello. He could be charming and serviceable, providing materials and advice as he did with all the above. Yet, he could also be extremely critical, accusing liberation heroes like San Martin, Bolívar, and Rivadavia of becoming either despots or obstacles to the greatest felicity of people.[18]

Bentham's legacy and impact on Latin American policy makers can be summarized in four points. First, the rule of greatest happiness to the greatest number of people implies the duty to adopt laws fostering the welfare of individuals in society. He was aware that this principle required a sacrifice of the ruling few. Second, "the possession of a common body of laws" would bring about both "a bond of union" and a common convenience that may be called "an intercommunity of laws." Third, the law must be written clearly, so that every citizen can understand it and "the burden upon individual memory and attention [should be] as light as possible." In Bentham's view nobody should ever be punished or disbarred of a right because of ignorance. And finally, "almost any law is better than none." A comprehensive code, excellent for one state, would be equally adequate anywhere else, regardless of country differences in tradition or condition. The arithmetic of good and evil, universal utility, and pain and pleasure were crucial for Bentham, and they help us measure happiness and draft effective and all-comprehensive codes. In turn, corruption and despotism were the greatest dangers.

In a continent where classical Judeo-Christian (mainly Thomist) and Aristotelian principles and values had traditionally prevailed, Bentham and Mill's utilitarianism was a breadth of fresh air, together with social contract and Kantian ideals from the Enlightenment—one more reason to be disliked among colonial statesmen, religious conservatives, and nonreformers.

MODERNIZATION PIONEERS

From the classical humanism, rationalism, and liberalism of the Renaissance, and away from the "Aristotelian Christianity of scholasticism," the New World moved vigorously into the Enlightenment: mainly, scientific understanding, technological innovation, and empirical philosophy. With the Spanish-American expeditions and *tertulias* (study circles) of the late 1700s, the revolutionaries had grown both outraged and fascinated with Europe's scientific movement against absolute monarchy and the power of the Church. Freedom, justice, and an open trade of inventions, knowledge, and ideas, including the printing of books and newspapers free from the Inquisition, were first-ranked priorities among the Latin American patriots and liberators.

Our leaders knew all too well the response of Church and civil authorities to change and innovation (such as Copernicus' revolution), leading to the imprisonment, torture, and death of prominent scientists simply because of their ideas. The burning at the stake of Copernicans such as Giordano Bruno (1600), Lucilio Vanini (1619), and Fontainier (1621) were often typical examples of teachers such as José Celestino Mutis, Simón Rodriguez, and Andrés Bello in Spanish America, and of humanists who explained the horrific censure and abuses of religious intolerance. Obviously, young intellectuals in the New World had little in common with the orthodoxy of Christianity, its doctrines, and its institutions.

From the French rationalism of Descartes to the British empiricism, starting with Bacon, Locke, and Hume, the new Latin American republics gradually received the influence of the German romanticism, idealism, and socialism of Kant, Hegel, and Marx. French propagandists, essayists, and journalists such as Voltaire, Rousseau, Diderot, D'Alembert, La Mettrie, and Marat, among others, had already captivated and alerted the continent's rulers and intellectuals, infusing ideals of fundamental change. And the social scenario could not be more challenging, active, and explosive: three major revolutions, the Industrial, the American, and the French, showing the creative and also the destructive power of the Enlightenment and industrial modernization while leading the way of the Latin American revolts of the early 1800s.

Yet, when the new republics came about, the promises of independence continued to remain largely unfulfilled. Engulfed in an endless chain of wars that lasted at least fifty years, a few nations, with the help of visionary front-runners, managed to reverse the vicious cycle of violence. One of the best examples was Argentina with her luminary modernists Bartolomé Mitre (1821–1906) and Domingo Faustino Sarmiento (1830–1890). By 1870s, the new Latin American missionaries of peace, order, and progress were vehemently liberal, pro-education, pro-technology, and pro-trade. As in the Renaissance, when the invention of the printing press had been a key development, these leaders took on the newspapers as the principal vehicle of expression.

Seeking social reforms and civilization, Sarmiento wrote about the role of newspapers in *El Zonda* (1839): "[the press] is a gripping and impetuous burst that destroys everything that is not firmly in place. A paper is a man, a citizen, and a civilization; it is the past and the present, the criminal and great actions, as well as the need of individuals and governments. The contemporary history, the history of all times, humanity in general, and the measure of a people's civilization are all part of a newspaper."[19] Before long, Juan Manuel de Rosas' dictatorship censored *El Zonda*, a periodical founded by Sarmiento in his hometown *San Juan*.

Once in Chile, as an exile, Sarmiento devoted his journalistic columns to the importance of order, legality, liberty, and the discussion of modern ideas. Like his predecessor (Mitre), Sarmiento and a handful of Latin American modernization leaders began working on the assumption that social reality follows the rules of reason and science, not divinity. Notions of human society as a mechanism and complete confidence in the progress of new sciences and technology became pillars of the new political thinking of reformation (*regeneración*).

The search for order, harmony, and lawfulness in all public matters, whether economic, political, or cultural, raised themselves as a priority. Natural rights and the rule of reason, as opposed to the barbarism of previous decades, turned into the appropriate route to deliver the promised equality, liberty, universal education, and democracy the independence process had promised. The future will show that the continuous adoption of scientific methods and practices would generate technology for the benefit of humanity, with the understanding of man's natural laws and natural rights as the foundation of a world of democracy and peace.[20]

In practice, the political *tertulias*, coffee-shop activism, and literary journalism of the independence were hereby giving way to the positivistic, mass-oriented, and empirical rationalism of modern scientific thought. More than Bentham, the focus was now on Auguste Comte and his sociological approach of positivist attitude whereby empirical sciences are the only adequate source of knowledge. Suddenly, the Declaration of Independence of the United States made much more sense than the European precedents and experiences; apparently, nowhere was this commitment greater than in the United States of America.[21]

Domingo Faustino Sarmiento recommended the adoption of the United States as a model. First, he proposed to imitate this country's political constitution and laws. Second, he wanted Argentina to follow the U.S. program of land distribution, immigration, and colonization. And the use of education for democracy, safety, and freedom, plus the emphasis on easy communications—canals, railroads, and mails—should, as in the United States, be basis for prosperity in Argentina. Things he most admired from the United States were her liberty, laws, educational system, the urge for growth, and the increasing material well-being of the average citizen. Because of this fondness, critics often labeled him as "a fanatic Yankee admirer."[22]

In open confrontation with the prestigious educator and jurist Andrés Bello, Sarmiento believed that the "disorder, prostration, and decomposition of the new republics" could be overcome mainly by learning from Europe and the United States, and going beyond encyclopedic ideas. As a man who grew up in the ideals but also apprehensions of the independence, Bello was far more cautious about such openness with Europe and the United States. Modernists and nonmodernists agreed, however, that after decades of independence, Latin America "offered a sad spectacle" of underdevelopment.

Although serious constitutional, internal, and foreign disputes marked the adoption of new media technologies and ideologies in the late 1800s, the modernization ideal is not a phenomenon of the twentieth century as often believed, primarily in Argentina, Mexico, and Brazil. Daniel Lerner did not bring modernization to the Americas in the post-World War II era, looking at the discourse for progress taking place in the Americas in the late nineteenth century. His equation: new media technologies, urbanization, and literacy equals economic growth and democracy was already present in Sarmiento's and other leading views a hundred years before. True, industrialization was then barely noticeable, but it was the preeminent goal of the Latin American forerunners of modern change in this region. Import-substitution industrialization arrived in various countries, including Argentina, Brazil, and Mexico, soon after the 1929 stock market crash.[23]

Nearly sixty years before, however, leading advocates of modernity considered railroads, the mail, terrestrial telegraph, and submarine lines as well as newspapers as the key requirements for progress in developing countries. President Sarmiento in Argentina, for example, "was responsible for laying the foundations of a federal telegraph that began operation in 1870," bringing serious competition to small systems run by provinces, railroads, and private companies.[24] The urge for progress, order, and profitability imposed upon the nineteenth-century republics resulted in the immediate need to modernize and expand communication networks. New, ample, low-cost, and efficient communication channels were a singular priority at that time.

The need for modernizing the economy and solving pressing social needs after the devastation of the war turned new technologies into a symbol of social prosperity and integration. Telecommunication systems, with the support of newspapers, supposedly fostered improved state functions and operations, including the implementation of agricultural, educational, commercial, industrial, defense, social welfare, and other government programs and activities.

The end of the monarchy and the initiation of her true independence in 1889 made similar assumptions in Brazil. Order, progress, and educational reform represented the dominant republican spirit, to such an extent that the first two concepts were actually stamped in the Brazilian flag designed by positivist painter Décio Vilares. Like Sarmiento and Mitre in Argentina, middle-class intellectuals, such as Benjamin Constant Botelho de Magalhaes, Miguel Lemos, and Raimundo Texeira Mendes, also promoted the Brazilian positivistic thinking exemplified in the modern media and other technologies of the time.[25] At one point, it was hoped that improved media and information would help to reduce the entrenched violence, cultural "parochialism," and "xenophobia" of the first half of the century. Ever since, the equalizing function of technology has been a popular cliché among technocrats, bureaucrats, and policy makers interested in media innovation as a rationale to further economic development, public opinion, and orderly change.

In Mexico, the positivistic approach imported during the late 1860s by Gabino Barreda, an educator and philosopher who met Comte in Paris, dominated the liberal reform of the *Porfiriato*, the dictatorial government of Porfirio Díaz (1830–1915) who ruled the nation with a strong fist. During his two presidencies, twenty-one years in power altogether, social order and material progress were undertaken with undeniable success, though at the expense of press freedom and other civil liberties. Advised by an educated elite of experts and intellectuals known as the *científicos* (scientists), Díaz built a prosperous country of wealth for the few and extreme misery for the many, particularly Indians and peasants.[26] Industry, railroads, and telegraph lines flourished during the Díaz regime.

Increasingly, state authorities and entrepreneurs began assuming that telecommunications and the mass media made economies more productive, markets more profitable, and education systems more effective. New communication services would bring adequate answers to specific problems. Whether it was by overcoming infrastructure problems or administrative deficiencies, the modernizing spirit of transportation and telecommunications were to provide political and economic advancement. From there on, the assumption would always be progress, peace, and the collective actualization of happiness through (media) technology. For the modernization ideologues, the function of communication was to educate and inform, enhancing the ability to live in an orderly, democratic, and peaceful society.[27]

HERE COMES INNOVATION

Lima's first railroad terminal, built in 1851, may well symbolize the beginning of the modernization era in South America. One of the earliest Latin American stations, connecting the Peruvian capital with the port of Callao, this building marked the dawn of the revolutionary communication and transportation technologies in Latin America. As in Europe and the United States, the railroads brought along the telegraph, enhancing not only government and private communication but also newspaper operations. Not coincidentally, Lima's principal daily *El Comecio* was a pioneer in the use of wire services twenty-five years later, buying in weekly basis news reports from the French Havas, German Wolff, and the British Reuters.[28] Most of the Latin American papers that employed wire services introduced them during the 1890s and early 1900s. *El Universal* of Caracas, for example, inaugurated its operations with a combination of Associated Press (AP), Wolff, and Reuters wire feeds in 1909.[29]

In Colombia, presidents Tomás Cipriano de Mosquera and Manuel Murillo Toro also brought significant modernization to the country's ports, railways, and postal system. In consonance, reformers moved to guarantee "absolute" freedom of the press in both the 1851 and 1863 constitutions, just as Costa Rica, El Salvador, Guatemala, Honduras, and Nicaragua had done in the constitution of their Federal Republic of Central America in 1824.[30] In this memorable document, article 175 stated that "[n]either the Congress, nor the Assemblies, nor any other authority may [. . .] limit *on any pretext, or in any case, freedom of thought, of speech, of writing, or of the press.*"[31] Even the Catholic church had its preeminence denied, explained Professor Paul Wellen, since the Central American Magna Carta encouraged the "tolerance of all religious cults." Eventually, conservative values, religious fanaticism, and state censorship would prevail in most, if not all, of these countries by the end of this century and beyond.

In colonial times, the spread of postal communications, books, and newspapers depended on the development of transportation systems, so the arrival of both railroads and telegraph wires were a giant step in the more efficient distribution of printed information. Seven years after its inauguration by former president Bartolomé Mitre in Argentina, for example, the prestigious daily *La Nación* (1870) featured a series of national and international correspondents linked via telegraph, including reports from the Middle East and North Africa.[32] Introducing this news service to its readers, La Nación announced: "[Our newspaper] just negotiated a contract with Havas-Reuter to receive daily telegrams from Europe with the Old World's most important political news and events. As long as the transatlantic cable works, the telegraph service will come without interruption. When the news story demands it, we will publish a same day bulletin that will be handed out to our subscribers asking for them."[33] Actually, because of the significant role of technology, many newspapers honored such telecommunication carriers by calling themselves *"Post," "Daily Mail,"* or *"Courier,"* and by mid-1800s *"Railroad,"* or *"Telegraph."*[34]

In Latin America, the name *ferrocarril* (railroad), adopted by several papers, sought to capitalize on evolving expectations of power, self-sufficiency, and technological progress in their respective countries.[35] Some examples are the Chilean *El Ferrocarril* of Santiago (1855), short before the arrival of both the railroad and the telegraph in this South American country; the *El Ferrocarril* (1869) of Montevideo, Uruguay; and the Bolivian *El Ferrocarril* (1873) of Potosí and *El Ferrocarril* of Cochabamba (1907). Other newspapers chose to honor different technological innovations such as the Venezuelan *El Fonógrafo* (The Phonograph), founded by Eduardo López Rivas in Maracaibo (1879) or the Peruvian *La Luz Eléctrica* (The Electric Power, 1885), an anarchist newspaper directed by Mariano Torres.

It is worth noticing that the Spaniard Francisco Salvá y Campillo developed in the first half of the 1700s a system that used wires to transmit alphabetic signals, but neither his name nor his proposal reached Spanish America during the *Despotic Enlightenment* of the colonial times. Although an eighteenth-century European invention (created separately but simultaneously in Britain, Switzerland, France, and Germany), the telegraph is for most Latin Americans an exclusive achievement of Samuel Morse. In any case, innovatory newspapers began to use this telecommunication technology by mid-1870.

That same decade, *La Opinión Nacional*, a liberal Venezuelan paper, put in place one of Latin America's first steam-powered printing presses. Led by General Tomás Cipriano de Mosquera (1863–1864 and 1866–1868), Colombian and pro-federal liberals also launched a modernization period known as the *Olimpo Radical* years, two decades of building railroad lines including one in the former state of Panama. In 1865, Manuel Murillo Toro, another federalist liberal, built the first Colombia telegraph line, connecting Bogotá with the port of Nare in the Magdalena River.[36]

Before the 1870s, few Latin American newspapers could claim any noted technological advancement. In Costa Rica, the Constitution of 1871 planned for a global modernization in all fields, but a truly technical newspaper such as *La Información* was not possible until 1908. Until the firm wave of railroad and telegraph construction arrived, the Latin American press remained technologically poor, thin, and limited to a small number of subscribers. The isolation because of the lack of media infrastructure continued to be a major obstacle for social development in most provinces and localities. But, during the last two decades of the nineteenth century, a numbers of countries and publications showed some significant improvements, principally in the most populated, economically prosperous, and educated nations.

Levels of trade and natural resources appeared positively related to media modernization, triggering a lasting inequality among Latin American countries. Argentina, for example, witnessed the relative benefits of its historical contact with Britain, hosting technologies that smaller, poorer, or more enclosed nations were unlikely to attract. On May 1, 1860, industrialist Miguel Mulhall and his *The Standard and River Plate News* brought a linotype press to promote commercial and technological innovations, including running water and gas lights. Next door, in Uruguay, *El Siglo* of Montevideo also purchased a steam-powered press in order to produce up to 2,400 papers per hour, bringing a new era of printing in this small but active southern South American nation. *El Siglo* advocated a press modernization model based on combinations of new technologies, additional subscriptions, and increased commercial announcements.[37]

In turn, Chile's *El Mercurio* sprang as a newspaper venture decidedly interested in copying the news and corporate archetypes of the *New York Herald*. Modern equipment, business approaches, and photo techniques employed in the U.S. Age of Yellow Journalism came to Chile through *El Mercurio*, consolidating closer news connections with North America as the Argentine *La Nación* did with Europe in the 1870s. By then, the Associated Press was on increasingly comparable footing with the European news agencies operating in Latin America. Focused on providing the fastest news and as ambitious as *The New York Herald*, *El Mercurio* concentrated on winning more readers to attract larger advertising revenues. How to present the news became the utmost priority, with dailies and magazines working on mastering their photography and even color formats. Alberto Urdaneta's *Papel Periódico Ilustrado* (Illustrated Periodical Paper, 1881) in Colombia and the Peruvian *La Prensa* (1903) were good examples of the U.S. modernizing trend. Another case, this time in Mexico, is Juan de Ribera's daily *El Monitor*.[38]

A most interesting period in the history of Latin American journalism is also the reformation era of Mexico's president Porfirio Díaz. The significance of the *Porfiriato*, wrote Toussaint, "is its transitional character between the [Mexican] journalism of the past and of the present times."[39] Before Díaz's first presidency (1876), Mexico was a predominantly rural and dispersed country. Barely starting as a transportation alternative, the railroad, along with the newspaper, usually distributed by mail, were media of the largest cities, primarily Mexico City, Puebla, Morelia,

Guadalajara, and Mérida. Other obstacles against the efficacy of newspapers included the low literacy levels (14 percent of the national population in 1895), the reduced market for news publications (an elite which represented less than 10 percent of the country's population), and the miserable salaries or extreme poverty of the general population. A newspaper would easily cost them more than a kilo of corn.[40]

Still, in 1894, some periodicals such as *El Imparcial*, *El Monitor del Pueblo*, and *El Noticioso* reached a circulation of 20,000 papers each. For a worker with three or more children, "spending money on a newspaper was something inconceivable."[41] Only the wealthy and occasionally the middle class could regularly afford a newspaper. Usually, politicians, government officials, clerics, merchants, industrialists, teachers, and affluent students made up the readership, that is, in addition to the journalists themselves. But, when the working class was interested in a publication, they found the way to read it. Pro-working class papers, such as *El Socialista*, *El Hijo del Trabajo* (The Work's Son), *El Hijo del Ahuizote* (The Otter's Son),[42] and *Regeneración*, had loyal readers among Indians, peasants, and city workers.

In the late 1890s, it was common to see laborers in clandestine places free of their oppressors, forming groups of thirty or more people to read and memorize the content of newspapers. As news was verbally relayed to other workers in nearby villages, a single issue could have a significant circulation. The worker's press might have been limited in funds and technology, but it had a significant acceptance and influence among the lower income.[43] Although proportionally less numerous in readers and titles than southern South America, Mexico had a remarkable growth of publications during the *Porfiriato*. Just Guadalajara, capital of the state of Jalisco and the country's second media center, had 100,000 inhabitants, fourteen printing presses, and at least twenty titles in 1900. Second to Brazil, Mexico was Latin America's most populous nation by the turn of the nineteenth century.

CENSORSHIP USHERS ANOTHER CENTURY

Except for the relative modernization of a handful of countries and the short-lived innovation experiences of a few others, both Latin America and the Caribbean are a frustrating chain of human servitude, violence, caudillos, racism, despotism, oligarchies, alien interventions, and complete censorship, following their independence wars.

In Haiti, masses are treated as ignorant children who are allowed "no voice in the debates to decide the direction of the new republic."[44] The old saying that *no one is free because freedom has not extended her influence to this place* is more evident in the Caribbean than anywhere else during this period. Sadly, this maxim is still true in many Caribbean nations, especially Haiti.

Strongmen or *caudillos*, often military ones, also reigned in the young republics of this continent and many well into their twentieth-century maturity. Furthermore, there is a continuous repression of blacks by government authorities and white oligarchies long after the abolition of slavery. Every country has tales to tell about their eccentric and abusive rulers, such as Pedro Santana, Buenaventura Baez, and Ulises Heureaux in the Dominican Republic; Antonio Guzmán Blanco in Venezuela; Juan Manuel Rosas in Argentina; and Antonio López de Santa Anna in Mexico, to name a few. Between 1830 and 1925, Ecuador was governed by forty different regimes, and the constant struggle for power among regional military chiefs was the norm. The same occurred in Venezuela and especially in Peru "where caudillos outnumbered civilian presidents."[45]

Professor Wellen recounts one incredible episode in Nicaragua. He writes: "In the mid-19th century the exercise of intellectual and political freedom was adversely affected by direct U.S. military intervention. In 1855 the U.S. millionaire Cornelius Vanderbilt founded the expedition of the freebooter William Walker, who landed with a mercenary force, declared himself president of Nicaragua, made English the official language, reinstituted slavery, and closed down opposition newspapers. The newspaper editor Mateo Mayorga was executed by a firing squad, but Walker was defeated and himself executed in 1860, after he had failed to capture Costa Rica."[46]

Another character is José Gaspar Rodriguez de Francia in Paraguay, one of the founding fathers of Paraguay, who managed to attain absolute powers from the country's legislature and soon after declared himself *El Supremo* (The Supreme), a dictator for life.[47] It goes without saying what these dictators did to their people and their liberties, for, as Blanco in Venezuela, he simply "silenced the press through widespread confiscation[s] and the imprisonment of journalists."[48] If there was any modernization, it did not extend to politics, and that was precisely the case of the lengthy and powerful dictatorship of Mexican general Porfirio Díaz, who "imposed law and order with total censorship."[49]

The subsidies and publications of the Mexican government during *Porfirio's* dictatorship brought about a media bonanza that was possible only at the expense of the freedom of expression. Critics of the regime also flourished but not without paying a price. In 1902, *El Hijo del Ahuizote* had its press confiscated and its editors Jesus Martínez-Carrión and Daniel Cabrera incarcerated. This flaming and transparent weekly proved that order and modernization made up an agenda of narrow meaning, one in which dissidence and criticism were not truly welcome.

Silencing and repressive schemes tend to trigger stronger reactions in Latin America. Within a few years, both editors managed to bounce back with two more radical newspapers: *El Colmillo Público* (The Public Fang, 1903–1906) and *El Ahuizote Jacobino* (The Jabobin Ahuizote, 1904–1905).

Cabrera's paper, the second one, became one of the most prominent satirical publications of the time, a model against mighty dictators such as Porfirio Díaz.[50]

Mexico is also a country that in the nineteenth century presented a puzzling paradox of its constitution and civil rights. On the one hand, it retained a strong reverence for colonial traditions, such as religious practices that changed little after her independence from Spain. On the other hand, it showed a liberal and secular vocation that was the envy of the region's innovators. The Church claimed that Catholicism was incompatible with liberalism, while liberals argued that religious beliefs were barriers to a progressive state administration. In both sides, however, intolerance and censorship were the rule of the game. In the end, Mexico is able to move forward through the tortuous path of liberal conservatives clashing with conservative liberals.[51]

In October 1824, the Mexican Political Constitution gave the nation her republican structure, federalism, and early basic liberties. Condoning religious censorship by banning any creed other than the Catholic faith, this charter nominally guaranteed freedom of the press as a fundamental right. The secularization of society, the protection of individual rights, and the supremacy of the state as conductors of private and public life were all part of this document. But, after forty-eight presidencies (eleven of them in the hands of the dictator Antonio López de Santa Anna) and more than half a dozen constitutional congresses in less than thirty years, this constitution fell into fast erosion.

Following the 1810 Revolution, Mexico had legally and philosophically embraced the liberal views of the press, primarily those of England. But, the culture of an effective press freedom did not receive much support in the Mexican Union. Jeremy Bentham, the British jurist and philosopher, had recommended, even the Mexicans themselves, that the liberty of the press was a *sine qua non* for achieving useful social goals and reforms. Aware of the difficulties to draft a law protecting this liberty, he had recommended the press to be free from any required government licensing with prevention preferable to punishment.[52] Not without trying, Mexico and other sister nations could not meet such high standards.

In 1857, a new and decidedly liberal constitution tried to amend the structural mistakes of the past. It began with little auguries of success, for only 55 of the 155 drafters took part in the constitutional deliberations. Yet, it introduced radical reforms that confronted the conservatism of Iturbide's imperial constitution of 1821 and the ambiguities of the 1824 charter of independence. One of the primary goals of the 1857 *Carta* was to effectively defeat the political power of the ecclesiastics.[53]

To begin with, the new charter, known as the *Constitution of Reform*, declared its liberalism by defining individual rights as the base and purpose of all social institutions, including the public powers (art. 1). The state was simply a guarantor of such human rights, and it was obligated to facilitate and implement the fulfillment of individual prerogatives such as the right to freedom of expression. For the first time and for the next sixty years (1957–1917), the Mexican society would try to live under a system of legal equality, free from the colonial anachronism of inflexible religious cannons, civil privileges, and societal discrimination. Publishers and journalists would no longer have to fear the concerted action of government, military, and church authorities, imposing the death penalty to those accused of heresy and libel.[54]

Hand in hand with the freedom of commerce, industry, and profession, President Benito Juárez reestablished the right to print in classical liberal terms during the late 1850s. In fact, after the French invasion of the 1860s and shortly before his reelection, he even defended an "absolute" freedom of the press. Prestigious journalists, such as Francisco Zarco, Gabino Barreda, and Miguel Lerdo de Tejada, editors of the influential *El Siglo XIX* and *El Monitor*, helped the president in his new administration.[55] But, a liberal successor, Don Porfirio Díaz, radically changed this attitude in the mid-1880s, enacting a *Ley de Imprenta* (press law) that authorized government authorities to incarcerate reporters without any due process or judicial review. Filomeno Mata, founder of *El Diario del Hogar*, a family newspaper often known as *El Diario de los Frijoles* for its kitchen recipes, exemplified the vicious intolerance, official repression, and repeated arrests of the time.[56]

When violence and persecution were not the option, the charge was usually seditious libel or defamation. For almost thirty years, journalists and press organizations endured the confiscation, closures, and arrests ordered by a government that excused abuse and repression with progress and modernization. Even liberal newspapers such as the renowned *Siglo XIX* disappeared. In 1896, this historic paper and also the popular *El monitor Republicano* were not only closed down but also replaced by state-subsidized publications such as the so-called *El Imparcial* and *El Mundo*. Rafael Reyes Spíndola, head of *El Imparcial*, emerged as the man who introduced Mexico to the concept of modern journalism, importing the first linotypes and organizational techniques of the U.S. press. These included a mass and industrial appeal, a dynamic news production, and a philosophy of conglomerate power. Indeed, strategic business alliances helped *El Imparcial* to use *El Heraldo*, *El Mundo Ilustrado*, and *El Cómico* as satellite business partners.[57]

The rest was a story of intermittent harassment, attacks, and suppressions of the opposition press. Numerous publications appeared and disappeared to attack the regime, but newspapers such as *Juan Panadero*, *Regeneración*, *El Hijo del Ahuizote*, and *El Colmillo Público* waged their war against Díaz openly or clandestinely inside Mexico or in exile from the United States.

Meanwhile, in the other extreme of the continent, the press faced somewhat less confrontational but equally effective repressive tactics. In Uruguay and Argentina, for example, newspaper commentary lived between the criminal codes of defamation and the private "codes of honor." Public scandal usually originated in journalistic disputes, and ended up in court whenever the slander was not considered a "gentleman" or was unable to duel because of physical disability, excessive age, or any religious or public impediment. In fact, journalists such as the Italo-Uruguayan Salvador "Totó" Nicosía of Montevideo's *L'Indipendente* had become expert duelists, and at age 28 he had already sorted out fourteen of these deadly contests before his challenge to the congressman David Buchelli.[58] More frequently, however, and because of the nature of their job, newspapermen were targets rather than initiators of duels.

For a journalist, it was easier to avoid a defamation lawsuit than a duel. Editors, reporters, and columnists had learned to shield themselves by publishing anonymous columns or under pen names. Their criticism was also routinely hidden in statements subject to interpretation, making difficult for the plaintiff, if not impossible, to prove any actual defamation. Provided that the criminal court was a functioning tribunal, these two requirements, the source of the libel and the falsity of the defamation, were difficult to prove. But, fair trials in courts, in highly publicized and politically charged scandals, were rarely the case.

Theoretically, truth was also a widely accepted defense in advanced Latin American libel systems. In Argentina, for instance, judges by the turn of the nineteenth century were already demanding that public official plaintiffs proved the *"animus injuriandi,"* that is, the intention to offend, including evidence that the defendant knew the charges were false.[59] Unlike the then common law libel of the United States, the burden of the proof was already on the accuser and not on the accused. Thus, the actual malice test of current press laws was neither entirely new nor as revolutionary as modern scholars made it sound like. Even so, it was harder at that time to distinguish between public and private life, and the truth defense was valid only in public conduct cases. Private causes, which any plaintiff could successfully argue, did not accept truth as a defense.

Duels, on the contrary, posed an even greater threat to nineteenth-century Latin American journalists. In these challenges, the burden of proving the truth was on the reporters if they wanted to refuse the duel. A challenge, by definition, was *prima facie* evidence that defamation had occurred, and they faced the court of public opinion for cowardice, which was a charge difficult to live with for any honorable person. If a journalist wanted to avoid a duel, he would have to sincerely retract his assertions, declaring that the challenger was an honorable individual free of any wrongdoing. Proof of the legitimacy of the retraction, of the respect for privacy, and of the lack of justification for the challenge was normally warranted as well. A retraction did not dishonor a journalist if sincere, otherwise it could have exactly the opposite effect, exposing the writer to the greatest contempt, especially if public opinion believed the news story as clearly insulting.[60]

Latin Americans did not go as far as the French and Italian duel laws. For the latter, publishers and editors were responsible for all unsigned articles, even when the author came forward to accept the challenge. Journalists in many European countries were not considered sufficiently honorable to accept duels. In Argentina and Uruguay, newspapermen enjoyed a somewhat greater legal reputation, but they were expected to defend their honor, and refusals perceived as cowardly were devastating for their personal and professional position.[61]

The newspaper became the political and propaganda tool *par excellence*, aided in the most stable nations by improved distribution networks of passengers, messages, and cargo, such as railroad, telegraph, and limited telephone systems. Increased levels of regulation, bureaucratic growth, and government monitoring also accompanied the emergence of socialist and anarchist ideas in Latin America's late nineteenth-century society.[62] Failing to learn from their historical and cultural heritage and from their conflicts with Europe and Anglo-America, most Latin American states lived a nineteenth century "full of dictatorships and caudillos, wars with neighboring countries, and economic and political instability."

Although moments of bonanza and democracy visited various nations, "[war and repression] blocked any sustained growth of the media, particularly the press, promoting the consolidation of newspapers."[63] In the nineteenth century, many Latin American charters tried hard though unsuccessfully to fully protect fundamental civil rights of expression, including the prescription of an "absolute freedom" of the press and speech, or as they said, "without any limitation."[64]

Chapter 5

How Not to Start a Century

If anyone had further doubts, the Spanish-American War (1895–1902) proved the real grip of the United States in Latin America. In U.S. schools, Cuba is not instantly recognized as part of this historic neocolonial war, a reason why Cubans make every effort to call this war *La Guerra Hispano-Cubana-Americana*. Echoing this sentiment, historian Philip S. Foner titled his book on the subject as *La Guerra Hispano Cubana Americana y el nacimiento del imperialismo norteamericano* (The Spanish *Cuban* American War and the birth of U.S. Imperialism).[1] By then, most nations in continental Latin America had been already freed from colonialism and slavery, but the U.S. press and audience were still thinking in U.S.–European terms.

For those following the Monroe Doctrine, this "Spanish-American" War simply confirmed the old ambitions of the U.S. expansionism in the Western Hemisphere, a geopolitics boiling as an aftermath of the Revolutionary War. New York City newspapers such as Hearst's (*Morning*) *Journal* and Pulitzer's (*Sunday*) *World* played a pivotal role in the emergence of the United States as a world empire. Advocating a military intervention that would forever change life in this continent, the *New York Sun*, the *New York Journal*, the *New York World*, and the *Chicago Tribune*, among many others, actively fanned and promoted the "Manifest Destiny," that pernicious policy that can be traced back to the Mexican-American War and the War of 1812.

Still, brilliant pages of the U.S. *Yellow Journalism* spread a media exposé of scandals, profits, and innovations throughout the hemisphere, bringing news-hungry countries such as Mexico, Argentina, and Brazil into the orbit of Anglo-American jingoism. Even distant nations of the Southern Cone in South America, including Chile and Uruguay, became secret admirers of the New York dailies, their impetus and their dynamism.

NUESTRA AMÉRICA AND MARTI

When U.S. America was honoring Joseph Pulitzer (1847–1911) as a giant of modern journalism, along with William Randolph Hearst (1863–1951), Latin Americans revered their hero-journalist José Martí (1853–1895). An editor, poet, jurist, and art critic José Julián Martí Pérez, the last one of the continent's great liberators of the nineteenth century, claimed that the entire continent should be a land of freedom for all. Not only the wealthy and white but also the poor, according to Martí, including Native Indians, blacks, and every mixed-blood person breathing in "Our America," should enjoy the liberty and independence many patriots had fought and died for. Martí inherited this famous motto of *Nuestra América* from his beloved inspiration, the early heroes of the Latin American independence. "We must make the Indians walk ahead so that America can march forward. We need this great and dormant race to wake up from its horror," stated Martí, writing for the Mexican *La Revista Universal* and its politico-literary *boletines* (bulletins).[2] For this cause of freedom and equality, he had to give his life in 1895.

In Mexico and Guatemala, where he lived between 1875 and 1879, Martí corroborated the beauty of journalism and his Native America. The path of "Our America," he noted, "could not be other than the one opened through the harvest of our capacities, rejecting the imported if it is not adaptable to our own realities."[3] In the Indian ruins of these countries, the Cuban hero admired their intelligence and imagination, their artistic creativity, and the search for the new. Impressed by the pre-Columbian books, he wrote:

> We cannot read one of these fine old parchment covered books without a feeling of tenderness. Like a beautiful novel, [they tell the story] of the Americas, of the Indians, their cities and festivals, the greatness of their arts, and the graciousness of their customs. Some of these Indians lived isolated and simple lives, going naked and lacking the necessities of life as newly born nations do. Others were nations already formed. Their creations resemble those of [our] nations only in the way one man resembles another. Friends are made by reading these ancient books, [by learning] about their vice-ridden cities defending themselves against the powerful men of the north.[4]

In Chichén Itzá, Martí compared the past of the Mayas and of capital cities with a broken book, torn, mud stained, and with its pages lying around or buried in the ground. Just like Miranda, Bolívar, or San Martín, José Martí's love for America was incomparable to any other emotion and commitment. Even his family suffered the big sacrifices for the motherland. Actually, in Havana, his hometown, Martí began his journalistic career publishing *La Patria Libre* (The Free Motherland). At the age of 16, he somehow knew his mission was to help free his country regardless of the sacrifices.

In *El Diablo Cojuelo* and *La Patria Libre*, two modest newspapers published during his high school years, Martí commented on the extreme alternatives of young Cubans of the time: either colonial domination or independence. Taking advantage of a *Ley de Imprenta* (Free Press Law) issued by Captain General Domingo Dulce in 1869, Fermín Valdés Dominguez and Martí published the single issue of *El Diablo Cojuelo* (The Limping Devil), "a short collection of anecdotes and puns on freedom of the press."[5] In the one issue of *La Patria Libre*, the young editor published satirical and dramatic remarks against the government. In fact, because of the above-mentioned press law, which lasted only thirty-three days, more than a 100 newspapers, leaflets, and magazines rose up to speak against the Spanish government, asking for freedom and autonomy under different formulas and terms.[6]

Accused of writing a treasonous letter against a member of the army, Martí was arrested on October 4, 1869. Six months later, at seventeen years of age, he was sentenced to six years in prison. Martí purged nearly one year of hard labor in Cuba, first in a stone quarry and then in a farm prison, before being deported to Spain on May 31, 1871. Once in the peninsula, his writings showed the endurance of the imprisonment, the intolerance for the injustice, and the sensibility of a person who witnessed and experienced the abuse of men and children. The chains left in him physical pains that lasted for the rest of his life.

In a prose published soon after his arrival to Madrid (1871), *El Presidio Político en Cuba* (The Political Imprisonment in Cuba), the young Cuban poet demanded: "[Spain], take off the shackles from the elderly, the children, and the mentally insane. Take away the stick from the miserable jailers and you will make [Cubans like me], who had not learned to hate in spite of your lashes, insults, and chains, forget some of their bitter days."[7] Deploring the so-called *Integridad Nacional* preached by the Spanish government, Martí denounced the torture and death of fellow prisoners such as the seventy-six-year-old Nicolás del Castillo, the twelve-year-old Lino Figueredo, and the eleven-year-old Juan de Dios, among others. All of them had been sentenced to ten years in prison supposedly for political reasons. The children of Cuba, cried Martí, should write on the first pages of their country's history the pains of Castillo, Figueredo, and Juan de Dios.[8]

Luckily for the New World, Martí survived this ordeal, being deported to Spain within the first year of his sentence. In the peninsula, he actively collaborated with pro-democracy papers such as *La Soberanía Nacional* of Cadiz, where he published parts of his *Political Imprisonment* essay. Other writings appeared in the liberals *La Discusión*, *La República Ibérica*, *La Cuestión Cubana*, and *El Jurado Federal*, before moving to Mexico and Guatemala from where he emerged as a mature journalist and leader. Siding with both the political and economic liberalism of the time, Martí challenged the authoritarian modernization of Porfirio Díaz. For him, freedom of thought and expression deserved protection from the petty and low blows of greed, power, and competition, and Díaz's regime represented for the Cuban leader a poisonous combination.

In 1878, following the *Pacto de Zanjón*, which offered an amnesty to political exiles ending with the ten-year war of *Guerra Grande* (1868–1878), Martí returned to Cuba with his wife Carmen Zayas-Bazán. She was pregnant with José Martí Jr., the hero's only son. Political stands admired by fellow countrymen quickly got him in trouble in Havana, especially with the Captain General Blanco who personally listened to one of his speeches. On September 17, 1879, he was once again arrested and deported to Spain. But, by January 1880, Martí was in New York City looking for the headquarters of his dreamed revolution. At that time, numerous Cubans were already living in New York, Philadelphia, Baltimore, Boston, and various towns of Florida, especially Tampa and Key West.

Convinced that Cuba and all Latin America required more indigenous than imported solutions for their independence and development, the "Apostle" of freedom (as disciple Gonzalo de Quesada y Aróstegui baptized him) planned for a free Cuba where liberty moved within democratic legal frameworks. Like Francisco de Miranda 100 years earlier, Martí had come to the United States looking for temporary shelter and political support. Both the founding fathers were anticlerical but respectful of religion, lovers of science and education, and passionate for the arts, particularly music, painting, and literature. Still, neither one trusted the U.S. government as a sincere ally. And in Martí's case, he feared the domination of Cuban politics and economics by Anglo-America, warning against one-crop states for its vulnerability to the ambitions of powerful neighbors.[9]

In 1886, when French envoy engineer Ferdinand de Lesseps presented the Statute of Liberty in New York City, Martí, working for the *New York Sun*, covered the news as an event of great continental significance. As Lesseps noted, the statute was to honor not just liberty in America but also the friendship between the Anglo, French, and Latin American cultures and communities. Proud of being a Cuban and a Latin American, Martí highlighted this mostly forgotten message. He saw himself as a citizen of this continent and as a person obligated to fight stereotypes against Latin Americans. During his time, dominant Protestant prejudices regularly condemned in the United States, including New York City, Latin

Americans, and other immigrants to the greatest social obscurity. And occasionally, the contempt was openly disclosed.

In 1889, for instance, New York's *The Evening Post*, along with Philadelphia's *The Manufacturer*, published articles calling Cubans "incapable people who, by nature and experience, could not carry out the obligations of citizenship in a free republic."[10] Promptly, Martí reacted with his *Vindicación de Cuba* (Vindication of Cuba, 1889), a pamphlet that included translations of the attacks and his response to each and every one of them. Yet, either for intellectual admiration or economic interest, or for both, Martí was invited to write for *The Hour* magazine and the prestigious *New York Sun* and *New York Herald*.

In the *Sun*, editor Charles A. Dana supported and encouraged the Cuban ideologue, knowing that Martí could bring valuable unorthodox views to his paper. Interested in a dynamic *New Journalism*, Dana's paper was in need of fresh ideas and appeals. Martí could be both, for he was committed to write pieces favorable and unfavorable to the United States. Over time, however, the *Sun* grew increasingly conservative and antilabor, ending in the same deceits and jingoism of Hearst's *The New York Journal* and Pulitzer's *The New York World*.[11]

Throughout the 1880s, the Cuban martyr devoted all energies to the huge demands of literature and the news. Naturally, politics and the freedom of his motherland were always center stage. In this decade, Martí's journalistic personality reached the highest levels, receiving continental acclaim for his articles and chronicles in various Latin American newspapers. In addition to contributions in New York's Spanish publications, notably the magazine *La América*, *El Latino Americano*, and *El Economista Americano*, his writings traveled around Central and South America in dozens of newspapers, including Argentina's *La Nación*, Uruguay's *La Opinión Pública*, Mexico's *El Partido Liberal*, and Honduras' *La República*.

His underlined theme was usually the same: to teach Anglo-Americans about Latin America and to enlighten Latin Americans about the life and government of the United States. In criticizing or praising the United States, he pointed out, "one should not exaggerate her faults by denying all her virtues nor should we hide her failings by preaching them as qualities."[12] The inauguration year of the Statute of Liberty (1886), universal symbol of freedom and independence, particularly freedom of the press, was for Marti the year of his consecration as a model hemispheric journalist.

Four years later though being Cuban, he had been formally appointed consul of both Argentina and Paraguay in New York, representative of Uruguay to the 1890 International Monetary Conference, and representative of the Buenos Aires Press Association in the United States and Canada. He was also named president of the Hispanic American Literary

Society in New York. In 1891, he resigned all of these honors, focusing his attention on the creation of the *Partido Revolutionario Cubano* (Cuban Revolutionary Party 1892) and the Cuban independence. He died in action in *Dos Rios*, Cuba, on May 19, 1895.

THE SPANISH *CUBAN* AMERICAN WAR

As mentioned earlier, the Spanish-American War is a misnomer. It leaves out the most important actor of the conflict: Cuba. The Cubans were the first and the most interested in defeating the Spaniards, and they wanted to end colonialism in the island. Yet, in practical terms, both economically and politically, the so-called Spanish-American War is an accurate reflection of the conflict between a dying global empire and a new, vigorous, and ambitious neighbor.

Although the animosity against Spain was a function of jingoistic images planted by the press, trade and militaristic adventure inclined average Americans toward the Cubans. Informed and educated Americans, however, knew that this particular confrontation, as the previous Mexican-American War, was mainly about foreign intervention, greed, and power. The U.S. readers, mostly through exaggerated news reports, understood the Spanish treatment of its colony and increased their animosity toward Spain. But the convergence of all these factors, not all of them virtuous, made U.S. Americans rally behind their troops, supporting an intervention that U.S. secretary of state John Hay (1898–1905) called "a splendid little war."[13]

The Cuban revolutionaries launched a decisive independence offensive in February 1895. Ready to join the battlefield, the great Martí reminded his friend Gonzalo de Quesada (writing from the Dominican Republic), that: "[A] newspaper is life. Don't let the rising [spirit] fall. To constantly emphasize [unity] in *Patria* [is] most important. [N]o one should ever dare to believe in this hour of common effort, that confessed revolutionary Cubans might have the slightest resentment, censorship, and distancing, or the slightest bitterness and arrogance against tacit brother Cubans."[14]

With his Revolutionary Party came the first issue of *Patria* (March 14, 1892), a publication that resembled in name and philosophy Martí's *La Patria Libre* during his school years. Days before the revolution, his then mature *Patria*, warned fellow combatants that "a mistake in Cuba [would be] a mistake in America, a mistake in modern humanity."[15] A journalism of the highest quality was *Patria*'s goal, telling everyone what might be needed and beneficial to all rather than a few. After all, there is no better throne than a good newspaper, wrote Martí, a place where reading is made truly available to the poor of will, time, or money.[16]

Yellow journalists, in the meantime, were blindly interested in scandals for profits, circulation, and business competition, pushing their publics

into a frenzied imperialistic mentality. As a reporting trend, the Age of
Yellow Journalism had clearly distinguishing boundaries with the previous New Journalism of the original Joseph Pulitzer and the muckrakers
of the early 1900s. For one thing the last two had a definite sense of social conscience. Less interested in a war with Spain over Cuba, President
Grover Cleveland asked "U.S. citizens to refrain from giving aid and comfort to Cuban rebels" in June 1895.[17] But the yellow journalists encouraged
by imperialists such as Theodore Roosevelt and Henry Cabot Lodge kept
their competitive snowball and pressure.

On April 6, 1896, the U.S. Congress granted the Cuban insurgency belligerent status. And thirteen months later federal legislators appropriated
50,000 dollars for relief of U.S. citizens in Cuba, adding to the significant
sums already given by U.S. sugar planters who wanted to protect their
properties from the possible burning by the rebels. Ultimately, what government and private actors pretended was to dominate and control the
island.[18]

Not all newspapers in the United States, however, agreed with the imperialistic plot of the pro-intervention enthusiasts. Contrary to the journals the *World* and the *Sun*, dailies such as the *New York Herald, Chicago
Times-Herald, Boston Herald, San Francisco Chronicle,* and *Milwaukee Sentinel* opposed their country's interventionism, while the *Chicago Tribune,
New Orleans Times-Democrat, Atlanta Constitution,* and *Indianapolis Journal*
vigorously championed it. Others that remained noninterventionists included *The New York Times, The New York Tribune,* the *Chicago Daily News,*
and *Boston Transcript.*[19] Actually, the last article Martí wrote was for *The
New York Herald,* a noninterventionist daily. On May 2, 1895, two and a
half weeks before his death in action, he mailed a letter to the *Herald's*
director explaining the objectives of the Cuban offensive.[20]

Ruling businessmen and politicians in the United States were less interested in Cuba's independence. Their goal was to take control of an island that enjoyed a privileged strategic position for the nation's business
and military projections in the Americas. On June 7, 1897, John Sherman,
President McKinley's secretary of state, officially complained to Spain of
the brutality of Captain General Valeriano Weyler against Cuban civilians.
As senator of Ohio, Sherman had been the one introducing the memorable Antitrust Act of 1890. Within ten months of this complaint, the U.S.
government declared war with Spain, sending to the island navy troops
and battleships, including the legendary Maine, infantry and cavalrymen,
and yellow reporters and photojournalists, primarily from the New York
papers.

On February 17, 1898, twenty-four hours after the Maine exploded
killing 260 sailors, the *New York Journal* initiated its famous "Remember the Maine" campaign. Jingoistic newspapers charged that a Spanish
mine destroyed the warship with its crew, using assistant secretary of the

Navy and future president Theodore Roosevelt as main source for their assertions. Soon after, Roosevelt quit his post to join the war, commanding as a lieutenant colonel of the so-called Rough Riders, a volunteer cavalry unit. On September 6, 1901, the "speak softly but carry a big stick" president, the youngest in the history of the American Union, took office after his predecessor William McKinley was fatally shot while attending a reception of the Pan-American Exhibition in Buffalo, New York. Anarchist Leon Czolgosz was the murderer.[21]

Although far from anarchism, José Martí was a resolute and pro-working class leader. He knew of the abuses of the emerging and wild capitalism, of the industrialized societies where unions and workers waged as fair a struggle as the war against colonialism in his native country. In 1886, the year of the Statute of Liberty, demonstrations and strikes ended up with police officers shooting against crowds. One tragic episode took place during a strike at the McCormick Reaper Manufacturing Company in Chicago, where six people died and a dozen more were wounded. A subsequent riot in Chicago's *Haymarket Square* resulted in seven officers killed and fifty others wounded. Eight anarchists, including that day's speaker Samuel Fielden, were arrested. Three months later, all workers were sentenced, except for the one who committed suicide. Four were sentenced to death; two, including Fielden, were convicted to life imprisonment, and the last one, to serve fifteen years in prison. Marti wrote on April 22:

> Everything ties me up to New York, at least for some years of my life: Everything ties me up to this cup of poison. You [my dearest friend Manuel Mercado] don't know it well, because you have not battled [in this city] as I have done it. [E]verything ties me up to this city: the political mistakes of our countries, the proximity to that land of mine which I love so much, [and] the disgust to live in countries where I can't take a practical or mechanical art with me. Mine is only another little intelligence that in these countries abound, and from which you can't make a living unless you rent it or sell it for some kind of government use—something precluded to foreigners. Everything ties up, and for the time being, to New York.[22]

The day before his death, writing once again to Mecado, José Martí reminded all Latin Americans about the danger of further annexations of territory in the Americas by the United States. To stop on time the force of imperialism in the Antilles and continental Latin America, the brutal and stormy power of the north that despised us, is what I have done until now and will continue to do, affirmed Martí. "I lived inside the monster, and I know its guts," he added.[23] Martí was acutely apprehensive after talking with Eugene Bryson, a *New York Herald* correspondent who updated him of the annexation fury of imperialistic politicians and yellow journalists in the United States.

The Cuban patriot was altruistically interested in a genuine independence, not only for Cuba but also for the Caribbean and rest of Latin America. If our independence revolution succeeded, thought Martí, the Antilles would be free, Latin America's independence would also be saved, and perhaps, the course toward a more equitable world would be set in motion if not accelerated. Anglo-America would also save her honor, since, at this point in time, "it is already doubtful and damaged," he wrote.[24]

NEWS FROM THE PANAMA CANAL

Colombia, a northwestern South American country with an ideal geographic location, was also at war by the turn of the century. With long coasts in both the Caribbean and the Pacific, and with the narrowest strip of land between the two oceans (the *Departamento de Panamá*), the Colombian territory became after Cuba the target of the United States. With trade in mind, Spain defeated, and the critical isthmus of the Western Hemisphere under their control, the U.S. government and trusts focused all their energies in building a canal. It would surely place the Union at the level, if not ahead, of commercial and military European powers such as England, France, and Germany.

During the Spanish Cuban American War, the battleship *Oregon* spent sixty-eight days, sailing from the West Coast of the United States to the ports of Cuba all around the Southern Cone of South America. Now that the United States was an empire with dominions in both oceans, leading U.S. officials and entrepreneurs agreed that a canal across Central America must be built quickly. Jeremy Bentham's prediction of the early 1820s was becoming a reality: whoever built and controlled first a water passage in the middle Americas would be an unchallenged world power for decades to come. Indeed, Bentham thought that Spanish America would not be able to carry out this project without assistance from the Anglo-American United States.[25]

Since the Spanish conquest, there had been plans to build a canal connecting the Pacific and Atlantic oceans. By 1528, the Spanish Crown had four projects on the table. One talked about a canal through a lake of Nicaragua; a second one used the Chagres River in Panama; a third project hoped to cut across the Isthmus of Tehuantepec; and the fourth one drew an unclear line from the Nombre de Dios to Panama City.[26] In the early 1800s two more plans concentrated solely on the Tierra Firme of Panama.

Even before Argentina or Mexico had their first railroad tracks, New York City financiers made possible the construction of forty-eight miles of a railway linking Panama City with the Caribbean. The interoceanic line

took four years of hard labor (1851–1855) and its unreasonable administration quickly led to both a massive riot and the landing of U.S. troops in
Panama. This event is historically known as the *Watermelon War*, a protest
whereby a passenger refused to pay charges imposed on a watermelon he
carried. Still, the prosperity was increasingly felt in the isthmus, a province
where the anti-Colombian sentiment grew day by day and where newspapers, founded during the emerging bonanza, fueled the spirit of region-
alism. One of these dailies, among the oldest in Latin America, was the
Estrella de Panamá y Star-Herald, established in 1849.[27]

Inaugurated by J. B. Bidleman & Company, the *Estrella* or *Star* began in
1849 as the English-speaking *Panama Star*, generating an intricate series of
papers including the Spanish *Estrella de Panamá*, the *Panama Herald*, *the Star
y Herald*, and finally the *Estrella de Panamá y Star-Herald* (1894). Commander Edmund B. Green, L. A. Middleton, James Middleton, Luis Boardman
Boyd, and John Powers were some of the early publishers, until a merged
version ended up in the hands of José Gabriel Duque in 1894. Heavily
influenced by Anglo-American designs and ideas, the Panamanian press
played a powerful role in the separation of Panama from Colombia. Actually, a member of *La Estrella*'s founding family, Federico Boyd, was
part of the triumvirate that ruled Panama right after its independence in
1903.[28] It is also noteworthy that Martí's columns were also printed in this
daily.

During the ten-year administration of Colombian president Rafael
Núñez (1884–1894), *the Star y Herald* was the center of a public scandal that
forced Governor General Santodomingo Vila to resign. Colombia was then
making efforts to keep in closer touch with her provinces, but the external
debt (nearly 3 million pounds plus interests), the meager army, and the
poverty and isolation of its population contributed to alienate distant and
wanted places like Panama.[29] In spite of a radical constitutional reform
(1886) and a new state philosophy of centralized government and a de-
centralized administration, Colombia could hardly exercise her national
sovereignty. Worse than everything, another internal conflict, known as
the *Thousand Days War*, broke out in October 1899, leaving the country at
the mercy of foreign powers, primarily the United States.

With just 650 kilometers of railways and colonial type of roads, Colombia, a country of the size of Texas and California combined, could barely
place her exports at river and ocean ports. The country, like most of Latin
America, was way behind the communication infrastructure needed to
minimally promote some kind of industrialization. Although Panama re-
volted as early as 1840 because of its isolation, Bogotá, either federal or
centralist, failed to open up any functional path with the so-called *Distrito Nacional* (National District). The central government relied on rudimentary maritime communications that only increased Colombia's vulnerability. As liberal General Rafael Reyes (1904–1910) pointed out in

his inaugural presidential speech, in the Panama separation's aftermath, it was not about freedom bringing us progress but about progress bringing us freedom.[30]

Once in power, former president José Manuel Marroquín (1900–1904) began to suspect a foreign invasion. International observers and the press kept criticizing Colombia as an eventual second Bolivia. And U.S. newspapers, including *The New York Times*, speculated that Colombians were vulgar deceivers and that they could lose both their Atlantic and Pacific coastlines (more than 2,500 kilometers).[31] Anyone, with minimal knowledge of diplomacy and the Monroe Doctrine, knew that the United States wanted a canal in Panama for obvious geopolitical, economic, technical, and military reasons.

Yet, the Colombian government did little to neutralize the U.S. threat. Not even a competent and coordinated embassy was appointed in Washington, DC. On the contrary, the able ambassador and negotiator Carlos Martínez Silva had to leave his post. He had significantly advanced the transfer of the bankrupted canal concession from the French to the United States, which the conservative Colombian government apparently endorsed by granting the French a six-year extension to facilitate such a transfer. Even Manuel María Aya, columnist of the newspaper *Sumapaz*, an organ of the liberal guerrillas fighting against the government at that time, had a practical solution: "It is very difficult to keep—wrote Aya— what everybody wish for. Let's give the United States sovereignty over the Panama Canal, in exchange for concession rights of $100 million dollars."[32]

A local visionary of the time, Santiago Pérez Triana, also excluded by Marroquin's political jealousies, explained the Colombian crisis as follows:

> Modern imperialism, that is, the fervent extension of the power to conquer and colonize, usually employs all sort of means to achieve its objectives. Had not been by the confronting impetus and appetites of several voracious rivals, there would be not a piece of land in Iberian America without a foreign flag. The Monroe Doctrine is simply one of those means of international rivalry. The truth is that our precarious sovereignties are not defended by force, because we don't have it. We have been and will probably be saved by such external rivalries on which our artificial and insecure equilibrium depends on.[33]

Great Britain, France, and Germany were also extremely interested in a canal of their own in Central America. For that purpose, though with very unfortunate results, the French began digging in Panama in 1878. After 20,000 men died of malaria and yellow fever, the French abandoned their venture in 1889, leaving Ferdinand de Lesseps, the great engineer of the Suez Canal, nearly bankrupt.[34]

The British, on the other hand, landed troops in Nicaragua in 1894, arguing that they just wanted to collect a compensation for improprieties of this country against the Crown's diplomats. The German emperor, according to the official Colombian paper *La Opinión*, was also anxious about developing energy, infrastructure, and transportation projects in Latin America. Everyone, especially the United States, knew that the Europeans' intentions were to deploy their men and build a canal through the Central American Republic.[35]

Even countries like Venezuela, Ecuador, and Nicaragua came to support the liberal rebels of the *Thousand Days War* against the Colombian authorities, trying to get a foothold in the eventual canal rights. The façade was the revival of the historic *Gran Colombian* Republic, with Nicaragua as a new member. In 1900, combined troops of Colombian with either Ecuadorian or Venezuelan soldiers invaded the country, and on November 12, 1902, the U.S.-controlled *Star & Herald* announced the Nicaraguan support for the Colombian insurgents.[36]

In every case, the United States brought up the Monroe Doctrine as a legal impediment and in 1896, two years before the *Guerra Hispano-Cubano-Americana* (Spanish-American War), U.S. Marines finally invaded Nicaragua with the ludicrous excuse of protecting U.S. citizens and property.[37] Once the United States had militarily and/or diplomatically defeated Spain, Britain, and France in the Caribbean, the coast was clear to trap Colombia.

Throughout this process the North American press paid the State Department a great service, hailing or sounding the alarm whenever the U.S. forces made or needed to make a move in order to secure its influence abroad.[38] Knowledge of the region among reporters was poor, confusing countries, peoples, and nationalities. In the Spanish-American War, for instance, yellow journalists often and inadvertently used the Puerto Rican flag to represent Cuban forces.

Having concluded the Spanish-American War in December 1898, the U.S. military turned its attention to Colombia's *Thousand Days War* (1899–1902). For Colombians, this was the longest, most destructive, and more costly confrontation of the 1800s, ending with bullets a century that endured eight national civil wars, fourteen provincial civil wars, two international wars with Ecuador, and three military coups. On October 18, 1899, the telegraph of *Villeta, Cundinamarca*, a vacation spot near Bogotá, informed Colombian president Manuel Antonio Sanclemente that a new war had started. Before going silent, the message read: "I run to hide the telegraph apparatuses."[39] The *Thousand Days War*, one of South America's most devastating conflicts, claimed between 60,000 and 180,000 fatalities, and material losses between 250 and 375 million pesos.[40]

Not surprisingly, though conveniently for his imperialist plans, President Theodore Roosevelt openly referred to Colombians as "a nation of barbarians," people in need of civilization by the Anglo-American race.[41] The Colombian rulers were for him a group of Sicilian or Calabrian bandits. If Mexicans had contempt for Hernán Cortés, Colombians felt the same way about Mr. Theodore Roosevelt, his personality, and his administration. In the Colombian archives, there have always been two Roosevelts: "Teddy" the horrible, and Franklin D. Roosevelt, the neighborly.

On November 21, 1902, commanders of the liberal guerrillas signed the peace agreement with the Colombian government, ending the *Thousand Days War* aboard the battleship *Wisconsin*. The United States became not only the uncontested world power of the Western Hemisphere but also its police force, especially within and around Panama. Indeed, U.S. troops landed in the former Colombian Department both on November 25, 1901, and on September 20, 1902, supposedly "to maintain order."[42]

Anglo-American policy makers, whenever Panama was at issue, had nothing but derogatory words against Colombians and other Latin Americans. The U.S. passion for the canal transpired in public declarations such as those of President William H. Taft, who, seeking reelection in 1914, thanked Theodore Roosevelt for freeing the canal from "such a tiny republic (Colombia) of subnormal civilization and morality."[43] Forty-five years earlier (1869), Secretary of State William Seward initiated the canal's campaign with an identical slogan. "We, Americans, are charged with responsibilities of establishing on the American continent a higher condition of civilization and freedom."[44] In the obtuse logic of the Manifest Destiny, "being North Americans the freest of all governmental systems, the world would be served by a canal that made the exporting of both the system's freedoms and goods easier and cheaper."[45]

Panama separated from Colombia with an U.S.-supported insurgency on November 3, 1903. In compensation, Colombians received 25 million dollars and the right to move through the canal, and without cost, exports, passengers, troops, and warships. Cargoes such as oil, salt, and coal would be exempted from duties and their transportation costs would be half of what similar U.S. products had to pay. Before the Panamanian independence, U.S. diplomats thought they would have to pay between 60 and 100 million dollars.[46]

SELF-CENSORSHIP TAKES CENTER STAGE

Like Pulitzer, but well beyond him, José Martí believed that the press should not be a mere vehicle of news nor a servant of meager and egoistic interests. Good newspapers in Martí's thinking were those that served their community and readers, contributing to improve life, our environments, and our societies. The press, teaching, and academia were for Martí a unity that would help citizens understand the reality of their countries. In addition to being watchdogs of the motherland, true newspapers were those that served the people with creativity, generosity, honor, and justice. Journalists who cannot love humankind do not deserve to write, stated Martí.[47]

For the Cuban patriot, liberty, the mother of all rights, inevitably results in peace and wealth. But, the highest level of liberty is achieved only when used to give freedom to those who have less or no liberty at all. According to the Martían code, based on a study by Martínez-Fortún y Foyo, honorable people look forward to, fight, and if necessary die for *true* freedom, that is, for the right of all peoples, not just some, or ours, to enjoy the full benefit of civil liberties. A real journalist, like any honest thinker and creator, cannot be vile and indifferent to human pain. Liberty, wrote Martí, particularly of the press, must be full and sincere. Societies will never be free of tyrants if their public liberties are not vigilantly protected and guaranteed.[48] This has become a sound advice, especially nowadays, both in Anglo- and Latin America.

In his view, freedom should be a constant and daily practice otherwise it will degenerate into an empty formula. If journalists do not help to raise the spirit of the ignorant or less-educated mass, they are voluntarily renouncing their freedom. One of the most consistent themes in the Cuban hero's communication philosophy is the role of the press as an educator. Consequently, if the press, being greedy, condones monopoly and oppression, it is not worthy of being called a press. Any nation for him began in its principles of justice, so it was inconceivable to have writers or reporters not committed to the remedies of social injustice.[49]

As a jurist, graduated from the *Universidad de Zaragoza* in Spain, he believed that freedom of the press and all public liberties could only reign in a world of competitive but even rights. He also recognized the existence of these human prerogatives as natural rights, but their guarantee depends upon the capacity to secure freedom against the ambitions of the greedy. In fact, the purpose of the law, including press laws, should be to secure and expand public wealth rather than to fight for stingy private riches.[50]

A critical man by definition, José Martí vigorously resisted all forms of censorship or restraint. The very nature of this practice was so repulsive to him that even as an art critic, at the time synonymous of a *censor* (a man who criticized), he preferred to keep quiet when having something to condemn and talking openly and graciously when he wanted to praise. In 1882, when former Argentine president Bartolomé Mitre wrote a letter to Martí, apologizing, as a director of the newspaper *La Nación*, for cutting parts of the Cuban journalist's first contribution to his daily (*Carta*), José Martí warmly responded:

Dear Friend:

Being my thinking the way it is, you did well in slowing down my first *Carta* [Letter], for which publication I am deeply thankful. [I]t is my fault not to be able to conceive anything in remnants. [Y]ou tell me that you are giving me the freedom to censor whatever my pen, writing about this world, finds deserving of censorship. But, this is a most painful task for me. In my opinion, criticism is simply the mere exercise of judgment. When criticizing theatrical dramas, keeping silent about how bad they were was my way of saying so. Since applause is the form of approval, it seems that silence is a good enough way of disapproval. [Mr. Mitre,] don't fear the abundance of my [potentially censurable writings]. [I]f there are any censrable contents, they will censor by themselves.[51]

Bartolomé Mitre had deleted certain passages "for his extreme radicalism in the form and his conclusions about the social and political organization of the United States."[52] He thought Martí's assertions could give the false impression, locally and abroad, that *La Nación* was about to initiate a campaign against the United States as a world's political, social, and market center which was contrary to what this daily believed.

Martí confronted various instances of both censorship and self-censorship in Mexico, Guatemala, and Venezuela. In Caracas, for example, he could publish only two numbers of the *Revista Venezolana* (Venezuelan magazine). Unfortunately for Martí, the eulogy to the Venezuelan poet and jurist Cecilio Acosta, published on July 21, 1881, caught the attention of the country's three times president Antonio Guzmán Blanco (1829–1899). An expert of intrigue and propaganda like his father, the liberal Guzmán-Blanco considered Martí a dangerous foreigner, and after a personal interview with the Cuban writer, the latter decided to leave Venezuela and return to New York.[53]

All too well, Martí knew what it was like to work in countries of strong caudillos. Like Porfirio Díaz in México, Guzmán Blanco was a vertical figure of the top-down modernization that built factories, railroads, and telegraph lines, subsidizing friendly presses and closing opposition newspapers. After a few months in Caracas and shattered dreams of a South American–Caribbean media project, he decided to return to New York, accepting a request to regularly contribute to the Venezuelan *La Opinión Nacional*. Fausto Teodoro de Aldrey, the publisher, wanted him to send news stories from around the world which he received in the form of vivid and successful Martían chronicles.

But Aldrey's journalistic guidelines, both his and his son's, became so limiting and censoring that Martí decided to stop writing for *La Opinión* less than a year later. As he put it, "what a huge torment is feeling able to write the greatest and being forced to write the puerile."[54] Although personally and professionally they both were far from Mitre's leadership, the Venezuelan publishers also wanted Martí to write ultimately friendly columns to the *status quo*. In the last issue of the *Revista Universal* (November 19, 1876) and in *El Federalista*, Martí had clearly resolved this apparent conflict, preferring to leave his beloved friends and American republics rather than endorsing what he considered unjust.

The same occurred to him in Guatemala, where he could not publish his planned *Revista Guatemalteca* (1878) because a fellow Cuban and loyal friend, director of the *Escuela Normal* where Martí worked, was forced to quit for ideological differences with the Guatemalan president. A truly useful magazine, to be printed in the context of an educational institution such as the *Normal*, could not be possible in an atmosphere of high-level official harassment. Even in the United States, Martí complained about Dana, the *Sun*'s editor's journalistic schemes; Dana's stubborn press formulas were ultimately in conflict with Martí's open, literary, and critical journalism of the late 1800s.

In spite of the increasing voices of modernity, which Martí, like most advanced leaders of the time, fully supported, Latin America continued to breed *caudillos* that censored people and the press. In Colombia, for instance, the *Regeneración*'s ultraconservative censorship took over during the late 1800s. President *Rafael Núñez*, its principal exponent, believed that printing presses were incompatible with progress. For him, a libertarian press was a source of war, ceaseless friction, and lack of respect. Consequently, the *Regeneración* was a time for heavy censorship and totalitarianism.

Under the excuse of "a free but responsible" press (art. 42 of the National Constitution), constant suspensions, premature closures, and an unrelenting official harassment targeted opposition newspapers. One of its legendary victims was the existing liberal daily *El Espectador*, Colombia's oldest newspaper. Denouncing the abuses of the Núñez administration in 1887, and challenging the republic's narrow centralism, publisher Fidel Cano launched both *El Espectador* and *La Consigna*, the latter in association with liberal hero of *The Thousand Days War*, Rafael Uribe Uribe.

The Ministry of Interior mailed a kind dispatch to *El Correo Nacional*: "I share with you this executive order whereby your newspaper is suspended. It will be published tomorrow, so I sent it in advance for you to make proper arrangements."[55] Right after the painful *Thousand-Day* civil war (1899–1902) and the separation of Panama, national governments decided that to foster communication technology and infrastructure was the way to go, primarily in connection to foreign centers. "It is not liberty what generates power," wrote again historian Luis Ospina Vásquez, commenting on the ideas of Colombian president Rafael Reyes (1904–1909); quite the contrary, "it is progress what brings about freedom," they said.[56]

Social science professor Alcira Argumedo of the University of Buenos Aires, author of *Los silencios y las voces en América Latina* (Silences and voices in Latin America), argues that our America's spirit is the sum of all Native, Creole, and Black resistance to colonialism, a worldview where thoughts of extraordinary leaders converge into a collective sentiment (from Tupac Amaru, Artigas, Dorrego, and San Martín to Bolívar, Simón Rodríguez, Hidalgo, Morelos y Martí, just to name a few). In fact, in academic circles, she says, "it is difficult to accept that Tupac Amaru's thinking has an equivalence to his contemporary Immanuel Kant; or that it is possible to compare Bolívar, Artigas, Hidalgo, and Morelos with Hegel, or José Martí and Leandro Alem with Weber. Nevertheless, when discrimination and the scorn against the poor are once again in vogue, the legacy of these Latin American leaders gain a special significance, in particular when it comes to tracing a different future for Latin America."[57]

Surviving grandparents can sit down today with their grandchildren in Latin America or elsewhere, and tell them, out of personal experience, how not to start a new century. The vicious circle of war waiting on the early 1900s resembles the turn of the twentieth century. Deep inequalities and poverty, human rights and corporate abuses, oligarchical greed, widespread corruption, dangerous pollution, and technological advances with no popular progress marked the last 100 years from beginning to end. It has been a comparably stagnant reality where decent levels of existence, human dignity, and the liberty to effectively express their mind are distant promises for most people.

If the year 1900 welcomed the planet with the tragic Balkan wars, leading humanity into the devastating World War I and World War II and the bloody prelude of Franco's Spain plus the violent aftermaths of Palestine, Korea, Vietnam, South Africa, Central America, and the Southern Cone, the revamped war against terrorism after 9/11 is indeed a sordid legacy for the new generations.

At least, this is the prevailing perception, since a so-called "terrorism index," announced by *Foreign Policy* magazine in Washington D.C., recently reported that 79 percent of surveyed U.S. American experts (intelligence agents, military veterans, scholars, and journalists, both liberal and conservative) believe that a new mass terrorist attack is unavoidable within five years and that the world is more dangerous for the United States because of terrorism.[58] The Incas, on the other hand, observes Argumedo, used to believe that every 500 years the world turned upside down. Hopefully, since after so much war it is the time for peace, we will see the Inca prophecy fulfilled, rather than the U.S. prediction.[59]

Chapter 6

Hot and Cold Wars, Warm Presses

Before World War I, Latin Americans tended to admire Europe more than the United States in most fields, including journalism. Yet, Anglo-America and particularly New York City enjoyed a dynamic and increasing reputation among innovators who foresaw North America playing a greater and influential role in international affairs. Following the Panama Canal crisis, both Latin Americans and Europeans knew that the United States had the technological, military, and economic capability to not only achieve but also secure a dominant position in the Western Hemisphere. Few, if anyone, however, would have ever guessed that the United States would finish the century as the uncontested global power it is today.

THE OLD PARADIGM DIES

Europe may have been the cradle of modern concepts of freedom and liberty but, at the turn of the twentieth century, the Old Continent suffered from a poor image in terms of the respect and protection of civil liberties, particularly freedom of expression. Traditional rulers in European states continued to "detest the idea of a free press," so much that aristocrats considered it "the greatest and most urgent evil, the most malignant and formidable enemy to the constitution."[1] Dictators such as Spanish prime minister General Ramón María de Naváez (1844–1866), Duke of Valencia, had come to declare that "it [was] not enough to confiscate newspapers, for [rulers] must also kill all the journalists," and it was not a joke.[2]

The same continent, where the Age of Enlightenment had warned countries not to restrain thoughts and opinions, for they would fall into stupidity, superstition, and barbarism, was the same geography where authorities, primarily in Spain, France, Austria, Germany, England, and Switzerland, used the death penalty to sanction speakers for treason, heresy, and seditious libel. Licensing, book burning, tax penalties, import prohibitions, administrative restraints or crackdowns, and other forms of censorship and self-censorship became customary in Europe, pushing repressive measures even in remaining colonial enclaves, with some of them found in the Americas as late as the Cold War.[3] We still have a few.

Regulation of the European press was in full force in the late 1800s, notably in Spain, France, Germany, Russia, Serbia, and Austria. In Spain, for example, there had been at least fifteen major press laws and decrees throughout the nineteenth century, and in France, a major press law reform (1881) supposedly passed to clarify confusions on speech and media regulation among judges, lawyers, and journalists. France and Spain, in addition to England, Germany, and Italy, had been the most legally influential nineteenth-century models in Latin America. A reflection of this legal dependence is the continuous effort of Latin American republics to replicate media policy frameworks of leading European nations.

There is a definite reason why European authorities became active against the press: the spreading of Marxism and anarchism, being both quite different as political philosophies. According to the late and distinguished professor Everett M. Rogers, father of diffusionism in modern development studies, Karl Marx's critical thinking along with Charles Darwin's evolutionary theory and Sigmund Freud's psychoanalytic method are the pillars of communication study. "They are the three most important theorists of the past century," wrote Rogers in 1994, "[t]heir ideas crossed the Atlantic and had important impacts on the beginnings of social science in America."[4] A 1990 survey of area journals and scholars in Latin America showed that after the Belgian Armand Mattelart, writers such as Karl Marx, Eliseo Verón, Daniel Lerner, Luis Ramiro Beltrán, Wilbur Schramm, Antonio Gramsci, Herbert Schiller, Paulo Freire, Everett Rogers, and Umberto Eco were leading individual influences.[5] The Frankfurt School and most Latin American media approaches, particularly the dependency, alternative communication, and statist theories, drank at one point from the fountain of Marxism.

If Darwin was condemned by religious leaders and Freud had his books burned, Marx, stated Rogers, "faced exile from his native Germany for his revolutionary political views—first to Paris, then to Belgium, and finally to London." In the United States, college professors, filmmakers, and writers, among other intellectuals, "were fired, ridiculed, and persecuted in various ways" for sharing his ideas. Both Marx and Freud had also been discriminated against as Jews. "One might think that [Marxism] would be studied carefully by all students of social science; yet in many countries, Marx's books [have been] banned," commented Rogers.[6]

In an interesting anthology, Spanish author Vicente Romano writes why "Marx's and Engels' texts about journalism, the press, and communication are one of the least known and analyzed aspects of these great thinkers and revolutionaries. Even Marxists themselves ignore the fact that journalism played an important role in the lives of Marx and Engels, giving their journalistic works a marginal or secondary status. Yet, if their first profession was to be revolutionaries, their second one was to be journalists, the only activity providing Marx with some remuneration throughout his life, from a young age to his older days."[7] In fact, he says, both leaders not only edited newspapers and magazines but also contributed to numerous European and North American press organizations, including *The New York Daily Tribune* (between 1851 and 1862).[8]

In sum, Marxism gradually became an inspiration for the national workers' press in the Americas, although not all newspapers called *El Obrero* (The Worker) or *La Voz del Pueblo* (The People's Voice) were necessarily socialists nor Marxists. In 1855, the seventeen-year-old and pro-Mexican journalist Francisco Ramírez founded *El Clamor Público* (The Public Clamor) in Los Angeles, denouncing how the Anglo-American conquerors of California "treated [Mexicans] 'worse than slaves.' The U.S. democracy," wrote Ramírez, "is a 'lynchocracy.' [H]e move[d] back to Mexico, urging others to do the same."[9]

In 1869, also as a teenager, the last great liberator José Martí published the one and only issue of *La Patria Libre* (The Free Fatherland), for which he was jailed and eventually expatriated. Then, in January 1880, after persecutions in Mexico and Guatemala, José Martí arrived in New York City, wherefrom he sent Cubans and other Latin Americans stories about labor strikes, lynchings, an earthquake, and notes about the Statute of Liberty and Brooklyn Bridge.[10]

Near the turn of the century, explain professors Douglas M. Fraleigh and Joseph S. Tuman, industrial workers, itinerants, immigrants, and people of color posed a significant threat to social order in the United States, seeking "to abolish capitalism and replace it with egalitarian socialism."[11] Martí was living in New York then when Eugene Debs, the socialist labor leader who eventually received more than 900,000 votes in a presidential election while in prison, organized the Pullman strike in 1894, "a major protest by railroad workers that halted rail traffic in Chicago until it was broken by federal troops."[12] That same year, Martí planned to launch an expedition to liberate Cuba but he was intercepted in Fernandina, Florida. Like Debs, the Cuban "apostle" had also supported several labor strikes, particularly one at the tobacco factory "*La Rosa Española*" in Key West in January 1894, where he confronted Spanish strikebreakers.[13]

Marxism, socialism, and labor movements were obviously not strange to Martí, nor were they to the history of journalism, even after the fall of the Berlin Wall. As Professor Bryant Jennings and Dr. Dora

Miron concluded in a media theory survey published in 2004, after the agenda setting, uses and gratifications, and cultivation theories, Marxism continues to be the most popular mass communications perspective of modern times.

Few scholars and practitioners, however, know how Marx and Engels conceptualized the role of the mass media in society. How many critics or followers know that Marx believed that "the lack of freedom of the press was a serious impediment for the advancement of a democratic movement?"[14]

For Marx, journalism and public opinion were intimately connected to the issue of freedom. The print media, as a form and instrument of expression, were on the one hand a social activity and on the other, a matter of power and social class. Thus, he wrote, "the first freedom of the press is not to become a [commercial] industry. A journalist, as any author, can only be really free when supported by the knowledge of objective needs, making decisions based on that [objective reality]."[15] We could even find traces of the theory of objective journalism in Marxism. Years later, Vladimir Ilyich Ulyanov, Lenin, did much to trivialize the original Marxist media approach, implementing the notion of a journalist simply as a collective organizer, educator, and propagandist. Why should anyone care about Marxist media views in contemporary society? Just as the numerous defenders of liberalism and the media marketplace, Marxism continues to exert a significant influence on critical observers of the status quo.

It is not Marxism, however, that represents a most intriguing episode in the history of the region's news media before World War I (that is, besides the absorbing events of the Mexican Revolution of 1910), it is the launching of a journalism education crusade in the United States to influence the world as far as China, beginning with the already mentioned Missouri School (September 14, 1908) and the Columbia University Graduate School of Journalism (September 30, 1912).[16] One of the first Latin Americans to graduate from the influential Columbia University J-School was the Puerto Rican Manuel Barbosa (Class of 1924), son of the prominent politician José Celso Barbosa, a so-called "Man of the People."

Children of the first black to attend the also prestigious Jesuit Seminary in Puerto Rico, the Barbosas learned much about both impediments for workers to become professionals and the problems of racial prejudice. Founder of the Republican Party and the newspaper *El Tiempo*, Don José Celso, and his two journalist sons (Pedro Juan and Manuel) promoted the cause of statehood, even if U.S. citizens and their press could not distinguish between the flag of Cuba and the flag of Puerto Rico.[17] In fact, as mentioned earlier, in a Harper's Weekly's article about the Cuban liberation against Spain (*"Insurgent cavalry drawn up for a charge"*), Frederic Remington mistakenly painted the Cuban flag in Puerto Rico's colors.[18]

Despite the educational flaws of the dynamic new and yellow journalism, Joseph Pulitzer's immortal image and Walter Williams's lasting philosophy gradually impacted Latin American print and broadcast media in significant ways. Journalism courses or schools had been created in Missouri, Wisconsin, New York, and Virginia (today's Washington and Lee University in honor of newspaper education pioneer, General Robert E. Lee) because, before 1910, "conditions in education for journalism were bad."[19] In a personal mission, for instance, Dean Williams, not Mary Gardner, traveled for the first time to Mexico City in order to train reporters on the expanding philosophy of the U.S. model of journalism education.

He lectured in March 1926 at the National University of Mexico, with translations by the young Mexican reporter Antonio Vargas of *El Universal*, the same newspaper in which *Señorita Bringas*, a socialist and a correspondent to several U.S. newspapers, had written extensively about education, politics, and famous literary figures. Williams discovered how different, wordy, and creative Latin American journalists could be when his ten-minute presentation turned into a fifty-minute translation by Vargas. "Many practicing journalists attended the course," wrote Henry Lepidus, "and those who satisfactorily passed an examination on it at the end were awarded suitable diplomas."[20] As credentials in journalism grew more and more fashionable, schools of journalism and, eventually, of communication became commonplace across Latin America and the Caribbean. Yet, the region's first J-School emerged in Argentina, not Mexico.

Thus, it was not a coincidence that the earliest Maria Moors Cabot Prize for distinguished contributions to "Inter-American understanding," the oldest international award in journalism (since 1939), had been granted to the Sunday editor of the Argentinean daily *La Prensa*, Mr. José Santos Gollan. Another gold medal went in the same ceremony to the already mentioned Don Luis Miró Quesada, president of the board in *El Comercio*, the legendary Peruvian daily, founded exactly a hundred years before this reputable academic consecration.

Since then, prominent editors and reporters from Alaska to Patagonia have marched across the solemn rotunda of Columbia University's Low Memorial Library, including the memorable Rafael Heliodoro Valle (a Honduran bibliographer and correspondent in Mexico), Elmano Cardim (managing editor, *Jornal do Comércio*, Brazil), Jorge Délano (cartoonist and editor, *Topaze Magazine*, Chile), Jules Dubois (Latin America correspondent, *The Chicago Tribune*), Arturo Schaerer (editor, *La Tribuna*, Paraguay), Tad Szulc (Latin America correspondent, *The New York Times*), Alejandro Carrión (columnist, *El Universo*, Ecuador), Germán Arciniegas (columnist *Cuadernos*, Colombia), James Nelson Goodsell (editor, *The Christian Science Monitor*), Alceu Amoroso (an essayist and literary critic from Rio de Janeiro, Brazil), John D. Harbron (associate editor, *The Toronto Telegram*, Canada), Julio Scherer-García (general director, *El Excélsior*, Mexico), Arturo-Uslar-Pietri (editor-in-chief, *El Nacional*, Venezuela), and many others.

In the beginning, Columbia University's Graduate J-School had a tendency to praise media owners, publishers, and politicians more than newsroom reporters. Powerful Latin American media figures obviously popped up, such as Agustín E. Edwards (*El Mercurio*, Chile), Enrique Santos Montejo (*El Tiempo*, Colombia), Luis Mitre (*La Nación*, Argentina), Alberto Lleras Camargo (*Pan American Union*), Roberto Marinho (*O Globo*, Brazil), Emilio Azcárraga Vidaurreta (*Cadena Radiodifusora Mexicana* and *Telesistema Mexicano*, Mexico), Eduardo Santos (*El Tiempo*, Colombia), Rómulo O'Farrill (*Novedades*, Mexico), Rodolfo Junco de la Vega (*El Norte* and *El Sol*, Mexico), and John S. Knight (*The Knight Newspapers* and *The Miami Herald*). Even the once well-financed Monsignor José Joaquín Salcedo (*Acción Cultural Popular*, Colombia) received a medal in his golden days.

In time, the school realized that it was far more rewarding to condecorate career columnists and newsmen and women, not politicians or media moguls. One brilliant winner, Colombian columnist Daniel Samper Pizano, wrote in a humorous note soon after the ceremony (his *Al fin y al Cabot*), "it was much more difficult for me to obtain my high school diploma in Bogotá [Colombia] than to come up to the podium of one of the world's top universities, dressed as a medieval "scholar," and return condecorated and graduated. Indeed, . . . to get my high school diploma I had to pay and pass [all kinds of exams in physics, chemistry, trigonometry, biology, Latin and French]; for the one in journalism, all I had to do was to write a couple of pages for which they pay me—badly—but, nonetheless, paid me."[21]

Not only people but also organizations in the news business started to receive condecorations and diplomas for their innovation, following World War I. Within two years of the First Journalism Congress of Washington DC (February 1922), the City of Quito, for instance, awarded Carlos Mantilla of *El Comercio* and his sons a "Golden Medal and Diploma" because of their company's modernization, both physically and technologically, turning the newspaper into an ideal enterprise in Ecuador.[22] By then, and in practice (not necessarily in theory), the old European news media paradigm was falling behind in "modern" Latin America.

THE U.S. MODEL ARRIVES

Because of admiration, fear, or respect, prominent state reformers such as Bartolomé Mitre and Domingo Faustino Sarmiento in Argentina, Porfirio Díaz in Mexico, Antonio Guzmán Blanco in Venezuela, and

Rafael Reyes in Colombia, among others, began to look more closely at the Anglo-American experience. The purpose was to emulate North American innovation processes and approaches in order to promote similar developments in their own republics. Economic regulation since the civil war (1861–1865) drew an increasing attention, if not a fascination in various Latin American states. To imitate and implement successful U.S. American formulas became the basic goal of several Latin American rulers.

Evidently, the United States represented an interesting alternative to European models, but it was also a social and legal system full of major contradictions and struggles. Justice Oliver Wendell Holmes Jr. and his father, the writer and physician Oliver Wendell Holmes (1809–1894), clearly exemplified the inconsistencies of Anglo-America in their family evolution.

Reluctant to condemn slavery in the late 1800s, Oliver Wendell Holmes Sr., the "doctor-poet" as Martí called him, was nonetheless a harsh critic of dominant Calvinist dogmas of New English and particularly Bostonian aristocrats like himself. Holmes' devotion for newspapers was also noteworthy, and Jeffersonian type of statements, such as the one made during the civil war about bread and newspapers being the only needs of man, caused admiration among literary critics like Martí. "Everything else we can do without," said Holmes.[23]

But, other Holmesian statements greatly worried Latin American leaders and intellectuals like Martí. As Holmes once affirmed: "We [U.S. Americans] are today's Romans, and both war and conquests will be our constant activities. We are the Romans of the modern world—the great assimilating people. Conflicts and conquests are of course necessary accidents with us."[24] Still, his reputation as a lively writer and a free press defender made Holmes an eclectic man, a middle ground fellow as José Martí commented in *La Opinión Nacional* of Montevideo.[25]

Oliver Wedell Holmes Jr., the influential and charismatic Associate Justice of the U.S. Supreme Court, grew up in this environment. For thirty years (1902–1932), his opinions and dissents would shake the highest court of the Union, introducing lasting liberal rationales on free press and speech cases. Holmes, the justice, stood up against monopoly powers, the abuse of workers, and the blinded reliance on laissez-faire dogmas espoused by Spencerian legal theorists. A modern advocate of the free marketplace of ideas borrowed from John Milton's *Areopagitica*, Justice Holmes favored the public interest and the protection of the weak whenever the balance of competition had been broken.[26] Even so, concerning Latin America, his debut as a Supreme Court justice served to further colonize Puerto Rico, not free it.

At the peak of the Anglo-American industrialization and the advance of its hemispheric power, Justice Holmes, based on the tradition of both Milton's defense for a free press and the commerce clause of the U.S. Constitution (art. 1, sec. 8, cl. 3), formulated two major theories that would eventually impact the entire continent: the *Clear and Present Danger Doctrine* and the *Marketplace of Ideas* concept. These rationales, proposed in the *Red Scare* era of socialist and anarchist worker's movements during World War I, would be gradually adopted in the Americas during the second half of the twentieth century—especially the marketplace of ideas.

Used for the first time in 1919, this metaphor argued "that the ultimate good desired is better reached by free trade in ideas. [And] that the best test of truth is the power of the thought to get itself accepted in competition of the market."[27] Holmes' marketplace theory intended, on the one hand, to tolerate unorthodox or unpopular expression that the majority found offensive while promoting, on the other hand, the remedy of more speech rather than less to counteract bad or harmful ideas.

The prominent jurist employed this concept after the U.S. Supreme Court had produced a series of unanimous convictions against speeches and publications of activists of the working class (some of them leading socialists), misusing another approach, the clear and present danger test. According to Holmes, the question was whether the words used created a clear and present danger bringing about the substantive evils Congress had the right to prevent.[28] Within one week in 1919, the top federal court turned his doctrine into a repressive "bad tendency test" that served to convict activists such as Eugene V. Debs for their political beliefs.

In *Schenck* v. *United States*, Holmes delivered the opinion of the court, joining later the unanimous decisions in *Frohwerk*[29] and *Debs*.[30] A Socialist Party candidate, the imprisoned Eugene Debs received nearly one million votes for president in 1920. But in *Abrams* v. *United States*, Holmes and his fellow Justice Louis Brandeis finally realized the danger of the legal distortion of "automatic" convictions, filing historical dissents for the marketplace and the clear and present danger tests in *Abrams* and *Gitlow* v. *New York* (1925). In this last case, he reminded the court that speech or press convictions under the clear and present danger doctrine required proof of an imminent danger.

Eventually, Latin America would pay close attention to the U.S. First Amendment debate, particularly, though not exclusively, during the last quarter of the twentieth century. In 1917, by the time Schenck was being tried in the United States, Mexico also had serious challenges regarding the use of printed and verbal communications in political and war contexts. Hoping to stop remaining passions, imminent dangers, and further confrontations of the 1910 Revolution, the government of President Venustiano Carranza passed the still existing *Ley de Imprenta de 1917* (Press Law of 1917). After revolutionary leaders Pancho Villa and Emiliano Zapata had been practically but not totally defeated by Carranza's forces, the federal government proscribed media attacks to privacy, morality, and the public order. To guarantee the public peace, the Press Law of 1917 ordered that:

> All malicious expression publicly made by means of speeches, yelling, singing, threats, writings, printings, drawings, lithography, photography, cinematography, engravings, or any other form, with the purpose to disparage, ridicule, or destroy the country's fundamental institutions; or to offend the Mexican nation or the public entities that form her ... shall be subject to a fine and an arrest minimum of one month and maximum of eleven months.[31]

Article 3, numeral 2 of the same law also prohibits as a breach of the public peace all media expressions that advise, incite, or provoke, directly or indirectly, members of the army to disobedience, rebellion, or dispersion. Or when communications invite the general public to anarchy, sedition, or rebellion, or to disobedience against the law and the legitimate authorities. In the same token, insults against the public authorities to generate hatred, contempt, or ridicule of public offices, the army or any public official will also be subject to the penalties mentioned above.[32] In Mexico there were fears of clear, patent, and imminent dangers, but unlike Holmes' dissenting opinions in the United States, the Mexican federal authorities were interested in silencing speech rather than finding a broader definition of this right.

From railway and telegraph laws to monopoly regulation, Mexico borrowed evolving U.S. media policy principles in the early 1900s. In her Constitution of 1917, article 28 prescribed that in the United Mexican States, either monopolies or monopolistic practices were to be severely sanctioned. With authorities effectively prosecuting any concentration of economic power in a few hands, antimonopoly laws were expected to condemn any exclusive industry or trade advantage to one or several individuals in detriment of the general public or any social class.[33]

Going beyond the unprecedented remedy of the U.S. Sherman Act of 1890, and from a social rather than the purely individual, natural rights perspective of the laissez-faire approach, the Mexican Constitution granted federal authorities ample powers to pursue the public, national, and people's interest.[34] Of the fairly small group of Latin American nations with antimonopoly laws (Brazil, Colombia, Chile, Guatemala, Haiti, Peru, and Venezuela), legally, that is, theoretically, Mexico emerged as a pioneer and model example of antitrust regulation. Unfortunately, telecommunications (one of several strategic areas) were excluded from the antimonopoly philosophy of the 1917 Constitution, including mail, telegraph, and radiotelegraph services.[35]

By the mid-1950s, and violating the supreme Mexican law, the Adolfo Ruiz Cortines administration (1952–1958) approved the merger of the *Telesistema Mexicano* (*TSM*). The Mexican telesystem combined the Azcárraga family concessions, XEW-TV (channel 2) and XHGC-TV (channel 5), with the O'Farrill family's XH-TV (channel 4), Mexico's television pioneer. Channel 4, inaugurated on August 31, 1950, also emerged as Latin America's first operational television station, three weeks before *Tupi-TV* of Brazil and two months ahead of *Union Radio TV* of Cuba.[36]

The antimonopoly exemption for television, invented by the government, revolved around the legal fiction that the above Mexican channels were separately licensed, operated, and administrated, when, in practice, Emilio Azcárraga Vidaurreta effectively controlled the three concessions. During the next four decades, television would be a puppet of the state; conversely, in a significant degree, every president would also be a puppet of television. President Miguel Alemán Valdés (1946–1952) and his political and economic interests in O'Farrill's television venture constituted an obvious example of the latter.[37] In 1993, via-satellite communications expanded the list of strategic areas exempted from the antimonopoly clause of article 28, but two years later, as part of the dominant privatization of the late twentieth century, both railroads and satellite communications were taken off the roll to promote these industries' competition and commercialization.[38]

For the most part, up to the 1980s, the vast majority of Latin American countries followed the state intervention of the Roman law tradition in communications, mostly the French, Italian, and German systems. British models and principles were also used in balancing public and private interests. But, without critical legal inquiries like those advanced by Holmes and Brandeis in the United States, the Latin American press laws systematically sanctioned expressions that posed a threat to public order, religious morality, and individual honor. With the exception of Colombia and Jamaica, press rules of *Desacato*, punishing any contempt against government authorities, not just judges, plagued the Latin American media throughout the nineteenth and twentieth centuries.[39] The U.S. legal, as opposed to the economic, technological, and professional media frameworks, would not be evident or even dominant in Latin American communication until the deregulatory, technocratic, and overly commercial spirit of the Reagan years.

SMALL PROGRESS, BIG RESTRAINTS

Industry, education, and telecommunication progress began a firm upward trend with President Rafael Reyes (1904–1909) in Colombia. Yet, government censorship against the media remained equally strong. Nevertheless, if a newspaper were to be fined for any reason, the publication would try to stay on after the penalty; if suspended, it would also carry on until a new suspension. In those years, new journals emerged every time a newspaper was forced to close. That was the dynamics of the Colombian opposition press in the early 1900s.

From Rafael Núñez's *Regeneration* (1884–1894) to Miguel Abadía-Méndez's *Banana-Styled Republic* (1926–1930), imprisonment, exile, and administrative repression dominated. For a painful period of four decades, these two presidents and their colleagues, including presidents Miguel Antonio Caro (1894–1898), Jose Vicente Concha (1914–1918), Marco Fidel Suárez (1918–1921), and Pedro Nel Ospina (1922–1926), silenced dissenting voices against their programs or concepts of national unity.[40]

During Núñez and Caro's presidency, law 61 of 1888, known as *"Ley de los Caballos"* (Law of the Horses), imposed physical isolation, expulsion from the country, incarceration, and suspension of political rights with cynical regularity. The crime to punish was to dare criticizing the regime, altering the public tranquility and order. A transitory provision of the 1886 Constitution, *article K*, along with *Decree 635* of the same year and the Penal Code (1837), which was reformed to include the death penalty, brought the political and press repression to terrifying levels. Article K prescribed that until a press law was adopted, the government was authorized to both prevent and repress the abuses of newspapers. Thus, to write against Núñez or Caro was a mortal gamble.[41]

One prominent example of the (conservative) persecution against opposition newspapers at that time was *El Espectador*. Born in Medellín on March 22, 1887, this Liberal Party became an immediate target after declaring that its goal was to denounce the authoritarian regime of General Rafael Núñez and his conservative centralization policies. In 1887, Cano also launched *La Consigna*, a newspaper in association with the Liberal *caudillo* Rafael Uribe Uribe. Favoring openness, free commerce, and free enterprise, both newspapers promised to inform Colombians with a partisan and patriotic liberal criteria.

The regeneration leaders of the Conservative Party deplored the tone of these and other liberal publications. By the turn of the twentieth century, opposition newspapers such as *El Relator, El Demócrata, El Correo Nacional, El Gladiador, Voz del Tiempo, El Constitucional, El 93, El Contemporáneo, El Progreso, El Reproductor, El Posta, El Republicano, El Derecho, El Debate, La Consigna*, and *El Espectador* had all been suspended. Their editors, including the prestigious Santiago Pérez, Rafael Uribe Uribe, Fidel Cano, Santos Acosta, the "Indian" Uribe, Jose María Vargas-Vila, and Cesar Conto, among others, had also been jailed or exiled. President Caro's argument was that the opposition had unfortunately preferred to be "revolutionary rather than reasonable," and that security imperatives "fully justify the suspension of a newspaper."[42]

In this early combination of *reasonableness* with a sort of *clear and present danger* doctrine in press cases, Caro concluded: "The instinct of social preservation have always spoken against the propagation of subversive and immoral writings."[43] Similarly, Núñez had also declared that the printing press was incompatible with the lengthy task of governing, and that newspapers were elements of war not peace, just like secret clubs, continuous elections, and congresses independent of executive authorities.[44] Not surprisingly, *Don* Fidel Cano, founder of *El Espectador*, labeled the infamous *Ley 61 de 1888* as the Law of the Horses, for only "blinded animals" like carriage horses in a street could be so narrow in scope.

The modernizing General Reyes, authoritarian and almost Prussian in his government style, also relied on the above-mentioned statute. But, opposition newspapers failed to recognize the revolutionary departures of this administration from the past, primarily Reyes' sense of a national and capitalistic modernity beyond the agrarian provincialism of his predecessors. During the first quarter of the twentieth century, Colombian publications mirrored a polity where imperialistic pressures, internal battles, and widespread inequality dominated. The country's semi-industrialized and foreign-owned businesses gradually resulted in masses of overexploited and underpaid workers. Union papers such as *El Socialista, El Obrero Moderno* (the Modern Worker), *El Ideal Obrero* (The Ideal Worker), and so on, began to emerge.

One interesting exception was the legalistic government of the liberal Carlos E. Restrepo (1910–1914). In spite of strong pressures from both the Church and the national conservative opposition, Restrepo tenaciously defended press freedom and other civil liberties. "I am Catholic" he once said, "but as a head of state who respects the constitution I cannot turn myself into the Pope of any creed. If freedom of the press in modern nations is not the first liberty, press freedom is indeed the pillar, the essential condition of all of them." Newspapers must be free, he added, and "they should be responsible only to the judicial power."[45] Restrepo's civilized government and his respect for freedom of the press were however the exception, not the rule.

Like General Reyes, though less amicably and diplomatically, *caudillo* and President Eloy Alfaro (1895–1901 and 1906–1911) led an administration of "liberals" in Ecuador that combined brutal force, Liberal politics, infrastructure development, and censorship all at the same time. On July 1, 1908, cheering the completion of the Quito–Guayaquil Railroad (*The Guayaquil and Quito Railway Company*), Ecuadorian ambassador to Colombia General Julio Andrade pointed out: "This morning was officially inaugurated the railroad that links my country's capital [Quito] with the Pacific Coast (Guayaquil). Its construction began forty years ago and since 1897 efforts have gone uninterrupted. The railroad exists thanks to British and U.S. capital and entrepreneurs, and [it represents] truth, progress, and man to man and people to people cooperation. Let's have a toast in honor of our respective presidents, Reyes, the patriot, and Alfaro, the fighter, whom history might not catalogue as great men, but that we are in our own right to call them useful for both Colombia and Ecuador."[46]

Echoing the official enthusiasm, the prestigious Ecuadorian daily *El Comercio* agreed that the railroad would be the base of any future progress in commerce and agriculture, science, the arts, and other expressions of human activity.[47] Railroads, according to this paper, were "a divine monster" as much as "a redemption," for they would enhance commerce as a source of hope in a lasting political, cultural, and economic stability. Ultimately, that was the reason why this daily adopted the name of *El Comercio*, convinced that freedom of the press was also a column in any free-trade, liberal, and commercial social system. Quito's *El Comercio* had been founded along this philosophy on January 1, 1906.

Still, eighteen months before the conclusion of the Quito line, this same daily denounced that the *Guayaquil and Quito Company* had been a corrupted and detrimental project to the treasury of a poor country like Ecuador. Without investing any capital (for the slow construction had been entirely financed with government bonds), this company basically "fills their pockets with as much money as they could get their hands on."[48] This depravity was partly attributed to General Alfaro's dictatorship.

Ecuador, commented *El Comercio*, "supposedly a free nation," brought back by the will of the army a president interested in disorder, official abuse, and robbery.[49] Five years later, General Eloy Alfaro, a Liberal opposed to individual and constitutional guarantees, had to resign, taking political asylum in the Chilean embassy. On that day (August 12, 1911), *El Comercio* applauded the Ecuadorian military and congressional demands for the president's resignation, as follows:

> Sovereignty, an indispensable element in the organization of a state ... is based in the preservation of order within the limits of liberty, justice, and the law. [D]eadly threatened by the oligarchy and by an infamous autocracy, Gen. Alfaro's designation is the only legitimate means to [restore] the constitutional and republican life in Ecuador. [He], Gen. Alfaro, created this situation after prostrating the people with a vicious, fraudulent, and tyrannical administration, devoted to illegality in order to perpetuate himself in power.[50]

Lynched by a mob of fellow partisans on January 28, 1912, Alfaro's body was disrobed, dragged through the streets, hacked to pieces, and incinerated.[51] Like Núñez in Colombia, General Alfaro's regime (coincidentally called *Regeneración* as well) ended its political cycle with the same and historic popular disdain, though more tragically. "With disgust," wrote the *Indio* Uribe on Núñez's death (1894), "the ground has swallowed up the [Colombian] monster of tyranny."[52]

REVOLUTION RESUMES

In Mexico, President Francisco I. Madero (1911–1913) led a social revolution that marked the history of this hemisphere. Launching innovative though extremely polarized journals, the *Revolution Mexicana* (1910–1917), strengthened three aspects of this country's journalism profession: the value of public opinion, the significant role of the printed word, and the importance of both technology and technique in news reporting.

In a statement that could be easily applied to most Latin American societies before the Cuban and Sandinista revolutions, Carlos Monsiváis, the thoughtful Mexican critic and author, explains his native country's uprising and early modernization as follows:

"Mexican culture has two big moments in the twentieth century that both defines it and organizes it. The first one is the Mexican Revolution, formally ending with the nineteenth century. [Abandoning] the idea of trying to be like France, [t]he Mexican Revolution, as [Octavio] Paz affirmed in *The Laberynth of Solitude*, brings up a grand revelation, the realization that things that could not emerge in the past because of the compulsion to imitate might suddenly come up. Now, anyone could see, better than ever, what the revolution meant in terms of new characters, new forms of speech previously repressed, new worldviews, and the way a revolution changed borders and the whole country.

To begin with—continues Monsiváis—hundreds of thousands of people, who lived in full or near-slavery conditions, either traveled for the first time, went out and saw different towns, experienced the railroad, or visited and admired the big cities. Between 1910 and 1930, this revolution changed situations and conditions, starting with the generational flows within the government [and the military]. It also unearthed something hidden, something real and uncertain: the nationalism, that is, that cultural [sentiment] that dominated from the 1920s to the 1950s. Curiously, it arose on behalf of the international proletarianism led by the muralist school of Diego Riovera, José Clemente Orozco, and David Alfaro Siqueiros, [...] proclaiming the existence of a rearranged nation, remade by the revolutionary movement."[53]

The second big moment, for both Mexico and Latin America, concludes Monsiváis, is when modernity arrives. "Being modern," he writes, "becomes [everyone's] and everyday's enterprise, a need to either break with or reconcile with the past, placing it in a museum." Surely, printing presses, books, newspapers, magazines, railroads, telegraph wires, telephone lines, and radio communications and broadcast stations come together to frame a future modernization paradigm, but technological progress will rarely go hand in hand with effective political or cultural openness and liberty in Latin America, if anywhere in the developing world.

During the *Porfiriato*, Madero's newspaper *El Demócrata* (1905), José María Pino Suarez's *El Peninsular* (1904), and *Savia Moderna* (1907), a publication where major revolutionary intellectuals collaborated, faced, like other opposition media, the harassment and intolerance of President Diaz's regime. In Madero's case, his campaign for political freedom including freedom to express ideas and opinions gained him the hatred of the dictator. Some of the other prominent revolutionaries, writing in *Savia Moderna*, also included Antonio Caso, Martí Luis Guzmán, José Vasconcelos, Alfonso Reyes, Alfonso Cravioto, and Miguel Alessio Robles. By February 1913, after fifteen months in the presidency following Diaz's resignation, Madero and his vice president Pino Suárez had been murdered.[54]

The beginning of this historical episode is closely tied to a journal article published in the United States, James Creelman's interview of Porfirio Diaz in *Pearson's Magazine* (1908). In it, the dictator announced that he would not run for reelection in 1910. Then, with Madero, the era of secret gatherings to read opposition papers, of *patrones* (bosses) also banning workers from reading and of fines and imprisonment against antigovernment journalists, was liberally ended. Madero's presidency and Francisco de León de la Barra's interim government (May through November 1911) immediately showed a substantial respect for the press, giving Mexico a Golden Age of media liberty rarely seen in this country. On July 5, the government secretary issued a notice inviting all newspapers to help guide the revolution and the people's passions and excitement.[55]

The opposition, however, was merciless with Madero. *El Imparcial*, *El País*, and *La Nación* of the Partido Nacional Católico (National Catholic Party) and the emotional *El Noticioso Mexicano*, *La Prensa*, *La Tribuna*, *El Mañana*, and *El Multicolor*, to name a few, mounted a propaganda campaign that Madero was unable to contain or neutralize. Unconvincingly supported by former *porfiristas*, his presidency grew dangerously unpopular with the public opinion. The greatest damage to his public image came from satirical papers such as *La Risa*, *Tilín-Tilín*, *La Sátira*, *Don Quijote*, and *El Mero Petatero*. In any case, this flourishing *Golden Age* saw the emergence of numerous journals, including the active *Regeneración*, *El Nacional*, *Diario Republicano*, *La Actualidad*, *La Ilustración Mexicana*, *La Guacamaya*, *El Siglo*, *Panchito*, *El Intransigente*, *El Ahuizote*, and *Azul* among others.[56]

Contemporary observers criticized the *maderists* for their lack of attention to the opposition. Government supporters claimed there was newspaper licentiousness rather than freedom of the press, and that the presidency was in danger because of the poor response to critical journals. One of the few and relatively effective pro-government publications was Gustavo Madero's *Nueva Era*, a newspaper that ended up burned down. Eventually, Madero lost not only the press and political battle but also his life. After President Madero's assassination, many opposition newspapers disappeared, such as Jesús M. Rábago's *El Mañana* and *El Multicolor*, owned by the Spaniard Mario Victoria. Others simply changed roles, becoming pro-government voices. A good example of the latter was Nemesio García Naranjo's *LaTribuna, El Noticioso Mexicano*, and *El Imparcial*, antimaderist publications that vigorously defended the Huerta administration.[57]

Once General Victoriano Huerta took over the president's office (1913–1914), the press receded to the times of appointed-state censors, servile pro-government newspapers, and military persecution, arrests, and expulsion of opposition writers. *El Voto* and *La Voz de Juárez*, for example, had their directors accused and arrested of complicity with Emiliano Zapata. Three types of periodicals dominated Huerta's one and a half years in power: first, the metropolitan press favoring the regime; then, the politically divided newspapers in exile, primarily in the United States; and finally, the foreign journals, led by *The Mexican Herald* which offered its columns to the revolutionaries. Metropolitan newspapers that loyally defended Huerta included *El Imparcial, El Noticioso, El Heraldo de Occidente, El Independiente*, and *La Tribuna*.[58]

The old and violent proverb of "eye for eye, tooth for tooth" dominated the Mexican press during Huerta's repressive months, until Venustiano Carranza forcefully took office in July 1914 bringing back a measure of press freedom, particularly in the first half of his presidency. With the support of the U.S. press, local intellectuals, and increasingly influential periodicals in the U.S.–Mexican border, such as *La República, El Progreso, La Voz de Sonora, El Paso del Norte*, and *El Demócrata*, Carranza promoted his policy of national unification and the rule of law. In fact, his newspaper *El Constitucionalista* (The Constitutionalist), founded on December 2, 1913, would be the central organ of the *Carrancistas*.

Confronting a scarcity of papers, the pro-Carranza newspapers promoted the new regime's social, legal, and economic reforms it considered viable and necessary. A nationalist propaganda campaign of Mexican unity, for instance, effectively aligned various revolutionary papers under the slogan of social reform, technological progress, and national modernity. Arms and newspapers became equally powerful instruments for Carranza in times of continuous unrest. Some of the most prominent constitutionalist newspapers included Los Angeles' *El Eco de México*, El

Paso's *El Paso del Norte*, San Antonio's *La Raza*, Merida's *La Voz de la Revolución*, and Veracruz's trilogy of *El Liberal*, *La Opinión*, and *El Dictámen*.

In time, Félix F. Palavicini, Carranza's secretary of public instruction, also built a network of newspapers based on the official Veracruz daily *El Pueblo* (1914), the newspapers *El Mexicano* and *Discusión*, and the prestigious *El Universal*, founded by Palavicini himself in Mexico DF (October 1916). The newspaper progress of the Mexican Revolution is actually well reflected in *El Universal*, a daily that combined measured politics with modern journalistic machinery and techniques imported from the United States.

Another icon of the Anglo-American news media influence would be Rafael Alducín's *Excelsior*, the renowned daily of Mexico's Federal District founded on March 18, 1917, which copied to the extreme both the format and the spirit of *The New York Times*. *El Universal* and *Excelsior* broke off the tradition of the politicized Porfirian and early revolutionary press, giving newspapers a corporate and business-oriented profile built upon U.S.-styled news, graphics, and editorials. In the late 1930s, José García Valseca masterly applied this profit-minded background to his popular journals *Paquito*, *Paquita*, and *Pepín*, building by 1948 a chain of twelve dailies—including the sports newspaper *Esto*—and several moneymaking magazines.[59]

The full-steam modernity in the Mexican press had come along with the 1917 Constitution. Freedom of the press was guaranteed on a conditional basis, maintaining the conventional pattern of a free but responsible press as prescribed by law. Although Carranza initiated his administration with the enthusiasm of an ample press freedom, an immediate confrontation with Zapata's *Tierra y Justicia* and Villa's *El Diario Oficial*, *Vida Nueva*, *La Convención*, *El Monitor*, and *La Opinión* forced Carranza to be only cautiously tolerant with newspapers. The Constitution of 1917 framed the press in these terms:

> The expression of ideas shall not be the subject of any judicial or administrative inquisition, unless it offends good morals, infringes the rights of others, incites to crime, or disrupts the public order (art. 6). The liberty to write and publish on any subject is inviolable. No law or authority may institute a prior restraint or demand from printers any bond or limit to their press freedom, except in cases of respect to private life and the public moral and peace. Under no circumstance could a printing press be confiscated as the instrument of the crime.[60]

This historic Latin American document linked not only freedom of the press but also other fundamental guarantees to social prerogatives such as the right to work, to receive an education, and to have means of production and community participation.[61] Statutory laws were to regulate the press on the basis of free but responsible communications. All malicious expressions, for example, damaging an individual's reputation or privacy or the social peace would be punished according to the revolution's *Ley de Imprenta* (Press Law of 1917). Malicious information could come in the form of verbal communications, signs, or other means such as writing, printing materials, drawings, photographs, lithographs, or any other form of public dissemination or transmission via mail, telegraph, telephone, radiotelegraph, or any messaging system.[62]

But, despite, or because of Carranza's rhetoric, the constitution, and the Press Law of 1917, the Mexican authorities and other social actors censored the print media with stubborn regularity. By December 1914, Colonel Pancho Martínez, a noted Zapatist journalist had already been assassinated, triggering all kinds of retaliations between Zapata's, Villa's, and the government's forces that led to mutual assaults of columnists and newspapers of all sides, including the closure of *El Monitor, El Norte,* and *El Radical.* Although prolific, the World War I and postwar years proved extremely conflictive in Mexico, generating an aggressive campaign against opposition papers such as the Catholic journals of the *Guerra Cristera* (The War on Christianity, mid-1920s). Editors, publishers, and journalists were either assassinated or attacked and their newspapers were closed down. Eventually, the Mexican media system would learn to live in this recurrent environment of government and ruling party violence and restrain.[63]

Other Latin American news media ventures endured comparably repressive practices in the World War I era. In Colombia, for instance, officials grew keenly apprehensive of political publications. Passionate and sensational newspapers including the *godos* (blue conservatives) and the *radicales* (red liberals), or better yet, the *Germanófilos* (pro-German) and *proaliados* (pro-allies), put censorship back in the Colombian agenda. After four years of a legalistic and pro-free press Restrepo presidency, the neutral Concha administration (1914–1918) had a hard time controlling not only Liberal, pro-allied, antigovernment newspapers but also *Germanófilos* pro-government publications. Even German radiotelegraph stations operating in Colombian soil posed a problem, for they allegedly helped fellow country warships in the Caribbean.

BROADCAST NEWS AND ENTREPRENEURS

There were so many emerging, simultaneous, and intertwined radio developments in Latin America and the Caribbean, states Mexican journalist and historian Fernando Mejía Barquera, that it is often difficult, if not arbitrary, to name someone as "the first radio broadcaster" in this or that country, this or that region.[64] Anyhow, and with peculiar accents, nation-states gradually introduced and expanded radiobroadcast services, beginning with amateur or government (usually, military) experimenters and ending with major media magnates. The same occurred in the United States with their inventors, engineers, merchants, and aficionados in industrial cities and their Navy research in the Great Lakes.[65]

Radio competition turned into a virtual war in various places, looking for profits and political gains through propaganda. Education, with rare exceptions like Chile, was an ephemeral rhetoric in Latin America. Radio characters ranged from gifted musicians and mass popular figures (e.g., the guitarist Andrés Segovia, the singer Carlos Gardel, and the boxer Jack Dempsey) to dull and imposing politicians, many of them military dictators. In Colombia, for instance, Gardel's accidental death fueled a new radio genre: news, that is, after half a decade of classical music, sports talk, radio reading, patriotic scores, and religious programming.[66] Technology, geopolitics, blood, presumed social impacts, local and alien commercial ambitions, and political manipulation erratically mixed in this *salpicón* (cocktail) of the emerging Latin American broadcasting. In most countries, politics and the new radio business "was as unpredictable as Popocatepetl."[67]

Radio broadcasting in Mexico goes back to the early 1920s during the presidency of General Alvaro Obregón. In August 1921, as part of the state of Veracruz's festivities to commemorate the *Tratados de Córdoba* (The Cordoba Treaties that sealed Mexico's independence), President Obregón hailed one of the country's first experimental radio broadcast transmissions. One month later, from the first floor of the *Teatro Ideal* of Mexico City, brothers Adolfo and Pedro Gómez-Fernández also experimented with a brief broadcast of two songs in which tenor José Mojica interpreted Paolo Tosti's Vorrei. Using a De Forest transmitter, with the financial support of businessman Pedro Barra Villela, the Gómez-Fernández brothers operated a local radio station that lasted nearly four months (September 1921 through January 1922).[68]

The educational and entrepreneurial initiative of public and private actors introduced radio broadcasting in the United Mexican States. Unlike newspapers and later television, this country's radio did not emerge as a centralized and mostly metropolitan medium. Provincial locations such as Pachuca, Cuernavaca, Morelia, San Luis Potosí, Chihuahua, and Ciudad Juárez were also broadcasting pioneers along with the Federal District, Guadalajara, and Veracruz. In Monterrey, state of Nuevo León, Constantino De Tárnava established regular late-night transmissions of classical music featuring soprano María Ytirría, pianist Carlos Pérez, tenor Aubrey Saint John Clerke, and poem reader Audoxio Villarreal. Engineer Constantino De Tárnava's station *TND* (Tárnava Notre Dame) was inaugurated on October 27, 1921, and his first experimental transmission can be traced back to the end of World War I.[69]

Another engineer, Salvador Francisco Domenzáin, is also a key figure in the early days of Mexico's radio industry. Not only did he contribute to pioneer radio broadcasting by inaugurating a station in the Federal District in 1922 but also helped the country to organize the *Liga Central Mexicana de Radio* (Mexican Central League of Radio, March 6, 1926). Actually, engineer Domenzáin founded the previous year the *Liga Nacional de Radio* (The National Radio League), paving the road for the subsequent merge of the Center of Engineers and the Mexican Central Club of Radio. Around that time, Domenzáin was also assisting the federal authorities to set up a transmitting/receiving station at the *Cancillería* (Foreign Relations Secretariat).

On March 19, 1923, with the support of the secretary of war and the navy, both Colonel José Fernando Ramírez and engineer José de la Herrán launched the JH radio station, named after the engineer's initials. It transmitted late night programs between 10 p.m. and midnight for nearly eight months. Almost simultaneously, Francisco C. Steffens inaugurated a SW station in the Federal District, featuring classical music programs every Sunday. Radio competition instantly increased with the same year's arrival of Raúl Azcárraga's *La Casa de la Radio* (The House of Radio, May 8) and the French-funded *CYB, La Estación de El Buen Tono* (The Good Sound Station, September 15).

Within a few months, Azcárraga's station, operating from his store of electronic appliances, merged with the prestigious Palavicini's *El Universal*. Its musical programming included high-profile artists, such as the famous Spanish guitarist Andrés Segovia, the Mexican composer Manuel M. Ponce, pianist Manuel Barajas, and poet Manuel Maples Arce who read his poem "Radio." Proud of their deal, *El Universal* wrote on its front page: "As the great U.S. newspapers do, *El Universal* [also] has a powerful broadcast radio station. It is set up in the nation's capital."[70] In response, the *Excélsior* also acquired a broadcast station half a year later.

These broadcast–newspaper combinations came to be known as the CYL and CYX radio stations, respectively. Their nomenclature, initially accepted by the ITU's Berne Conference of 1924, had to change to identifications beginning with the call letter X, following agreements signed at the 1929 International Telecommunication Conference in Washington, DC. The *Universal–Casa de la Radio* venture, however, disappeared in 1928.

On April 26, 1926, president and revolutionary leader Plutarco Elías-Calles (1924–1928) signed into law the *Ley de Comunicaciones Eléctricas* (Electrical Communications Act) that obviously included broadcasting. Adopted even before the U.S. Radio Act of 1927, article 12 of the Mexican Electronic media statute prescribed that radio transmissions could neither threat the state's national security nor attack, in any way, legitimate government authorities. Elías-Calles had made his political reputation as an anticlerical man who firmly believed in order, laws, and institutions.[71]

Mexico's radio broadcast industry experienced an exponential growth in the 1930s and in the subsequent two decades. On February 5, 1930, *Radio*

Mundial-XEN (World Radio) introduced one of the hemisphere's first all-news radio stations. Its owner and director was the media giant Don Félix F. Palavicini, founder of *El Universal* and former member of the 1917 Constitutional Assembly. An entrepreneur well acquainted with U.S. media formats and practices, he had purchased the station (formerly identified as CYS) from General Electric. By then, communication-related multinationals of the United States were all over Latin America and the Caribbean looking for and exploiting media business opportunities.

In 1897, the Western Union Telegraph had aggressively pursued and controlled Mexico's international telegraph service, and the telephone industry would remain foreign until the state acquired in 1958 controlling interest in Telmex over the historical ITT and Ericsson investments.[72] In the 1920s, with the arrival of broadcasting, RCA was also making concerted efforts to shape not only Mexico's but Latin America's broadcasting along North American patterns. The aim was "to open the region's radio systems to direct United States corporate investment and commercial development with minimal oversight."[73]

Commercialization, as opposed to its educational, scientific, and cultural origins, was clearly dominant of the Mexican radio enterprise by the early 1930s. On September 18, 1930, Emilio Azcárraga Vidaurreta, father of *El Tigre*, Televisa's owner and media mogul Emilio Azcárraga Milmo, inaugurated *La Voz de La América Latina-XEW* (The Voice of Latin America), a five-kilowatt broadcast station with national and cross-border audience ambitions. This dream, a Spanish-speaking broadcast service across the continent, would be the central theme of his family. To finance it, Azcárraga Vidaurreta used for the first time strategies to attract advertisers, persuading product manufacturers of the benefits in joining the news and entertainment radio bandwagon.[74]

Not surprisingly, the Mexican government came up with both incentive and controlling regulations on licensing and advertising in the first half of the 1930s. In 1931, the notion of broadcast permits was replaced with long-term concessions of up to fifty years, asserting the government's duty to protect the spectrum as a national public resource though creating favorable conditions for foreign investment. Chapter VI, Book V of the Law of General Means of Communications of 1933 (*Ley de Vías Generales de Comunicación*, July 10), ordered that broadcast stations could devote only 10 percent of their time to commercial announcements (art. 17).

This same statute guaranteed the federal authorities free access to all commercial frequencies, for which purpose the government created the so-called Press and Advertising Autonomous Department (*Departamento Autónomo de Prensa y Publicidad*—DAPP). Charged with managing the state's radio stations and the government's social communication policy, the DAPP was also organized to monitor and regulate the use of advertising in commercial and cultural broadcasting. In coordination with the National Revolutionary Party (*Partido Nacional Revolucionario-PNR*) and the Public Education Secretariat, the DAPP set out to promote government programs for national development. During the Lázaro Cádenas' presidency (1934–1940), radio stations from the above entities (*XEFO, XEUZ, XFX, XEDP,* and *XEXA*) were expected to work together for the same goals, primarily national unity, social progress, and public information.

In 1933, the federal government donated radio sets in rural villages hoping to lure peasants into listening to *SEP's* development programs (*Secretaría de Education Pública*) while enjoying the wonders of a new technology. The principal goal then was to foster harmony, public order, and both cultural and political unification. But, peasants did not listen, for there was no transmission of popular songs such as the revered *rancheras*—though recipients loved the radio sets. Eventually, development agencies incorporated popular themes of folk melodies and the *Charro* spirit (Mexico's cowboy), successfully standardizing and spreading a simplified message of national pride and unity.[75]

By 1939, the DAPP had disappeared, but its activities moved to the secretary of government. Production of the *Hora Nacional* (the National Hour), however, initiated by the DAPP two years before, went on until the 1990s, maintaining the philosophy of national unity and the tradition of Latin America's oldest broadcast program. Nevertheless, there was significant hesitation with the scope of this show. In sixty years, the program's title changed from "The National Hour" (1937) to "The Hour of the Mexican Republic's Government" (1949), and from "The Hour of Mexico" (1977) back to its original name of "National Hour."

Mexico, as the rest of Latin America, abided by the European principle that broadcasting was a public service, destined to serve and realize pro-social goals beyond private industry and/or individual ambitions. At the 1924 Inter-American Conference on Electrical Communications held in Mexico City, the nationalistic, Europeanized, and public service model formally defeated the evolving U.S. commercial broadcast paragon.[76] Officially, Mexico claimed to endorse any free-market competition consistent with the government's political and developmental ideals. Yet, in practice, the profit-oriented philosophy would quickly absorb the Mexican and Latin American broadcast systems. By 1940, the Mexican government had virtually stepped out of radio broadcasting, leaving most of the business to the already powerful entrepreneur Azcárraga Vidaurreta.

Network radio and subsequently television fell in the hands of a private oligopoly and monopoly in Mexico, heavily influenced by and dependent on U.S. technology, manufacturers, advertisers, training, program formats, and marketing. During the late 1930s and early 1940s, Mexican radio networks grew around *XEW*, Azcárraga's mother station, fourteen regional affiliates, and his Mexican Music Company, an RCA subsidiary. A second network of his property was built upon *XEQ*-Mexico City, making Azcárraga Vidaurreta the first president of the Radio Broadcasting Industry National Chamber in 1942 (CIR in Spanish).[77]

With more or less private competition, the introduction of radio broadcasting in Brazil (1922), Argentina (1923), Chile (1923), Peru (1925), Cuba (1925), Venezuela (1926), Colombia (1929), and other Latin American nations followed essentially the same Mexican pattern. "The absence of significant broadcasting developments in either Spain and Portugal," wrote Katz and Wedell, "coupled with the Pan-American links established since independence, caused Latin Americans to be greatly influenced by the United States in the institutionalization of their broadcasting systems. The majority of the South American countries were already within the sphere of influence of the United States, both politically and economically when broadcasting technology became commercially available," concluded these authors.[78]

There are some special features across the Latin American broadcasting systems in terms of policy, economics, political structure, and foreign influence. In Cuba, before Fidel Castro's revolution, the influence of the U.S. broadcasting system was overwhelming. The Mestre brothers and their *CMQ* network contributed to implant an overly commercialized broadcast system, turning the island into an experimental site of the U.S. broadcasting empire in Latin America. In fact, in the mid-1960s, Goar and Abel Mestre (the Czar) toured the region acquiring stations on behalf of the National Broadcasting Company (NBC)-owned *Cadena Panamericana de Televisión* (Pan-American TV Network).

This has been an expansion trend initiated by RCA radio in October 1940, launching shortwave rebroadcasting arrangements in twenty Latin American countries. CBS' *Cadena de las Americas* (The Chain of the Americas) and Crosley Broadcasting's *Cadena Radio Interamericana* (The Inter-American Radio Chain) followed suit within a few months. Clearly, radio broadcasting expanded rapidly in the Americas, and by 1934, there were at least sixty-eight radio stations in Mexico, fifty-seven in Chile, fifty-two in Cuba, forty-two in Brazil, forty in Argentina, and thirty-five in Uruguay, to name the most radio-seduced countries. Apparently, half of the radio receivers available in Latin America could pick up shortwave radio signals.[79]

Concerned with the Nazi, Fascist, and Falangist broadcast operations of the German, Italian, and Spanish dictatorships (wishing a return to the Aryan, Catholic, or Iberian–American empires with considerable sympathies in Latin America), the United States decided to launch a Pan-American crusade of hemispheric friendship. Privately and governmentally, U.S. authorities and entrepreneurs embarked themselves on a concerted propaganda campaign of press liberty, freedom of choice, and freedom of enterprise in the Americas. Although with mixed results in the beginning, the U.S. imperialism eventually came out triumphant after World War II. Not a single Latin American country was able to resist the selling, temptation, and domination of the economic, political, and cultural paradigms of Anglo-America, particularly in media affairs.[80]

In the late 1920s, Brazil introduced radio broadcasting as a private yet noncommercial enterprise, with stations owned and run by clubs or associations of listeners. In fact, up to the presidency and civil dictatorship of Getulio Vargas (1930–1945), the government had discouraged advertising, fostering education and culture in the airwaves over entertainment and profitability. By the late 1960s, following an even more repressive military era (1964–1985), the Brazilian federation was fully immersed into the U.S. broadcast model of commercialization, painfully twisted toward monopolization and political persecution.[81]

Chile is perhaps the most interesting case of the struggle between commercialization and educational interests in both radio and television broadcasting—that is, until General Augusto Pinochet's dictatorship (1973) which fractured the media and social history of this South American country. The Chilean broadcast radio, introduced as a mere private venture in the early 1920s, gradually grew more balanced in favor of public, educational, and community constituents because of governmental pressures. Political parties, religious groups, universities, and workers' unions received licenses to compete with commercial radio stations. Similarly, in Colombia, the first radio station (*HJN*) was created by the government to promote education (August 7, 1929). Yet, in the long run, not only Colombia but also Argentina, Peru, Venezuela, and most of the non-English-speaking nations of Latin America and the Caribbean switched to purely commercial broadcast systems, inspired and modeled after the spirit of mercantilism of the United States. Following World War II, the region's radio stations and networks became heavily Americanized and ultimately controlled by profit-oriented, oligarchic, and politically partisan groups.

In celebration of the sixty years of the *Radiodifusora Nacional de Colombia* (founded on February 1, 1940), the daily *El Tiempo* published an interview with Gustavo Samper, director of the National Institute of Radio and Television, *Inravisión*, the Colombian public broadcasting enterprise. Thanks to the *Radio Nacional*, as it is popularly known, ordinary Colombians learned about news immediacy, communication power, and even popular repression. Indeed, during the tragic *Bogotazo*, when the people's leader Jorge Eliécer Gaitán was assassinated downtown on April 9, 1948, several radio stations were taken over by members of the Liberal and [Communist] parties, calling for a national revolt against the ruthless Conservative government of President Mariano Ospina Pérez. When asked what to do with this historic network, Samper responded with another question: "Why can't an educational text go with an advertisement reading Coca-Cola? What's the problem?" "Commercialize National Radio" is his solution.[82]

In the *Bogotazo*, "comrades" and other rebels took over the frequencies under the Gaitanist motto of *"a la carga"* (charge), including the *Radio Nacional*, commented witnesses of the *9 de Abril 1948*, a video also featuring Gloria Gaitán, the caudillo's daughter.[83] Immediately, Colombian authorities, explained the historian Hernando Téllez, suspended all operation licenses, checking records of each station and news announcer as to whether or not reestablish the respective licenses.[84] Following this decision, "the government forced the creation of the National Association of Broadcasting (*Anradio*), demanding the obligatory affiliation of all stations to the new organization and giving licenses only to those which became Anradio affiliates."[85] When choosing its membership, Anradio received instructions from the Colombian Ministry of Communications, "effectively discriminating against anti-government ones."[86]

More than finding out who steered what and when in the history of Latin American and Caribbean broadcasting, it is far more challenging and interesting to uncover how and why prominent broadcasting events occurred the way they did, and who benefited from them. This is another book in itself, but some authors addressed the subject with considerable success in their publications, notably Elizabeth Fox and her well-known *Latin American Broadcasting: From Tango to Telenovela* (1997).[87]

In Argentina, a memorable case, "the state was interested in radio for geopolitical and nationalizing purposes in the early days," but, soon after, "private interests became more dominant," wrote Dr. Waisbord, formerly at Rutgers University and now with the Academy for Educational Development in Washington DC. In his view, "the commercial development and structure of broadcasting cannot be understood [in Argentina, Uruguay, and particularly Paraguay], without addressing the close relations between governments and media owners."[88] An obvious beneficiary was Juan Domingo Perón who used broadcasting for self-promotion, especially television, adding "this medium to [his] propaganda arsenal of newspapers and radio stations."[89]

Getulio Vargas did the same in Brazil during the 1930s, explains Professor Rosental Calmon Alves of the University of Texas at Austin, "grasp[ing] the power of radio and using it to impose his nationalist views [and government agenda]."[90] Tightly connected to politics and elections, the Brazilian broadcasting ended up exclusively concerned with both political power through news and economic gain through advertising. For decades, just like most other Latin American countries, Brazilian authorities tolerated the effective control of the airwaves by national and multinational sponsors, primarily foreign advertisers and advertising agencies. "The original plans for the educational use of radio were almost totally forgotten," concludes Alves.[91]

In Venezuela, radio was possible once Luis Roberto Scholtz and Alfredo Moller persuaded the "dictatorial trinity" of the Gómez family about the benefits of broadcasting for the country, more exactly both the three-time president General and Army Inspector Juan Vicente Gómez, and his son, General José Vicente Gómez. In other words, Venezuelans began their broadcasting history with a military station. His uncle, the late General Juan C. Gómez, had been assassinated (in the very presidential Palace of Miraflores) shortly before the launching of AYRE (May 1926), the first broadcast station, according to the Venezuelan Chamber of the Broadcasting Industry (*CVIR*, in Spanish). Moller, the station's presenter, "had to be extremely prudent in not broadcasting anything that could be interpreted as a criticism of the regime."[92]

As with Getulio Vargas' modernization and censorship machine (e.g., his *Departamento de Imprensa e Propaganda* and his alleged *A Voz do Brasil*), the Gómez dictatorship virtually wiped out any possibilities of dissent. For two years every morning, AYRE read the official news handed out by pro-governmental *El Nuevo Diario* (the New Daily), while Harry Wilson, the North American engineer who had been hired to set up the station in the corner of *El Tejar* and the *Nuevo Circo* building, sneaked in evening news received from foreign lands. As in Brazil, leftist youngsters organized in a student federation were the only vocal and courageous opposition to the tyrants, including the Venezuelan leaders and subsequent presidents Raúl Leoni and Rómulo Betancourt.[93] Then, on December 9, 1930, *Broadcasting Caracas*, today *Radio Caracas*, replaced the government's mouthpiece.

In the Caribbean, people have known all to well about criminal dictators and human rights abusers. Writing for the *Listín Diario* in the Dominican Republic, professor and author Andrés L. Mateo warned the region, and the hemisphere, not to forget Rafael Trujillo's *"Era" del Miedo* (Age of Fear), a long period of terror (1930–1961) built atop an authoritarian tradition and historic violence imposed as an inexorable fate. The dictator dominated all public and most private life with his slogan: "in this house the boss is Trujillo." In other words, Trujillism, sobs Mateo, "was bigger than Trujillo. Thus, not even twenty Vargas Llosas writing twenty more novels [like the *Danza del Chivo*] could barely describe the frightening reality lived in [the Dominican Republic] at that time." Nothing more ludicrous then, than to expect freedom of thought, speech, or the press in a dictatorial regime of that sort.[94]

On February 7, 1948, Jorge Eliécer Gaitan organized a massive and silent march in Bogotá, demanding an end to the official violence in the countryside through a historic "prayer of peace." Mr. President [Mariano Ospina-Pérez], yelled Gaitán, "under the weight of a deep emotion I bring myself before your excellency, interpreting the desire and the will of this immense mass, hiding its burning heart lacerated by so much injustice under a rousing silence, to ask for peace and mercy for our nation."[95] As Fidel Castro put it in an interview with the conservative daily *El Siglo*, when he arrived to Colombia's capital, liberal newspapers were vividly denouncing the 20 to 30 peasants murdered every day in the rural areas. His eloquent rhetoric in criminal trials and public speeches broadcasted throughout the country had also made him extremely popular; he was a brilliant politician, a brilliant speaker, and a brilliant lawyer, said Castro.[96]

As a revolution, the *Bogotazo* was especially clear. Gaitán had explained in open squares and the mass media that there were only two parties in contemporary society: the liberal and conservative parties of the exploiters and the liberal and conservative parties of the exploited. Oligarchies, he said, would love to have "all anguished people in silence for them to split the profits of the public treasury, satisfying their petty political and economic interests. [T]he small oligarchies of the liberals procure and receive their contracts, while the small conservative oligarchies offer and give them those contracts." Instead, Gaitán liked to speak of "the clamorous silence of the noble people," silence as a popular mandate that could turn to thunder if overlooked, and where the future of the Americas ultimately rests upon.[97]

Sociologist Alfredo Molano comments that elites and government propaganda had to give Jorge Eliécer Gaitán bad labels in order to neutralize him, the famous name-calling technique as old as the Catholic Church's *Congregatio de Propaganda Fide* of the early 1600s. "Since calling Gaitán demagogue, populist, communist, and even fascist did not work, killing him was the only way to stop him," concluded Molano.[98] There are less passionate and academic reasons, or as Gaitán would say, *frías explicaciones* (cold explanations) for the ongoing injustice, most of them revolving around free marketplace concepts, including the free marketplace of ideas. But, not even Justice Oliver Wendell Holmes had been free from political ideology, as he secured his post in the U.S. Supreme Court after agreeing with Teddy Roosevelt to tax American colonies such as Puerto Rico without their residents having the right to vote in a U.S. election, something that many democrats of their time considered "unconstitutional and imperialistic."[99]

Professor Joseph D. Straubhaar, a reputable Latin American, currently at the University of Texas at Austin, summarized the region's radio industry, arguing that it "set a pattern for broadcasting in most of South America: a predominance of entertainment over education or cultural programs, a clear dominance of advertising-supported stations, a tendency to import a good deal of materials as well as program ideas; and countervailing tendency to use a great deal of national and local material as well. [C]ommercial radio was widely successful because it fit well into the developing South American market economies."[100]

Recognizing the wisdom of "several researchers who make a strong case that the activity of U.S. radio networks" helped draw Latin American nations toward commercialization in the 1930s and 1940s, Straubhaar also highlights the presence of U.S. advertising agencies, U.S. advertisers or corporations, and U.S. technologies, programs, and approaches as basic components of the Latin American consumer media system. Yet, removed from definite dependency conclusions, this scholar contributed relevant ideas of cultural proximities and reversed competition roles, accounting for developing-country gains in international markets and counteracting actions against excessive foreign program imports that dependency researchers could not immediately explain.

An expert of *telenovelas*, Joseph Straubhhar, explains *radionovelas* as the origin of drama in Latin American broadcasting, a fascinating fusion resulting from multiple influences coming from France, Cuba, Mexico, and Argentina, among others. Particularly important, he observes, "were scripts imported from Cuba, where *radionovelas* were first developed as a Latin American form of the U.S. soap opera, sponsored by Colgate, the U.S. corporation which wanted to sell soap in Latin America with the same advertising vehicle that had proved successful in the United States."[101]

Gaitán would probably lean toward a simpler but equally powerful explanation of the essential character of Latin American mass media: that they are mainly tools of the aristocracy to exploit miserable masses. As Professor Gonzalo Soruco pointed out at the University of Western Ontario in Canada: "the early days of the [Latin American] republics saw the press turned into an organ of political parties used mostly to vilify opposition politicians. Beginning in the twentieth century, the press has become the organ of the elites and the rich, often used as a party organ espousing the political ideology of the owners—at times turning into a product that entertains rather than informs the readers."[102] Ana María Miralles would be even more succinct: the Latin American news media moved from the early gazettes and the confrontation against absolute colonial powers to a republican party press, a depoliticized or commercialized news industry, and finally a mostly concentrated or monopolized communications media.[103]

In communication terms, it is not unjustified to emphasize the history of Spanish America, primarily Mexico, the former *Gran Colombia*, and the Argentine confederation over the Brazilian past, for the latter has a shorter experience with both civil administration and the mass media. After all, the Brazilian territory was a laggard in setting up a printing press, in abolishing slavery, in obtaining open independence, and in adopting a constitution free from colonial influences. Yet, in spite of these factors, the Brazilian federation always generated much curiosity long before modernization monarchs and rulers, such as Pedro II (1825–1891) and Getúlio Vargas (1882–1954).

As Paleologo pointed out, "we [Brazilians] were practically unknown in the continent for we had never worried about making ourselves known with our neighbors. For our brothers of race, we felt an absolute indifference, and our focus was always placed in both Europe and the United States. What did we know about Latin America? Nothing. We, Brazilians, knew more details of the social history of the principal European countries and North America than about our Latin American brothers."[104] On the contrary, Hispanic Americans were rather interested in Brazil, in her different history, language, and cultural traditions. Not surprisingly, international editions of magazines such as *O Jornal*, *Brasil en América Latina*, and *O Cruzeiro Internacional* had a significant success in Latin America following World War II. *O Cruzeiro*, for instance, founded in 1928, sold up to 700,000 issues among Hispanic American readers, particularly in South America.[105] Because of her distance and sporadic interaction with Spanish-speaking nations situated north to the Panama Canal or in the Caribbean Basin, Brazil often generated less interest than Mexico, Central America, Cuba, Hispaniola, and other Caribbean islands.

Naturally, much has changed in the Federative Republic (formerly United States) of Brazil since the end of the military arrogance, persecution, and censorship of the Cold War years, particularly after the corrupted administration of the impeached president Fernando Collor de Mello (1990–1992), the first popularly elected president in twenty-six years. With Vice President Itamar Franco as head of state (December 1992), Brazil initiated an ascending world reputation as a stable democracy, free from coups and anticoups, marshals and generals, and the authoritarian populism, sudden resignations, and democratic-elected presidents unable to finish their terms. For good and for bad, the mass media had always been center stage in the Brazilian political process.

Commercial and public radio networks emerged as a vital media system in leading Latin American nations during the 1940s and 1950s, although the former quickly dwarfed the latter in most, if not all, countries. In Brazil, for example, the immediate winners were "*Emissoras Asociadas* (Assis Chateaubriand-Diários Associados Group), *Rádio Bandeirantes* (Grupo Carvalho), and *Rádio Globo* (linked with the newspaper *O'Globo*'s owner Roberto Marinho) [especially, the last two which are the most popular today]."[106] In fact, the *Sistema Globo de Rádio* (113 owned and affiliated radio stations), *Divisão de Rádio da RBS*, *Jornal do Brasil*, and *Rede Manchete de Rádio* became "major media conglomerates."[107]

Journalist Rosental Calmon Alves, formerly with the Rio de Janeiro's *Jornal de Brasil* and currently Knight Chair in journalism and director of the *Knight Center for Journalism in the Americas* at the University of Texas–Austin, explains how radio networks evolved from the amateur days and President Vargas' authoritarianism (e.g., his *Rádio Nacional*) to subsequent radio ventures fully run by U.S. companies or national commercial chains, the latter conveniently promoted and controlled by military dictators. As in other South American nations, audiences grew up listening to the *Reporter Esso*, a prominent radio newscast produced by the United Press International, marketed by McCann Ericksson, and supported by Standard Oil's Esso subsidiary. In 2002, notes Alves, "Brazil had 1452 radio stations, including a few national chains, such as *Globo, Bandeirantes, Jovem Pan, Antena 1,* and *Cidade.*"[108]

In Perú, the *Peruvian Broadcasting Company* had been airing radio programs since June 15, 1925, including daily news read from newspapers, primarily *El Comercio*. Over a decade later (1936), *Radio Weston's La Revista Oral*, a verbal magazine, introduced Peruvian audiences to more elaborate and profitable radio news information with editorial commentary.[109] Also, in Colombia, the so-called *Colombian Radio and Electric Corporation* (not *Corporación Radio Eléctrica Colombiana*) introduced *La Voz de Bogotá*, the country's first private commercial radio station, with apparent U.S. support in order to raise its status. Typical of the country's and region's early Americanization, the "Colombian Broadcasting," "Santander Broadcasting," "Broadcasting Caracas," and other Anglicized brand names proliferated. Many were truly influenced by U.S. interests, such as *La Voz de la Victor*, a pioneer radio station established in 1933; indeed, *RCA Victor* was RCA's voice, not *La Voz* (voice) of Colombians.[110]

In Mexico, the daily *El Universal* y Raúl Azcárraga's *La Casa del Radio*, a store selling electronic devices, formed a joint venture. On May 8, 1923, the newspaper announces in a front-page story: "just like the biggest newspapers in North America, the *Universal Ilustrado* now counts on a powerful radio broadcast station [CYL] in the Republic's capital city." Four months later, "El Buen Tono" (CYB, later XEB), a major news radio station known today as *La B Grande de México* and originally set up with French capital, emerged to effectively compete. The daily *Excélsior* had similar aspirations with its CYX station, although the real character would be Emilio Azcárraga Vidaurreta who, in 1930, launched his business-oriented "*La Voz de la América Latina desde México* (XEW, or simply *La W*)."[111]

From the start, inspired in neighboring Anglo-American models, Mexican entrepreneurs have also had this ambition of commercially and, why not, politically exploiting Latin America and the Caribbean through the airwaves. *La W*, located on 16 September Street, no. 23, atop Azcárraga's Theater Olimpia, was only a baby step. Within the next forty years, Don Emilio masterminded a *Telesistema Mexicano* (TSM), a *Televisa Group*, a Spanish International Network (*SIN*, later *Univision*), and a *Satélite Latinoamericano* (*Satelat*, his Latin American satellite system) with one goal in mind: money. The "tiger," Azcárraga's nickname, pioneered the introduction of advertising strategies, with news and entertainment as primary foundations of the industry. Unsurprisingly, in 1941, he was elected president of the Mexican Chamber of the Radio Broadcasting Industry (CIR, *Cámara Nacional de la Industria de la Radiodifusión*, later *CIRT*).

By then, Mr. Azcárraga Sr. already had two leading stations XEW, with regional stations, and XEQ, a second national network.[112]

Cuban radio pioneers are also key players in this game of commercial broadcast empires, particularly the Mestre and Cisneros families. Dating back to the Cuban Telephone Company's PWX station (1922), a subsidiary of the legendary International Telephone and Telegraph (ITT) Corp., and the Havana daily *Diario de la Marina*'s station 2-AZ (1923), both *CMQ* (1933) and *Radio Habana Cuba* (*RHC*)-*Cadena Azul* (1940) also depended on U.S. advertisers, namely, the soap manufacturers Crusellas (a Colgate-Palmolive's subsidiary) and Sabates, the latter owned by Procter and Gamble.

On Emilio Azcárraga's advice (1942–1943), then in program exchanges with the NBC, the Mestre brothers, primarily with Goar's leadership, a Yale University business graduate, purchased CMQ and turned it into "Cuba's undisputed premier [radio] network."[113] Goar Mestre would soon so flourish in the broadcast industry as to become the so-called Czar of Latin American television during the heyday of the U.S. TV network expansion in the early to mid-1960s. In the same token, the Cisneros brothers, Diego and Antonio, acquired *Venevisión* in Caracas, formerly called *Televisa* (1960), a secured venture with juicy profits from a Pepsi–Cola franchise, among other businesses.[114]

Throughout the 1930s, Azcárraga, comments Professor Joy Elizabeth Hayes of the University of Iowa, a visiting Fulbright scholar at the *Universidad de Monterrey*, built two powerful radio networks relying on his Mexican Music Company, an RCA subsidiary. It is important to consider, writes Hayes, that following World War I, the Radio Corporation of America had "begun a concerted effort to shape Latin American broadcasting along North American lines," that is, planting open "radio systems to direct United States corporate investment and commercial[ization] with minimal government oversight."[115] In just a decade, after some resistance from federal authorities, a proliferation of commercial stations, and an increasing consolidation of the industry's ownership, the Mexican public sector "stepped out of radio as a broadcaster in its own right, leaving the medium in the hands of Azcárraga and other commercial broadcasters whose interests were closely allied to those of the state."[116]

In Colombia, radio networking began in 1940, based on active stations dating back to 1930, especially after the commemoration of Liberator Simón Bolívar's death centennial. *La Voz de Bogotá* (HKF), *Radio Manizales*, *Ecos de Occidente*, *La Voz de Antioquia*, *La Voz de la Víctor*, and others were created by entrepreneurs connected to foreign businesses, notably the Victor Talking Machine, RCA, the Dutch Phillips Company, and the Standard Oil Company (with its *Reporter Esso*), to name a few. When not heading to the United States or Great Britain's *BBC*, a number of radio announcers and producers flew to Mexico excited to receive training at Azcárraga's *La*

Voz de la América Latina."[117] By 1940, the *Alfombra Mágica* (The Magic Carpet), *Cadena Azul Bayer*, Bedout, Kresto, and Bolívar networks operated with alien sponsorship or ownership. Notice how names were Hispanized as a consequence of a Colombian law prohibiting foreign trade names in 1936.

Still, foreign influences, primarily from Anglo-America and Britain, but also from Mexico, Cuba, and in less extent Argentina (e.g., *RL1 Radio El Mundo* and *LR4 Radio Belgrano*), remained strong, especially during World War II and its propaganda machine when the U.S. Office of Inter-American Affairs, under Forney A. Rankin, sponsored the diffusion of NBC's and CBS's training and programming activities in the Americas. In 1941, William S. Paley traveled the whole continent, promoting his CBS *Cadena de las Américas*, a business campaign to which NBC responded with a regionwide *Cadena Panamericana*. A historic radio station in Chile, *Radio Cooperativa Vitalicia*, today simply *Radio Cooperativa*, agreed to serve as an early NBC affiliate.[118] Here, once again, the *Reporter Esso* is the star program. Nevertheless, as Téllez put it in his book, results were "discouraging" for both U.S. networks in the Americas, especially in Colombia where local networks rejected any direct affiliation.[119] Influences became then more subtle and oblique.

On September 1, 1948, partly as a new commercial strategy, partly as a response to *El Bogotazo* and other internal and external unrest, local Colombian entrepreneurs in Medellín and Bogotá decided to launch a new network: *Emisoras Nuevo Mundo*, later *Caracol*, the so-called "First Colombian Radio Network." What looks peculiar is the tone of its inaugural broadcast, which proudly proclaimed radio networking as an industry from and for the New World.

That day the station's director stated, "*Emisoras Nuevo Mundo* are born neither as the product of a simple investment desire [to make money] nor as a satisfying and transitory hobby. [This network is] ... a powerful weapon to gather people around truth, democracy, and solidarity. [Broadcasting] is an instrument for peace, education, culture, and healthy entertainment, but it is also a dangerous weapon of inconceivable danger in irresponsible hands. Because of radio experiences in foreign countries, for good and evil, we, preoccupied with our immediate Colombian reality, have decided to create a network that fills the gaps and problems of our broadcasting industry."

In a significant remark, this Colombian commercial network concluded: "Broadcasting, as a popular diffusion tool financed through private means, is not a public service, but it has the obligation to serve the public, to honor its mission of serving the public according to national interests of sovereignty and defense. As a potent and resounding voice in a sovereign, independent, and democratic nation [like Colombia], *Emisoras Nuevo Mundo* will not betray the motherland and her glories, raising itself as one more voice in the universal chorus of a New World's unity and friendship with other peoples in the Greater Colombia, Central America and the Caribbean, the North and the South of this continent."[120]

Caracol, whose roots go as deep as the 1932's *Compañia Radiodifusora de Medellín*, met the immediate competition of the *Radio Cadena Nacional* (*RCN*, the National Radio Network, February 1949), although both subsequently affiliated to the government-imposed *Anradio*, a National Broadcasting Association created to censor radio stations following the assassination of Jorge Eliécer Gaitán.

Since then, like in many corners of the Western Hemisphere, there has been great suspicion for industry mass media associations, including the Inter-American Press Association (*IAPA* or *SIP*, in Spanish) and *AIR* to which *Anradio* belongs. As a matter of fact, in 1958, after ten years of violence, political restraints, and big brother pressures, Bernardo Tobón de la Roche, owner of *Todelar*, Colombia's third major network, decided to create his own association, the National Radio Federation-*Federadio*. The *Todelar* chain had been launched in 1953.

In 1946, a first Inter-American Congress of Broadcasters gathered in Mexico to establish the Inter-American Association, the *Sociedad Interamericana de Radiodifusión*, currently the International Broadcasting Association (AIR, in Spanish), headquartered in Montevideo, Uruguay. Far less influential and organized than its counterpart the *Sociedad Interamericana de Prensa* (SIP), founded in 1926 (currently at the Jules Dubois Building in Miami, Florida), the AIR relied on both Goar Mestre and Emilio Azcárraga as founding members. Goar presided the organization from 1948 to 1953, and Don Emilio became the boss from 1953 to 1955. Fifty broadcasters from eighteen Latin American countries accepted Mr. Lorenzo Balerio Sicco's invitation, AIR's first president and organizer from Uruguay (although he also represented Bolivia).[121]

Although a truncated organization oftentimes, AIR president Andrés García Lavín (1991–1995) aptly described the region's mass media as an industry with a singular majority ownership and participation from private investors. As he explained, "many people are too poor to buy newspapers, so the printed press, like television, has had to concentrate in those countries with the largest populations and the highest incomes, such as Brazil and Mexico, which alone boast more than half of the [Latin America's] daily newspapers and television channels."[122] Because of deep poverty and inequality, the situation has probably gotten worse, not better, in the last decade.

In this overly commercialized and politically unstable environment, educational broadcasting did not stand a chance. Yet, creative projects usually emerged in difficult circumstances. On May 25, 1948, the Colombian Ministry of Communication granted *Radio Sutatenza* a license as a short-wave rural radiophonic school for adult education, approving the creation of an *Acción Cultural Popular* (ACPO, Popular Cultural Action) a year later. This institution was set out to improve rural literacy nationwide, although as AED Vice President and Health Communication Officer Reynaldo Pareja once observed peasants were encouraged to nurture "a vision of themselves and of the world" distanced from the "struggle of classes" and "the economic or political factors controlled and manipulated by the ruling elite."[123]

On the contrary, Monsignor José Joaquín Salcedo always saw his initiative as a "Revolution of Hope," grounded on good, solid, and traditional Catholic values. An amateur radio operator since October 1947, this curate or *Vicario Cooperador* of Sutatenza never imagined he would soon be flying to the United States to present his ideas before the United Nations, the World Bank, the Inter-American Development Bank, the U.S. Agency for International Development (USAID), the United States Information Service (USIS), and the Voice of America. With his Simón Bolívar Foundation in New York, he would also touch base with General Electric (for transmitters and transistor radio receivers), Pepsico, American Express, Chase Manhattan International, Rockefeller Brothers, General Mills, H.J. Heinz Co., Xerox, and other multinationals.[124]

In 1968, Pope Paul VI blessed *Radio Sutatenza*'s new and impressive facilities in rural Cundinamarca, not far from Bogotá, an international center where communication development practitioners and scholars from around the world came to learn about the successes of the radiophonic-school model ultimately framed by Daniel Lerner's modernization (1958) and Everett Rogers' diffusion of innovation (1962) paradigms. In accordance to prevailing UNESCO mass media development assumptions and programs, Sutatenza's format spread in Asia, primarily India, Latin America, and Africa.[125] A UNESCO survey, in 1971, reports that radiophonic schools have emerged in Mexico (1961), Cuba (1962), Brazil (1965), Peru (1965), Guatemala (1966), Jamaica (1966), Chile (1969), Ecuador (1971), and Paraguay (1971), most of them under the auspices of the Catholic Church.[126]

With the exception of HCJB, *La Voz de los Andes*, transmitting from Quito, Ecuador, since 1931, the spread of Pentecostal radio networks has been a more recent albeit rapidly growing phenomenon, making thousands of "disciples of Jesus Christ" out of listeners in Latin America and elsewhere.[127] Brazil is probably one of the most successful and typical examples. Even if the Catholic Church remains dominant with over 110 stations around the country, since the 1980s, "the expansion of evangelical Protestant sects in Brazil included in their strategy the acquisition of numerous radio stations, [...] broadcasting regularly on more than 60 radio stations in almost all states. The still-predominant Catholic Church—writes Professor Alves—had already obtained its ... own record of using radio, but it was caught by surprise when the evangelical network reached proportions that had been unimaginable in [this country] just a few years earlier."[128]

Although popular and supported as a nonprofit organization since 1961, ACPO's *Sutantenza* began a steady financial crisis and declined after its commercialization in 1980, which commercial networks bitterly opposed. Still, Monsignor Salcedo, the "multimedia Quixote," according to documentarian Mauricio Salas, continued to work with all enthusiasm until death, explaining in his Flagler Street office in Miami how proud he was of the remaining ACUDE (Assist) and AVANCE (Advance) projects in Venezuela and Honduras, respectively. His newspaper *El Campesino* had a circulation of over 70,000 copies (Unesco said 3 to 5 million copies annually), and his *cartillas* (booklets) also ran in the millions. It is indeed an irony that this historic international enterprise closed down quietly, "with most of [its] facilities [being] sold to the commercial Caracol network of Colombia."[129]

Bolivia is a different but also a remarkable early case of alternative radio for participatory and democratic communications: *Las Radios Mineras* (The Tin Miners's Radio Stations), particularly in traditional mining districts such as Potosí and Oruro around the 1952 Bolivian Revolution. Actually, like in Colombia, these popular radio stations began to emerge in the late 1940s. The most historic station surfaced in Catavi in 1949, and during three decades names like *Radio Animas*, *Radio Pio XII*, *Radio Nacional de Huanuni*, *La Voz del Minero*, *Radio Vanguardia de Colquiri*, and *Radio 21 de Diciembre*, among others, courageously appeared to report on the erratic and corruptive politics of the Bolivian aristocracy and worked as telephone or postal services.[130]

Defying the commercial pressures of globalization and the "creed" of modernization scholars with their "biblical" prescription, the miners' radio stations fiercely resisted all kinds of political and economic repression from dictators, especially General Hugo Banzer's (1971–1978) and General Luis García-Meza with his Interior Minister Coronel Luis Arce-Gómez's, the latter extradited and convicted for narcotrafficking in the United States.[131]

After several decades of market-power abuses, a number of Latin American countries decided to enact U.S.-styled antimonopoly laws trying to control the number of licenses one company may hold and hoping to neutralize the control of domestic and/or alien conglomerates, but these statutes, as in the United States, have been mostly innocuous since conglomerates easily avoid the rules through skillful and twisted affiliation contracts.[132]

A GIANT WAKES UP

Although Brazil had a media history of roughly one and a half centuries before World War II, this sleeping giant did not truly awake in world and Latin American contexts until Nazi submarines showed up at its shores—four centuries after colonization.[133] During the fifteen years of the Vargas regime (1930–1945), a modernizing though repressive era comparable to the *Porfiriato* in Mexico, the Brazilian press and society prospered both economically and technologically along the lines of Anglo-America but in hemispheric isolation.

In the so-called *Estado Novo* (New State), launched by Vargas with a coup d'état in 1937, Brazilians experienced a complex mix of middle-class nationalism, anticommunism, militarism, and corporate statism. Business power, regulatory abuses, press censorship, and infrastructure and technological progress were also features of the historic Vargas dictatorship. But, Brazil's cosmopolitanism, civil liberties, and international projection would not come until the presidency of Juscelino Kubitschek (1956–1961) and his *Partido Social Democrático (PSD)*. Kubitschek's dream of a powerful and influential South American republic is the image of Brazil many Anglos and Latin Americans continue to have, despite decades of a most bloody and repressive military regime initiated in 1964, often referred as "the 1964 Revolution."

Yet, pre-World War II media developments also made history in Brazil, although they are usually little known beyond her borders. One media icon, for example, is the historic *Diario de Pernambuco*, a governmental daily founded by Antonio José de Miranda Falcáo on November 7, 1825, which sought a *liberdade de imprensa* (free press) based on commercial announcements (*anúncios*). In spite of its imperial and orthodox views, the *Diario* published contributions by prominent and progressive Brazilian journalists such as Assis Chateaubriand, Antonio Freyre, Ulises Costa, Alfredo Carvalho, and Manuel Oliveira Lima, among many others.[134] In 1938, Assis Chateaubriand, led the country's pioneer and most influential radio network of the time, *Diários e Emissoras Associadas*, formed by twelve newspapers, five radio stations, and one magazine.[135]

The *Diario de Pernambuco* faded away once modern metropolitan newspapers such as *O Globo*, the *Jornal do Brasil*, and the *Folha de Sao Paulo* came about overshadowing nearly 130 years of old biases (*parcialidades*), inquiries, defamation, and public order issues.[136] Brazil's legendary interest for commerce, similar to the United States and in contrast with the closed-port heritage of Spanish America, also had in Pernambuco's *Jornal do Comércio* a major journalistic precedent. This paper goes back to the *Folha Mercantil* of 1824 and the *Diario Mercantil* of 1827, emerging around the same time of Hispanic America's oldest postcolonial newspapers such as Lima's *El Peruano* (1825) and Valparaiso's *El Mercurio* (1827).

As previous traditional newspapers and literary publications, radio broadcasting in Brazil also emerged with strong political, cultural, and educational tones. Government reactions to broadcasting resulted in authoritarian, conservative, and paternalistic regulations, affected by public interest expectations. But, interestingly, unlike the predominant commercial start of various Latin American nations, notably Argentina, Peru, Colombia, and Venezuela, Brazil launched her radio industry as an educational, community-owned, and not for profit venture. Member-supported associations, such as the pioneer club established by educator Roquette Pinto and astronomer Henry Moritze in 1923, characterized the early days of Brazilian broadcasting.[137] That is, until a federal law of 1932, introducing the use of advertising for commercial broadcasts effectively killed the private community spirit and initiative.

Government regulation, substantial in what worried the Vargas regime, that is to say, politics rather than industry mechanics, centered on censoring content, particularly after the Constitutionalist's Revolution of 1932 when students in Sao Paulo used a radio station (*Radio Record*) to demand liberty for Brazil.[138] For that purpose, following his coup and the new constitution of 1937, President Getúlio Vargas organized the above-mentioned *Departmento de Imprensa e Propaganda* (DIP, 1939) to control news and information and promote his concept of Brazilian culture, order, and morality.[139]

Persecution and assassination attempts against journalists plus norms imposed on foreign investment, public order, government access, right of reply, and defamation dominated the press during the World War II years (see art. 12, cl. 14 of the 1937 Political Constitution of Brazil).[140] In less than nine months in 1943, the *DIP* reported "2,256 incidents of censorship of the words of songs and 1,088 cases of censorship of recordings of radio programs."[141] Curiously, the only regulations on the new broadcasting technology were decrees 20,047 of 1931 and 21,111 of 1932, prescribing national interest and licensing obligations, respectively. As often occurred with new technologies, radio broadcasting activities remained mostly unregulated, especially after permitting advertising in 1932.

Before the noted media take-off of the mid-1960s, the U.S. commercial model visibly seduced the Brazilian press. A corporate, sensational, monopolistic, and apolitical format gradually set out to dominate the practice of conventional journalism, with authorities supervising and, if necessary, repressing civil rights on national integrity and security grounds. Kubitsckek's presidency, as mentioned above, was a significant exception, reversed in its liberal achievements by a lasting, U.S-supported, and regionally damaging military coup (1964) that would orchestrate the Southern Cone's "Dirty War" of the 1970s.[142] For the next two decades, the Brazilian press would live a dual life of liberal constitutionalism in media and economics and a fascistic integralism in mass media politics and regulation.

Eventually, this dualism made possible the growth, concentration, and expansion of the powerful *Rede Globo*. Currently, the Globo Network consists of at least eight wholly owned television stations, seventy-four affiliates, and 1,500 satellite rebroadcasting antennas. Other holdings include one of the country's four largest dailies (*O Globo*), one of the two main national cable networks, and dozens of radio stations and magazines (*Marie Claire, Criativo, Globo Ciência, Globo Rural*, etc.).[143]

JOURNALISM EDUCATION COMES TO PLAY

Since its origins in the 1930s, journalism and mass communication education in Latin America and the Caribbean was a topic of heated regional and hemispheric debates. Discussions concerned matters such as secular and religious values in education, domestic, and transnational journalistic influences, humanistic versus behavioral science training, and freedom of the press versus press responsibility. These same factors would have a direct and profound impact in the Cold War and post-Cold War transformations on Latin America's journalism and mass communication teaching.

Journalism education in the region traces its roots to Argentina, Brazil, and Mexico, as they excelled regionally for their university dynamism and mass media advancement. On April 27, 1934, the *Argentine Círculo de Periodistas de la Plata* (The La Plata Circle of Journalists) founded the region's first *Escuela Superior de Periodismo* (Higher School of Journalism). Although initiated by a professional organization, university officials insisted on a liberally based social preparation in the humanities and social sciences.[144] A month later, on May 25, the Catholic Church sponsored another program in Buenos Aires, *the Escuela Superior de Periodismo of the Instituto Grafotécnico* (Higher School of Journalism of the Graphic–Technical Institute). This program was geared toward skills training, although it also instilled students with a sense of social responsibility.

Public universities emphasized liberal education and minimized skills training since state educational institutions were steeped in the tradition of the European academy. Private Catholic universities, on the other hand, emphasized both social and private concerns. They justified a skill-based education as a means for trained journalists to correct social ills while promoting private industry developments.[145] This distinction, however, established a dichotomy of Latin American journalism education along lines of secular versus religious emphases and skill-based versus liberally based dichotomies, although the lines were not always clear.[146]

In Brazil, the *Universidade Federal del Distrito do Rio de Janeiro* (Federal University of the District of Rio de Janeiro) offered journalism courses as early as 1935. It was not until May 13, 1943, when the *Facultad Nacional de Filosofía* (National College of Philosophy) of the *Universidade do Brasil* in Rio de Janeiro created a journalism program that stressed humanistic training similar to that in the Italian, French, and Iberian academies.[147] The first Mexican school, in the meantime, was inaugurated at the *Universidad Femenina* (Women's University) in 1936 as part of the National

Autonomous University in Mexico City (UNAM).[148] The decision to establish journalism programs in women's schools suggested a low academic esteem for the craft among Mexicans.[149] More highly regarded curricula, however, emerged with stronger government support at *the Universidad Nacional Autónoma de México* in 1951 and the *Universidad Veracruzana* in 1954.

For many Mexicans, however, if not most of them, the first true professional school of journalism was the *Acción Católica Mexicana*'s Carlos Septién García, founded on May 30, 1949. As the *ACM*'s president Luis Beltrán y Mendoza then pointed out, the country needed "a school to prepare young, honest, and skillful journalists, inspired in the public good [...] to best serve Mexico's goals." It began with four professors and twenty-five students. One of the inaugural and resounding lessons's was journalist Septién-García's lecture on *Cómo hacer un periódico* (how to make a newspaper), in which he spoke of three types of journalism: informative journalism (typically, Latin American), doctrinary journalism (European), and technical-scientific or modern journalism (Anglo-American). Although profoundly religious and loyal a so-called journalism priesthood, the school became independent of the Mexican Catholic Action in 1964.[150] Apart from Brazil, Argentina, and Mexico, no other Latin American country had a journalism program before the Second World War. During World War II, Venezuela's Universidad Central (1941) and Cuba's *Escuela Professional de Periodismo Manuel Márquez Sterling* (MMS Professional School of Journalism, 1942) reactivated the process of forming journalism schools in the region.[151] Other programs followed in Ecuador, Colombia, and Peru in 1945 and in Venezuela and Chile in 1947.[152]

Journalism programs in the region's smaller nations, including most Central American republics, were initiated after the world wars. The first journalism courses appeared in Guatemala's *Universidad de San Carlos* in 1952. The program was housed in the humanities program.[153] By the mid–1960s, national universities in Central America such as the *Universidad de El Salvador* (1955), Nicaragua's *Universidad Centroamericana* (1960), and the *Universidad de Costa Rica* (1967) graduated their first students in this field.[154] In the English-speaking Caribbean, the University of West Indies at Mona, Jamaica, began offering a one-year journalism program in 1974. Within a couple of years, this undergraduate diploma was expanded to a three-year degree leading to a Bachelor of Arts in communication.[155]

Journalism programs in Central America and the Caribbean have suffered and continue to suffer from a lack of resources. The poor state of journalism education in the island of Hispaniola, shared by the Dominican Republic and Haiti, underscores the region's problems. The first journalism school in the Dominican Republic was inaugurated in 1960. Alisky criticized the program for devoting too much attention to print journalism, while poor Dominicans relied on radio and television for news.[156] The situation is worse in Haiti. Habermann noted that the typical Haitian journalist has no formal training in journalism or a related field and that he/she holds several other jobs to make ends meet. The poorly equipped School of Journalism and Mass Communication at the University of Haiti, established in 1980, offered few skills courses and "is considered by media owners and journalists alike as useless for the training of media professionals."[157] Mostly part-time faculty including the dean staffs its Department of Communication Sciences.

THE SWEET AND SOUR *COLEGIOS*

The establishment of journalism organizations known as *colegios* following World War II also contributed to program growth. In most cases, these organizations required journalists to have a journalism degree from a recognized domestic university in order to practice. Universities and many journalists lobbied for the creation of *colegios*, claiming that press guilds would improve "professional" standards in the region. Others, however, believed that for universities, *colegios* had the potential to increase student enrollment, while for journalists these entities effectively restricted the number of reporters in the market, creating conditions to raise salaries.[158]

Media owners in the region fiercely opposed such *colegios*, exploiting Cold War rhetoric by claiming they were *de facto* "licensing" of journalists and a threat to press freedom. In the United Nations, Communist bloc and Third World countries endorsed the establishment of these associations, reinforcing the view among U.S. media professionals, journalists, and educators that *colegios* posed a threat to press freedom.[159] Knudson was rather cynical of the owners' claims, arguing that they feared *colegios* simply because they would increase labor expenses. Within a few years, the region's *colegio* laws represented a case where domestic labor disputes and academic politics became entangled in the international Cold War debate. Ironically, the *colegio* that caused the most international controversy was Costa Rica's, the region's most respected democracy for its press freedoms.

By the end of the Cold War, the heated international debate over *colegios* gradually subsided, even though some of them survived unchanged until now.[160] In 1999, Bolivia, through the *Federación de Trabajadores de la Prensa* (Press Workers Federation of Bolivia) and law 494 of 1979, and Cuba, by means of the *Unión de Periodistas de Cuba* (UPEC, Union of Journalist of Cuba), had *colegios*. Also, Venezuela and her *Colegio Nacional de Periodistas* (CNP), organized by the *Ley de Ejercicio del Periodismo* (Law of the Journalism Practice, 1994), and Honduras, following the *Ley Orgánica del Colegio de Periodistas* (Organic Law of the Journalists Guild, 972), require professional degrees and registration for practicing journalists.[161]

Because of the deregulation of the mid- and late 1980s, forced by the renewed U.S. media innovation and privatization of the world's regional markets, Latin American countries that had full-force *colegios*, such as Chile, Colombia, Costa Rica, Peru, Dominican Republic, and Uruguay, ended up changing their press legislation. Chile's Political Constitution of 1980, for instance, drafted and approved during General Augusto Pinochet's dictatorship, barred any person from being compelled to belong to any association.[162] Yet, the Chilean journalism profession and the educational authorities continued to assume that a professional journalist was a person only with a "Social Communication" degree in hand. In 1988, a proposed *Law of Opinion and Information Liberties and of the Practice of Journalism* explicitly included a communication degree as a requirement to legally practice this profession in Chile.

Following in part the Chilean pattern, the Inter-American Court of Human Rights (1986) recommended that any form of obligatory *colegiación* be considered both unconstitutional and against international law. Since then, the Dominican Republic's Supreme Court (1989), Peru's Constitution of 1993, Costa Rica's Supreme Court (May 1995), and Colombia's Constitutional Court (March 1998) ruled their respective press laws unconstitutional, either partially or entirely. Colombia's top constitutional tribunal, for instance, threw out Law 51 of 1975 (the Colombian press statute) using the balancing of interests approach.

The law, argued the Constitutional Court, may in fact require diplomas of expertise, giving authorities the power to inspect and monitor the practice of any profession. If the occupation, art, or activity does not represent a social risk, it may be practiced freely. But, if the profession implies any danger for society, the Colombian Congress is also free to regulate it. That is, authorities may only require sufficient certification when the goal is to avoid any potential and actual social danger. Conceivably, in the case of journalism, there may be a social danger created with false or mistaken information. But, in balancing the freedom to express ideas or information with the eventual social danger caused by any unprofessional communication, the Colombian Constitutional Court preferred to defend the former one. The right to freedom of the press is then paramount to any apparent need to regulate the professional practice of journalism through academic requirements such as a university degree.[163]

Similar arguments have been used in Peru, Costa Rica, and the Dominican Republic on this issue, ordering, at least in theory, their domestic legal systems to observe and respect international treaties such as the Inter-American Convention on Human Rights. Without *colegio* laws, other Latin American nations, including Argentina, Brasil, Ecuador, Haiti, Guatemala, and Panama, require either identification cards, diploma registration, or degree conditions for certain press-related jobs in government offices. Yet, an increasing group of countries, namely Uruguay, Paraguay, Nicaragua, Mexico, Chile, Costa Rica, and El Salvador, have decided to follow, with or without *colegios*, the open, private, free marketplace, nonunionized, and unregulated professional steaming from the United States, Canada, and the English-speaking Caribbean.[164]

In short, this controversy practically ended when the Inter-American Court of Human Rights, based in San José Costa Rica, unanimously ruled in the case *Stephen Schmidt v. Colegio de Periodistas* (1985) that the mandatory *colegiación* of journalists "denies access to the full use of the mass media as a form of self-expression or diffusing information, including the people's right (a collective prerogative) to receive information without restrictions."[165] Mr. Schmidt of the *Tico Times* had been criminally accused in April 1980 of practicing journalism illegally, as he was not an official member of the Costa Rican journalists' guild (*colegio*). The penal district court ruled in Schmidt's favor, arguing that he had merely exercised a basic human right, but the Costa Rican Supreme Court of Justice reversed the lower court's judgment, sentencing the reporter to three months in prison.

Under pressure, primarily from Inter-American Press Association, the government of Costa Rica filed a formal consultation to the Inter-American Court of Human Rights, which ultimately declared all national laws of colegiación unconstitutional. Nevertheless, pockets of discontent and opposition with this international jurisprudence continue to dominate in some circles. Incidentally, it is in this type of outcome in which anyone can recognize the valuable contributions of the SIP/IAPA, a significantly more open entity in recent times, to the free flow of information, but when it comes to touching the economic and political sensibilities of its members, such as the underresearched issue of print media conglomerates and their dominance, the organization lacks credibility.

In the mutual bickering of mass media owners versus governments, when not acting as allies, heads of state and other critics have strongly criticized the IAPA as an organism "that defends the interests of companies, and not the genuine liberty of expression."[166] In fact, Argentinean president Néstor Kirchner recently and harshly criticized the IAPA as an institution that turned its back on Argentina during the last military dictatorships, that tacitly became an accomplice of the disappearances during the dirty war, and that only cares about the commercial interests of its funding members. Yet, popular presidents also have a lengthy history of media censorship, collusion, and intolerance as to fully believe in or sympathize with their claims.

In any case, professor Mary Gardner, the memorable IAPA's historian, can rest in peace for her long fight against *colegios* as a form of licensing journalists' echoes throughout the Americas today more than ever before.

THE TV DREAM AND NIGHTMARE

More than a remarkable economical, political, or institutional revolution, Latin American television emerged as a noted technological event of lasting cultural implications. Television stations simply replicated and exacerbated what radio broadcasting had done twenty to thirty years earlier.

Television advertising, to name an important feature, was only more ambitious, sophisticated, and alienating than during the radio days. Naturally, radio-advertising revenue suffered greatly once television came about. Commercial television programming, appealing and entertaining as it was thanks to its novel images and sounds, showed however little innovation in formats and themes. Radio and film audiences in Latin America could easily associate the U.S.-imported television productions to old, local, and foreign-influenced radio programs. In Latin America, as elsewhere in this hemisphere, sports, comedies, *radionovelas*, live musicals, sponsored talks, trivia contests, and practically every other show were not an invention of television.[167]

TV broadcasters in Latin America rarely offer a groundbreaking achievement and, comparably to their U.S. counterparts, they keep operating in the same lines of the regularly criticized North American "wasteland," including new media versions, such as satellite, cable, and other wireless subscription-based services. The only relative exception to this middle of the road, if not mediocre, but profitable industry is the homegrown telenovela. And even here, as Brazilian actress Sonia Braga has pointed out, both television and film productions are unimaginative in the final analysis. As with Univision and other Hispanic channels in U.S. America, it appears that the Latin American and Caribbean tube is designed to be a below-average performer, cutting costs while securing ads and profits.

Although not very creative, children programming probably constituted the only genuinely innovative TV format, for radio and newspapers paid little or no attention to young audiences before the arrival of television technologies. The English-speaking rock and roll and the U.S.-styled disk jockey that seduced millions of Latin American adolescents and children did not firmly take place until the first half of the 1960s. Alfonso Lizarazo, for example, a popular South American disk jockey of the late 1960s, introduced the practice of moving from radio to television musicals in Colombia—a sort of homegrown Ed Sullivan show.[168]

In the same token, television was organizationally and managerially almost identical to broadcast radio, following even more tightly the internal

structure, ownership patterns, profit motives, commercial spirit, and social and political roles of radio networking. With television, unlike radio,
the U.S. broadcast model became fully dominant. Also, being more capital
intensive, television turned even more elitist, concentrated, and discriminatory than radio, favoring urban, white, and higher income populations.
For nearly two and a half decades, that is, up to the early 1970s when big
sports such as the Olympics and the World Soccer Cup brought million
of viewers, television was a technology of limited access and coverage in
both rural and densely populated and impoverished urban areas. In many
countries and numerous settings, it continues to be the case in spite of the
Internet excitement.

So, the true revolution of television was originally technological, as it
is now the case with the Internet in Latin America. Other dominant features, such as the way of conducting media businesses, media diplomacy,
and media politics and censorship, including most notably the dominance
of U.S. private and commercial operations and practices, were simply
transferred from radio to television. And these same patterns are being
transferred once again into the new technologies of 2000, even more in-
sidiously dominated by monopolistic interest and multinationals operating primarily though not exclusively from the United States. The fact
that either guerrillas or narcotraffickers, new elites on their own terms,
used for public relations purposes these new technologies does not make
them more democratic. Eventually, the technological impact of television resulted in damaging perceptions of cultural inferiority, mental dependency, social inequality, political manipulation, misinformation, alien-
ation, lack of access, distortion of values, and polarized conflicts, among
others.

As the broadcast radio industry in Mexico and most of Latin
America, television stations also emerged with variations of public interest, educational, and state goals and controls. But, within a few years,
the domestic television scene was all private commercialization, cos-
mopolitism, and elitism. A vertical and often manipulative monologue
of closed monopolies, U.S. imports, and nepotism at the highest levels of
private and governmental media entities and authorities dominated the
new and supposedly promising television industry. In Mexico, to cite a revealing case, President Miguel Alemán introduced television with a State
of the Union speech in 1950 after a comparison of two broadcast systems
by the National Institute of Fine Arts: the BBC and the U.S. commercial
models. Naturally, considering the history and status of Mexico's radio
industry, the latter was chosen as the most convenient and comparable.[169]

Initially, Alemán favored his friend Rómulo O'Farrill in the licensing
process, giving this newspaper publisher the honor of inaugurating the
first television concession of Latin America. *XH-TV*, the *Canal 4* (channel 4), began its official transmissions on August 31, 1950, nine months

after the granting of the license by the Mexican communication authorities. Brazil's *TV Tupi* and Cuba's *Union Radio-TV* would follow suit on September 18 and October 1950, respectively. Emilio Azcárraga Vidaurreta had to wait until July 1950 for the license approval and in March 1951 he launched *XEW-TV (Canal 2)*, learning that only media that are loyal to the president would do well in business. In fact, while O'Farrill had faithfully supported in his newspaper *Novedades* the presidential candidacy of Manuel Avila-Camacho (1940–1946), of which Alemán had been the campaign manager, Azcárraga Vidaurreta decided to support the opposition.[170]

By 1955, eventually with Alemán on board, O'Farrill and Azcárraga merged in a most powerful television monopoly, the *Telesistema Mexicano (TSM)*, one that would reign unchallenged in Mexico for the next forty years. In it, the Azcárraga family ended up with the upper hand and taking revenge for not being the first in this business. This network, later called *Televisa (Televisión Vía Satellite)*, would also turn into a hemispheric media empire that controlled dozens of radio and TV stations, satellite facilities, printed publications, an international news service *(ECO)*, and dominant interests in the U.S. *Univisión* chain, formerly known as the *Spanish International Network (SIN)*. At the dawn of the twenty-first century, *Televisa* also produced 35,000 hours of television broadcast a year, exported programming to fifty countries, covered the world with more than 100 correspondents, and transmitted satellite signals to forty-seven countries in three continents.[171]

The Mexican government, except for the timid exceptions of presidents Luis Echeverría-Alvarez (1970–1976) and José lópez Portillo (1976–1982), traditionally and often enthusiastically nurtured this monopoly. Presidents Adolfo Ruiz-Cortines (1952–1958), Adolfo López Mateos (1958–1964), and Gustavo Díaz-Ordaz (1964–1970) were especially supportive of a television monopoly that submerged Mexico into a manipulative regime of self-censorship in broadcast news, dominated by big corporate party (PRI), and state interests which lasted until the mid-1990s. Relaxing the nationalism and public service philosophy defined by the Law of Communication of 1940, which banned any licensing to foreign stations, the Mexican federal government enacted the Federal Broadcasting Law of 1960, giving *Televisa* the necessary space to expand its business across borders via microwave and satellite communications.

Leading Latin American countries, namely Brazil (September 1950), Cuba (October 1950, nearly a decade before the revolution), and Argentina (1951), tried to match Mexico's early start. Early adopters, following the big three pioneers and Cuba, were Venezuela (November 1952), the Dominican Republic (1952), Colombia (June 1954), and Uruguay (1955). The first Central American nations to inaugurate a television station were El Salvador, Guatemala, and Nicaragua (all in 1956), even before Peru

(1958), Chile, Ecuador, Honduras, and Panama that introduced this service in 1959. Relative latecomers would be Costa Rica (1960), Trinidad and
Tobago (the first English-speaking country with an operational TV channel, 1962), Jamaica (1963), Barbados (1964), Paraguay and Antigua (both in
1965), St. Lucia (1967), Surinam (1968), and Bolivia (1969). By 1984, a few
Caribbean states, Anguilla, Guyana, Dominica, Granada, and Belize, were
without a television transmitter in their territories. Belize was apparently
one of the latest in setting up a TV station in 1986.[172]

In the spread of television more than radio, the region presented evident
patterns of a hemispheric transnational diffusion and domination, resulting in common features of TV development in the most media influential
Latin American countries. To begin with, the adoption of television came
as a result of the political ambitions of exclusive modernizing elites under
restrictive civilian authority or military rule. Indeed, Mexico's dominance
by the PRI imposed a style of vertical, commercial, and state-controlled
television that many Latin American nations replicated, particularly in
terms of domestic security, national sovereignty, and profitability interests
and values. In addition to a virtually unregulated advertising industry,
Mexico's Federal Broadcasting Law of 1960 synthesized the state expectations with radio and television, focusing on the promotion of public order,
state propaganda, private gain, and suppression of critical views.

In fact, dictators General Juan Domingo Perón (1946–1955 and
1973–1974) in Argentina, General Marcos Pérez-Jiménez (1952–1958) in
Venezuela, and General Gustavo Rojas-Pinilla (1954–1957) in Colombia
introduced television for government and ruling party propaganda purposes. In Brazil, Army General and President Eurico Gaspar Dutra (1946–
1951), who had actively participated in the construction of Dictator
Getúlio Vargas' *Estado Novo*, also launched television for obvious political
gains and motives. In all these cases, including Mexico's Alemán administration, the agenda had been technological progress and modernization
(more a myth than reality at that time), internal order, and an intuitive
sense of territorial sovereignty and national security.[173]

Once the early dictatorial rhetoric of public services and state-controlled
television enterprises faded, the television industry in most Latin
American countries became easy prey of the voracious U.S. television expansionism. For slightly over a decade, both Chile and Uruguay stood
out as two significant exceptions to the fully dominant U.S. commercial
broadcast model. In Chile, for instance, the government of President Jorge
Alessandri (1958–1964) bravely resisted the modernization course, refusing to grant licenses for what he considered was the banal, mediocre, and
superfluous commercial television industry, unnecessary for a poor country in need of resolving serious socioeconomic problems.[174]

Unlike most states in Latin America, the Chilean government believed
in a strong broadcasting system, supporting the public function of culture

and mass education. Following a television decree issued by the previous Carlos Ibañez administration (1952–1958) that banned the licensing of foreign stations, Alessandri's presidency authorized Chilean universities to set up television channels to foster education, the arts, technology, and political independence and pluralism. The first stations began to operate in 1959. In a rare but interesting coalition of Christian democrats, conservatives, socialists, communists, and radicals, the country "rejected private commercial television on the grounds that it would favor big business and encourage mass audiences at the expense of educational and cultural programming."[175]

Even so, for more than a decade, Alessandri's Television Law of 1958 was repeatedly violated by TV stations that raised funds through commercial advertising without any legal punishment. This anomalous situation, corrected in the Television Statute of 1970, also sought to give television stations greater private control and economic independence before the inauguration of President Salvador Allende (1970–1973). The center-right and Chilean conservatives, rallying behind the elderly Alessandri, feared that Allende and his leftist front *Unidad Popular* would disrupt the balance of power that had "smoothly" run the country during the last two decades. The military was especially outraged of a socialist president elected by a narrow margin of less than 40,000 votes. Curiously, twelve years earlier, Allende had lost the presidency to Alessandri in a similarly close election. Afraid of the potential manipulation of both universities and television stations by the left, leaving President Eduardo Frei (1964–1970) sanctioned the above-mentioned Television Law of 1970, taking various executive powers in broadcasting away from the presidency.[176]

In any case, Chile's educational television philosophy is one of the most profound attempts at building a broadcast system separate from the private, commercialized, and free-market model imposed by the United States in Latin America. Other experiences like channel 5 in Uruguay, a television station created in 1963 under the *Servicio Oficial de Difusión Radio Eléctrica* (*SODRE*, Official Service of Radio Electric Diffusion), advocated a public broadcasting monopoly similar to the BBC in Great Britain. Colombia's efforts of an alternative broadcast structure also resulted in a so-called hybrid or mixed system where government authorities owned and administered television frequencies and studios. Through the *Instituto Nacional de Radio y Televisión* (*INRAVISION*, National Institute of Radio and Television), the government had and continue to grant concessions to private programmers for their commercial exploitation. In the end, every educational television endeavor in Latin America succumbed to the new and inflexible patterns of commercial market laws, dominated by monopolistic groups, U.S. program imports, and both hard and soft-sell advertising campaigns.[177]

Guillermo Orozco, the prestigious Mexican communication researcher with the *Universidad de Guadalajara*, argues that there have been seven types of television in Latin America: television as an institution, television as a mass medium, television as culture, television as language, television as a referent, and above all, a television as a market and as a political arena. In fact, he wrote, it is more and more evident that the Latin American television activity is essentially or primarily mercantilistic, followed by a political drama where television companies have won the power to advance their profit-making and strategic ambitions in public life with an effectiveness never seen before. *Rede Globo* in Brazil and *Televisa* in Mexico are the two colossuses of this evolving television business power in Latin America.[178]

With a cost-effective, that is, a bland menu of dramatized series, hard or "reality" news, and *telenovelas*, the cultural catalizer which became the region's successful market story both nationally and internationally, *la televisión sigue más viva que nunca* (television is more alive than ever) concludes Orozco – for those who mechanically like to kill old media when new technologies arrive. Curiously, in the case of Latin American television, new media such as satellite TV and various forms of codified cable seemed to have lost the battle, despite strong appearances in Mexico and Argentina (over 1.5 million subscribers in 1994).[179]

Professor Nora Mazziotti of the *Universidad de Buenos Aires* (*UBA*) and the National University of La Matanza in Argentina deplores how *livianos* (light) are both the Argentine television programming and the studies or journalistic writings about it. In recent times, she says, Argentine television is increasingly dominated by gossip, infotaintment, pseudo journalism, talk shows with celebrities, reality game shows, and self-improvement programs making up a virtual *telebasura* (tele-trash), an array of national, Latin American, or North American enlatados (canned programming) such as Susana Giménez's *Hola, Susana*, the Mexican *Chavo del Ocho*, *Los Simpson*, and the Colombian re-run *Betty, la fea*, to name a few.

Telenovelas are a remarkable genre in the history of Latin American television, either Argentinean, Colombian, or (co)produced anywhere else, except when recycled as a mechanism to more cheaply fill broadcast schedules. From the experimental times of the Argentinean television during Peronism (1951-1960) to its consolidation years of local channels connected to NBC, ABC, CBS and the Time-Life Group (1960-1973), national talent from film, theater, and the musical arts flourished to build a tradition of TV writers, actors, and directors, nurturing the telenovela and other homegrown formats. In fact, broadcaster Alejandro Romay is credited with having launched an Argentinean-styled television competing with that Cuban TV of Channel 13 (Goar Mestre's) "that does not invent anything but only brings recipes originated in the United States to seduce our public."[180]

Then, the military dictatorship and statization of the mid-1970s to early 1980s (exactly, 1974-1983) would come to censor the telenovela because of its immorality, lack of ethics, poor taste, mass appeal, and continuing reference to social conflict, particularly, issues of free love, pregnancy, abortion, extramarital relationships, and situations of social tragedy, bankruptcy, and frustration. Once the *Malvinas* (Falklands) war broke out, censorship was tightly and quickly extended to the broadcast news. The goal was to put the national television industry in exile, concludes Mazziotti.

The rest of the story is a re-privatization (1984-1994), overcommercialization, and trivialization of this country's TV industry, framed by incidents of deep pocket corruption, concentration, and transnationalization. Channel 13, for instance, ends in the coffers of the *Grupo Clarín*, "Hispanic America's largest-circulation daily," while the multinationals JP Morgan, *Telefónica* of Spain, and the Australian Prime TV companies grow more popular. It is what Mazziotti calls the period of "atomization" where media acquisitions and alliances dominate the marketplace, assisted by an increasing number of independent producers.[181]

According to Orozco, the history of television in Latin America revolves around four poles: as an open propaganda instrument of dictatorial governments; as a tool of subtle ideological manipulations and transnational interests; as a mechanism of secrecy, favoring the status quo while hiding significant news and social movements; and, lately, as a platform of gossip, infotainment, and comedic portrayals of public life.[182] In Brazil, with unique features, television also lands in the lap of Roberto Marinho's *Globo* network, after a long and intimate collaboration with military dictators and corrupt or less corrupt civilian governments afterwards.

Under the military, wrote the influential Spanish theorist Jesús Martín-Barbero, who made his career in Colombia since 1963, Brazilian television transformed "the mass into the people and the people into the nation."[183] "The next stage was the commercialization of culture in which the media took on the 'economic function' of creating a consumer society," commented John Sinclair of Victoria University of Technology in Melbourne, Australia.

After defeating the early monopolistic hegemony of the São Paulo-based *TV Tupi* of Francisco de Assis Chateubriand's *Diários Associados* (technically assisted by General Electric), *Rede Globo*, tied to the Time-Life Group, dominated throughout the dictatorship and until today, despite the competitive resistance, sometimes united, others dispersed, from *Editora Avril*, the *Jornal do Brasil* Group, the Grupo Silvio Santos' *SBT* (the Sistema Brasileiro de Televisão), the Grupo (Adolpho) Bloch's *Rede Manchete*, the Saad family's *Rede Bandeirantes*, and the religious *Rede Vida* of the Catholic Church and *Rede Record* of the Pentecostal *Igreja*

Universal do Reino de Deus. This last chain, founded in 1953 by the Machado de Carvalho family, but sold to pastor Edir Macedo's IURD in 1989, is about to become the second most popular television network in Brazil.[184]

Until his recent death at 98 (August 8, 2003), Roberto Marinho has been the South American icon of success among television entrepreneuers in Latin America, the "Citizen Kane" of Brazil, "indispensable to understand the game of media and power," wrote Colombian journalist Gerardo Reyes, a Maria Moors Cabot award winner working with *El Nuevo Herald* in Miami. To many, Marinho was even more influential and astute than "The Tiger," Don Emilio Azcárraga Milmo and his cubs. One way or another, and since the mid-1960s, South American television investors have either mimicked or envied the evolution of this businessman in the broadcast industry, with only some apparent exceptions in Colombia and Chile.[185]

The late Roberto Marinho brought political propaganda, modernization and transnationalization, and the populism of sports and telenovelas to a level of mastery Latin Americans had not known before, even with U.S. multinationals and tall merchants in the region, such as, the Azcárragas, the Mestres, and the Cisneros. Other media kings or emperors, such as the Colombian Julio Mario Santo Domingo, owner of the *Caracol* network, are actual dwarfs before Marinho. In *Los Dueños de América Latina* (The Owners of Latin America), Gerardo Reyes profiles the life of this and other contemporary Latin American broadcast media moguls, including Gustavo Cisneros (*Venevisión*, *Direct TV Latin America*, *Playboy TV Latin America*, and part of *Univision*, *Caracol Televisión*, and *Chilevisión*) and Ricardo Salinas (*TV Azteca*).

North and South, although in different ways, the Marihnos, the Mestres, the Azacárragas, and the Cisneros-types of families converged in a feast of profit-making ventures and television trivia, with noteworthy exceptions. If in Chile, the government insisted in a television model run by universities, out of fears of comercialization and high doses of both political conservatism and paternalism, Colombia promoted a so-called "mixed system" just to control and censor the new medium. In the end, the commercial TV enterprise dominated fueled by popular entertainment events and advertising such as the summer olympics and the world soccer cups. As the television consultant and author Valerio Fuenzalida pointed out, in Chile, the World Soccer Cup of 1962 "propelled the consolidation" of the country's television activity, "demanding technical equipment and professionalization in order to serve both internal TV transmissions and foreign television services."[186] Something similar occurred in Mexico with its 1970 World Soccer Cup and in Argentina with the televised World Soccer Cup of 1978 under military rule, to name a few cases.

BIG BUSINESS NEWS FROM SPACE

Speculation about the use of satellites and their paradox began in the Americas right after the memorable October 4, 1957. In Colombia, for instance, the daily *El Tiempo* stated: "in just one day, a dividing line has been drawn in the development of mankind. There is something heroic and at the same time something satanic in Sputnik's accomplishment."[187] As in the old times of telegraphy, many argued that space telecommunications were good for social progress in poor countries. Others, on the contrary, rejected this assumption as a modernization dream Latin Americans were in no position to equitably bring about either collectively or individually. Like every new technology in this region, the issue of satellites ultimately ended up "engulfed in a magic nimbus of power," full of empty promises and formulations.[188]

The adoption of satellite technologies in Latin America did not come overnight or as a simple process. Tortuous as the history of Mexico's *Morelos*, *Solidaridad*, and *Panamsat* satellites was the introduction of the Brazilian *Brasilsat* and Argentinean *Nahuel* space systems. Yet, investing comparable time and resources, other Latin American nations saw that their projects failed, notably Colombia's *Satcol* and both the Andean *Cóndor* and the Antillean *Carisat*. New technologies, especially those expensive and sophisticated, have rarely been an equalizer in Latin America. Actually, they have often been an increased source of discrimination and inequality across and within countries and communities.

The early days of this region in space communications were marked by government-sponsored researches, bilateral agreements with the United States, and intraregional competition. As early as February 1959, the University of Chile negotiated with NASA a project to track and receive radio signals from satellites. The plan included studies on the outer-space portion of the earth's atmosphere and its effect on weather, the nature of radiation from outer space, and the provision of information that would permit future exploratory flights beyond the earth.[189] Back then, Chile expected to make leading improvements in domestic and international communications.

This bilateral media cooperation may be traced back to years before NASA and Sputnik. On November 15, 1956, the Inter-American Geodetic Survey and the *Instituto Geográfico Militar de Chile* (The Geographic Military Institute of Chile) signed a previous accord that eventually made Chile the first Latin American country with a permanent satellite earth station by the end of the following decade. Immediately, other countries followed suit. Trying not to fall behind its neighbor, Argentina set up an "optical satellite tracking station" at *Villa Dolores* in the province of *Córboba*, linking the Smithsonian Institution and the *Observatorio*

Astronómico de la Universidad Nacional (Astronomical Observatory of Cordoba's National University). Inaugurated on October 23, 1959, this two-year experiment intended to share mutual benefits and experiences from the operation of distant satellite infrastructures.[190]

These bilateral treaties represented for the U.S. additional strategic sites toward the completion of an inter-American satellite information network. For the Latin American countries, it meant an opportunity to learn "hands-on" about a revolutionary and otherwise inaccessible space technology. On February 26, 1960, Ecuador authorized NASA to build and operate an experimental antenna atop the *Cotopaxi* snow-covered peak (the so-called Quito Tracking Station Facility). A permit extended in exchange for Ecuadorian personnel trained in the use of satellite telecommunication equipment. Weeks later, on April 12, the Mexican government also agreed to the construction of a ground station at *Empalme-Guaymas* in the State of Sonora, but under the explicit condition of working on peaceful and scientific purposes (that is to say, no military applications).[191]

At this point, two interesting patterns dominated in the inter-American communications diplomacy. Whereas U.S. entities favorably negotiated communication technology agreements on country-by-country basis, influential Latin American governments also began to gravitate around high-tech military objectives, displaying a strong regional competition for leadership in space telecommunications. At first, Argentina and Brazil appeared more determined than Mexico in taking full advantage of any available satellite technology and information. Various Argentinean and Brazilian actors including the private sector were ready to organize national space committees, offering local scientists opportunities to work with American, Soviet, and European experts on satellite communications.[192]

When the U.S.-led *Comisión Interamericana de Investigaciones Espaciales* (Inter-American Space Research Commission) was founded in Buenos Aires in 1960, the Latin American "space powers," primarily Argentina, Brazil, and Chile, rallied behind it. They persuaded other South American countries such as Peru, Uruguay, and Bolivia to join the United States in a vast campaign promoting space research throughout the continent.[193] Not until 1964 would Mexico become part of this regional commission after substantial reforms to accommodate unwilling members.

The late 1950s and early 1960s were times of active participation, experimentation, and competition, not just simple contemplation in the satellite field, primarily among the "big three" Latin American states (Brazil, Argentina, and Mexico). On July 13, 1961, however, Brazil took a definite lead, announcing a memorandum of understanding between NASA and the Brazilian *Departamento de Correios e Telegrafos* (DPTC). Promising to interconnect points of the Brazilian territory with North America and Europe via satellite, this experiment, the world's first *active* communication satellite test, planned to deliver intercontinental transmissions of telephone, telegraph, and television signals.[194]

On July 10, 1962, using the historic NASA/AT&T's *Telstar I*, Latin America was in fact inaugurated to the new era of satellite communications. Just like France, England, Italy, and Sweden came ahead in Europe with NASA's assistance, Brazil emerged as the region's satellite front-runner, acting as a testing site for the *Telstar*'s intercontinental experiment. Temporarily linked to the United States, Great Britain, France, and Italy, via satellite voice, television, facsimile, and data, Brazil's participation in this exchange symbolized the beginning of space communications in Latin America and in the Caribbean.[195]

One week before the enactment of the U.S. Communication Satellite Act (*COMSAT*), Brazil adopted its *Código Brasileiro de Telecomunicacôes* (Law 4117 of 1962). This document, the first of its kind in Latin America, had a significant regional impact for it became the backbone of the Brazilian telecommunications policy and the model of future Latin American telecommunication regulations.[196] Major developments such as the country's nationalization of the telephone system, the creation of both *EMBRATEL* (the Brazilian Telecommunications Enterprise) and the specialized Ministry of Communications philosophy, and the implementation of new services such as direct dialing, color television, and satellite networking were all framed by the 1962 code. That same year, successful transmissions using RCA/NASA's *Relay I* brought back to Brazil longer and improved North American satellite TV signals, sealing Brazil's regional superiority in communication technology.

By 1967, seven countries of the region extended contracts to the COMSAT corporation, seeking expertise in the planning, bidding, offer evaluation, acquisition, and construction of satellite antennas, including testing and installation of required telecommunication equipment.[197] A U.S. Senate report in 1961 predicted that Latin America and the Caribbean would be the most dynamic satellite market after Europe, and until 1970 it was. Chile, Panama, Brazil, Colombia, Venezuela, Jamaica, and Ecuador all purchased their first earth stations from U.S. manufacturers in the late 1960s. Actually, the amount of antennas sold in Latin America at that time equaled the number of orders placed in Western Europe.

Because of their geopolitical concerns and contacts with the United States, Panama and Chile purchased the region's first space communication antennas, just a few months ahead of Brazil, Mexico, and Argentina. On July 22, 1968, twelve months after the contract award, GTE built Chile's *Longovillo 1*. And two months later, Page Communications erected the first Panamanian dish at *Utibe*.[198]

In Chile, long-term research with space technologies and the extreme distance from the world centers of power, limiting the modernization prospects of the upper class, played an influential role in the Chilean decision to acquire an international antenna first than anybody else. These same factors were present in Argentina and Brazil but cool relations with the U.S. government contributed to delay in their respective space media plans. On the contrary, Panama's geopolitical importance mixed with innovation influences from the U.S. Canal Zone framed this country's early adoption of a satellite station. Panama had for years enjoyed the reputation of a well-served developing country in the mass media and telecommunications, exhibiting telephone-density levels comparable to those of many Western industrialized countries.

In September 1968, Mexico inaugurated a satellite center for the intercontinental transmission of the XIX Summer Olympiad. *Tulancingo 1*, built by *Mitsubishi Shojikaisa Limited* in the state of Hidalgo, would be the world's largest earth station ever built: 105 feet in diameter and 330 tons of weight supported by 1,200 additional tons of steel and concrete.[199] This antenna was connected to the INTELSAT III series, a satellite of which exploded in mid-air on its September 19 launching a few days before the inauguration of the Olympic Games' television transmissions.[200]

In Brazil, the historic date came in February 1969. Hughes Communication International built *Tangua 1* near Rio de Janeiro, while Argentina preferred the Italian subsidiary *Satellite Telecommunications Systems S.p.a.* for the construction of her *Balcarce 1*, the first South American antenna awarded to a European contractor. Set up by the *Rio de la Plata*, this space station cost 6 million dollars. Aides of the American Embassy in Buenos Aires complained that the multimillion contract had been given to the Italian company simply because Italy, not the United States, was Argentina's best trading partner.[201]

Meantime, all Andean countries except Bolivia acquired their international satellite stations between 1969 and 1971. Peru was first with *Lurín 1*, built by NEC in July 1969. Then came Colombia in March 1970 with her *Chocontá 1* (an ITT Space Communications antenna), Venezuela's *Camatagua 1*, sold by GTE in November 1970, and Ecuador's *Quito* station, assembled in 1972. Most other Latin American and Caribbean states also began joining INTELSAT not only as countries but also as user-members in the early 1970s. In the English-speaking Caribbean, for instance, the first countries to have a satellite antenna were Trinidad and Tobago (*Matura Point*, November 1971), Jamaica (*Prospect Pen*, December 1971), and Barbados (*Congor Bay*, October 1972).[202]

More cosmopolitan nations like Uruguay and Costa Rica surprisingly came late to this global field. Costa Rica, for instance, purchased her *Tarbaca* station in 1981, even after latecomers such as El Salvador (1979), Guyana (1979), Suriname (1979), Bolivia (1980), and Guatemala (1980) joined in. Uruguay, a higher income nation when compared to others in the region, also put off all plans to buy her *Manga* station until December 1980, and depended on Argentina's satellite-to-microwave relays across the La Plata river.[203] Like Cuba, a user-member since 1979, Uruguay did not even belong to INTELSAT when it decided to acquire her own antenna.

THE TELEVISED-SPORTS JACKPOT

Long before imported television series and news, Latin America received live via-satellite sports transmissions. As the 1964 Tokyo Olympiad, when the United States tested the efficacy of its emerging geosynchronous satellite program, the 1968 Olympic Games in Mexico City served to try out NASA's ATS (Applications Technology Satellite) series in the Americas. As the first country to use in this region an Applications Technology Satellite (*ATS-3*), Mexico delivered televised and other satellite signals about the Olympics to both Western Europe and the United States.[204] Later in 1968, Brazil also relied on this spacecraft to run an experimental study for the reception of telephone calls and text. And ten years later, this same VHF artifact was still being used in the Caribbean, linking Jamaica, Barbados, and St. Lucia in an educational project, even though the satellite had been planned to last only eighteen months.[205]

What sealed the term "via satellite" in the minds of millions of Latin Americans, however, was not the intercontinental televised transmission of the 1968 Olympics, Pope Paul VI's visit to Colombia (also in 1968), or Armstrong's landing on the Moon (July 20, 1969). The key event, especially for marketers and advertisers, was the live television coverage of the 1970 World Soccer Cup: "*Fútbol México-70.*" That summer, millions of homes followed for three weeks live scenes of *Pelé* and his Brazilian team winning the legendary "Jules Rimet" cup, an event that tangibly represented the debut of international television in Latin America both technologically and economically.

This sports-satellite symbiosis played a determinant role in Mexico's decision to launch a domestic satellite system in 1985. In fact, some Latin American scholars are convinced that international competitions such as the Olympic Games and the world soccer cups have been ideal occasions to foster media technology invasions worldwide.[206] Technology sellers and their buyers, usually state agencies, often defend new technologies as beneficial to the adopting country by definition. Following the 1986 version of the World Soccer Cup—once again—in Mexico, local officials justified the acquisition of the *Morelos* satellite system as a great image tool. In their view, thanks to the massive audience of this popular event, "2.8 billion people around the globe could watch, via-satellite, how Mexicans overcame crises and natural tragedies" including a devastating earthquake killing nearly 100,000 people months before the championship.[207]

Similar claims surfaced in South America during the early stages of the same tournament, originally offered to Colombia. As a Colombian minister of education noted, events like the World Cup represented a unique opportunity for countries in need of a better image abroad.[208] Government officials of the Liberal Party's Turbay administration (1978–1982) favored in unison the *Satélite Colombiano (Satcol)*, assuring that there will be innumerable benefits to the country with a national satellite network in orbit. But, Colombian president Belisario Betancur (1982–1986) rejected both the *Satcol* project and the XIII version of the World Cup *Colombia-86*, immediately after taking office (September/October 1982).[209] His decision brought as much praise as condemnation, with Betancur arguing that it was far better to say "*yes* to Gabriel García Marquez's Nobel Prize (1982), *no* to the via-satellite World Cup."[210]

Despite the enormous popularity of this sport in Colombia, critics, including the Betancur presidency, feared an economic disaster similar to Argentina's, where the 1978 World Cup reported huge losses. Still, officials in both Mexico and Argentina had little misgivings regarding the implications of this Cup–satellite television events, posing no reservations to the modernization pressures applied by the powerful *FIFA* (Fédération Internationale de Football Association).

THE SHOCK OF CHILE'S 9–11

Millions of Latin Americans, especially those in their 40s and older, immediately associate September 11 not only with New York's World Trade Center and the Pentagon in Washington D.C., but also with the aerial bombing of the *Palacio de la Moneda*, Chile's presidential palace in 1973. Following that tragic event, which killed the democratically elected and socialist President Salvador Allende, over 3000 people (the final count will never be known) lost their lives in a violent operation orchestrated by the recently-appointed Army Commander in Chief General Augusto Pinochet Ugarte, a man who had sworn loyalty a few days before the attack. In fact, people continued to disappear during the next two decades (1973-1990), many of them thrown to the middle of the ocean in barrels filled with cement, according to Manuel Contreras, the former chief of the secret policy agency DINA, who had kept silent for over thirty years.[211]

Televisión Nacional de Chile (TVN), the state-owned TV netwok, released "an hour-by-hour story with photos and video (including the palkacio de la Moneda bombing by air)" in September 2003, along with detailed everyday accounts of the military coup in the newspapers *La Tercera*, *La Segunda*, and *Radio Cooperativa*, including president Allende's last speech.[212] Declassified documents in the United States point to the historic daily *El Mercurio* as receiving financial support from the CIA and the State Department to mount a propaganda campaign against the leftist head of state while supporting the dictatorship for years to come. In his *El Mercurio File*, Peter Kornbluth of the *Columbia Journalism Review* writes:

"September 11, a day of infamy in the U.S., is also a dark day in the history of Chile. Although former U.S. officials such as Henry Kissinger have insisted that Washington had no involvement in the military takeover, and was trying only to preserve democracy in Chile, CIA and White House records show how the CIA used Chilean media to undermine the democratically elected government of Socialist Salvador Allende, an operation that played a significant role in setting the stage for the military coup of 11 September 1973. From these documents emerges the story of the agency's main propaganda project—authorized at the highest level of the U.S. government—which relied upon Chile's leading newspaper, *El Mercurio*, and its well-connected owner Agustín Edwards, [a] Chilean Rupert Murdoch."

"Even before Allende was inaugurated as president of Chile"—continues Kornbluth—"Edwards came to Washington and discussed with the CIA the 'timing for possible military action' to prevent Allende from taking office. President Nixon directly authorized massive funding to the newspaper. The White House approved close to \$2 million dollars—a significant sum went into Chilean currency in the black market. Secret CIA cables from mid-1973 identified *El Mercurio* as among 'the most militant parts of the opposition' pushing for military intervention to overthrow Allende."[213]

And this is only one case of the dirty Cold War that infested South America through the deadly *Operación Condor*, a military violence and state of mind eventually spread all over Latin America in the 1960s, 1970s, and 1980s.[214] After a brief dream with globalization following the fall of the Berlin Wall, national security campaigns remerged to fuel the endless war againt terrorism, a new type of cold war with destructive and intermittent hot flashes.

Chapter 7

Dreaming a Fair World

With the decolonization of the 1950s, 1960s, and 1970s, people of the Third World pictured once again the possibility of self-defining governments and social models, distancing themselves from those imposed by Europeans and U.S. Americans. Another European power, the USSR, now turned "dictatorship of the proletariat," became an added source of pressure. Local and foreign powers, acting on their interests, at odds or in concert, but from their privileged positions, moved quickly to stir the popular ambition of freedom, making a mockery of the word. Apparently, Latin American society was(is) destined to face greater pains and upheavals before peaceful civility reigns, accepting the need for a realignment of resources, responsibilites, and benefits.

From the spotty modernization of the early Cold War years to the global *techno-modernization* of the late 1990s, going through periods of dependency, statistism, and cultural critiques, Latin Americans, like most in the planet, have essentially failed to erect communities with basic human rights guaranteed for all, including essential, effective, and affordable communications. Efforts to come up with equitable, participatory, and community media systems run into the fierce opposition of elitist, alien, and greedy private interests. As the stakes were high and the challenges strong, those in power rarely, if ever, weighed the advantages of a postcolonial mentality in future business.

The feasibility of fair and even marketplaces, even if more profitable, was a worthless fantasy for multinational media owners and entrepreneurs in Latin America. Global business often, if not always, implied the sacrifice of regional and local needs. As an Andean project manager noted years ago, "every time a new integration initiative has been generated, foreign [and domestic] multinational interests orchestrate a campaign to undermine it."[1]

But critical media observers refused to accept such a *status quo* and inequality. Many understood that poor communications historically contributed to erode democratic values and institutions, and that *incommunication* led to dead-end crises, deprivation, and confrontation. Journalists and other media people knew all too well that poverty, authoritarianism, corruption, narcotrafficking, and human rights abuses, in addition to the increasingly endemic violence, were intimately connected to the mass media and vice versa. Although the last fifty years witnessed enormous efforts and advances in media technologies, millions of individuals and groups in the Americas remained virtually disconnected from the comforts of modern life. How to put the mass media and other communications to work for the benefit of the majority was and still is the mystery in this field.

WHAT GLOBALIZATION OFFERS

In the 1960s, transnational television emerged as the heart of the region's press and telecommunication media agenda. U.S. corporations such as NBC's *Cadena Panamericana*, CBS' *Cadena de las Américas*, and ABC's *Worldvision Group* took center stage to build inter-American networks of hemispheric coverage. In 1969, for example, ABC had organized both a South American (*LATINO*) and a Caribbean (*CATVN*) television network that included direct investments in thirteen countries. In South America, ABC was in Argentina (channel 9), Chile (channels 4 and 13), Colombia (channel 9), Ecuador (channels 3, 6, and 7), Uruguay (channel 12), and Venezuela (channel 4). In Central America and the Caribbean, the U.S. network had invested in Costa Rica (channel 7), the Dominican Republic (channel 7), El Salvador (channels 2 and 4), Guatemala (channel 3), Honduras (channel 5), the Dutch Antilles (channel 2), and Panama (channel 2) (Beltrán & de Cardona, 1979, p. 35). More recent sources indicate that by 1964, the ABC's *Worldvision Group* already had forty-eight station affiliations in twenty-one Latin American and Caribbean countries.[2]

Thirty years later, U.S. transnational corporations, consolidated in global satellite, cable, and Internet joint ventures, came back to take on the old dream of international channels operated from Miami, New York, Atlanta, or Los Angeles. Thanks to the denationalization, privatization, and market openness at the end of the Cold War, North American television signals flooded the Latin American spectrum. One prominent example is *Time Warner*, the world's largest media consortium, delivering among many other media services Turner's *CNN en Español*, *Cartoon Network*, *TNT-Latin America*, *HBO-Latin America*, and *Cinemax-Latin America*. In 1996, HBO president Jeffrey Bewkes believed that the expansion of his channel and the parent company was in fact "a Manifest Destiny."[3]

Strategic alliances with powerful multinationals such as AT&T, TCI, Bell South, Viacom, and Sony, to name a few, made of *Time Warner* a giant that renders any aspiration to a robust and competitive video market in Latin America mostly, if not entirely, futile—especially when conglomerates the size of *Disney* and its popular productions (*Disney studios, ESPN,* and *ABC*), Viacom's *MTV, Nickelodeon,* and *USA Network-Latin America,* and *News Corporation's Sky Latin America* and *Fox-Latin America* are the only possible competitors,[4] that is, if these companies choose to effectively compete rather than to peacefully coexist, as is typical of oligopolies.

Mexico's *Televisa,* Brazil's *Globo,* and in much less extent Venezuela's *Venevision* or *Cisneros* Group are the only ones in position to offer some hemispheric competition to the megaconglomerates based in the United States. And even so, they are likely to do so only in alliance with Anglo-American or British media corporations rather than alone. In fact, the *Televisa Group,* the largest Third World media company along with Brazil's *Globo,* is a "1.3 billion conglomerate that includes two TV national networks (*Cadena Canal 2* and *Cadena Canal 5*), a regional TV network (*Cadena Canal 4*), and the influential Mexico City's *Canal 9.*"

Televisa controls 80 percent of Mexico's television and 70 percent of the country's newspaper and magazine publishing markets, in addition to cable, radio, and satellite networks as well as programming, record, film, and advertising production and distribution companies. It also sells news and entertainment programs via satellite to ninety countries in association with Rupert Murdoch's News Corporation, the U.S. cable giant TCI, and Brazil's Globo organization.[5] *Eco/Galavisión,* a via-satellite channel initiated in 1989, *Univisión* (in association with Venezuela's Venevisión), and Alpha Lyracom's *Pan-American Satellite Corporation,* the world's first private regional satellite since 1985, are also essential components of the Mexican conglomerate.[6]

Unlike South America, where educational and state goals played a significant role in satellite projects such as *ASCEND* (Advanced System of Communication and Education for National Development), *SERLA,* (*Sistema de Educación Regional Latinoamericano*), and *SACI* (Sistema Avançado de Comunicaçoes Interdisciplinares), the Mexican satellite television policy was entirely profit oriented. *Televisa* and *Univision,* formerly known as the Spanish International Network (*SIN*), regarded any regional, intergovernmental, or national development space project as essentially a waste of time.[7]

Records show, on the other hand, that the *Telesistema Mexicano* proposed the idea of an inter-American satellite TV network, connecting all Spanish-speaking countries of the continent with U.S. and Canadian assistance and participation, as early as 1961. The plan is historically known as project *SARIT*: the *Satélite Artificial de la Red Interamericana de*

Telecomunicaciones (The Artificial Satellite of the Inter-American Telecommunications Network).[8] Yet, this ambitious enterprise never went beyond an outline. By the mid-1970s, however, *SIN* became "the first U.S. commercial network to broadcast regularly to its affiliates" live programming from Mexico City via satellite.[9]

Throughout the satellite boom, the Mexican government also had different ideas from its Latin American peers. Rather than a public multilateral project and in conjunction with the private sector, namely *Televisa*, the federal Mexican authorities pushed for a mixed inter-American or an Iberian-American satellite television system based in Mexico City. The televised transmission of the Pope's visit to South America and the Olympic Games had been a living proof of Mexico's comparative advantages at the regional level. Her proximity to the United States and Hollywood, geographic and historical centrality in the Americas, contacts and knowledge of the Hispanic market in North America, and the fact that Mexico City has been a traditional dubbing and distribution center for U.S. television producers turned Mexico into an ideal place.

Televisa dreamed of a commercial satellite network connecting TV stations in Spanish across the hemisphere, including the United States and from Mexico's capital city. A first step in this direction was the Third Iberian-American Workshop of Via-Satellite Communications held in Mexico City between March 15 and 20, 1971, where industry representatives from the host country, Spain, and seven more Latin American nations including Argentina and Brazil gathered to inaugurate *the Organización Iberoamericana de Televisión (OTI)*. This private entity, the Iberian American Television Organization, intended to facilitate the transmission and selling of satellite-delivered television programs in the region's Hispanic and Luso-Brazilian worlds.

It is not coincidental that on November 15, 1971, the Soviet Union inaugurated *Intersputnik* (today, the *Intersputnik International Organization of Space Communications*), a satellite network with Cuba as a founding member, initiating the transmission of color television programs from the very *Plaza de la Revolución* to Moscow (November 1973/January 1974).[10] Unlike other media forms of expression like music (the famous *Nueva Trova Cubana*) and the *Nuevo Cine Latinoamericano* (the New Latin American Film), little can be said about socialist Cuba and its mass media, except that it has been heavily monitored and repressed by the Cuban Communist Party since 1959.

With OTI, established in Mexico, *Televisa* moved to take advantage of an INTELSAT offer granting favorable conditions for future Iberian-American television transmissions, a proposal announced during a previous workshop in Caracas. On October 12, 1974, the Mexican *Secretaria de Comunicaciones y Transportes* (SCT) finally signed the *Tlatelolco* convention, endorsing the rental of any needed satellite capacity in INTELSAT. On paper, this represented the launching of the (*Satélite Latinoamericano*)

SATELAT, the first entirely commercial and mostly private satellite venture of the hemisphere.

In April 1969, representatives of the U.S. Communication Satellite Corporation (*COMSAT*), General Electric International, and Hughes Aircraft, along with prestigious U.S. institutions such as the Ford Foundation and Stanford University, had proposed in Santiago, Chile, a private continental satellite. After a meeting with faculty and administrators of some private Latin American universities, the idea was to establish a so-called *Centro Audiovisual Internacional Via-Satelite* (*CAVISAT*, or Via-Satellite Audiovisual Center).

CAVISAT sought to deliver satellite educational programs and degrees to Latin American students in their home countries, and eventually, other kinds of televised materials. But, within a few months, the plan felt apart. As the U.S. partners in *CAVISAT* threatened to impose the project ("come what may, at their own expense if necessary, and whether Latin Americans like or not"), Latin American officials moved quickly to denounce it as "an Anglo-American plan for the ideological occupation of the continent."[11] At that point, Emilio Azcárraga Vidaurreta, the father, suspected that going north first was better than going south. In other words, from the beginning, his original target was the Spanish-speaking population living in the United States.

Close and long standing connections with U.S. media manufacturers, producers, and advertisers, such as Hughes Aircraft, General Electric, RCA, J. Walter Thompson, Colgate-Palmolive, and the like, also made *SATELAT* a suspicious project for other Latin Americans, and far less Latin American of what it sounded like. Actually, the initiative generated a significant animosity among government officials opposed to the presumptuous Emilio Azcárraga Milmo and his *Televisa* network. The Hughes Aircraft Company, for instance, was a key factor in making the monumental *Estadio Azteca* (Mexico City's soccer stadium) and the 1970 World Soccer Cup an extraordinary success for both Azcarraga and *Televisa*. They had already tested the huge potential of a televised world cup in 1962, when after videotaping the principal matches of the *Copa Mundial de Chile*, numerous Latin American and European countries approached *Televisa* to purchase copies of the games.[12]

In the mid-1970s, *SATELAT*, the so-called Latin American satellite, nominally 52 percent owned by the Mexican government and 48 percent the property of *Televisa*, jumped into the regional market with the *Canal Nuevo Mundo* after a false start in the *OTI* and a few stations in Spain.[13] With the collaboration of Mexico's news agency *Notimex* and the *Banco Nacional Cinematográfico* (the National Film Industry), *SATELAT* began its regionwide distribution of television programs such as *América, Magia y Encuentro* (America, Magic, and Encounter).

A menu of variety shows featuring live cultural traditions of Latin American countries, including *América sin Fronteras* (The Americas without Borders), a program that connected via satellite two or more points of the continent, was meant to be *SATELAT*'s line of programming. In the end, the satellite venture failed as lack of profits and the *SCT*'s refusal to underwrite future transponder renewals with *INTELSAT* killed the initiative.

Trying to compete with the Mexican media moguls, both the Brazilian government and the Globo network also planned to get into space and export their programming and services as soon as possible. In 1973, the Brazilian Ministry of Communications formally initiated feasibility studies for a *Sistema Brasileiro de Telecomunicaoes por Satellite* (*SBTS*), a national system registered at the ITU (International Telecommunication Union) in less than three years and placed under the responsibility of Brazilian telecommunication enterprise *EMBRATEL*.[14]

The Brazilians began working on a telecommunications plan in the Northeastern State of Rio Grande do Norte in the late 1960s. The already mentioned advanced system of interdisciplinary communications *SACI/EXERN* set off to demonstrate "how satellite distribution of televised classes could improve the quality of in-school education for primary students in rural areas."[15] The project also expected to combine social development goals with profit-oriented services.

Before long, the latter took center stage and *Globo*'s prominent role in the Brazilian television and telecommunications structure dominated. Whereas the Brazilian federal government focused on the propaganda gains of a satellite TV network in times of a bloody dictatorship and anticommunism, *Globo* concentrated on its profits, its evolving national market monopoly, and its international perspectives. Eventually, Roberto Marinho, a latecomer in broadcasting fully supported by the military and a 5-million-dollar contract with *Time-Life Inc.*, would turn his *Globo Group* into a Brazilian media giant with exports to 130 countries by the mid-1990s.[16]

In time, other television actors, most notably the Miami-based *Telemundo/Telenoticias* network, originally created in Puerto Rico, then managed from New York, but more recently owned by Sony and CBS, also emerged to compete for Latin American audiences. The dream of a pan-Latino news and entertainment service like *Sur*, an interesting venture operating from Lima, Peru, or the U.S.–Venezuelan channel *Gems International* and the Colombian broadcast networks *Caracol* and *RCN* continue to be the theme of numerous Latin American television entrepreneurs.

Noticias NBC, for instance, inaugurated in April 1993, has been one of the resounding failures of the ongoing hemispheric channels in the Americas. It shut down its Latin American news offices and operations of North Carolina in the late 1990s. In unexplainable management decisions, which tell much about the knowledge or willingness to learn about this region, NBC insisted in running the *Canal* from its headquarters in Charlotte, North Carolina. A town little known for its cosmopolitanism,

let alone its Latin Americanism, NBC had enormous problems both re-
cruiting and retaining its Spanish–Portuguese-speaking talent or keeping the pulse of the region. Although salaries were competitive, Latin
American employees felt alienated and isolated, flying back to Miami or
elsewhere as soon as they got an offer from any Hispanic station.

The goal of any hemispheric TV channel today is to hit the jackpot
of an open minded, empathic, and profitable channel capable of entic-
ing the elusive Latin American viewers and markets. Theoretically, the
main business appeal is the roughly 70 million TV households of Latin
America, an audience equivalent in size to nearly 80 percent of the U.S.
television marketplace. Some authors claimed that only Mexico had up to
50 million TV households in 1995, sixteen million of them color television
sets. With a 95 percent penetration, these figures also included 1.7 million
cable subscribers.[17] In the early 1990s, Carlos Díaz, president of Turner
International, speculated that "in about 15 more years there would be 25
million subscription TV viewers in Latin America."[18] With the exception
of Argentina and its remarkable 61 percent cable penetration, however, almost five million subscribers, the rest of Latin America in the year 2000
was rather shy of such an expectation.[19]

How Latin America should respond to the avalanche of foreign programs from space was the main concern of the region's policy makers,
scholars, and other researchers in the early and mid-1970s. How to respond to this "invasion" of channels in the good sense of the word (freedom of choice) but also in the bad sense of the word (cultural alien-
ation)? Years ago, Nobel Prize winner Gabriel García Márquez, a McBride
Commission member, suggested that there could be as many responses
as countries in the hemisphere. Yet, discussions on the implications of
new technologies in Latin American society have for some time revolved
around six major tendencies: modernization, dependency, semiotic, cultural, alternative, and state-oriented perspectives.

FAR FROM INDEPENDENCE

The ideological spectrum of Latin American communication has always
been more complex than normally assumed. In criticizing new media diffusion predictions, *dependency* theorists have traditionally asserted that
the acquisition of such technologies is usually the result of ultimately
damaging, mechanically imported, and imposed ideals of modernization. In this perspective, telecommunication and mass media technologies,
including the Internet, are essentially imperialist tools whereby foreign
governments and multinationals perpetuate their global economy and
politics.

That communication is still dominated by imported models, technologies, and practices is the most serious problem for numerous media observers in Latin America. Many of them continue to believe that unless

Latin American and other developing countries manage to create spaces of self-governance, advancing cooperative efforts without the tutelage and dominance of foreign powers (the United States and others), little hope exists of truly free communication systems in this continent. One situation that remains the same over the years, even decades, is that new media technologies normally imply for the buyer quasi-monopolistic offers with painful terms and conditions in technological dependence.

In the last twenty-five years, top officials of the Caribbean Development Bank, the Caribbean Institute of Mass Communication, and the Caribbean Association of Media Workers have expressed deep concerns about the dependent status of their countries. For them, the extent of the influence of foreign broadcasting and the effects of the new satellite technology, with its invasion of airwaves and markets on behalf of dominant external services, is not necessarily good news for the region.[20]

Since the mid-1960s, critics in Latin America have repeatedly denounced dependency on new media technologies as a form of control and domination: a technological, political, and cultural subjection to world centers of power largely responsible for the region's poverty and stagnation. In spite of the formulations and revisions of the Cold War and post-Cold War years, media dependency is stubbornly reflected in developing societies like those of Latin America. The influence of multinational merchants and their products remain as overwhelming and oppressive as in the early days of the modern industrialization. The purpose and spirit of current information and program flows, fostering consumption and orderly markets, remain virtually unchanged in their selling campaign of values, doctrines, and the way of life of commercialism.

In dependency critiques, new media technologies are mainly another source of social inequality and discrimination. It is through glamorous telecommunication media news and entertainment, states Souki-Oliveira, that the privileges of modern strata are reinforced, forcing the importation of luxurious technologies that increase the region's debt and social prostration. At first glance, the fascination for newer and better communications appears beneficial to all, but over the years, technology innovation results in the same detrimental effect of further social disparities, discrimination, and frustration.[21]

Yet, who could ever reject technology and speedy telecommunications as a sign and eventual realization of progress! But, though the potential of telecommunication for human understanding is unquestionable, in many, if not most countries, mass media technologies including computer-generated advertising have produced a system that contributed to the overall impoverishment of millions of Latin Americans, threatening to send them back to preindustrial dependency.[22]

Researchers in the dependency tradition continue to agree that the insertion of new media technologies in the era of globalization is as ill conceived as in the massive adoption of traditional technologies in first

half of the 1900s. In spite of valuable examples of popular and native autochthonous creativity, fashion and imitation still dominate the spread of
new media technologies in Latin America.[23] As a matter of fact, reminds
Jiménez, in Latin America the transfer of press and electronic media has
always had little to do with either autonomy or originality. Sadly, technology innovation has been an activity permanently characterized by imitation and analogy, with contents, objectives, and practices framed by pervasive atmospheres of political subordination.[24]

Summarizing the fear of dependency and subordination in the United
Nations, a Colombian delegate once affirmed, "we feel that the right to
a free flow of information was adopted to protect an individual against
all forms of subjugation. Broadcasting [and other telecommunications],
regardless of frontiers, can, in the final analysis, be one of them. This
is specially so if [the mass media] are left in the hands of a few privileged [people], who can persuade, create habits, set trends, and arouse
a homogeneous awareness among individuals across vast continental
areas. This could [certainly] apply to Latin America—from Mexico to
Chile—which speaks the same language and has the same color television
system."[25]

On the contrary, according to modernization experts, the need for
progress urges developing countries to quickly modernize and expand
communication networks with new media technologies. The assumption
being that social and economic efficiency is all about fast, low-cost, and
high-quality communications.[26] For years, governments in Latin America
have invested millions on mass media technologies convinced that it
would bring significant advancement in education, agriculture, health,
commerce, industry, and other public services and operations. For example, Daniel Lerner's modernization logic has now mutated to the Internet,
promising all kinds of economic, education, and political benefits to those
who move quickly to embrace it.

At one point, satellite communications were told to end parochialism
and xenophobia. Today, nonetheless, top producers and heavy users of
space technology and satellite news and entertainment experience a resurgence of the old hatreds against foreign peoples and cultures. The equalizing function of satellites and previous telecommunications, a popular
cliché among international experts in the 1960s, is as remote as in those
days.

In Mexico, where a domestic satellite system was presented as an ideal
solution to the economic and social stagnation of the 1980s, the secretary
of communication and transportation pledged that *Morelos* would foster
social prosperity and integration. Promising an equal access to the implicit
benefits of telecommunications, namely education, health, food, electricity, security, and tourism, the government predicted an effective decentralization of both state and federal programs. The new satellite infrastructure was supposed to especially benefit the people of the rural areas, in

particular those located in remote hard-reaching places where until now basic mass media and telecommunication services were unavailable.[27]

Similar assertions surfaced in Brazil where satellite media was expected to bring remarkable progress in national sovereignty, security, and identity. *TV Globo* proclaimed in the mid-1980s that "thanks to the regular and efficient use of satellites, true network television was once and for all a consolidated enterprise [in Brazil]. With *Brasilsat* in continuous operation, the *Globo* network is able to serve large urban centers and also the most distant regions of the country—a potential audience of at least 80 million people covered by *Globo* signals."[28]

Unfortunately, this same grand technology also helped to create a media giant capable of manipulating viewers for their commercial exploitation and voters in both military transfers during the lengthy dictatorship and the subsequent election of the impeached civilian president Fernando Collor de Mello in the early 1990s. Since 1964, and faithful to the modernization paradigm, the Brazilian military and subsequent civilian rulers have put much emphasis in the geopolitical advantages of unifying the land and the people through television via satellite.[29]

Everywhere, the logic is always the same: progress, peace, and happiness through information technology innovations, a beautiful dream of material gratification and individual liberty. As a Mexican newspaper publisher once pointed out in a U.S. symposium: "the function of communication is to assure that modern technological complexes available today contribute to educate and inform the people, enhancing their ability to live a democratic and peaceful life in order."[30]

In the end, reasons favoring any new media technology revolved around one fundamental assumption: media modernization as a magic multiplier and a progress generator. As a SELA (Latin American Economic System) report noted, the decade of the 1960s is a memorable time when prospects to overcome poverty and underdevelopment reached the highest point. Such confidence on the potential transforming capacity of mass communications, trumpeted by CIESPAL, UNESCO, and the OAS, spread the enchanting melody of the mass media as an accelerator of social development. This campaign created the conditions for the importation of modern communication technologies throughout the region, bringing transistor radio and television broadcasting, telecommunications, and color television to fight backwardness.[31] Yet, in the era of the Internet, mergers and markets, rather than poverty and inequality, are the dominant themes of the ongoing modernization.

ALTERNATIVE PERSPECTIVES

Community-oriented and alternative communicators see the media landscape with different eyes. For them, modern communication technologies are simply authoritarian or vertical solutions to serious and delicate problems. They stubbornly rely on limited, mechanistic, and apocalyptic assumptions, including classical Marxist views, promising much but delivering little, particularly in areas of great need.

Although alternative communicologists tend to favor modest mass media such as "independent" newspapers, "free" radio stations, graffiti, popular theater, amateur video, and the like, big technologies are considered suitable if arranged to promote true democratic change. Instead of socially selective and alienating, new media technologies are expected to be horizontal vehicles of popular participation. *Alternativists* are ready to support the introduction of new media services whenever adopters employ a different perspective, one where modern media and technological progress work as a tool of radically different objectives from the commercial goals of ongoing transnational communications.[32]

Not long ago, the CELAM (*Consejo Episcopal Latinoamericano*), a prominent sponsor of alternative media projects, admitted that today's communications have indeed reached amazing global dimensions, thanks to the rapid technological improvement of message-delivery systems. However, this spectacular expansion, with new press, information, and telecommunication services stretching the oral, written, and audiovisual word to unprecedented frontiers, is still characterized by uniformity and homogenization. So, in spite of this impressive technological growth, a simple question remains. Can vast marginal and isolated masses protect themselves from the penetrating and often destructive influence of global communications?[33]

Alternative communications are often praised in the Americas for challenging the big media's monopolistic controls, for emerging as new vehicles of expression trying to consolidate democracy by means of self-determination, and cultural sovereignty and autonomy.[34] The nature and substance of their work have often generated a deep respect for small and often more influential and credible alternative media, such as union newspapers, rural broadcast stations, street theaters, amateur video productions, and popular singing. These are channels known for giving the poor an access to voice and to speak without insurmountable and discriminatory filters against the poor, the illiterate, and the less developed.

In this theory, the bottom line is to confront the *status quo*. Top-down perspectives like the information society and its global telecommunication revolution are criticized as authoritarian forms of message production and delivery. The purpose is to open up choices, not necessarily to dethrone the big media. Alternative communicators also intend to demystify technologies devoted to patterns of mercantilism, abuse, and self-censorship. An extremely harmful implication of today's media revolution is that the telecommunication economy, with its scientists, technicians, and business people as preeminent class, can live without the impoverished and the uneducated.[35]

Regrettably, the propaganda of grand media technologies are every time more and more arrogant, more vertical, with the technology purposes, dynamics, and operations more and more divorced from the majority.[36] The global village philosophy is "not the clean, antiseptic and apolitical society people have been told it is, where democracy and freedom rules. Capitalism is the real name of the game and profitability is its main motif, [a] society where exploitation of the working class is the main feature."[37] Consequently, a global village will always be if the ultimate goal is to use the power of technology for the mercantilistic persuasion of receivers. Press and telecommunication technologies are never democratic if they are not effectively popular in character.[38]

Rules on technology access and innovation contribute little to the cause of democratization if they fail to address the concerns of the poor. The right to communicate is neither authentically democratic nor truly popular unless the disadvantaged and the people who have no voice are the axle of the regulation. A renewed interest in popular cultures and expressions generated in the 1980s new research philosophies among Latin Americans. Imperialism and dependency began to be gradually replaced with the concepts like transnationalization, denationalization, and hegemony. Because of the prominence of the media in contemporary societies and the vagueness of our knowledge in this field, Latin Americans felt the need to rethink and reconceptualize their social problems, free of any universal or metaphysical imperatives.[39]

Media technologies for the *culturalists* are realities explained by intricate social conditions and contradictions, including, but not exclusively, class struggles. New media are simply forms of social engagement in which domination is secured by transcending dominance as such while converting itself into hegemony.[40] In other words, new instruments of mass communication are only cultural tools to legitimatize political power, institutions, and domination, although in less obvious ways.[41] For example, satellite television is less about national objectives such as solving administration deficiencies, lack of integration, or loss of sovereignty and independence, it is ultimately a question of making television an apparatus of cultural hegemony, "accentuating the cultural backwardness of the receiving state."[42] In this perspective, we have become "slaves of technology," victims of an explosion of new media systems in which the underlying themes are coercion, discrimination, and concentration.

The purpose of the *cultural hegemony* theory is to explain deeper ongoing changes, such as urban developments and cultural industries that include the effects of modern media. New and revolutionary technologies are among Latin American culturalists forms of social dispersion, an urban plot offering symbolic and heterogeneous messages fed by constant mutations of local, national, and transnational media networks.[43] Cultural hegemonists are keenly interested in informal interactions where elitist, popular, and mass communications blend themselves into new genres of expression, but they are also intrigued with the study of transnational messages removed from territorial boundaries such as the so-called denationalized subcultures.[44]

In Mexico, for instance, the combination of television and satellites is said to have facilitated a progressive cultural denationalization of the country, a media structure where broadcasting and other telecommunications have for decades promoted cultural patterns of avaricious consumerism, gender inequality, and the unqualified admiration of imported values. Distortions in education, language, eating habits, and commercial anxieties are major concerns in the globalization of new media technologies, although the meltdown of ideological frontiers, chauvinistic values, and narrow cultural interactions are seen as positive contributions.[45]

In sum, modern technologies are mere instruments of cultural hegemony: forms of mediation of connection transforming TV networks, satellites, computers, video games, etc. into a hegemonic machinery carrying values, images, spaces, and attitudes which benefit only those having access to and control over these devices.[46] Popular culture is a key notion in contemporary societies for it may reconcile the conflict between the technologically modern and the culturally significant. In fact, this is an unresolved and ongoing struggle reflected in the states' difficulty to attain both legitimacy and consensus versus the people's inability to overcome social obstacles and frustrations with working alternatives.[47]

New media technologies are never neutral if they are part of abusive schemes to take advantage of and to dominate, exploit, and profit from others. Some of these abuses are the imposition of social norms and values, the homogenization and control of thoughts and expression, and the reduction of dissension to technical and moral standards in concert with the system's needs and interests. In fact, press and other mass communication technologies have too often been dedicated to the consolidation of a conformity that favors the privileged over the impoverished.[48]

Even so, defensive positions such as the traditional cultural invasion and technological dependency find little echo nowadays. They are seen as immaterial concepts among the *culturalists*. "Inflammatory" descriptions such as cultural imperialism, technological aggression, ideological penetration, and so forth can no longer play the role of the Pandora's box from which all explanations to Latin America's problems are extracted, noted Schwarz and Jaramillo.[49]

In the cultural hegemony theory, communication progress comes not only from the introduction of new media technologies as leading practice but also from the way media are appropriated in the daily life of the family, the neighborhood, the community, the nation, and the global environment.[50] Live television transmissions of the World Soccer Cup, for instance, in every four years is a vivid example of how the new mass culture of television is appropriated by thousands of viewers. The narrative genre of televised sports is gradually transformed by the people into a tradition of myth and melodrama in which fans develop a collective cultural identity through satellite images.

In semiotic analysis, an influential antecedent to the cultural studies tradition, media technologies are systems of signification carrying implicit or explicit functions in need of both disclosure and separation from their actual contents. In turn, ideology is the background of every communication process and event where audiences are encouraged to maintain a creative integrity by resisting the manipulations of those who pretend to control their minds. Semioticians are especially interested in the manipulative power of the media. From birth to death, argues Moragas-Spa, societies are subjected to an endless net of signs and vehicles through which small groups advance their own objectives. If taken off guard, individuals face the risk of becoming true robots, manipulated by symbols where semiotics could be the antidote against such an exploitation of individual life.[51]

Members of the Latin American semiotics school have traditionally opposed the way new media implant hidden biases in society. For decades and without effective resistance, wrote Pasquali, new communication technologies and their programs have diffused latent notions of inequality, discrimination, power, violence, and justifications for crushing the weak. Permissive minds are dominated by elitist manipulations of the mass media, while rebellious ones are condemned to a silent ostracism.[52] More than channels through which communication is delivered, radio, television, satellite, cable, and the Internet are ideological places where content is often created as a form of scientific rhetoric.[53]

For the Latin American semiologist, it is imperative to unravel the true functions of every media structure, studying technology as a potential carrier of social distortions. The goal is to get to the heart of every technology artifact so that the real meaning of what they truly represent can be empirically defined. For example, the interdisciplinary convergence of both media linguistics and the semiotics of culture may be the most appropriate way to learn the effects of television as an instrument of power.[54] The assumption being that all television technologies and discourses, artistic or lyrical, aesthetic or metaphysical, are the great myth of modern life: a myth in which technological modernity is just one of many bourgeois tales.[55]

In the Latin American semiology research, dependency on foreign technologies is not a mere economic and political condition. It is a cultural handicap insofar as signs and contents are not really indigenous but those of external societies with totally different interests. So, not until countries manage to redefine and explain the local symbiosis between culture, people, technology, and society, technological dependency will be a phenomenon poorly understood in Latin America.[56]

The modernizing spirit of the new media has always been criticized by semiologists for their limited and positivistic prescriptions, a technocratic reasoning generally built on one-sided, simplistic, and isolated assumptions.[57] For a semiotician, the role of the telecommunication media cannot be effectively evaluated unless a rediscovery of their social function is seriously undertaken, breaking with the imitative practices for years imposed during the introduction of previous technologies. Press and telecommunication services are thus instruments of a cybernetic spectacle where facts are routinely transformed into artificial realities, and where audiences are massively narcotized to the effects of violence, consumerism, sexual exploitation, and other antisocial forms of expression.[58]

Media technologies are in the semiology tradition, rarely regarded as all-powerful instruments, for the idea of the supremacy of the media over the audience is amply rejected. As mentioned earlier, semiologists are more interested in the internal dynamics of messages hidden in all electronic means than in the intricacies of technology *per se*. As Silva explains, communication has become a matter of mediations or interconnections rather than actual operations; that is, communication technologies are a matter of culture.[59] The impact of media technologies is also a subject of appeal in semiotics, for it is intimately connected to its theory of signs and symbols. The development of an applied semiotics of technology is then a clear trend in the field, with semioticians expecting to understand and explain someday the codes, routines, and social production rules of technological objects.

A satellite news or entertainment channel, for example, is certainly much more than a pure hardware: it is a sign, a symbol, and a cultural process of signification beyond the physical transmission of transnational messages through space. If countries want to respond to the cultural needs and implications of these services in their societies, it is imperative that they clarify the role and influence of these services and artifacts through a pragmatic semiology. The game of appearances that First World media innovations impose on developing countries everyday must be adequately interpreted, administered, and organized by the latter.[60]

Finally, the interactive is a major issue in semiotic studies of media power. As Vilches states, in the process of communication "the interactivity produced by new information technologies may well represent the ultimate relativity of canonical concepts such as author [source], reader [audience], message, text, and the like."[61] What the semiotic research intends to do is to come up with a new social reading of technology: a "semio-anthropology" of the electronic media where ideological constructions and manipulations are explained in semantic terms. In an information and postmaterialistic society led by technological change, the relationship between semiotics, telecommunication, and mass media may offer important solutions to neutralize the negative cultural effects of the new media.[62]

IN SEARCH OF GLOBAL HUMANISM

Free from the fatalism of the Cold War critical analyses, a numbers of Latin American scholars are now dedicated to learn more about the existing competition among industrialized nations. The idea is to find opportunities in which without radical confrontations with the north, developing nations can truly benefit from multilateral negotiations. Open and guaranteed communications for all are arguably the road toward the achievement of an effective progress and integration throughout Latin America.[63]

In the English-speaking Caribbean, for example, governments have recognized that introducing new and sophisticated technologies, leaping to modernity, is a prominent duty, though not without programs taking into account the Caribbean reality and needs.[64] States, it is argued, have a primary responsibility of procuring not only the best possible technology transfer but also the best protection of the material and cultural interests of their nationals. Whereas the role of state institutions and their capacity to promote progress in democratic contexts is a key factor, communication integration and the enactment of a nondiscriminatory right to communicate are also fundamental considerations. It is the poor understanding of both the decisive roles of the state and the need for democratic communications what frequently makes development projects fail in Latin America.

The *statist* approach, a historically oriented research, has for decades worked on comparative media systems and regulations in Latin America. Only more recently, their scope have transcended the domains of traditional legalities toward more comprehensive mass media and telecommunication policy studies.[65]

Based on imported European and Anglo-American regulatory principles, most notably from France, Spain, Italy, Germany, and the United States, a number of Latin American statist researchers have supported the need for self-defined media policies led by a patriotic and democratic state. The expectation is that national or regional regulatory structures should generate an equitable and universal access to media technology based on basic human rights and rules of reciprocity, cooperation, and participation.[66] Yet, outside forces are not considered unwelcome in this theory, for domestic factors also play a major role in causing positive and negative change.

Unlike libertarian doctrines where individual privileges are the central and many times only consideration, in the statist approach individuals are part of a larger picture of public law with immanent relationships between rights and responsibilities. In principle, communication is a public service where states have the obligation and exclusive jurisdiction to enact and execute media rules, provided there is a democratically elected administration acting as legitimate representative of civil society.[67]

Ideas of deregulation, privatization, and denationalization are then viewed with suspicion, for independent states are not expected to achieve development and integration by giving away national sovereignty (authorizing mergers, buyouts, takeovers, and the like).[68] Still, privatization is not an entirely rejected concept. Quite the contrary, criticism against statist systems as inherently bureaucratic, paternalistic, or corrupt is usually contested with decentralization, selective privatization, and market-driven arguments. Not even modernization reforms are precluded as a line of action in state interventionism platforms, as long as states guarantee democratic forms of social change and development.[69]

Statist ideologues embrace change, freedom, and democracy as faithfully as technological progress, management effectiveness, and economic efficiency. However, in their opinion, it is time to put aside the concept that communication is merely a business, or news a merchandise. It is time for fundamental changes in the way media channels operate, putting them at the service of society and the promotion (not distortion) of civic consciousness, cultural pride, peace, and social solidarity.[70] Cautious but effective state action is thus recommended when acquiring or accepting new media technologies, for the state may no longer be an spectator in areas where scientific progress and relevant institutions are favoring only a handful of individuals, not the general public.

Systems based on the invisible laws of an unregulated marketplace are intolerably libertarian and permissive for this research philosophy. The dream of a new order is not over yet. No matter how tempting it is to say that the New World Information and Communication Order (NWICO) is either dead or agonizing, its agenda in Latin America just lies dormant in the midst of fashionable, pressing, and ultimately alienating technocratic needs.[71] With increasing pessimism for the return to hard-line laissez-faire models, Latin American *statist* positions soon hope to demonstrate that what the region needs are truly democratic, integrating, and autonomous media structures.[72] In this school of thought, the state is the only entity powerful enough to carry out and guarantee effective reforms of social democratization, provided that all sectors are allowed to join the process without an illegitimate exercise of power.

A voluminous criticism, however, challenges the wisdom of placing any social strategy on the full command of the state. Policy makers and planners should always remember, warns Fernández-Areal, that individual rights exist independently of the state. Otherwise, there would be a high risk of falling into "the fascist tendency, totalitarian in nature, of making the state a whole, and the individual part of that state without other rights than obeying the establishment."[73]

Certainly, there are problems with state-centered solutions, commented Martín-Barbero. A major one is the hypocritical vision of the state held by both the right and the left. The former denies the social origin of the state, hiding its relationship with the class interests in society. In contrast, the latter identifies the state exclusively with the hegemonic class, defending its legitimacy, however, every time it collectivizes things.[74]

Even so, the statist theory continues to endorse the importance of a democratic state in overcoming national and regional poverty and stagnation. Communication channels and integration are also believed to create favorable conditions for improved and horizontal multilateral exchanges among developing countries, as well as between them and the industrialized world.[75] Otherwise, it will be difficult to see real progress in Latin America, a region still seriously "dismembered, disintegrated, and kept away from greater possibilities of development."[76]

Chapter 8

One Step Forward, Dozen Backward

Journalists and other media professionals generally believe that the situation of freedom of the press in Latin America is better today than it was nearly fifteen years ago. The return of democracy to the Southern Cone in South America, not only in Argentina, Brazil, and Chile but also in Perú, Bolivia, Paraguay, and Uruguay, is typically cited as a remarkable case of liberal advancement and reform. Similarly, significant political improvements in Central America and the Caribbean (although the recently democratized Haiti has fallen back into a political limbo), particularly in Nicaragua, El Salvador, and Panama, are hailed as evidence of democratic progress. But millions of residents in the Americas, actually the majority, are not entirely convinced of such gains in the region's democratization.

A stubborn poverty, exacerbated and finally recognized as a serious problem in the world's news agenda, following disturbing numbers of casualties and human sufferings due to natural disasters; the unrelenting levels of localized war and terrorism, internal armed conflicts, violence, and disregard for basic human rights including shocking abuses of women, children, the elderly, immigrants, and detainees; the erosion of democratic values and institutions, deepened by uncontrolled cases of public and private corruption, often linked to criminal activity such as the illegal trade of individuals for sexual exploitation, of narcotics, and of weapons, among other felonies; and the environmental degradation, such as the admitted pollution and global warming, heightened by threats of new or renewed epidemics and natural or man-made ecological disasters are all reasons for apprehension, if not pessimism among present and future generations.

That military coups are seemingly a thing of the past and that communication technology has had a remarkable twentieth century cannot be placed in doubt, but is that a guarantee for a brighter and harmonious future?

PROGRESS AND CONCERNS

In Mexico, where the election of President Vicente Fox brought to an end the undemocratic tradition of seventy-one years of *dedazos* (by the *Institutional Revolutionary Party*'s elite pointing at the new president), impoverished people, at least 40 million Mexicans, are still waiting on the promised materialization of social justice. In fact, over one-third of the country's total population living in extreme poverty are losing their patience with the alleged growth and advancement of the market democracy, particularly when during the fortunes of globalization they saw their salaries lose instead of gaining value.[1]

In a country where under the Partido Revolucionario Institucional (*PRI*) lived the appearance of democracy, combining state paternalism with selective repression, expectations were high around the newly and truly elected president. One party leader, Ana Teresa Aranda, a Senate candidate for the winning National Action Party (*PAN*), hailed how millions of Mexicans could not believe their eyes: a peaceful and effective transition of power from the *PRI* to the *PAN*. "I started to cry," declared Aranda, "just thinking that the injustices, arrogance, corruption, and tremendous marginalization of the poor that has been part of our lives for so long and now it was coming to an end. For all of us, it was like turning a new page, so we could live a new life in this country."[2]

One of those powerful expectations was a new and vigorous foreign policy defending freedom of speech and of the press throughout Latin America, challenging Castro's regime in Cuba and the Peruvian government of the three times president Alberto Fujimori, reelected in a phony election just weeks before Fox's landmark victory. In the case of Peru, the new Mexican leadership was to back the Organization of American States(OAS)'s condemnation of Fujimori's reelection. In the Cuban case, Fox's presidency was also expected to actively denounce Cuba's persecution and the censorship of dissenting voices.[3] After much praising and fanfare in both Mexico and the rest of the Americas for President Fox's assumption to power on December 1, 2000, his *sexenio* (six-year term) ended in significant disappointment, judged as an administration that mostly benefited the wealthy through the North American Free Trade Agreement (NAFTA) and with a country plagued with government scandals and corruption and assailed by narcotraffickers. His administration will go down in history as it began, a first democratically elected president after seven decades of PRI's control, but little else.

The end of former civilian or military dictatorships, the rapid adoption of new communication technologies, the spread of Anglo-American First Amendment values, and the importation of innovative news, opinion polls, media marketing, advertising, and public relations techniques flooded the region. Reformulated or neoliberal approaches to democracy brought in the late 1990s pragmatic, if not cynical, notions of capitalism to Latin America. Print and broadcast media, primarily daily newspapers, magazines, satellite, television, and radio stations, also experienced concentration maneuvers and infusions of large amounts of private capital including significant foreign investments in hardware and software developments.[4]

Two major changes stand out in Latin America and, to less extent, in the Caribbean in the last fifteen years. One is technology, specially the Internet with its multiple services and applications. The other is the definite trend toward more democratic governments, away from either ruthless military regimes or orthodox Marxist–Leninist systems. Yet, the ongoing privatization, globalization, and democratization have done little, if anything, to reduce poverty and effectively increase access for dissenting voices or tolerance for diverse ideas.

In fact, democracies are not turning out to be as strong as we had thought. In Peru, for example, President Alberto Fujimori managed to openly machinate his reelection for a third term, without major national and international consequences. Like Fujimori, President Fernado Henrique Cardoso in Brazil and former presidents Carlos Saúl Menem of Argentina and Ernesto Pérez Balladares of Panama also introduced constitutional changes in order to facilitate their reelections. An epidemic of presidential maneuvers by incumbents came close to eroding the region's democratic gains in several electoral processes, casting doubts on the true value of the people's vote and will.

One of the model Latin American democracies of the post-Cold War era, the Chilean administration of former president Eduardo Frei Jr., son of the prominent president Eduardo Frei (1964–1970), proved in 1999 that Chile was not as democratic as regularly assumed. Journalist Alejandra Matus, the first Chilean granted political asylum by the U.S. government following the Pinochet regime, had her book *El Libro Negro de la Justicia Chilena* (The Black Book of Chilean Justice) banned and confiscated by her country's authorities. This revealing critique of the Chilean justice system, skillfully marketed by the editorial house (*Planeta*) as "Chile's prohibited book that can be read in Argentina," was also widely distributed through the Internet. The author dedicated this publication to Daniel Martínez, Miguel Yunisic, and Rodolfo Sesnic, journalists who died covering the arrogance and abuse of the judicial system in this South American democracy.[5]

In this instance, Chile resembled more the Cuban media control than the professed democracy of the late twentieth-century Latin American democracies. Not only in Cuba or Chile but also elsewhere in this continent, the Internet has been the only available escape to certain press stories that otherwise would have been suppressed by government or private authorities. Actually, observes David Adams, Latin American correspondent of the *St. Petersburg Times* in Florida, the Internet "offers the ideal opportunity for dissident media to get their voice out of the country." Cuba is the perfect example. Journalists that are not able to exercise their profession are able to send articles out of Cuba via the Internet, which is something they would not have been able to do before. And I am sure that in other parts of Latin America, the same applies.[6]

The advancement of Latin America's democracy and freedom of the press is both notable and undeniable, but there is so much room for improvement. Violence against journalists, threats from armed groups including guerrilla, drug-related, and military and paramilitary forces, as well as open intimidation tactics from public and private sources continue to be serious obstacles. The increasing self-censorship generated from powerful media and other conglomerates, the systematic use of judicial threats and constraints such as libel lawsuits, national security statutes, and treason charges, and the lack of access to government and corporate information are also hideous forms of control. Perhaps, the progress is simply a transition from the blatant official censorship, killings, torture, and disappearances of the past to the "more sophisticated, more subtle, less brutal, less violent" censorship of the recent times.[7] After September 11, 2001, and the global and the endless war against terrorism, at least, as stated by the present George W. Bush administration, censorship, and other public and private restrictions to the right to communicate heightened throughout the planet.

A 2004 report of the Committee to Protect Journalist (CPJ) declared that journalists in the Americas came under increased attacks for reporting on "political corruption, drugtrafficking and organized crime."[8] In 2003, the CPJ's assessment was that violence and repression continued unabated and even increased, eroding the trust in journalists and opening doors for government authorities to confront the media relying on archaic press laws. In 2002, journalists felt vulnerable to legal and physical assaults, and in 2001, with 9/11 fresh in people's minds and the public official's agenda, violence including murder and intimidating verbal attacks against the press proliferated. In sum, although democratic rights had been expanding in the region, with the absence of military dictatorship and improved technology such as the Internet, "press freedom has not always improved as a result."[9]

Media professionals in the Caribbean, for example, continue to complain about the ever-increasing media ownership run by smaller elites, the lack of access to public information, the resilient politicization and partisanship of communications, and the inadequacy of libel, obscenity, privacy, antimonopoly, national defense, and security regulations. Low salaries, ethical problems, deficient training, and a weak infrastructure for the provision of services to the entire population are also frustrating problems. The news media, particularly the newspaper reporters, have also identified the need to curve government abuses, media concentration, the failing adoption of new communication technologies, and the Caribbean region's atomization as primary challenges to begin the millennium.[10]

In turn, self-censorship, corruption, official constraints, and selective violence and intimidation are some of the ongoing challenges in Central America, a region that largely overcame the horrors of war, torture, and terrorism as ways to settle political and ideological differences. Persisting problems in the region's mass media, however, are the internal and external government pressures, the low educational level of the audience, the poor salaries and preparation of mass media workers, and the economic weaknesses of various media organizations particularly those speaking for the poor.[11]

PREFERRING FREEDOM

Right after World War II, U.S. corporate and government circles began considering the opportunity and convenience of First Amendment principles and customs in international law. Perhaps, article 19 of the Universal Declaration of Human Rights could be instrumental in spreading free-market, private enterprise, and anticommunist values.[12]

Conventional Latin American reporters, especially in the post-Cold War years, are prone to echo the importation of a U.S. First Amendment spirit in their countries as an effective mechanism to combat abusive government practices and interference against press entities and operations. But, more critical reporters are not as enthusiastic as their pro-First Amendment colleagues and media employers. The opposition, more than political or ideological, is ultimately historical, philosophical, and cultural.

To accept any First Amendment construct as a manifest media destiny would be intolerable for a Latin American willing to see balanced and reciprocal communication relations between the North and the South. Unless such a First Amendment spirit results from a negotiated multilateral framework, equitable and beneficial to all parties in comparable stature, a free and autonomous Latin American mind could not possibly accept that type of legal, philosophical, and cultural intrusion. Historically, and unlike the United States, Latin American and Caribbean media realities were not erected on purely free-market, competitive, and individualistic principles. On the contrary, "although commercialization has greatly permeated the mass media throughout the Americas, few countries would renounce the notion that information [and entertainment are] above all service[s] to the public."[13]

If the U.S. federal media system seems institutionally arranged to be suspicious of the government, the Latin American countries appear structurally designed to trust the state as defender of the public good. Consequently, whereas in the United States the principal threat is a monopolistic practice likely to disrupt the natural order of the marketplace, in Latin America the evil is any form of authoritarianism or dictatorship abusing power and breaking the public trust in the democratic institutions. Judicially, if the Anglo-American press is individual based, market driven, and ethically rather than legally responsible, the Latin American press system is socially centered, service oriented, and legally rather than morally accountable.[14]

For nearly two centuries, the United States and Latin America have sharply differed on their press responsibility standards, though, not necessarily, on their political and social expectations of the mass media. Unlike the common law and particularly the Anglo-American legal system, where communication follows a linear mix of commercial liberal precedents, the media law of Latin America has been based upon Roman–Canonical, Spanish, and Napoleonic principles. After World War II, and clearly within the last two decades, the United States stepped up its legal influence, pushing for the global harmonization of media regulation as part of the explosion of new communication technologies.

Americanized in their media and economics, a few Latin American countries are increasingly determined to redefine their information frameworks, introducing U.S.-styled provisions and interpretations. The majority still remain, however, clinched to their old notions of press responsibility or vigilant as to what to do with their media systems. Proclamations such as the First Amendment, protecting freedom of speech or of the press in a single clause, are the exception in Latin America. Unlike the seemingly unconditional statement of the Bill of Rights, most Latin American constitutions guarantee freedom on conditional basis. A review of seventeen charters in this region revealed that only two, Brazil and Nicaragua, have press mandates without explicit legal responsibilities, just like the First Amendment. The other fifteen constitutions maintain the well-known pattern of a *free but responsible press as prescribed by law.*

Other Federal Charters such as those of Argentina and Mexico were also extensively patterned on the U.S. Constitution.[15] Beginning with the stipulation "all residents of the nation enjoy the following rights in accordance with the law" (in the same paragraph which guarantees the rights to work, own property, and petition along with those of teaching, trading, traveling, and professing a religion), article 14 of the Argentine Constitution secures the right to "publish ideas through the press without prior censorship."[16] This provision comes from the federal charter of 1853. Yet, because of the Argentine dependence on subsequent statutory rules, the press faces greater legal threats in Argentina than in the United States.

Currently, evolving statutes on criminal libel, the exercise of journalism, and taxes on newspaper advertising are the biggest concerns of the Argentine press.

Another federal charter modeled after the U.S. Constitution is the political constitution of the United Mexican States. Passed during the 1910 Revolution (February 5, 1917), this *Carta Magna* has governed Mexico with a marked social and secular emphasis. Freedom of the press among Mexicans is philosophically an individual right similar to the liberties of thought, creed, and intimacy, linked to social prerogatives such as the right to work, to have an education, and to have means of production, social participation, and the like.[17] This element of social rights, comparable to the UN covenants of 1966, is one of the greatest contributions of the Mexican history to the theory of mass media law in Latin America.

Regrettably, the Mexican press law is also the typical example of a conditional system where the logic *"libre sí, pero ...* (free yes, but)" dominates. Article 6 of the 1917 Constitution as amended states: "the expression of ideas shall not be subject to any judicial or administrative investigation, *unless* it offends good morals, infringes the rights of others, incites to crime, or disturbs the public order."[18] To any conventional lawyer in the Americas, this construction appears obvious, for "it would be incongruous to give the mass media a special treatment excluding them from all legal [responsibilities]."[19]

In the Roman law tradition, the exercise of every right carries along correlative duties and obligations, which is the reason why Mexico's and most other Latin American constitutions have traditionally imposed implicit or explicit responsibilities upon the press. Also, the French Revolution helps us to explain why Latin America followed this archetype. As "the true paper basis of all paper constitutions" according to Carlyle,[20] newly independent states in Spanish America adopted article 11 of the Declaration of the Rights of Man and the Citizen almost *verbatim.* Published in 1794 by Antonio Nariño in New Granada (today, Colombia), this declaration proclaims that "the free communication of thoughts and opinions is one of the most precious rights of man; therefore, every citizen shall be able to freely speak, write, and print, *responding for the abuses of this freedom as determined by law."*[21]

Article 7 of the Mexican Constitution falls in the trap of professing a free press with broad exceptions, such as the respect for privacy, proper morals, and peace, among others. Although very significant, these and other exemptions are poorly defined not only in Mexico but also in most Latin American nations. Not surprisingly, Mexican reporters and media organizations keep raising loud complaints against governmental intrusions, physical attacks, and intimidations perpetrated by public officials criticized for corruption and other wrongdoings.[22]

The right to communicate requires a *sui generis* treatment in information societies neither the French revolutionaries nor the ancient Romans dreamed of. Creating a special media legislation is one of the greatest challenges of developing nations in the coming century, provided they want to openly and democratically communicate nationally and internationally. This is not to say that countries need to replicate the U.S. regulatory system, insofar as the philosophy of social-oriented goals seems a fruitful approach in genuine democratic conditions.

In 1998, for example, a legislative initiative known as the *Law of Social Communications* was moving to repeal in the Mexican Congress the Press Law of 1917. Trying to reform and modernize the country's broadcast licensing system, information access laws, and monitoring of print and electronic media operations, the Mexican lawmakers finally realized that maintaining a historic but vaguely defined constitutional standard of the press, dating back to the revolution, was damaging to the Union's communications and society. Still, coming up with the "right" statute, a ritual that has rendered mostly negative results in the past, may not be the smartest way to go about it. What Mexico could do is to follow the example of a few Latin American counterparts and *redefine* its constitutional right to communicate.

Brazil is perhaps the best example in this regard. In 1988, the Brazilian Constitutional Assembly announced in article 5, clause 9, that "[t]he expression of any intellectual, artistic, scientific, and communication activity is free, without the need for licensing or censorship."[23] Virtues of this definition are both its ample scope and its positive rather than negative tone, giving little room to subsequent restrictions and manipulations. But, is freedom of expression absolute in Brazil? Not at all. As top judicial authorities agree in advanced democracies, such as the United States, freedom of expression is not an absolute right. As the Brazilian Constitution also points out, based on more experienced countries, expressions may only be regulated to protect life, liberty, equality, safety, and *priority*, which is an intriguing term used by the Brazilians depending on how it is implemented.

Colombia is another example of a noteworthy but less successful effort to redefine freedom of the press. In 1991, its National Constitutional Assembly adopted a series of innovative provisions that replaced a more than 100-year-old standard of the press. Article 20 declares that "everyone has the freedom to express and diffuse his/her thought and opinions, to inform and receive impartial and truthful information, and to create means of mass communication. These rights," prescribes the new Colombian charter, "are free and have social responsibility. The right of reply is guaranteed on equitable basis, [while] there will be no censorship."[24] This definition is radically different from the former constitution of 1886, which called for "a free press in times of peace but responsible by law when threatening the people's reputation, social order, or public tranquility."[25]

The grand difference is the new concept of press responsibility. As in Mexico, *social* responsibility of the mass media is now critical in Colombia, especially when there is a pressing need to strengthen or rebuild democracy. Sadly, except for the antimonopoly controls and the right to create means of mass communication (also present in the Peruvian and Chilean constitutions), Colombian lawmakers are not regulating the media with any clear community development in mind. More than to promote progress, legislators picture social responsibility as a way to impose greater liabilities upon the press. Overlooking average individuals, media disputes have been focused on libel lawsuits filed by government officials and politicians, members of the church, and even well-known drug lords. This is in addition to the physical attacks (nearly 100 reporters killed between 1986 and 1996), the government harassment, the guerilla and paramilitary violence, and the increasing self-censorship of the 1990s.

With its thirty reporters murdered between 1995 and 2004, Colombia remains as the deadliest country for reporters in the Americas and the world's third most dangerous after Iraq (thirty-eight) and Algeria (thirty-three). As deadly as Russia (both now at thirty-one when adding journalists killed in 2005), the Colombian intolerance is followed by Brazil (twelve) and Mexico (ten) in Latin America. There have been more reporters killed in Brazil than in Afghanistan, and as many in Mexico as in this southern Asian Islamic Republic.[26]

A misguided social responsibility could be less of a problem when compared to the likely distortions of the right to communicate coming from the *truthful* and *impartial information* clauses of the 1991 Constitution. In practice, the new charter is asking the Colombian courts to get involved with content, to prove in judicial settings two of the most difficult notions in the world of journalism: *truth* and *impartiality*. In arduous reports, such as government corruption, journalists are lucky if they have half-truths, a defense which may not be valid in Colombia. Consequently, the more the Colombian judiciary deals with news content, the higher the risk to commit state censorship.

Recent approaches recommend that the emphasis on journalism should be on ethics and professionalism, not impartiality. Can a journalist be both partial and professional? Less conventional circles tend to answer yes. Conceivably, a "green press" story on deforestation could be slanted against timber companies but effectively competent. Besides, how could anyone be impartial on a report covering the revival of *Muerte a Secuestradores (MAS, Death to Kidnappers)*, a paramilitary squad which murdered hundreds of innocent people in Colombia's drug-related terrorism? What the law should expect are news reports with sufficient professional standards.

In any case, constitutional definitions of freedom of the press are not merely a game of words or legalistic deliberation. With numerous national charters reenacted or amended, writings on basic human rights such as freedom of expression play a fundamental role in the future of developing democracies. What is the repercussion, for example, political and otherwise, of the Nicaraguan Constitution which holds that people have the "right to freely express thoughts and opinions in public or in private, individually or collectively, in verbal, written, or any other form"?[27] Curiously, this document follows the liberal design of the First Amendment while condemning the United States as an imperialistic power in the orthodox style of a former Soviet ally. With no particular press exceptions or responsibilities, the Nicaraguan Political Constitution also precludes the state from establishing an "official" religion, something that no other Latin American country, except Cuba, has ever dared to do.

Much can be said as well about the Constitution of the Province of Córdoba in Argentina, where, in the name of God (which in the Argentine Republic officially means the Catholic, apostolic, and Roman faith [art. 2 of the Federal Constitution]), freedom of expression is defined almost identically to the First Amendment: "The Legislature shall not enact laws that abridge freedom of the press."[28] Talking about the internationalization of the First Amendment, this kind of writing tends to contradict the regulatory spirit and assumptions of almost every Latin American Constitution. Unlike the U.S. law, which is market driven, individual based, and morally accountable, the press law of Latin America is public service oriented, social centered, and legally more than ethically responsible. Clearly, there is much to explore in this fertile ground of Latin America's constitutional media law.

PRESS RESPONSIBILITY AS CENSORSHIP

There are various effective and sophisticated ways to silence the press in Latin America. With the excuse of irresponsibility, journalists in this region have been and are being murdered, disappeared, held hostage, attacked, officially harassed, sued, openly or quietly censored, fired, blacklisted, and verbally or physically threatened. Mexico, for instance, is the hemisphere's most experienced country with the press. Yet, it is currently one of the most hostile and intolerant nations with the mass media. It was the continent's first American territory to introduce the printing press (1535) and the region's first to have a newspaper (1722) after New England; nevertheless, reports on plain censorship and other human rights violations dominate the Mexican media landscape. Regular transgressions, according to the Inter-American Press Association (IAPA) and Human Rights Watch, include the lack of safety for journalists, access to public information, and legal guarantees for media members and organizations.

In 1998–1999, two journalists, a native and a foreigner (U.S. correspondent for the *San Antonio Express News*, Phillip True) were murdered. The Mexican reporter, chief of the daily *Frontera Chica* of Ciudad Victoria, state of Tamaulipas, was shot at point-blank range by three gunmen who presumably belong to the judicial police.[29] Although a helper of the poor, there are suspicions of his apparent connections to the local mafia. True's murder, on the other hand, is also unresolved, as there are conflicting official versions on his assassination. Killings, death threats, torture by police and prosecutors, forced confessions, illegal detentions, and "disappearances," along with unjustified convictions, are thus ways to impose "responsibility" upon Mexican communities and civic rights leaders including journalists.[30]

In spite of much talked about democratic progress in Mexico, reporters generally feel unprotected, fearing punitive manipulations of statutes such as the Press Law and the Penal Code against their safety and activities. Asking for guarantees to access public information, media professionals and organizations have firmly denounced ongoing attempts to enact a new Law of Social Communication, which includes a national commission to control both print and electronic media services. The use of intimidating and capricious libel lawsuits by public officials and Mexican tycoons is also an epidemic in this Latin American nation. Mexican courts, especially in the poor and rural south, in the industrialized region of Morelos and Jalisco, and in the northern borders of Baja California and Tamaulipas, are little relief to human rights abuses. As residents know in these states, judicial processes are often failing and distorted.[31]

In November 1998, after years of pressures to privatize the *Productora e Importadora de Papel S.A.(PIPSA)*, a state-owned manufacturer and importer of newsprint, the government agreed to sell the sixty-four-year-old company. *PIPSA* was purchased by the *Durango Industrial Group (Gidusa)* for U.S. 105 million dollars, ending with an anachronistic institution and one of the biggest headaches of newspapers.[32] Although the original purpose of *PIPSA* was to encourage publication by supplying inexpensive newsprint, the system grew into a corrupted mechanism of dependence on paper and state advertising. Part of this entity's heritage is also the long history of *embutes* (bribes to reporters and editors), *gacetillas* (paid public advertisements), and self-censorship.[33] In an orchestrated fashion, "responsible" media enjoy not only political and governmental benefits but also substantial revenues.

The above problems, however, are not exclusive of Mexico. Like today's tight Mexican oligopoly or the former monopoly of *TELEVISA*, Argentina shows as well prominent levels of market concentration in the print and broadcast press. Private dominance began right after the auctioning of two major Buenos Aires stations in 1989 (Channels 11 and 13), following President Menem's approval in violation of the *Broadcasting Law of 1980* and regulatory bans on television ownership by newspapers. Channel 13 was sold to the *Grupo Clarín*, Argentina's most powerful media conglomerate, which, besides its influential daily, also controls radio stations, publishing houses, a news agency, and cellular and cable TV franchises.[34] Thus, the symbiotic, mutually beneficial, and ultimately soft journalism of Mexico's big press is also a prevalent feature in Argentina, despite apparent press–government quarrels at political levels. Economically, the "don't rock the boat" philosophy among media owners continues to dominate in Latin America.[35] Tense politics is simply bad for business, especially when state advertising is a significant source of revenue.

Nevertheless, members of the Argentine public powers use the intimidating tactics of libel lawsuits, fines, and legislative actions to insure a "responsible" news coverage and protect their names, territories, and political agendas (e.g., rules on hidden cameras to protect public officials). Calling the press scandalous and irresponsible in a recent libel case (*Menem* v. *Sanz*, 1998), President Menem and his brother (the plaintiff) accused the opposition media of waging a war against the presidential family. Discarding a long-standing judicial precedent (the *Campillay* decision), Argentina's Supreme Court convicted the director of *Revista Humor* for defamation, arguing that Eduardo Menem's careless story as a "corrupted" figure had been unlawful for it was published in a news report rather than an editorial. Ironically, this judgment came after the High Court had accepted the actual malice test of *NY Times* v. *Sullivan* as a valid defense.[36]

Libel in Colombia, as in Mexico and Argentina, is also a crime against an individual's moral integrity. Other felonies and misdemeanors construing nonresponsible uses of the mass media include incitements to violence and economic panic, insults to patriotic emblems, and breaches of judicial secrecy (*reserva del sumario*). False news, obscene content, and journalistic blackmailing (threatening someone with the power of the press) are additional offenses punishable with fines and/or imprisonment.

In an overly commercialized environment, Colombian defenses against defamation are limited when compared to systems where libel is a civil matter. News on social issues are exempted from libel prosecution, but media services are frequently asked to prove the full truth of their assertions. Forcing the press to retract without having to show actual malice, public officials and public figures often demonstrate that freedom of expression in Colombians is mostly a privilege, not a right.

Historically, Colombia has been a tragic case of silencing journalists with murder. Yet, while physical attacks on the press are increasingly worrisome in Argentina and very serious in Mexico, Colombia's press safety is showing signs of improvement in recent months. Thirteen journalists were murdered in 1998 alone, but no reporters had been assassinated in the year 1999. Indeed, as the IAPA reported in Montego Bay, Jamaica: "Colombia has experienced one of the calmest periods in the past fifteen years. In the [last six months], no journalist was killed … [and] there were no terrorist attacks against the media [something] exceptional in the context of the growing domestic war."[37] Even the IAPA and its mostly absolutist standards look with optimism and hope at the future of the Colombian press.

Trying to procure a new media philosophy, Colombians are making efforts to define communication as a competitive, participatory, and socially responsible activity. Their goal is to replace enduring dogmas of order, morality, and emergency with fresh notions of meaningful freedom, sovereignty, and fairness. But, neither the Supreme Court nor the newly created Constitutional Court has yet managed to decide what the 1991 constitutional rhetoric really means. For years, social responsibility has been an attractive but disappointing theory in Colombia, insofar as there are no clear guidelines on *when* and *how* reporters are deemed responsible.

Legal redefinitions rarely bring immediate change, if at all, but they play an influential role in the process of human transformation. So, if Colombia and other countries of the region want to fulfill their constitutional promises, they need to concentrate on closing the gaps between the rich and the poor, guaranteeing basic rights to ordinary people.

INVITED TO JOIN ENDLESS WARS

The trade of illegal drugs was a taboo subject in the Colombian media until the early 1980s. One of the first reporters to put his life in danger publishing stories on the trafficking of marihuana from the *Sierra Nevada de Santa Marta* (a natural reserve by the northern Andes) was the Colombian José Cervantes-Angulo. His book, *La Noche de las Luciérnagas* (The Night of the Fireflies), was printed in Bogotá in 1980. In this 300-page book the author detailed the smuggling of narcotics initiated by American citizens, including Cuban Americans who because of their bilingual skills and Florida connections were highly instrumental in such a trade in the Caribbean.[38] It is not an exaggeration noted Leonidas O. Gómez (1991), a Colombian journalist working in New York and author of the book *Cartel: Historia de la Droga*, to say that Cervantes is one of the lucky reporters who after writing extensively about drug lords and their businesses is safe and alive.[39]

From the early 1970s, provincial newspapers printed bloody reports about the killings of entire families connected to the exportation of illegal drugs. Such stories progressively appeared in the newsrooms of major cities once narcotrafficking began to penetrate different strata of the Colombian society. In the beginning, only sensational tabloids, magazines, and radio newscasts paid particular attention to the violence among *marimberos* (marihuana traders). Drug-related news were then insignificant episodes from the underground world and its scandals. News on this issue were quickly dismissed as common, curious, or folk events typical of a developing country. Even televisions use the rise of the *clase emergente* (sudden wealthy individuals from drugtrafficking), as a colloquial theme. The *narco* was a humorous topic for the increasingly successful *telenovelas*, if at all. The drug issue was a rumor or an anecdote, rarely a fact and even less a concern.

As early as September 1974, opposition media such as the leftist *Revista Alternativa*, directed by today's star columnist and director of *El Tiempo* Enrique Santos Calderón, in association with the novelist Gabriel García Márquez, accused the former president Julio César Turbay Ayala (1978–1982) of ties with the mob. An early cover, showed Turbay Ayala, temporary substitute for President López Michelsen (1974–1978), holding a gun with a legend: *El Padrino Designado* (the Appointed Padrino). This pictured episode appeared years before García Márquez won the Nobel Prize. A terrorist explosion partially destroyed the offices of *Alternativa* in December 1976. It was never known who engineered it, though, years later, organizations combining narcotraffickers and fascistic paramilitary sympathizers openly expressed their disgust for left-wing publications.

That drugtrafficking was first uncovered by either sensationalist tabloids or radical Marxist media largely explained why the established press did not pay serious attention to the advances of drugtrafficking in this country. A magazine of the upper class that also but cautiously criticized links of the Turbay presidency with the mafia of illegal drugs was the *Revista Nueva Frontera*, directed by former president Carlos Lleras Restrepo. After losing to Turbay the presidential election of 1978, Lleras maintained against the latter a very critical stand. Still, his prestigious political magazine was also regarded as a mere resented opposition.

On September 14, 1979, negotiations for an extradition treaty of Colombian criminals to the United States took place and were barely reported by the local press. Colombians did not know of its approval or ratification by the legislative branch. Within the next fifteen years, thousands of Colombian citizens were murdered because of this document. On November 7, 1985, the Palace of Justice was assaulted and burned by an *M-19* commando, including files of major narcotraffickers waiting to be extradited. That night, in an unprecedented display of force that killed at least sixty people including seventeen Supreme Court Justices among other people who disappeared, the army took not only physical control of the palace but also political command of the nation.

Echoes of Chief Justice Alfonso Reyes Echandía, pleading President Belisario Betancur (1982–1986) over the radio to stop the fire and army assault, would torment Colombia for generations to come. Sixteen months earlier, broadcasters also shocked Colombians with the assassination of Justice Minister Rodrigo Lara Bonilla by the Medellín Cartel. The extradition was the main reason behind the murder. This was the tragic episode that plunged Colombia into a long decade of widespread narcoterrorism.

Neither the U.S. Drug Enforcement Administration (DEA) nor the intelligence offices of Colombia came first to denounce the drug cartels; it was just one man: journalist Luis Carlos Galán.[40] For the dominant media, Galán was unreliable. He was too young and against the traditional political system. The only influential medium to back him up was *El Espectador*. Emulating Lara-Bonilla, Luis Carlos Galán, former columnist of the *Nueva Frontera* magazine and presidential candidate for the *Nuevo Liberalismo*, heroically confronted the corrupting power of the cartels. During a political rally in Antioquia in 1979, homeland to the Medellín Cartel, Galán openly rejected Pablo Escobar as a member of his party.

In September 1983, *El Espectador* published a front-page story with the criminal history of then congressman Pablo Escobar. He got elected through one of the traditional liberalists Galán wanted to eradicate. Two months later, the assertive anchor Juan Guillermo Ríos interviewed Carlos Lehder, the first "extraditable" convicted to more than 100 years in prison in the United States. Explosive opinions by Lehder in the daily *El Tiempo*, the political magazine *Semana*, and the radio networks *Caracol* and *RCN* soon focused the attention of fellow narcotraffickers on reporters. Lehder labeled himself as a Nazi admirer, a people's politician, and a crusader against traitors such as those defending the extradition.

During the second half of the 1980s, thousands of innocent Colombians were killed by the cartels including at least seventy reporters, and 1986 was probably the worst year for Colombian journalism. On July 16, drug lord Evaristo Porras allegedly ordered the assassination of correspondent Roberto Camacho Prada of *El Espectador* in Leticia, capital of the Colombian Amazon. Two months later, Raúl Echavarría, subdirector of Cali's daily *Occidente*, was also murdered. Cali was the headquarters of powerful drug cartel formed by Rodriguez Orejuela family. Journalist Fabio Castillo of *El Espectador* had to leave the country for publishing his book *Los Jinetes de la Cocaína* (The Riders of Cocaine), a detailed chronology of the Colombian drug lords including the Cali Cartel.[41]

On December 17, 1986, newspaper director Guillermo Cano was machine-gunned in front of *El Espectador*. One week before Christmas, young *sicarios* of the Medellín Cartel approached Cano on a motorcycle and shot him to death. Cano was mounting a defense on extradition as a resource to fight back the drug mafia. On September 2, 1989, the *Extraditables* tried to finish Cano's *El Espectador* by blowing up the newspaper's building with a truck loaded with dynamite.

On August 18, 1989, Colombians mourned the assassination of presidential candidate Luis Carlos Galán. Television images of the political rally where he was viciously machine-gunned near Bogotá will be a lasting proof of the high level of violence reached in modern Colombia. One year later, another murder would horrify the nation. Television journalist Diana Turbay, news director of the *Noticiero Criptón* in Bogotá and daughter of former president Julio César Turbay, was killed in a cross fire between the police and the *Extraditables*, the squadron set up by Pablo Escobar. *Noticia de un Secuestro* (News of a Kidnaping), a García Marquez's chronicle, describes this painful episode.[42]

The same month Diana Turbay was abducted, columnist Francisco Santos of *El Tiempo* and Maruja Pachón, sister of dead leader Luis Carlos Galán, were kidnapped, among other reporters. About the same time, a new assassination plot was executed against the prestigious broadcast journalist Yamid Amat. Fortunately, the paid criminals failed in the Amat conspiracy, while Santos, Pachón, and other captive journalists were safely released as part of ongoing negotiations with the Medellín Cartel.

More than 100 reporters have been killed within the last ten years. During the Samper administration, the bloodshed of journalists diminished but did not stop. On November 2, 1995, the journalist, former ambassador to the United States, and three times presidential candidate Alvaro Gómez Hurtado was also assassinated in front of his students at the Sergio Arboleda University. He was the most influential conservative leader of recent times, former president of the assembly that approved the current 1991 Constitution, and editor of the daily newspaper *El Nuevo Siglo*. He made the new constitution possible through an alliance with once guerrilla *comandante* Antonio Navarro Wolf of the *M-19*, now a political party. Gómez had been kidnapped by the *M-19* in June 1988.

In Colombia, it is trivial to talk about government censorship, harassment, self-censorship, and human rights abuses in the midst of such violence. Yet, as President Gaviria (1990–1994) did in the early 1990s, Samper deepened the restrictions on the press with antiterrorist decrees banning live news on subversive acts or interviews with narcotraffickers or guerrilla groups. Defamation lawsuits by suspected narcotraffickers or corrupted politicians have forced the mass media to retract their reports. In many cases, media inaccuracies and sensationalism have been notorious as well.

Illegal searches, discrimination, obstacles to gather information, and the more sophisticated commercial boycott of opposition newspapers have been common practices among government and economic groups supporting the regime. *La Prensa*, for example, closed down in 1996, and *El Espectador* has publicly admitted to be near bankruptcy because of the lack of advertising orchestrated by both the Samper government and its wealthy and monopolisitic supporters.

In contrast, at least, in the initial stages, the origins of drug-related news in Peru have been closely tied to the history of the guerrillas, primarily *Sendero Luminoso* and the *Tupac Amaru* (MRTA) movement. By the late 1970s, headlines about guerrilla attacks in coca-growing zones began to timidly appear. Shining Path (*Sendero*) gained influence among producers and traffickers of coca leaf and paste, notably Colombian drug dealers. Once again, urban mass media paid little attention to the narcoviolence in both the *sierra* (mountainous countryside) and the jungle. The dominant press was too busy with the delicate transition from a radical military *Revolutionary Government* to a moderate dictatorship. Former president General Francisco Morales Bermúdez (1975–1980) had just given back leading newspapers to their private owners, as they had been previously expropriated by General Juan Velasco Alvarado (1968–1975).[43]

Starting in 1982, Gustavo Gorriti, an investigative reporter of the magazine *Caretas*, courageously denounced the corruption of government supporters by drugtrafficking. His first target was Carlos Lanberg Meléndez, a millionaire close to the Morales Bermúdez regime and the leadership of the *Alianza Popular Revolucionaria Americana (APRA)*. Eventually, with his life threatened, Gorriti left the country. Gorriti's articles helped to try and convict Lanberg to fifteen years in prison, blocking the formation of a drug ring that could have been as powerful as the Cali and Medellín cartels.[44]

Isolation in the Amazon jungle facilitated the operations of dangerous illegal drugtraffickers. One of them was Evaristo Porras who controlled in 1982 the flow of coca paste from Peru and Bolivia through Leticia, a Colombian port on the Amazon River. In 1983, Carlos Veuque, editor of the Peruvian magazine *Selva*, was brutally beaten for reporting on such trafficking, and Edgar Puerto Carrero, correspondent of the Lima daily *La República*, survived a dynamite explosion to his car. Correspondent Roberto Camacho Prada of the Colombian daily *El Espectador* was not as lucky. He was assassinated in Leticia along with three paperboys in 1986. Allegedly, the assassin acted under Porras' command.

The Peruvian cocaine industry has been fragmented, unorganized, and mainly controlled by Colombians; however, drug proceeds infiltrated national elites and the media industry. Tainted contributions to PR and electoral campaigns and purchase by nacortraffickers of broadcast stations, advertising agencies, or pro-drug reports in the mass media were commonplace since the early 1980s.[45] Still, the bulk of media professionals not only rejected but also denounced the temptation of narcodollars.

In 1987, Raúl González, columnist of the revista *Que Hacer*, condemned the relation of coca and subversion in the *Alto Huallaga*. Tocache, a densely cultivated area with coca bushes and no paved roads in this valley, became a mixed town of peasants, guerrillas, and drug dealers with lots of satellite antennas, pornographic theaters, prostitution houses, and stores selling cameras, VCRs, computers, and latest model Nissan jeeps. "Taxes" on crops and the movement of unrefined coca helped armed groups proliferate, though the *narcos*–guerrilla liaison is far more complex than what conventional foreign media usually reports. Poverty and isolation, lack of government, and the corruption of political and military authorities, seduced by profits from so-called operation rights, contributed to consolidate narcotrafficking as a solid underground industry. Drug dealing flourished in the mid- to late 1980s. It was the time of President Alan García, one of the most corrupted administrations in the modern history of Peru.[46]

Apart from Colombia, Peru has been the country most afflicted by narcoterrorism. Between 1988 and 1996, at least eighteen journalists were killed and an equal number disappeared. Hugo Bustíos, for instance, correspondent of *Caretas*, was killed by an army officer in Huanta, Department of Ayacucho, in 1988. Four years later, Pedro Yaurí of *Radio Universal* was executed by the paramilitary in Huacho, Department of Lima. Both were running inquiries on antiguerrilla campaigns.

That same year (1992), a bomb destroyed the offices of *Canal 2*, killing broadcast journalist Alejandro Pérez and three security employees. In August, outspoken radio reporter Adolfo Izuisa was stabbed to death for commenting on the narco–guerrilla war in Juanjui, a provincial city in the Department of San Martin. Five months before, his eldest child had also been killed by terrorists. A 1996 congressional amnesty excuses civilians, the military, and the police of crimes committed during antiguerrilla actions. This legislation is likely to leave many murders unpunished.

Freedom of the press did not improve with the now three times president Alberto Fujimori (1990 to present). Actually, it got worse. By means of a "self-coup" on April 5, 1992, Fujimori suspended the 1979 Constitution and dissolved both the congress and the judiciary. A new national charter allowing his immediate reelection, the death penalty, and the stronger role of the armed forces was approved by a new congress in October 1993. Following the coup, journalist Gustavo Gorriti was detained and later released under rising international pressure. He had published in *Caretas* an investigative report questioning assistant president Vladimiro Montesinos' excessive power.

A restructured Supreme Court also upheld a conviction against *Caretas'* editor Enrique Zileri for libeling Montesinos, whom he called the "Rasputin" of Peru. In May 1995, a criminal judge opened yet another suspicious investigation, charging this magazine's editorial board with defaming an already convicted drugtrafficker (Carlos Lanberg). The judge issued a U.S. 45,000-dollar impoundment order. *Caretas* was the one that first uncovered some of Lanberg's illegal activities in the early 1980s.

After lifting censorship during a visit to the influential daily *El Comercio* of Lima (1992), government harassment against opposition media continued. Complaints about official violence, illegal detention, frivolous lawsuits, and unfounded accusations of terrorism are regularly reported by press and human rights monitors inside and outside the country. Other restrictions include rules on either taxes, access to and dissemination of information, manipulation of *colegios* (to "improve" the quality of journalism), or discrimination of journalists by public offices.[47]

Freedom of expression is a narrow right in Peru. Press rights are fully guaranteed only to those favoring government positions. On May 6, 1996, critics of the Fujimori regime such as writer and former presidential candidate Mario Vargas Llosa, his journalist son Alvaro Vargas Llosa, and Ramón Ramírez Erazo, editor of *La Nación*, a daily newspaper in Lima, were separately charged in court with crimes against national security, treason, and lack of respect for state authorities, particularly the president. There is a sizable list of journalists either accused or convicted of collaborating with the terrorists. One of them, Jesús Alfonso Castiglione, was sentenced in 1995 to twenty-years in prison "by a faceless, Star Chamber tribunal, from which the press [was] barred."[48] Within press circles, Castiglione is considered a "prisoner of conscience."

In the last seven years, the Inter-American Press Association (IAPA) has cited Peru as a country where the media is prevented from circulating freely and is repeatedly censored. The IAPA's 1996 report asked the Peruvian authorities to apply antiterrorist laws fairly and respect human rights. As of this writing, President Fujimori is in the midst of an international scandal for trying to censor *Canal 2*, an independent television station in Lima. Its owner, Baruch Ivcher, an Israeli-born and long-time naturalized Peruvian citizen, has been one of the most persecuted media characters of the last decade in this Andean nation.

Dozens of criminal charges are pending against Ivcher, his wife, and his daughters, as he continued to criticize in exile the Fujimori presidency, Mr. Montesinos, and the secret police forces. According to Ivcher, the Fujimori regime and in particular Montesinos have been involved in drug dealings and gruesome violations of human rights. Some of the facts denounced by Ivcher were the brutal murder of secret agent Leonor La Rosa and the torturing of her colleague Mariela Barreto. In the early 1990s, Ivcher hired journalist José Arrieta as chief of Channel 2's investigative unit. Arrieta, also in exile, was the reporter who first discovered the bodies of the professor and six students abducted from *La Cantuta* University, a disappearance and murder case that government authorities denied until the very end in the early 1990s.

Is Colombia, on the other hand, the second oldest democracy of Latin America in danger of destruction? The year 2000 began with the U.S. Congress debating the approval of a 1.2-billion-dollar packet to help Colombia combat illegal drug production and trafficking, confronting as well the insurgent guerrillas, the paramilitary, and the abuses of human rights.

The fight against poverty is more timidly implied in this assistance, as President Andrés Pastrana (1998–2002) looks for donors among European countries to tackle the social recovery front. For years, the U.S. government has been primarily, if not exclusively, interested in drug-related urgencies. This aid comes after the U.S. Congress decertified Colombia on two consecutive occasions as an uncooperative state in the war against drugs, as a narcodemocracy where even its president was at one time at the mercy of drug cartels by accepting donations of up to 6 million dollars in a 1994 election.

Drug corruption, a seemingly unmanageable problem in Colombia, is becoming a serious if not a critical issue in other Latin American nations as well. For the first time in the Andean world, a head of state was indicted for drug-related crimes, whereas prestigious politicians such as former defense minister Fernando Botero Jr. had been either charged or arrested for funneling illegal campaign funds. A one-time national hero, current ambassador to Mexico, and former attorney general Gustavo De Greiff was also implicated in the Cali Cartel's apparatus.[49] General Miguel Maza Márquez, a warrior against Pablo Escobar while director of the National Security Department *DAS*, reportedly accepted drug money to give up his candidacy to the Liberal nominee, former president Ernesto Samper.[50] Top officials such as former minister of the interior and presidential candidate Horacio Serpa were also investigated for fraud or illicit enrichment.[51]

The Liberal Party was not alone in the once cynical drug rush of Colombia. Harry Beda-Malca, a local chapter organizer of the Andrés Pastrana campaign (close runner-up in the last presidential race), is accused of laundering 5 million dollars a month through a pirate subsidiary of a Miami-based bank.[52] And media owner Alvaro Pava, former senator and officer of the Pastrana team, allegedly agreed to a U.S. 600,000-dollar electoral donation from the Cali Cartel provided that the Samper headquarters received the same amount.[53]

"Today's Colombia is made up of not only heroes but also drug dealers, militiamen, and guerrillas," affirmed Garcia Márquez a decade ago.[54] It has not essentially changed since then, although the news protagonism around narcotrafficking has mostly emigrated to the U.S.–Mexican border due to heightened drug violence in this area, further affecting, if not infesting, both countries.[55] Former prosecutor general Alfonso Valdivieso, then a presidential candidate, was convinced that "the time to end the horrible twenty-year nightmare of complacency with drug trafficking" had arrived in Colombia.[56] Indeed, for two decades, paraphrasing Archbishop Pedro Rubiano, drug corruption had been an elephant sitting in the presidential palace's foyer but undetected. A good example was retired Army Sergeant Justo Pastor Perafán, charged with narcotrafficking in Bogotá. Perafán, an unknown drug dealer until the mid-1990s, amassed a 1-billion-dollar fortune without being noticed.[57]

Thousands of Colombians, particularly members of the elite, were as responsible as their rulers for the moral erosion of the country. As former president Ernesto Samper (1994–1998) recognized, Colombians could not be hypocrites anymore, for the country was invaded by drug dealers. This society, he said, "went about tolerating narcotrafficking in such a way that what we need is an escape for all of us, not just me."[58] As a solution, presidential candidate Alvaro Gómez-Hurtado proposed in 1990 a "National Salvation Movement." Five years later, on November 2, 1995, he was assassinated.

Could Colombians stop this madness? In 1993 the Gaviria administration (1990–1994) ruled that media violence enhanced real violence, banning live broadcasts of terrorists' and subversive acts including communiques and interviews with either drugtraffickers or guerrilla groups.[59] But a democracy such as Colombia, weak and in fear, needed remedies far from media controls, beyond legal reforms or even presidential recalls. What this and other nations of the Americas required, or even better deserved, is a fresh social agenda rooted in the effective protection of fundamental liberties and guarantees.

JOURNALISM IN POVERTY AND VIOLENCE

In 1995, Colonel José Leonardo Gallego, director of the Colombian antinarcotics police, officially announced that over 8,400 individuals had fallen victims to the drug terrorism of the last decade. Forty percent of them had been killed including one minister of justice, one attorney general, four presidential candidates, eighteen magistrates, fifteen judges, and hundreds of police officers, public officials, party militants, journalists, workers, teachers, children, housewives, and other civilians.[60] Unofficial sources raised the death toll as high as 60,000 people.[61] Private sources, including broadcast and print media, indicated that at one peak of the drug war between 1993 and 1994, 30,050 Colombians might have been killed, including 8,000 in Bogotá and roughly 1,200 individuals abducted for ransom purposes.[62]

Foreign commentators attribute this violence to the aggressive habits of Colombians such as historical radical politics and drugtrafficking, and to chronic abuses that turned this nation "into what may very well be the most dangerous country on earth."[63] But Colombians reject and even resent this categorization as simplistic and discriminatory, recognizing drugtrafficking however as the source of unheard human rights violations "starting with the most basic one, the right to live."[64]

Warmth and hospitality are historical values of the Colombian culture, but the new constitution (July 5, 1991) had to explicitly mandate every citizen to work for peace and the protection of fundamental rights as the basis for tolerance and coexistence. Five years into the enactment of the new Carta Magna, selective killings, kidnappings, and other forms of aggression continued. A 1995 report of a human rights monitor condemned Colombia as a nominal democracy where "torture remains a daily reality," where impunity is the rule, and "disposable people" (street children, homosexuals, beggars) are murdered in cleansing orgies "by paramilitary squads often linked to the military."[65] There is simply no peace, no democracy. It took drug cartels, death squads, guerrillas, *sicarios* (career criminals), and narcomilitary and political conspirators less than a decade to push Colombia down the present toboggan of death and inhumanity.

Under pressure and despite powerful incentives to look the other way, Colombian journalists maintain "a brave battle informing audiences on their government's corruption, narcotraffickers crimes, and the effect of using drugs at home and abroad."[66] In this struggle, Article 20 of the 1991 Constitution plays a pivotal role, guaranteeing the liberty to express and diffuse thoughts and opinions including the right to "disclose and receive truthful and impartial information" in Colombia.[67]

Replacing an 1886 system of freedom of expression, the current constitution conceives communication as an open, competitive, participatory, and socially responsible activity. Media corrections, for example, are now an explicit order (art. 20, cl. 2). A chapter on social, economic, and cultural rights also "protects" the freedom and independence of the journalism profession (art. 73). There are significant differences between Article 42 of the old *Carta* and Article 20 of the new Colombian constitution. For one thing, conventional notions of public order, social morality, and state of emergency have, at least on paper, given way to progressive ideas of popular freedom, impartiality, and equity.

The Colombian communication law continues to regard all media including the print press as a public interest function with key social obligations. What this means in concrete situations is for the courts to decide. Yet, the Colombian Supreme Court needs to promptly resolve essential issues, such as what is a "free but socially responsible" broadcast program? Soon after the enactment of the 1991 Constitution, the Gaviria administration set up an eighteen-member team of "experts" to preview hundreds of hours of TV programming each week. But, there was no clear standard of responsibility to use. For years, social responsibility in a commercialized environment like Colombia has been nothing but a disappointing theory.

Defamation, on the other hand, is still a crime in Colombia and its defenses limited when comparing to countries where libel is a civil matter. Government officials and public figures force the press to retract without proving actual malice. Ironically, even news media entities came to argue that the Samper administration was "too tolerant with [critics], letting them do and say whatever they want."[68] Unfortunately, freedom of expression is for many Colombians a privilege, not a right.

In 1991, the Colombian Constitution introduced innovations of major social importance. The People's Defender (Ombudsman), the *Fiscalía* (to reverse impunity), the Constitutional Court (to protect supreme laws), and the president's limited power to declare a state of commotion, ending of the pernicious state of siege of previous decades were among the most important. Also, the people's right to receive impartial information, to a *tutela* action (defending essential rights), and to a double citizenship (for integration purposes), in addition to basic economic and cultural immunities including the right to a healthy environment, were all new and revolutionary for the Colombian legal system.

Although there have been some positive results, much remains to be done. Popular access to the media and other cultural channels (information, education, technology, and the arts) is shrinking rather than expanding. The unequal distribution of wealth, the increasing gaps between the rich and the poor, and the persistent lack of elemental social rights (work, health, housing, and schooling) are huge barriers to the participatory society and the new constitution envisioned.

At first glance, enthusiastic trade, industry, and technological liberalizations gave the impression that Colombians were doing better. In reality, improvements, if any, have been insubstantial and limited to upper classes, better prepared for transnational businesses and opportunities. As most countries in this hemisphere, Colombia seems stranded in the emerging universal plutocracy critics talk about, a social strata, environment, and modus vivendi typified by extreme levels of income concentration, free-market speculation, technocratic power, and growing signs of intolerance and discrimination. A renewed law of the jungle has taken over primary notions of ethics, fairness, and humanity. If there is any sense of openness, wrote Pasquali, it is to fake a mostly superficial spirit of democracy or liberties built upon a ubiquitous system of societal preferences.[69]

In his inaugural speech former Colombian president Ernesto Samper promised an intriguing *Pacto Social*, a "contract with Colombia" whereby special attention would be paid to the poor. Unfortunately, in a matter of days, the pact turned into a painful display of corruption scandals, conspiracy plots, and criminal exposés involving the president himself. In this presidency, the social plan did not even take off.

Next to life and peace, sovereignty, or rather dignity, the right of the people to define their own future free from external interferences is an ardent aspiration in Colombia and other Latin American countries at this time. In fact, self-determination may be more important than freedom of the press, insofar as numerous Colombians continue to feel politically, economically, and even ethnically discriminated by world powers. In 1996, for instance, congressman Danny L. Burton proposed that U.S. Navy warplanes, stationed off the coasts of Colombia, Peru, and Bolivia, be used to spray coca-leaf and other illegal crops. These countries, he stated, "have no rockets to intercept our aircraft and I am positively sure they are not going to initiate a war against the U.S., if we break-in and eradicate the plantations."[70] Senator Burton ignored that Bolivia was a landlocked nation, but, U.S. foreign policy toward Latin America has normally been one of ignorance, disdain, and indifference.[71]

In the meantime, Colombians listen to the news. A National Household Survey by the U.S. Department of Health and Human Services (August 1996) found that the use of cocaine, LSD, and pot among teenagers rose 105 percent between 1992 and 1995.[72] Not coincidentally, a nationwide poll (Knight-Ridder/Princeton Survey Research, January 1996) showed that "crime and drugs" was the most important issue among U.S. voters in Mr. Clinton's reelection. It does not take a psychic to realize that cocaine is as easy to get in North America as "a pint of Hagen Dazs or a pack of Marlboro," concluded a special news report in National Public Radio.[73] So, Colombians have never wanted nor could they afford to be scapegoats of U.S. domestic politics. Actually, even U.S. newspapers have occasionally asked their country's presidential politics to "leave Colombia in peace."[74]

Self-determination is also a focal point in the Andes largely because of the lack of commitment of the developed world on issues like fighting poverty, drugtrafficking, and war in developing nations. If Colombians were to evaluate the performance of, say, the United States on these fronts, this union would surely fail. Who should examine the examiner questioned Daniel Samper, a Coors-Cabot Award winner and prominent Colombian journalist for years exiled in Spain. Because, judging by its actions in the war against illegal drugs, he observed, the United States has no moral standing to condemn anyone.[75]

The rights to a guaranteed life in peace must be a priority for true democratic progress in Colombia. The peace plan currently led by President Andrés Pastrana need to show tangible accomplishments if it is to maintain the support of Colombians, their neighbors, and the international community. It badly needs to secure a stable and progressive cease-fire, offering open amnesties, sanctioning hideous war crimes, and professionalizing the military. The justice system also needs to be revamped to vigorously and effectively fight kidnapping and narcotrafficking.

National sovereignty is to be protected as well, building on Pastrana's improvement of the Colombian image and diplomacy including the United States. Colombia must become a world champion of international law demanding committed action to fight the illegal drugs and arms trade worldwide. If the policy is to globally decriminalize this activity, the first steps should come from hegemonic powers rather than peripheral nations like Colombia.

Respect for human rights in Colombia also means the obligation to safe and ample freedom of expression, in particular the right to criticize government officials without intimidation. Article 20 of the 1991 Constitution must be interpreted to offer impoverished Colombians effective access to the mass media while dismantling monopolies and concentration in the communications industry including telecommunications, broadcasting, and the printing press. The social (legal) responsibility of the press may not be an excuse to censor speech. Unprotected forms of expression shall also be clearly and narrowly defined by the supreme and constitutional courts.

In the end, the key toward resolving Colombia's numerous problems (narcotrafficking included) is the right of impoverished people to participate in society, to profit from the national economy, and to receive equitable benefits in proportion to the ruling elites. As a 1996 Latin American presidential summit reminded in Cochabamba, Bolivia (*The Grupo de Rio*), the need for decisive action against absolute poverty is the only way out of most crises in this hemisphere. What is needed to start redefining the Americas' communication system is both ethical and competent action, guaranteeing basic individual, collective, and ecological rights for a fresh, equitable, self-determined, humanitarian, communitarian, and effectively democratic society.

FINAL REMARK

There is no point in denouncing and raising issues if they are not accompanied by proposed solutions, admonished the Colombian ethicist Javier Darío Restrepo at the already mentioned tenth anniversary of the New Iberian-American Journalism Foundation in Bogotá. For him, the journalism practice and theory ought to change something every day, particularly if it is to alleviate the life of those in crisis.

But, it would be pretentious and even arrogant for this book's author to start enumerating solutions right now. The scope of this volume was already too ambitious, though, hopefully, useful. His only recommendation is for current and future students to initiate the (re)writing of badly needed histories in the rich evolution of Latin American journalism. Some of the most urgent are the history of Native and Black American journalism to rescue centuries of unjustified and forced silence; the history of women journalists, since antiquity and colonial times; and the history of communication technology, free from modernization biases.

Other critical retrospectives could be the history of Latin American media thought during independence; the history of the regions media propaganda throughout the 1800s; the history of foreign intrusion and media manipulation, and the history of media commercialization and monopolization in Latin America and the Caribbean. A biography of common individuals contributing to the mass media would be a most welcome contribution, otherwise we run the risk of the Maya: dying with a history of only the powerful and the elite. There is so much to do. The inspiration should be not to let anyone or anything silence our sounds of freedom.

Notes

INTRODUCTION. WHEN GOOD NEWS IS BAD NEWS

1. Coe, 1999, p. 276.

2. Malvido, 1999; Velázquez-Yebra, 1999, 2000.

3. Browse *The Belize Times* (www.belizetimes.bz) and *The Belize News* online (www.belize.com).

4. Walter Williams' *The Journalist's Creed* is apparently the first code of ethics to spell out news-reporting principles in a single document. Since then (c. 1905), accuracy, fairness, independence, individual responsibility, public service, trust, patriotism, and world-comradeship have been popular professional standards. As the most important pronouncement of its kind, the Missouri School of Journalism celebrates the fact that this creed "adorns the walls of the National Press Club in Washington, D.C.—in bronze." Indeed, the University of Missouri (MU) at Columbia also regards its press program—established in 1908—as the world's first school of journalism. In *A Creed for My Profession* (1999), Ronald T. Farrar introduces both the Journalist's Creed and Williams as follows: if the former is one of the most widely circulated codes of professional ethics to this day, the latter is the man who authored and carried the message to nearly every country in which newspapers were published. Many believe MU president Williams invented journalism education, creating global organizations of reporters that "spread the gospel of professionalism throughout the world" (in www.umsystem.edu/upress/fall1998/farrar.htm, p. 1).

5. Ruge & Herrera, 2000. Also, Corzo-Gamboa, 2002, p. 2.

6. Velázquez-Yebra, 2000, p. 2.

7. The Xcaret Compendium of Mayan Hieroglyphic Writing. In Velásquez-Yebra, 1999, p. 2. See also Rodríguez-Ochoa, Marín, & Cerda-González, 1999.

8. Malvido, 1999.

9. Haw, 2005, p. 1.

10. Velásquez-Yebra, 1999, p. 2.

11. Musacchio, 2005, p. 2.

12. Kettunen, 1998, p. 1.

13. Saxon State and University Library–Dresden, 2001, p. 1. See Villacorta, Carlos A. & Villacorta, José Antonio, *Códices Mayas*, Ciudad de Guatemala: Tipografía Nacional, 1930.

14. In *Actualidades Arqueológicas*, with Robb, Matthew, 2000, p. 1. See also Grube, Nikolai & Robb, Matthew, *Yuri Valentinovich Knorosov* in Vail, Gabrielle & Macri, Marta J. (eds.), Language and dialect in the Maya hieroglyphic script, *Written Language and Literacy*, special issue, vol. 3, no. 1, 2000. Also see Malvido, 1999, and Audiffred, *Lo creado por una mente humana*, 2000.

In 1862, in the library of Madrid's *Real Academia de la Historia*, French Abbé Charles Etienne Brasseur de Bourbourg rediscovered "an anonymous copy work of several hands" from Bishop Diego de Landa's *Relación de las cosas de Yucatán* (c. 1566, in Coe, 1999, p. 100). The French cleric translated, annotated, and introduced this valuable account for publication in Paris (*Relation des choses de Yucatan de Diego de Landa*, Paris: Arthus Bertrand, 1864). It became a virtual Rosetta Stone for modern Mayanists. Spanish and subsequent English language editions based on this translation began to appear in 1884 (in de Landa, Friar Diego, *Yucatan, before and after the Conquest*, New York: Dover Publications, 1978, with notes by William Gates, pp. xiv–xv). As a matter of fact, this last book is a republication of an earlier edition by the Maya Society in 1937, one of the first Anglo-American versions of De Landa's masterpiece.

15. Coe, 1999, p. 146.

16. Kettunen, part II, 1998, p. 1.

17. Ruge & Herrera, 2000.

18. Watch Dr. Galina Ershova explaining the Berlin episode beside Knorosov in Ruge & Herrera, 2000.

19. Corzo-Gamboa, n.d., p. 2. Written apparently in the summer of 2000.

20. Ruge & Herrera, 2000.

21. Pinzón, 1988, p. 4.

22. Corzo-Gamboa, 2002, p. 3.

23. As quoted by Corzo-Gamboa, ibid.

24. See *La antigua escritura de los pueblos de América Central*. Go to UNNetCat, the Library Catalog of the University of Texas at Austin. http://utdirect.utexas.edu/lib/utnetcat/full.WBX?search_type=FL&search_text=KNOROSOV. See also Coe, 1999, pp. 145, 147, 155.

25. González-Prieto, n.d., pp. 1–2. See also Tuck, *The artist as Activist*, 2000, p. 1, and Aguirre-Quezada & González-Oropeza, 2004, p. 3.

26. *Pecesitos* or "little fish" was an epithet popularly used to designate members of the Partido Comunista (Communist Party) in Mexico, although it also refers to underground activities of the communists who virtually had to swim under water in order to express their views.

27. Doyle & Kornbluh, 1997, p. 3. More than 100,000 civilians lost their lives following the CIA (Central Intelligence Agency) destabilization campaign against Arbenz, a coup detailed in over 100,000 top secret pages. It is one of those tragic archives where one leave means at least one death. Other sources say 200,000 or even 250,000 people died in the bloody outcome of this military intervention. On May 23, 1997, the Clinton administration declassified some 1,400 pages in a

post-Cold War openness program of the Central Intelligence Agency. Thus, we now know that these records contain instructional guides on how to kill or "roll-up communists and collaborators," including the Guatemalan president. PBSUC-CESS became "the model for future CIA activities in Latin America."

28. Marcos Perez Jimenez Dies, 2001, p. 1.

29. Brewer, 1954, pp. 1, 9.

30. *Arqueología Mexicana*, 1997, pp. 22, 23.

31. Kettunen, 1998, part I, p. 2.

32. Ibid, part II, p. 2.

33. Ruge & Herrera, 2000.

34. *Timeline: Guatemala*, 2004, p. 3.

35. Coe, 1999, p. 275.

36. Jacobo Arbenz-Guzmán also received the *Aztec Eagle*, and the Haitian government bestowed upon him its *Order of the Great Cross* soon after. See *Mexico Honors Guatemala Chief* (April 15, 1953, p. 17) and *Haiti Honors Guatemala's Chief* (January 1, 1954, p. 3), both articles in *The New York Times*.

37. Corzo-Gamboa, 2002, p. 3.

38. Tradition of Dr. Linda Schele lives on, 1999, p. 1.

39. Xcaret dictionary of Mayan hieroglyphics, 1997, p. 2.

40. Ruge & Herrera, 2000; Hammond, 1999.

41. Velázquez-Yebra, 2000, p. 1.

42. Ruge & Herrera, 2000.

43. Coe, 1991, p. 39.

44. Corzo-Gamboa, 2005, p. 1.

45. Hammond, 1999, p. 8.

46. See Sergei M. Mironov visited Kovalevsky cemetery in St. Petersburg. Retrieved September 27, 2004, from: http://www.mironov.ru/english/news.phtml?id=8136

47. Racine, 2003, p. 80.

48. Altamirano, 2000, p. 1.

CHAPTER 1. WHOSE TRUTH ON *TRUE STREET*

1. Coe, 1999, p. 21.

2. Coe, 1994, p. 108.

3. Coe & Stone, 2001, p. 14. See also Coe & Kerr, 1998, p. 54.

4. Coe, 1991, p. 39.

5. Coe & Stone, 2001, p. 8.

6. Coe & Stone, 2001, pp. 13, 29, 33, 54, 100. Another instructive source is John Montgomery's *How to Read Maya Hieroglyphs*, New York: Hippocrene Books, 2002, and its companion, the *Dictionary of Maya Hieroglyphs*, published that same year.

7. Coe & Kerr, 1998, p. 31.

8. Coe, 1994, p. 60. Emphasis added.

9. Coe & Kerr, 2001, pp. 62, 70.

10. Brotherston, 1995, p. 10.

11. Coe, 1999, p. 7.

12. Coe & Kerr, 2001, p. 38.

13. Gardner, 1971, p. 4. Mary A. Gardner (1920–2004) was a true "pioneer," according to the *Lansing State Journal* and her colleagues. She taught at Michigan State University (MSU) for twenty-five years. The first woman to obtain a doctorate in journalism at the University of Minnesota, Dr. Gardner also became the first woman to earn tenure as a journalism professor at MSU and the first one to be elected president of the Association for Education in Journalism and Mass Communication (AEJMC). She helped establish one of the first journalism programs for Hispanics in the United States. As a U.S. Latin Americanists fluent in Spanish, Gardner spent many summers in the Americas, teaching students the importance of journalism accuracy and ethics (mainly in Monterrey and Guatemala City). For over two decades, she flew to Mexico and Central America to train reporters, including stops in Miami to conduct research about the IAPA's (Inter American Press Association's) headquarters. Before joining MSU, Professor Gardner taught at the University of Minnesota and the University of Texas–Austin, where she had an usual undergraduate student, Mr. Alejandro de la Vega of the *Grupo Reforma*. Eventually, he hired her to improve his newspaper chain, offering support to her in-site summer research.

An ideologically conservative scholar, Gardner was ready to confront colleagues and students with unorthodox views. In turn, her years in the Marine Corps and her passionate conservatism worried critical thinkers, particularly those from Latin America. Even so, when an MSU research team called her to join them for a USIA (United States Information Agency) study of television newscasts worldwide, Gardner vehemently rejected the invitation as a conflict of interest. "Press scholars should never accept government information agency support to fund their research," she told this author. Personal conversation with Gardner, April 1985. For specifics on Gardner's background, see also Burton, 2004, p. 1 and *Dr. Mary Gardner Dies at 84*, n.d., p. 1.

14. Schele & Freidel, 1990, p. 421, no. 15. Emphasis added.

15. Ibid., p. 97. Emphasis added.

16. Schele & Freidel, 1990. See also León-Portilla, 2001.

17. León-Portilla, 1986, pp. 11, 15.

18. Piña-Chan, *El Lenguaje de la Piedras*, 1993, p. 12.

19. Ibid., p. 15.

20. Stuart, 1998, p. 5.

21. Ibid., p. 11.

22. Coe, 1992, p. 171. See also Jansen, 1997, p. 44.

23. Boone & Mignolo, 1994, p. 51.

24. Ibid., p. 52.

25. See table of contents in Boone, 2000.

26. See Chapters 2 & 3 in León-Portilla, *Visión de los vencidos*, 2000, pp. xv, 20–21, 31. See also Montell, 2003, p. 37. See also León-Portilla, 2001. In this last book, the author recites revealing literary passages of the Mexica, the Maya, and other pre-Columbian cultures. There are valuable examples of poetic, sacred, historical, and political narratives and chronicles that speak of specific events such as the imprisonment of Cuauhtemoc, the fall of Tenochtitlan, the first encounters with the Spaniards, the Tlaxcalan conspirators, the smallpox epidemics, and many other issues of public importance. The fact that the language is lyrical does not mean it is not newsworthy.

27. Montell, 2003, p. 25.

28. Sullivan, 1996, p. 2.

29. León-Portilla, 2000, pp. xx, xxiv.

30. Cummins, 1994, p. 196. Read also Reid, James W., Ancient Peruvian textiles, *Latin American Art*, Spring 1990, pp. 55–59. In a lecture entitled "Icon and Narrative in the Moche Art of Peru," University of Miami, Professor Margaret A. Jackson stated that "recent studies suggest that the non-lettered Moche society employed a highly original system of iconic and narrative approaches to *communicate* an ideology that was both widespread and long-lived." The medium here is pottery. Emphasis added.

31. Cummins, 1994, p. 192. See also p. 207, in this publication.

32. Boone & Mignolo, 1994, p. 71.

33. León-Portilla, 2000, p. ix.

34. Gans, 1994, p. 274. Also review Gans, Herbert J., *deciding What's News*, New York: Pantheon, 1979.

35. Zelizer, 2004, p. 15.

36. Barnhurst, Kevin G., News as art. *Journalism Monographs*, no. 130, December 1991.

37. Zelizer, 2004, p. 24. To see the connection between books, chronicling, and news, read the recently published *Hard News: The Definite Account of the Extraordinary Upheaval at the New York Times* by Seth Mnookin (2004), a Washington Post's best seller.

38. Schele & Freidel, 1990, p. 16. Emphasis added.

39. Fash, 2001, p. 12. See also Coe & Kerr, 1998, p. 62.

40. Sharer, 1996, pp. 135, 179. Emphasis added.

41. León-Portilla, 1986, pp. 3, 9–10.

42. Brotherston, 1995, p. 11.

43. *Los nudos de los Incas cuentan historias*, 2005, p. 1. Using computers, scholars Gary Urton and Carrie J. Brezine of Harvard University analyzed twenty-one quipus found in Puruchuco, near Lima, establishing patterns in their knots.

44. Topical Currents, WLRN, 2005.

45. Robert E. Park (1864–1944), quoted in Chaffee & Rogers, 1997, p. 12.

46. Quoted in Zelizer, 2004, p. 87. Read Chapter 3 in this book, *History and journalism*, pp. 81–110.

47. Schele & Freidel, 1990, p. 46.

48. Jansen, Maarten, *Arqueología Mexicana*, January/February, 1997, pp. 14–15. The Selden, Bodley, and Nuttall codices are in England, while the Becker I and Vindobonense codices are in Austria. Of the Borgia Group, the Borgia, Vaticano B, and Cospi are in Italy, both the Laud and the Feryervary-Mayer are in England. Legally, the Aztec Tonalamatl de Aubin is on "temporary trust" to the National Museum of Anthropology in Mexico City. The Collection of Mexican Codices of the National Museum of Anthropology also classifies the *códices* as historical genealogical, historical ritual-calendaric, purely historical (chronicles), purely genealogical, cartographic-historical, economic, and botanical–medical. In *Memory of the World Register*, 1997, p. 8.

49. Coe & Kerr, 1998, p. 143.

50. Schele & Freidel, 1990. For a simple and accurate explanation of the manufacturing of paper, read Meeren, 1997.

51. Coe & Kerr, 1998, p. 151. See also León-Portilla, 1986, pp. 12, 42; Boone, 2000; Miller & Taube, 1993, pp. 65, 67.

52. Tarragó, 1996.

53. Berdan & Rieff-Anawalt, 1997, p. 231.

54. Coe, 1992, p. 79.

55. Brotherston, 1995, pp. 11, 13, 18.

56. Salas de León, 2001, p. 9. It is not conclusive yet if the *Tonalamatl de Aubin* is in fact pre-Columbian.

57. Ibid.

58. León-Portilla, 1988, p. 5. Emphasis added.

59. Márquez-Rodiles, 1974.

60. Coe & Kerr, 1998, p. 132.

61. Coe & Kerr, 1998, p. 133.

62. León-Portilla, 1986, p. 58.

63. Love, 1994, p. 3. Emphasis added.

64. Sharer, 1996, p. 202. See also Coe, 1998, p. 140.

65. Berdan & Rieff-Anawalt, 1997, p. 231.

66. Love, 1994, p. 5.

67. León-Portilla, 1986, p. 11.

68. Ibid. See also León-Portilla, 2001.

69. Ibid.

70. Galarza, 1997. See also Berdan & Rieff-Anawalt, 1997, p. 231.

71. Boone, 2000, back flap.

72. Schele & Freidel, 1990, p. 54.

73. Boone, 2000, back flap.

74. Jansen, 1991, p. 40.

75. León-Portilla, 1986, p. 119. See also Berdan & Rieff-Anawalt, 1997, pp. 14–15.

76. Muñoz-Fernández, 2005.

77. Berdan & Rieff-Anawalt, 1997, p. 15.

78. Muñoz-Fernández, 2005, p. 1. See also León-Portilla, 1986, p. 119.

79. Jansen, 1991, p. 41.

80. Love, 1994, p. 5.

81. Fash, 1991.

82. The Mayas: "Greeks of the New World," *Crow*, 1992, pp. 1–21. For details on Morley's work as a secret agent, read Harris, Charles H. & Sadler, Louis R., *Archaeologist was a Spy: Sylvanus G. Morley and the Office of Naval Intelligence*, Albuquerque, NM: University of New Mexico Press, 2003.

83. Ibid., 1991, p. 111.

84. Fash, 1991, p. 16.

85. Coe & Kerr, 1998, p. 99. See also Galarza, 1997, p. 8.

86. Schele & Freidel, 1990, p. 85.

87. Ibid., p. 76.

88. Ibid.

89. Robinson, 2002, p. 119.

90. Schele & Freidel, 1990, p. 18.

91. *Science Magazine*, 2002, p. 1984.

92. Report: First Vestiges of Writing, 2002, p. 1.

93. *Science Magazine*, 2002, p. 1984. Emphasis added.

94. Powers, 2002, p. 1.

95. Florida State University, 2002. Emphasis added.

96. From the Códice Matritense de la Real Academia de la Historia in León-Portilla, 1986, p. 10.

97. Schele & Freidel, 1990, p. 18. Archaeologist Alba Guadalupe Mastache of the INAH (Instituto Nacional de Antropología e Historia) reached an identical conclusion when writing: "Mexico and Central America are the cradle of one of the world's most important original civilizations, just as the Andean area, ancient Egypt, Mesopotamia, the Hindus Valley, and China." See *El Mexico Antiguo*, 1993, p. 5. Hers was the opening article published in the first issue of *Arqueología Mexicana*, the reputable Mexican academic journal of Mesoamerican studies launched in April 1993.

98. Start with, Karlen Mooradian's The Dawn of Printing (*Journalism Monograph*, May 1972, pp. 1–35), a survey about seals and stamps, and you can see how pre-Hispanic seals, beginning with the Olmecs, were not included in this retrospect. Still, visitors can see those seals even from the Andean region, when touring the pre-Columbian collection at the Museum House of the *Marquéz de San Jorge* in Bogota, Colombia.

99. Robinson, 2002, p. 252.

100. Stapley, 2000, p. 3.

101. Read archaeologist (and retired research chairman of the National Geographic Society) George Stuart in Evans & Webster, 2001, p. 784.

102. See the glyphs in Kaufman & Justeson, 2001, linked through *AncientScripts.com*, 2002, p. 5.

103. Evans & Webster, 2001, pp. 482–483.

104. Justeson & Kaufman, 1997, p. 8.

105. Stapley, 2000, p. 5. Emphasis added. See also Schuster, 1997.

106. Justeson & Kaufman, 1997, p. 6.

107. Robinson, 2002, p. 260. Read also, Schuster, Angela M. H. (1994, September/October). Case of the suspect stela, *Archaeology*, vol. 47, no. 5, pp. 51–53.

108. Mesoamerican relic provides new clues, 2004, p. 2.

109. Ibid., p. 1.

110. Evans & Webster, 2001, p. 482. Unlike "the relatively shorter Maya phrases," archaeologist Stephen Houston emphasizes that "the jaw-dropping attribute of the Isthmian writing system is how lengthy it is." Nevertheless, he does not dispute the authenticity of the stela. See Mesoamerican relic provides new clues, 2004, p. 2.

111. Saunders, 2005.

112. De la Fuente, 1995, pp. 9, 10.

113. Solanes-Carraro, 1993, p. 52. Cacaxtla is the archaeological site that Yuri V. Knorosov toured in the highlands of Mexico during his first visit to Mesoamerica. He knew that the Mayan murals, especially those in the eastern coast of Quintana Roo and Yucatan, such as Tancah and Tulum, reproduce "aspects of their everyday life, linked to their vision of a universe in perpetual movement" (Staines-Cicero, 1995, p. 61). In Tepantitla, a suburb of Teotihuacan, the *Tlalocan* murals or *Paradise of Tláloc* depicts a large number of ordinary people playing, singing, and dancing in a heaven of water, butterflies, plants, and flowers (Vela, 1993, p. 20). See also Angulo, 2001, pp. 57–59.

114. Fahmel-Beyer, 1995.

115. Angulo, 1995, p. 24. Emphasis added.

116. Whittaker, 1992, p. 7.

117. Taube, 2001, p. 58.

118. Coe, 1994, pp. 89, 104.

119. Taube, 2001, p. 58.

120. Schele & Freidel, 1990, p. 164. Read also Aguilar, 1992, p. 3 and *Fallece uno de los artífices de la antropología mexicana*, 2001, p. 2.

121. Coe & Kerr, 1998, p. 64. Read also Benítez, *La Tumba 7*, 1993.

122. Coe, 1994, p. 59.

123. Fahmel-Beyer, 1993, p. 25.

124. Whittaker, 1992, Figure 2.2.

125. Robinson, 2002.

126. Whittaker, 1992, pp. 5, 7.

127. Coe & Kerr, 1998, p. 63.

128. Piña-Chan, 1993, p. 9.

129. Schele & Freidel, 1990, p. 50.

130. Quoted in Coe & Kerr, 1998, p. 89. This Castilean priest (1540–1600), "the Plinio of the New World" in Von Humboldt's words, is most known for his travels and research across the Andes (between 1572 and 1586). His leading work, *Historia Natural y Moral de las Indias*, with timid traces of a theory of evolution, was published in Sevilla in 1590. Read Leandro Sequeiros, *Area de Filosofía*, Facultad de Teología de Granada, Spain, n.d. Retrieved September 4, 2005, from: http://www.jesuitas.info/documentos/Leandro_Sequeiros/jose_de_acosta.htm.

131. Stuart, 1999, p. 1.

132. Ibid., pp. 1–3.

133. Ibid.

134. See Códices prehispánicos in *Arqueología Mexicana*, vol. 4, no. 23, January/February, 1997, pp. 14–15.

135. Ojeda Díaz, 1997, p. 51.

136. In 1891, the old National Museum of Archaeology, History, and Ethnography acquired the *Colombino*, expanding the Boturini collection entrusted to this entity in the early 1800s. Read *UNESCO*, 1997, p. 7 and also Emeritus Librarian Oscar Zambrano in La Biblioteca Nacional de Antropolobía e Historia, la más antigua y completa de latinoamérica, *Sala de Prensa*, Mexico City, January 30, 2001, p. 1. Retrieved September 4, 2005, from: http://www.cnca.gob.mx/cnca/nuevo/2001/diarias/ene/310101/bnah.html.

137. Siebert, 2002. See also Furlong, 2005.

138. *English Summary: The Dresden Codex*, 2001, p. 1. Read the German version as well for it is updated.

139. See GIF 03 at *Gallery of Images from the Dresden Codex*. Retrieved May 16, 2000, from: www.astronomy.pomona.edu/archeo/dresden/dresden-tour.html.

140. According to Mexican historian, archaeologist, and art critic Salvador Toscano (1912–1949) in *English Summary*, 2001, p. 1.

141. GIF 8 in Gallery of Images from the Dresden Codex.

142. Villacorta & Villacorta, 1930, pp. 18, 148. Dr. Ernest Forstemann, director of the Royal Library of Dresden during the 1880s, was the first scholar to produce

a chromolithographic version of the codex and to discover the vigesimal counting system of the Maya along with other important mathematical issues in their calendar.

143. English Summary: The Dresden Codex, 2001.

144. East, 1999, p. 2.

145. Gilbert & Cotterell, 1996, p. 242.

146. See *Yun Kax*, *Ahpuch* (the divinity of death), and *Xaman Ek* (the divinity of rain, fertility, and the morning star) talking on the Dresden Codex, in Villacorta & Villacorta, 1930, pp. 12, 15, 68.

147. Boone, 1994, p. 22.

148. Coe, 1992, pp. 79–80.

149. Houston, 1994, p. 27.

150. Coe, 1992, p. 229.

151. Coe, 1992, p. 49.

152. *English Summary: The Dresden Codex*, 2001, p. 1. See also Coe & Kerr, 1998, pp. 175–176.

153. Coe, 1992, pp. 101, 105–106.

154. Baudez, 2002. For a sense of this issue of forgery in pre-Columbian archaeology, see the 2004 Sundance Film Festival selection "What Sebastian Dreamt," based on a novel of Guatemalan writer Rodrigo Rey Rosa.

155. Love, 1994, p. xv.

156. Ibid., p. xvi.

157. Rosny, 1887.

158. See images 1 & 12, Northwestern University Library, 2001. Retrieved from: http://digital.library.northwestern.edu/codex/page12.html.

159. Craine & Reindorp, 1979. The Pérez Codex, a nineteenth-century compilation (c. 1837) of early colonial Maya writings, now lost, is part of the Collection of Mexican Codices at the *Biblioteca Nacional de Antropología e Historia (BNAH)* of the National Museum of Anthropology in Mexico City.

160. Mesoamerican Codices in the University Libraries, 2001, p. 9.

161. Coe, 1992, pp. 105–106. See also Códices Prehispánicos in *Arqueología Mexicana*, 1997, pp. 14–15.

162. Schuster, 1999, p. 1. See also Coe & Kerr, 1998, p. 181.

163. Márquez-Rodiles, 1974, pp. 36–37.

164. Livraga, n.d. Retrieved on September 9, 2005. See also Mario Roso de Luna, *La ciencia hierática de los Mayas: Contribución para el estudio de los códices Anáhuac*, Madrid: Librería de Pueyo, 1911.

165. For images, see *The Grolier Codex*, 2002, or MARI, 2001.

166. An eleven-page Mayan codex fragment, 1971, pp. 1, 49.

167. Thompson, 1975.

168. CMC, 1999.

169. Baudez, 2002, pp. 3–4.

170. *Códices Prehispánicos* in *Arqueología Mexicana*, 1997, pp. 14–15, 34–43; Sotelo Santos, 1997. Also, Baudez, 2002, disputes the authenticity of this codex in his article *Venus y el Códice Grolier*.

171. Baudez, 2002, p. 4.

172. Aguilar, 1992, p. 4.

173. Riding, 1982, p. 1.

174. Ibid. Similar agreements are being discussed between Mexico and Spain, see Conclusiones del Tercer Encuentro de México y España sobre el Patrimonio Cultural, San cristóbal de las Casas, Chiapas in Noticias, *Actualidades Arqueológicas*, Instituto de Investigaciones Arqueológicas, UNAM, March/June, 2005. Retrieved December 20, 2005, from: http://morgan.iia.unam.mx/usr/Actualidades/notiesp.html

175. Dating back to 250 and 1200 CE, these pre-Columbian pieces survived the destruction of the twin towers on 9/11 (inside a U.S. Customs security vault). The objects had been seized in Miami three years before the terrorist attack. *Devuelven obras arqueológicas*, BBC Mundo.com, July 25, 2004, p. 1, and WLTV, Channel 23–Miami, Florida. Retrieved the same day from: http://news.bbc.co.uk/hi/spanish/news. See also Devolución de piezas refleja daños en patrimonio arqueológico salvadoreño, CNN en Español, June 28, 2001. Retrieved that same day from: http://www.cnnenespanol.com/2001/destinos/06/26/arqueologia_el.salvador.reut/index.html.

176. Chipp, 1988. Today, the Guernica is at the Reina Sofía Museum, despite Picxsso's desire of having the painting exhibited at the Prado.

177. Riding, 1995, p. 3.

178. In 1997, the late Dr. Carmen Cook the Leonard, former editor of the Mexican journal *Yan* (where Thompson published his diatribe against Knorosov in 1953), insisted that the *Penacho de Moctezuma* had not been "stolen." She argued that there was no need for Austria to return the gift, since the Penacho was one of 158 pieces the Aztec emperor gave to Hernán Cortés as a present in 1519. "Let's show our sense of justice and culture, acknowledging the nation of Austria as true owner of the headdress," she said. Lost for six decades at the Vienna Museum, from 1817 to 1878, curators rediscovered it and saved it. Half of its original gold ornaments had disappeared and were replaced with replicas in bronze.

179. The argument is that relics representing the essence of a given culture should return to their countries of origins and allow first heirs of these masterpieces to have easy access to them.

180. Villanueva-Castillo, 1991, p. 1.

181. See The British Musuem COMPASS Collections Online. Retrieved December 15, 2004, from: http://www.thebritishmuseum.ac.uk/compass/ixbin/goto?id=OBJ5907 "Accredited researchers must present a written application explaining the reasons why they require to consult the originals." It should be mentioned that "photographic material of virtually the whole collection" is available. For requirements to access the *Colección de Códices Originales Mexicanos* or the Collection of Mexican Codices at the National Museum of Anthropology and History's BNAH library, see *Memory of the World Register*, 1997, p. 11.

182. Chaffee & Rogers, 1997, p. 7.

183. Emery & Emery, 1984, p. 2.

184. Emery, Emery, & Roberts, 2000, pp. 4–5.

185. Gardner, 1971, p. 4.

186. Cabeza de Vaca, 1992. Also, read Núñez Cabeza de Vaca, 2001.

187. Chivelet, 2001, p. 10.

188. Núñez Cabeza de Vaca, 2001, p. 88.

189. Arce, Paulina, Los Chasquis del Tawantinsuyu, *Revista Ser Indígena*, September 3, 2005. See also Nabokov, 1981, and Peabody Museum of Archaeology

and Ethnography, 1999. Arce's article was retrieved September 25, 2005, from: http://revista.serindigenacl/props/public_html/?module=displaystory&story_id=772&format ...

190. Schele & Freidel, 1990, p. 15.

191. *Communication Abstracts*, 1979–1999, Thousand Oaks, CA: Sage Publications.

192. Knudson, 1998. For a starting point on the nexus Chiapas and the Maya, read *Four Creations: An Epic Story of the Chiapas Mayas*, edited and translated by Gary H. Gossen, with foreword by Miguel de León-Portilla, Norman, OK: University of Oklahoma, 2002.

193. Beginning this century, there has been increased levels of teaching and research on Latin American communication issues, but area studies still lag behind against intercultural needs and realities of Anglo-America in the Western Hemipshere. For example, less than 150 titles about U.S. Hispanics and Latin American nations appear in over 10,000 entries listed by *Communication Abstracts* between 2000 and 2004, a popular scholarly mass media index in the USA.

194. *Cricket*, vol. 32, no. 9, May 2005, pp. 36–41.

195. For a passionate discussion at the United Nations on who discovered America and 1992 as the year of the fifth centennial celebration of such a historic event, read the prologue in Huyghe, 1992.

196. Smithsonian Institution, 2000, p. 2. For a chronology of the Vikings, see Gotland University College, 1998.

197. Arciniegas, 1986, pp. 6–7.

198. Ingstad, 1977, p. 233.

199. Clark, 1994, pp. 56–57, 124–125.

200. Parks Canada, 2000.

201. *The Sagas of Icelanders*, 2000, p. ix. Start reading "The Vinland Sagas" at p. 626.

202. Almgren et al., 1991, p. 116; also Parks Canada, 2000. See also "Thorvald dies in the land of the one-legged," *The Sagas of Icelanders*, 2000, p. 634.

203. Read Thorvald explores lands and dies on Krossanes, *The Sagas of Icelanders*, 2000, p. 633.

204. Parks Canada, 2000, pp. 1–2.

205. Almgren et al., 1991, p. 119.

206. L'Anse aux Meadows Archeological Site, Parks Canada, 2000, p. 1.

207. Redmond, 1979. In contrast, read Chapter 3 in Landsverk, 1969, pp. 52–74. Unlike Redmond, Landsverk claims that there are four early eleventh-century rune stones in North America.

208. Two good examples are the books by Jacques de Mahieu: *Drakkars sur l'Amazone* (*Drakkares en el Amazonas: Los Vikingos en el Brasil* (Buenos Aires, Argentina: Hachette, 1977) and *El Imperio Vikingo de Tiahuanacu: América antes de Colón* (Barcelona, Spain: Ediciones Nuevo Arte Thor, 1985).

209. Bakken, 1998; Redmond, 1979.

210. Emphasis added. In Kensington Rune Stone Collection, Elwyn B. Robinson Department of Special Collections, Chester Fritz Library, University of North Dakota, Grand Forks, n.d., p. 1. Retrieved September 26, 2005, from: http://www.library.und.edu/Collections/og1040.html. For slightly different translations, see also Kjaer, 1994, p. 9, and Wahlgren, 1958 in either Bakken, 1998, p. 1, or Mills, 1997, p. 2. The word *skylar* or *sk(l)ar* has been routinely translated

as skerries (small, rocky islands) but that is an unlikely meaning, said engineer and language researcher Richard Nielsen.

211. See Holand, 1909, 1910, 1919a, 1919b, 1932, 1940a, 1940b; Wahlgren, 1958, 1986; Blegen, 1968; Landsverk, 1961, 1969; and Hall, 1982, 1994.

212. Holand, 1909, 1910, 1919a, 1919b; Blegen's *New Light on an Old Riddle*, MHS, 1968.

213. Wahlgren, 1958, pp. 179–180. In August 2001, news of another stone dated 1363 broke out. The rock had been found within one-fourth mile of the Kensington Rune Stone in Minnesota. Three months later, scholars Kari Ellen Gade, chairwoman of Germanic Studies at Indiana University, and Jana K. Schulman, associate professor of English at Southeastern Louisiana University, confessed to have forged the stone "for fun" with classmates during a University of Minnesota graduate seminar on runic inscriptions back in 1985. They wanted to cast doubt on the KRS and test whether people would believe a faked boulder was genuine. Sixteen years later, the forged stone showed up, and geologist Scott Wolter, a noted supporter of the KRS, came forward, examined, and declared the rock authentic. Following the professors' announcement, he immediately accepted it was not Viking. I'm not embarrassed, he said, but disappointed—"when I was in college I did some stupid things too. [T]here has been other fakes in the past." In Peg Meier's "2nd Runestone a hoax, say two who claim to have carved it," *Star Tribune*, Minneapolis, MN, November 6, 2001, p. 2. Retrieved September 26, 2005, from: http://listserv.tamu.edu/cgi/wa?A2=ind0111&L=arch-l&F=&S=& P=4732.

214. Smithsonian Institution, 1998, p. 2.

215. Read Hall, 1994.

216. In The Runes of the Kensington Rune Stone, *Historiska Museet*, Stockholm, Sweden, October 21, 2003. Retrieved September 26, 2005, from: http://www. historiska.se/exhibitions/kensington/en/art_runor.html. See also Kensington Runestone, *Wikipedia*. Retrieved September 26, 2005, from: http://en.wikipedia. org/wiki/kensington_Runestone.

217. Kensington Runestone, *Wikipedia*, p. 5.

218. Historiska Museet, 2003, p. 1.

219. Kjaer, 1994, p. 27.

220. Hola! 1992, p. 12.

221. Jansen, 1991, p. 15.

222. Fermín de los Reyes Gómez, *El libro en España y América: legislación y censura* (siglos XV a XVIII), Madrid: Arco, 2000.

223. Quote from Starr, Chester G., *A history of the ancient world*, New York: Oxford University Press, 1991, p. 19, in Fraleigh & Tuman, 1997, p. 31.

224. Coe, 1994, p. 160.

225. León-Portilla, 1986, p. 119.

226. Jansen, 1991, p. 14. As in Rome, censors emerged as a purely administrative office, creating rosters for political, military, and taxation purposes. In this capacity, they judge the morals as well as the public and private behavior of citizens. This is when censorship transforms from a merely technical to a content-based or political assessment.

227. Mann, 2005 (catalog review); Parry, 1990, p. 215. Read Chapter 11, *A Demographic Catastrophe*, in Parry, 1990, pp. 213–228. See also Chartol, 1982. *Le*

Genocide Amerindien: Coquete et Exploitation de L'Amerique an XVIe Siecle. Pointe-a-Pitre, Guadeloupe: CDDP, and *Este Libro* in Barba, E. M., et al. (eds.), *Iberoamérica,Una Comunidad*, vol. 1, Madrid: Ediciones de Cultura Hispánica, 1989.

228. Stannard, 1992a, pp. 1–6.

229. Andre Saint-Lu's "Acerca de algunas *contradicciones* lascasianas," *Estudios sobre Fray Bartolomé de las Casas*, 1974, p. 2.

230. Stannard, 1992a, p. 1.

231. Stannard, 1992b. A 1993 edition of this book dropped the name Columbus from its title.

232. Ibid., see the publisher's description.

233. Sullivan, 1996, p. 4.

234. Stannard, 1992b. See back cover.

235. Castro-Caycedo, 1991, pp. 556–557.

236. Cristobal, 1989, p. 100.

237. Promoting peace: President Clinton visits Rwanda, *Online News Hour, PBS*, March 25, 1998. p. 1. Retrieved on August 30, 2005, from: http://www.pbs.org/newshour/bb/africa/jan-june98/rwanda_3–25a.html.

238. Socolow, 2000, p. 5.

239. Ibid., p. 6.

240. Myers, 2003, back cover.

241. Socolow, 2000.

242. Lafaye, 2002, pp. 162, 164.

243. Montaner, 2001, pp. 91–95.

244. "Una mujer independiente se atrevió a vivir según sus reglas," *Clarín*, Buenos Aires, Argentina (http://www.servicios.clarin.com/notas/jsp/v7/notas/imprimir.jsp?padid=1125115). Read also "Bachelet, una mujer de lucha," *La Razón*, La Paz, Bolivia (http://www.larazon.com/versiones/20060116_005423/nota_249_238507.htm); "A leader making peace with Chile's past," *The New York Times* (http://www.nytimes.com/2006/01/16/international/americas/16winner.html?pagewanted=print). All rerieved on January 16, 2006.

245. Florida Department of State, 1993, p. 4.

246. Landa, translated by William Gates, 1978.

247. Myers, 2003, p. 25.

248. Jones, 2001, p. 10.

249. Myers, 2003, p. 23.

250. León-Portilla, 2002, p. 10.

251. Alberro, 1988, p. 169.

252. In 1820, a liberal revolution forced Spanish King Ferdinand VII to restore the Constitution of Cadiz of 1812, which he did. But a counterrevolution took place in the mid-1820s bringing back Spain to inquisitions of radicals that formally disappeared after his death in 1833. See Luvín-Guzmán, 2003, p. 27, and Roth, 1996. See also Meyer-Kayserling, R. G., Inquisition in Iberia, parts 1 & 2, *Jewish Encyclopedia*, International Society for Sephardic Progress. Retrieved August 30, 2005, from: http://www.isfsp.org/inquisition.html.

253. See Inquisition, *Encyclopedia Britannica Online*, retrieved August 10, 2004, from: htt://www.britannica.com, and Religion, Portugal, Country Studies, *Research Division of the Library of Congress*, retrieved August 10, 2004 from: http://countrystudies.us/portugal/56.htm.

254. Luvín-Guzmán, 2003, p. 6.

255. Unlike Portugal and Spain, the British abolished the Star Chamber in the first half of the seventeenth century (see Court of Star Chamber, Long Parliament, 1641, in *Encyclopedia Britannica*). Also, Luvín-Guzmán, 2003, pp. 4–6, and Star Chamber, *The Columbia Encyclopedia*, sixth edition, 2001–2005, Retrieved February 20, 2006, from: http://www.bartleby.com/65/st/StarCham.html.

256. Pérez, 2005, front flap.

257. Alberro, 1996, pp. 588–589. See also pp. 198, 592.

258. Lynch, 1986, p. 39. See also Alberro, 1996, pp. 589, 592.

259. Miller, 1975, p. 3.

260. Castro-Caycedo, 1991.

261. Parry, 1990, p. 215. Actually, read the entire Chapter 11, A Demographic Catastrophe, pp. 213–228.

262. Elisabeth Noelle-Neumann in Severin & Tankard, 2001, p. 273.

263. *Instrumentos de Tortura*, 2003, pp. 17–18. See also Luvín-Guzmán, 2003.

264. J. H. Plumb in Parry, 1990, p. 21. Also, Alberro, 1996, p. 78. See also *Historia de la Inquisición en el Perú*, 2003.

265. Ibid., p. 6; Alberro, 1996, p. 195.

266. Maya-Restrepo, *Magia y resistencia*, n.d., p. 1; *Brujería y reconstrucción*, p. 4.

267. Miller, 1975, pp. 83–84.

268. Sánchez i Cervelló, 1995.

269. Castañeda-Delgado, 1974.

270. *Historia de la Inquisición en el Perú*, 2003, p. 2. See also Castro, 2003. "Beatas, visionarios e imperialismo eclesiástico: María de Pizarro, Fray Francisco de la Cruz y otras inquisiciones," *Identidad, ciudadanía y participación popular desde la colonia al siglo XX*, La Paz, Bolivia: Asociación de Estudios Bolivianos/Plural, pp. 67–74.

271. Hamill Jr., 1974.

272. Adams, 1991, pp. ix, 14.

273. Lynch, 1986, p. 39.

274. Ibid., p. 45.

275. Bonilla, 1983. See also Lynch, 1986, p. 52.

276. Von Hagen, 1959, pp. 135–136.

277. See *Running in the Past: American Indian Running Traditions*, Peabody Museum, Harvard University, Cambridge, MA, virtual exhibition, March 31, 1999. Retrieved September 25, 2005, from: http"//www.peabody.harvard.edu/mcnh_running/.

278. Lafaye, 2002, p. 85. Author Manuel Josef de Ayala is one of those who persuaded that not until June 12, 1539, when the Sevillian Juan Cromberger signed a contract with its operator Juan Pablos to set up a shop, did Mexico City have a pringting press, twenty years after the conquest of Tenochtitlan (p. 215). In turn, read Eduardo Pogoriles, Distrito Federal, una ciudad labrada por la historia, *Clarin.com*. Retrieved January 27, 2006, from: http://www.clarin.com/supplementos/viajes/2006/01/22/v-01211.htm.

279. "Primera Imprenta," *Recorridos Turísticos: Calle de la Moneda*, Secretaria de Turismo, Gobierno Federal, Mexico. Retrieved January 27, 2006, from: http://www.mexicocity.gob.mx/Disfruta%201a%20ciudad/Recorridos%20turisticos/Calle%20 ... See also, Castañeda, Carlos E. (1940, November). "The beginning of

printing in America," *The Hispanic American Historical Review*, vol. 20, no. 4, pp. 671–685.

280. "La imprenta en México," *Biblioteca Palafoxiana de Puebla*. Retrieved January 27, 2006, from: http://www.bpm.gob.mx/inicio.asp.

281. For images of these books go to http://instructional1.calstatela.edu/bevans/

282. Epigrammata of Erasmus and Utopia of Thomas More, 1518. Retrieved January 28, 2006 from: http://instructonal1.calstate.edu/bevans/Art454L-01-MapsDocsEtc/Webpage-Info.00002.htm. See Lafaye, 2002, Appendix 6, pp. 166–169.

283. Doctrina Cristiana of Fray Pedro de Cordova O.P., 1544. Retrieved January 28, 2006 from: http://instructonal1.calstate.edu/bevans/Art454L-01-MapsDocsEtc/Webpage-Info.00008.htm.

284. Tarragó, 1996. Antonio Ricardo printed a similar newssheet in Lima, the Relación de Pedro Balaguer de Salcedo acerca de la entrada de Hawkins al estrecho de Magallanes, y derrota que el inglés padeció a manos de Don Nuño Beltrán de Castro (1594).

285. Avendaño-Amaya, 2004, p. 1.

286. Schilling, S. P., et al., "Report: Lahar hazards at Agua Volcano, Guatemala," *USGS Cascades Volcano Observatory*, Vancouver, Washington: U.S. Geological Survey.

287. Boorstin, 1983.

288. Tarragó, 1996, p. 25. See also Tamayo-Herrera, 1985, p. 150; Lafaye, 2002, p. 102.

289. "Efemérides: junio," *Biblioteca Nacional José Martí*, La Habana, Cuba. Retrieved January 29, 2006, from: http://www.bnjm.cu/efemerides/efemerides_junio.htm. See also Ambrosio Fornet, El Libro en Cuba: Siglos XVIII y XIX, La Habana, Cuba: Editorial letras Cubanas, 1994. See a fragment in *La Jiribilla*. Retrieved January 29, 2006 from: http://www.lajiribilla.cu/paraimprimir/nro51/1403_51_imp.html.

290. Cacua Prada, 1983, p. 10. See also "La Imprenta en Ambato," *Ilustre Municipalidad de Ambato*. Retrieved January 29, 2006, from: http"//www.ambato.gov.ec/imprenta.html.

291. Trenti-Rocamora, 1948. See also Norberto Firpo, "Para memoriosos," *LaNacion.com*, February 13, 2005. Retrieved January 29, 2006, from: http://www.lanacion.com.ar/Archivo/nota_id=679250 and Catálogo colectivo de impresos latinoamericanos, 1851, University of California–Riverside. Retrieved January 29, 2006 from: http://ccila.ucr.edu/CCILAAhome.html.

292. About the National Library of Brazil/Fundação Biblioteca Nacional, The Library of Congress. Retrieved April 21, 2006, from: http://international.loc.gov/intldl/brhtml/about/partners_fbn.html. See also National Library History, Conference of Directors of National Libraries (CDNL). Retrieved April 21, 2006, from: from http://concorcio.bn.br/cdnl/national_library.htm.

293. The Código Brasiliense at the John Carter Brown Library, Brown University, Providence, RI. Retrieved May 20, 2006, from: http://www.brown.edu/Facilities/John_Carter_Brown_Library/CB/impressao.htm. King João III had introduced the Inquisition in Portugal during the early 1500s.

294. Read the Código Brasiliense, p. 3.

295. Grases, 1967.

296. Lent, 1977.

297. Grases, 1967, p. 90.

298. Emery & Emery, 1984, pp. 28–29.

299. This historic publication, originally printed at the Empedradillo at today's Monte Piedad in front of the Zócalo and two blocks west to the Casa de la Primera Imprenta (the New World's first printing house), came to be suspended for lack of paper. Read Juan Ignacio María Castorena, Universidad de Monterrey. Retrieved May 17, 2006, from: http://www.udem.edu.mx/agencia/historia/personajes/castorena/.

300. Read Blackstead, Katharina J. (1996, December). Notre Dame acquires library of José Durand, no. 67, The University Libraries of Notre Dame, Indiana, p. 3. Retrieved May 21, 2006, from: http://www.library.nd.edu/advancement/documents/Access67December1996.pdf.

301. Several authors highlight the brief *Gazeta de Santafé de Bogotá* (1785) as the earliest newspaper of the capital of the Nuevo Reyno de Granada, but the *Papel Periódico* launched by Cuban Don Manuel del Socorro Rodríguez is conventionally regarded as the first true paper of present-day Colombia, a weekly modeled after the *Papel Periódico de la Havana*. See Cacua Prada, 1983, pp. 11, 13. See also, Badilla-Calderón, Annie (2000, January). Revista Latina de Comunicación Social, no. 25, Universidad de La Laguna, Tenerife, Spain, pp. 1–8. Retrieved May 18, 2006, from: http://ull.es/publicaciones/latina/aa2000yen/147badilla/147badilla3.html.
For the opposite view, read *Historia del periodismo mundial*, Biblioteca Luis Ángel Arango, Bogota, Colombia, pp. 1–4. Retrieved May 18, 2006, from: http://www.lablaa.org/blaavirtual/ayudadetareas/periodismo/per3.htm
This source also speaks of a first *Gaceta de Buenos Aires* in 1764 when most scholars agree that the first printing press came to this city not until 1780.
As far as Cuba is concerned, the Unión de Periodistas de Cuba (Union of Cuban Journalist, UPC), acknowledges May 17, 1764, as the first day for the *Gaceta de la Habana*, even if there is no material evidence to confirm it. See Unión de Periodistas de Cuba (2006, May). *Efemérides del periodismo en Cuba*. La Habana, Cuba: UPC. Retrieved May 21, 2006, from: http://www.cubaperiodistas.cu/008_efemerides/mayo.htm.
Other authors propose as well that Costa Rica is a newspaper pioneer with her *Gaceta Mensual* (1729), albeit most media historians affirm that the *Noticioso Universal* (1833) is the nation's first paper.

302. Checa-Godoy, 1993.

303. Villamarín-Carrascal, 2006, p. 2.

304. Reese, 1995, p. 54.

305. Portrait of Sor Juana Inés de la Cruz, Mexico, by Andrés Islas, 1772, Museo de América, Madrid, Spain. The other portrait is an anonymous oil painting, The Philadephia Museum of Art, Philadelphia, PA.

306. Cristina, 1984.

307. Glick, 1985, pp. 424–425.

308. Villamarín-Carrascal, 2006, pp. 2–3.

309. See Clément, Jean-Pierre (1997). *El Mercurio Peruano: 1790–1795*. Vol. 1: Estudio. Frankfurt, Germany/Madrid, Spain: Vervuert Verlagsgesellschaft. Also read, Zeta-Quindes, Rosa (2000). *El pensamiento ilustrado en el Mercurio Peruano: 1791–1794*. Piura, Peru: Universidad de Piura.

310. Cacua Prada, 1983, p. 17.

311. Cristina, 1984.

CHAPTER 2. A TASTE OF FREEDOM

1. Fraleigh & Tuman, 1997, p. 60.
2. Francois, 1994, pp. 28–29.
3. Egea-López, 1983. Read Miranda, Francisco de, *Peregrinaje por el país de la libertad racional, 1783–1784: diario de viaje a través de los Estados Unidos*, revised and organized by Josefina Rodríguez de Alonso, preface by J. L. Salcedo-Bastardo, Caracas, Venezuela: Oficina Central de Información, Dirección de Publicaciones, 1976. See also Miranda, Francisco de, *The Diary of Francisco de Miranda, Tour of the United States, 1783–1784*, the Spanish text edited, with introduction and notes, by William Spence Robertson, 1928; Miranda, Francisco de, *The New Democracy in America: Travels of Francisco de Miranda in the United States, 1783–1784*, translated by Judson P. Wood, edited by John S. Ezell, 1963; Costa, Sara A. *Francisco de Miranda: diario de viaje a Estados Unidos, 1783–1784*, Santiago, Chile: Dirección DIBAM, 1998.
4. Racine, 2003, p. 44. Original emphasis.
5. Ibid., p. 35. See also pp. 32, 39. The word silly is used by Racine, p. 41.
6. Lavretski, 1974, p. 40.
7. Ibid., p. 21. See also Robertson, 1909, pp. 217–218.
8. Racine, 2003, p. 15. See also Lavretski, 1991. For his impression of the Spanish military campaign in Northern Africa, read *El sitio de Melilla de 1774 a 1775); contiene el diario del ataque y defensa de la Plaza de Melilla contra el ejército del emperador de Marruecos, mandado por su misma persona desde el 9 de diciembre de 1774, escrito por Francisco Sebastián de Miranda, con notas retrospectivas, aclaraciones para la más clara inteligencia del texto, y documentos relacionados con la historia de este glorioso sitio*. Presentado por Rafael Fernández de Castro y Pedrera. Tánger, Marruecos: Larache, Artes Gráficas Boscá, 1939.
9. Racine, 2003, p. 22.
10. Lavretski, 1974, p. 44.
11. Robertson, 1909, p. 212.
12. Ibid., pp. 199–200.
13. Bushnell, 1974, p. 379. See also Robertson, 1909, p. 251, and Crow, 1992, p. 418.
14. Pueyrredón, Carlos Alberto, *El General Miranda: precursor, apóstol y mártir de la emancipación hispano-americana*, Buenos Aires, Argentina: Emecé editores, 1943. Also, Brandes, Elizabeth, *Francisco de Miranda: Apostle of South American Independence*, unknown binding, n.d.
15. Egea-López, 1983, p. 60. Also see Nucete-Sardi, 1950, pp. 80, 224.
16. Egea-López, 1983, p. 48.
17. Silva, 2002, pp. 122–123.
18. Ibid., p. 111.
19. Ibid., fn. 2 & p. 99.
20. Ibid., p. 101.
21. Ibid., p. 112.
22. Ibid., p. 117.
23. Lavretski, 1974, pp. 44–45.
24. Entry on December 8, 1783 in *Archivo del General Miranda*, 1929, p. 232.
25. Lavretski, 1974, pp. 45, 131.
26. Crow, 1992, p. 419.
27. Harrison & Gilbert, 1993, p. 371.

28. Ibid., p. 397.

29. Lavretski, 1974, p. 45.

30. Seigenthaler, 1991, p. 25.

31. Fraleigh & Tuman, 1997, pp. 69–70.

32. See Copyright Clause, U.S. Constitution, art. 1, sec. 8, cl. 8.

33. Schlesinger Jr., 1993, p. 189.

34. Restrepo-Piedrahita, 1986, p. 9.

35. Silva, 2002, p. 102, fn. 8. Also Díaz-Callejas, Apolinar (1998). Aproximación al tema de la enseñanza de la historia en Colombia. VI Congreso Iberoamericano de Academias de la Historia. Caracas, Venezuela, April 26–30, p. 2. Retrieved May 16, 2006, from: http://www.apolinardiaz.org/verdocumento.php?id_tema=5&id_documento=20.

36. Mier, 1998, pp. xvi–xviii.

37. See *Personajes y Museos*, Villa de Leyva, Colombia. Retrieved May 31, 2006, from: http://www.villa-de-leyva.com/museos.htm.

38. Fraleigh & Tuman, 1997, p. 67.

39. Ibid., pp. 74–75.

40. Lavretski, 1974, p. 82.

41. Harrison & Gilbert, 1993, p. 385.

42. Robertson, 1909, p. 273.

43. Carrasco, 1951, p. 385.

44. See Francisco de Miranda Colombeia, in Organization of American States, pp. 1–4. Retrieved January 31, 2006, from: http://www.venezuela-oas.org/Colombeia.htm. See also Lavretski, 1991, pp. 111–113.

45. See Carlyle, 1989 [1837], p. 229.

46. Cacua Prada, 1983, p. 19.

47. Cristina, 1984, pp. 582–586.

48. Rodríguez-Castelo, 1996, p. 83.

49. Glick, 1985, pp. 424–425.

50. Parry, 1990, p. 332. Read Rueda-Enciso, José E. (n.d.). Lozano, Jorge Tadeo (from the Círculo de Lectores' *Gran Enciclopedia de Colombia*), Bibliotexa Luis Angel Arango, Banco de la República, Bogotá, Colombia. Retrieved September 30, 2005, from: http://www.lablaa.org/blaavirtual/letra-b/biogcircu/lozajorg.htm.

51. Lavrin, 1974.

52. Ibid., 1996, p. 84.

53. Cristina, 1984, p. 585.

54. Cacua Prada, 1983, p. 26.

55. Ibid. See also Buitrago-López, 1980.

56. Cacua Prada, 1983, p. 26.

57. *Archivo del General Miranda*, vol. VII, 1929, p. 188.

58. Grases, 1967, p. 51.

59. Ibid., pp. 59–61. Emphasis added.

60. Avila, 1941, p. 6.

61. See facsimile in Salcedo-Bastardo, 1981, p. 61.

62. Ibid., pp. 61–62.

63. Egea-López, 1983, p. 68; Wolfram, 1943, p. 83.

64. Egea-López, 1983, p. 68.

65. Rodríguez de Alonso, 1982, p. 166.

66. Cacua Prada, 1983, p. 28.

67. *Correo del Orinoco*, June 27, 1818, p. 4.

68. *Correo del Orinoco*, October 27, 1821, p. 478.

69. Read *América del Norte* in *Correo del Orinoco*, March 27, 1819, pp. 93–95.

70. Read *Correo del Orinoco*, 1998 [1818–1822], pp. 144 & 271.

71. Bolívar, 1947 [1825], p. 1123.

72. Febres-Cordero, 1974, p. 203.

73. Henestrosa, 1990, p. 65.

74. Bolívar, 1947 [1824], p. 961.

75. Ibid., p. 714.

76. Ibid., 1160. Original emphasis.

77. Bolívar, 1947 [c. 1807], p. 29.

78. Bolívar, *Carta de Jamaica*, 1815.

79. Febres-Cordero, 1974, p. 71.

80. Collier, 1985, p. 205. Haiti means land of mountains in Arawak language and, with its revolution, it became the world's first black republic free of colonial domination. Like the rest of Latin America, often more dramatically, Haiti has suffered from civil wars, repressive leaders, and natural and environmental disasters throughout its republican life. See Touch of Haiti: Artists plan a museum in Orlando to share their love of their Native country, by Dickinson, Joy Wallace, *Orlando Sentinel*, Orange County news, Orlando Florida, September 25, 2005.

81. Making sure Latin Americans remember and celebrate the world's first black republic, the Inter-American Bank (IDB) recently honored the hero Alexandre Pétion for his and Haiti's contribution to the cause of independence, the abolition of slavery, and unity in the Americas. Next to a painting of Pétion, Haitian artist Pascal Smarth included portraits of Latin American heroes Simón Bolívar, José de San Martín, Miguel Hidalgo y Costilla, José Cecilio del Valle, José Gervasio Artigas, and Bernardo O'Higgins. Twice, Alexandre Pétion offered Bolívar asylum and provided him with weapons, ammunition, funds, food, and a printing press. Read *Inter- American Development Bank* (2003, May 22). IDB honors Haitian hero Alexandre Pétion. Washington D.C.: IDB Press Release.

82. Bolívar, 1947 [1816], p. 214.

83. Roca, 1976, p. 92.

84. Ocampo-López, 1984, p. 32.

85. Ibid., p. 29.

86. Pombo & Guerra, 1986, p. 383.

87. Ocampo-López, 1984, pp. 35–38.

88. Mier, 1998, p. xv.

89. Grases, 1967, p. 203.

90. Ibid., plate no. 71.

91. Ibid., pp. 138–139.

92. Ocampo-López, 1984.

93. Ibid., pp. 23, 27.

94. *Archivo del General Miranda*, vol. XV, 1929, p. 112.

95. Bolívar, *Carta de Jamaica*, in Grases, 1981, p. 177. Read also, Ballén, Rafael (2005). Incidencia del pensamiento político europeo en la formación del estado colombiano. *Diálogos de Saberes: Investigaciones y Ciencias Sociales*. Bogota,

Colombia: Universidad Libre/Grupo: Hombre, Sciedad y Estado. Retrieved April 2, 2006, from: http://dialnet.unirioja.es/servlet/busquedadoc?volver=1.

96. Martínez-Williams, 1987, p. 3.

97. Ibid., p. 4.

98. Beltrán, 2001, p. 147.

99. Silva, 1987/1988, p. 8. Also, *Camilo Henríquez Gonzalez: 1769–1825*, La Tercera, Enciclopedia escolar, Santiago, Chile, 2005, p. 2. Retrieved October 1, 2005, from: http://icarito.latercera.cl/biografias/1810-1830/bio/henriquez.htm.

100. Beltrán, 2001, pp. 144 & 146.

101. Ibid., p. 123.

102. Lynch, 1986, p. 39.

103. Historia, *Biblioteca Nacional de Perú*. Retrieved June 1, 2006, from: http://binape.perucultural.org.pe/.

104. Read Focus: Public libraries in South America in *IFLA Section of Public Libraries Newsletter*, no. 23, January 2001, p. 6. Retrieved June 26, 2006, from: http://www.ifla.org/VII/s8/news/00-23.pdf.

105. Lynch, 1986, p. 61. Also Rock, 1987, p. 88.

106. Adams, 191, p. 76.

107. Timmons, 1996, pp. 61 & 158–159.

108. Ibid., pp. 92–93.

109. Adams, 1991, p. 73.

110. Beltrán, 2001, p. 133.

111. In Oppenheimer, Andrés (2004, July 4). Latin America: Independence heroes revisited in a harsher light, Miami Herald/Keepmedia.com, Miami, Florida, p. 2. Retrieved July 20, 2005, from: http://www.keepmedia.com/pubs/MiamiHerald/2004/07/04/501443/print/.

112. Art. 16, Constitution of Cundinamarca in Pombo & Guerra, 1986, p. 313; also, in Buitrago-López, 1980, p. 8.

113. Art. 11 in Pombo & Guerra, 1986, p. 372; also in Buitrago-López, 1980, p. 8.

114. Febres-Cordero, 1974, p. 137.

115. Ibid., p. 140.

116. Goldstein, 1983.

117. Fraleigh & Tuman, 1997, p. 87.

118. Title 1, art. 28, Constitution of the State of Cartagena of Indies, 1812, in Pombo & Guerra, 1986, p. 102.

119. Arts. 3, 4, Provisional Constitution of the Antioquia Province, 1815 in Pombo & Guerra, 1986, p. 373.

120. See Federation Act of the United Provinces of the New Granada, 1811, and Constitution of the Republic of Tunja, 1811.

121. Buitrago-López, 1998, p. 14.

122. Febres-Cordero, 1974, p. 135. It is important to note that Juan Bautista Mariano Picornell y Gomilla was also a translator of the French Declaration of the Rights of Man and the Citizen in 1797, the so-called *Declaración de los derechos del hombre y del ciudadano con varias máximas republicanas y un discurso preliminar dirigido a los americanos* (French declaration with various maxims and a preliminary speech addressed to the Americans). Read Sambrano-Urdaneta, Oscar in Grases, Pedro (1979). Andrés Bello: Obra Literaria. Chronology, vol. 50. Caracas, Venezuela: Biblioteca Ayacucho.

123. Ibid.

124. Carlyle, 1989, p. 229.

125. Ocampo-López, 1984, p. 28.

126. Henestrosa, 1990.

127. Ibid., pp. 54–55.

128. Ocampo-López, 1984, p. 42; Paredes-Cruz, 1984, p. 27.

129. Sarmiento, 1951.

130. Febres-Cordero, 1974, p. 150.

CHAPTER 3. TAKEN BY WAR AND CENSORSHIP

1. During an interview in 1991, Mr. Bernays, a nephew of Sigmund Freud, reminded us that if propaganda *could be used for war, it can be used for peace.* Unfortunately, aggressive uses of the media remain the norm, especially now in the war against terrorism. Married to Doris E. Fleischman, Mr. Edward Bernays, a Cornell University graduate, died on March 9, 1995. Read Edward Bernays, "Father of Public Relations" and leader in opinion making, dies at 103, *The New York Times*, March 10, 1995, pp. 1–3. Retrieved June 30, 2006, from: http://www.nytimes.com/books/98/08/16/specials/bernays-obi.html.

2. Beltrán, pp. 114 & 147. Also, Rodríguez-Díaz, 1997, p. 20.

3. Rodríguez-Díaz, 1997, p. 97.

4. Ibid., pp. 98 & 99.

5. Read State of the Union Messages: President James Monroe (1823), *The American Presidency Project*. Retrieved July 4, 2006, from: http://www.ucsb.edu/sou.php. See also Chávez to deliver speech in Panama (in celebration of 180th Anniversary of the Anfictionic Congress), *El Universsal.com*, June 21, 2006, p. 1. Retrieved July 2, 2006, from: http://english.eluniversal.com/2006/06/21/en_pol_art_21A727753.shtml.

6. Read State of the Union Messages: President James K. Polk (1848), *The American Presidency Project*. Retrieved July 4, 2006, from: http://www.ucsb.edu/sou.php.

7. Read Moreno, 2004, presentation. Historian Jesús Velasco-Márquez calls this armed conflict not "the Mexican War" but "the U.S. War against Mexico," 1995, p. 7.

8. Moreno, 2004; Velasco-Márquez, 1995.

9. Velasco-Márquez, 1995, p. 5.

10. *Correo del Orinoco*, 1998, p. xii; McDowell, 2003, p. 6.

11. Schlesinger Jr., 1993, p. 250.

12. Singletary, 1960, pp. 13–14.

13. Schlesinger Jr., 1993; Singletary, 1960.

14. Singletary, 1960, p. 3.

15. Emery & Emery, 1984, p. 166.

16. Ibid.

17. Singletary, 1960, p. 15.

18. "Agustín de Iturbide," in *Encyclopedia Britannica*. Retrieved January 3, 2005, from: http://www.britannica.com/eb/print?tocId=9043055&fullArticle=false.

19. Schlesinger Jr., 1993, p. 250.

20. Ibid., pp. 249, 261. See also Cunliffe, 1993, p. 149.
21. Singletary, 1960, p. 15.
22. Bauer, 1974, p. 306.
23. Schlesinger Jr., 1993, pp. 250, 397.
24. Schlesinger, 1993, p. 178.
25. Emery & Emery, 1984, p. 166.
26. Bauer, 1974, p. 396.
27. Griffith, 1998, p. 168.
28. Davis & Wilburn Jr., 1991, p. 87.
29. Baur, 1994, p. 14.
30. Ibid., p. 11.
31. Baur, 1994, p. 13.
32. Ibid., p. 14.
33. Ibid.
34. Collier, 1974a, pp. 628–629.
35. SIDBOL, 1987, p. 7.
36. Ferreira, 1989.
37. Bauer, 1974, p. 327.
38. Emery & Emery, 1984, p. 167.
39. Henestrosa, 1990, pp. 142–143.
40. Checa-Godoy, 1993, pp. 52–55.
41. Singletary, 1960, p. 5. See also Bauer, 1974, p. 392.
42. See Civil Disobedience in Bode, 1982, pp. 110, 114, 115 throughout the nineteenth century. Original emphasis.
43. Cunliffe, 1993, p. 251.
44. Whitman, 1997, pp. 5–6.
45. Singletary, 1960, pp. 4–5.
46. Crow, 1992, p. 664.
47. Henestrosa, 1990, p. 154.
48. Ibid., p. 151.
49. Checa-Godoy, 1993.
50. Ibid.
51. Alvarez & Martínez-Riaza, 1992, p. 159.
52. Checa-Godoy, 1993.
53. Collier, 1974a; Alvarez & Martínez-Riaza, 1992, p. 142.
54. Alvarez & Martínez-Riaza, 1992, p. 149.
55. Ibid., p. 62.
56. Ibid.
57. See La Constitución de Cádiz de 1812 in Alvarez-Lejarza, 1958, pp. 252–300.
58. Ibid., pp. 307–310.
59. Bolívar, (1947[1829]), pp. 1301–1305.
60. Constitution for the Republic of Venezuela in Alvarez & Martínez-Riaza, 1992, p. 71.
61. Title VIII, art. 156, Constitución de la República de Colombia, 1821 in Pombo & Guerra, 1986, pp. 63–104.
62. Buitrago-López, 1998, p. 14.
63. Pombo & Guerra, 1986, pp. 113–114.

64. Speech to the Constitutional Congress of Bolivia. Bolívar, (1947[1799–1826]), vol. 2, pp. 1220–1221.

65. Roca, 1976.

66. Buitrago-López, 1998, p. 16.

67. Lombardi, 1974, p. 616; Alvarez & Martínez-Riaza, 1992, pp. 92–93.

68. Crow, 1992, p. 451.

69. Alvarez-Lejarza, 1958, pp. 395–396.

70. Art. 175, num. 1, in Alvarez-Lejarza, 1958, pp. 331–363.

71. Art. 1, *Decreto del Congreso Federal de 17 de Mayo de 1832*, ibid., pp. 397–398.

72. Ibid., p. 398.

73. Art. 12, ibid., p. 400.

74. Title III, arts. 25, 29, ibid., pp. 366–394.

75. Ibid.

76. Art. 29, Ibid., p. 427.

77. Bolívar, 1829.

78. Alvarez & Martínez-Riaza, 1992, p. 86.

79. Bauer, 1974, pp. 326, 371–372.

80. Alvarez & Martínez-Riaza, 1992, pp. 101–102; Collier, 1974b, p. 542.

81. Alvarez & Martínez-Riaza, 1992.

82. Ibid., p. 78.

83. Read *Bolivia* & *Chile* in Jones, 2001, pp. 260 & 465. O'Higgins banned books, theatrical works, carnival games, drums, "gyrating dances," and "extravagant clothes," during his supreme directorship.

84. Quoted by Oppenheimer, 2004, p. 2.

85. Pedro II, *The Columbia Encyclopedia*, sixth edition (2001–2005). Retrieved July 4, 2006, from: http://www.bartleby.com/65/pe/Pedro2.html. Read also Jones, 2001, pp. 283 & 585.

86. Read Joanne Hardwood's *Aztec and Maya Culture* in Jones, 2001, pp. 158–159.

CHAPTER 4. MODERNIZATION AND THE PRESS

1. Skidmore & Smith, 1992; Baur, 1994.

2. Alvarez & Martínez-Riaza, 1992, p. 75.

3. Beltrán, 1943, pp. 26, 29.

4. Henestrosa, 1990, pp. 37–38.

5. Wolfram, 1943, p. 19. In 1812, Henríquez, also a priest, published an extract of John Milton's *Areopagitica* in his *Aurora de Chile*, and two years later, this paper was closed down and replaced with the pro-Spanish *El Monitor Araucano*. See Jones, 2001, p. 465.

6. Beltrán, 1943, pp. 17–21; Henestrosa, 1990, pp. 35–36.

7. Checa-Godoy, 1993; Henestrosa, 1990, p. 46.

8. Otero, 1946, p. 223.

9. Checa-Godoy, 1993, p. 33.

10. Henestrosa, 1990, pp. 29.

11. Williford, 1980, pp. ix–xiv.

12. Popkin, 1999.

13. Otero, 1943, pp. 89–90.

14. Popkin, 1999.

15. Williford, 1980, p. xv.

16. Ibid., p. 10.

17. Ibid., pp. 28–29.

18. Ibid., p. 35.

19. Bucich, 1951, p. 22.

20. Lavine, 1984, pp. 144–145.

21. Ibid.; Otero, 1946, pp. 99–100.

22. Crow, 1992, pp. 601–602.

23. Skidmore & Smith, 1992, p. 53.

24. Baur, 1994, p. 12.

25. Conrad, 1974, pp. 352, 495; Otero, 1946, p. 100.

26. Berry, 1974, pp. 192–193.

27. Fuentes, 1988, p. 129.

28. Otero, 1946, p. 109. Interestingly, on May 4, 1839, both Manuel Amunátegui, a Chilean royalist who fought in the battle of Ayacucho, and Alejandro Villota, an Argentinean patriot in the same historic encounter, founded *El Comercio*, Peru's most prominent daily today. Few Latin American newspapers have such a long and intriguing origin of multiple nationalities and political passions. In fact, according to Professor Robert N. Pierce, during the 1930s, *El Comercio* was so far to the right that columnists praised Hitler and fascism. This daily has been owned by a family of a Panamanian descent, the legendary journalist Don José Antonio Miró Quesada (1845–1930). Read also, Salwen and Garrison, 1991, p. 117, and *Organización de Estados Iberoamericanos (OEI)* (2000–2006), Medios de comunicación y cultura, Regional Office, Lima, Peru. Retrieved July 4, 2006, from: http://www.campus-oei.org/cultura/peru/07.htm.

29. Alvarez & Martínez-Riaza, 1992, p. 132.

30. Jones, 2001, p. 546.

31. Ibid., p. 998.

32. Beltrán, 1943, p. 261; Alvarez & Martínez-Riaza, 1992, p. 155.

33. Beltrán, 1943, p. 262.

34. Frederick, 1993, p. 27.

35. Otero, 1946, p. 106.

36. Noam, 1998, p. 100.

37. Alvarez & Martínez-Riaza, 1992, pp. 158–159.

38. Emery & Emery, 1984, pp. 281, 333; Alvarez & Martínez-Riaza, 1992, pp. 158–159; Checa-Godoy, 1993, p. 180.

39. Toussaint, 1988, p. 2.

40. Ibid., p. 4.

41. Ibid., p. 5.

42. For the Aztecs, the otter was an animal that represented bad luck, bad presages, and an annoying character.

43. Toussaint, 1998, p. 5.

44. Jones, 2001, p. 1017.

45. Ibid., pp. 66, 181, 714, 683, & 1842.

46. Ibid., 1719.

47. Ibid., 1813.

48. Ibid., 2561.

49. Ibid., 1575.

50. Checa-Godoy, 1993, p. 181.

51. Rives-Sánchez, 2000, p. 15.

52. Williford, 1980.

53. Rives-Sánchez, 2000, p. 20.

54. Ibid.

55. Alvarez & Martínez-Riaza, 1992, p. 119.

56. Ross, 1965, pp. 21–22.

57. Ibid., p. 23.

58. Parker, 2000, pp. 2–3.

59. Ibid., p. 13.

60. Ibid.

61. Ibid., p. 12.

62. Alvarez & Martínez-Riaza, 1992; Baur, 1994.

63. Checa-Godoy, 1993, p. 133.

64. See arts. 6, 7, Constitution of the United States of Colombia in Buitrago-López, 1998, p. 19.

CHAPTER 5. HOW NOT TO START A CENTURY

1. See Foner, Philip S., *La Guerra Hispano Cubana Americana y el nacimiento del imperialismo nortemaericano*, Madrid: Ediciones Akal, 1975. See also Foner, Philip S., *The Spanish Cuban American War and the Birth of American Imperialism*, New York: Monthly Review Press, 1972.

2. Henríquez-Ureña, 1977, p. 15.

3. Ibid., pp. 14–15.

4. Martí, 1984, p. 3.

5. Gray, 1974, p. 358.

6. Otero, 1946, p. 258.

7. Bueno, 1982.

8. Ibid.

9. Gray, 1974, p. 359.

10. Henríquez-Ureña, 1977, p. 30.

11. Emery & Emery, 1984.

12. Bueno, 1982, p. 23.

13. Wade, 1993, p. 400.

14. Bueno, 1982, p. 293.

15. Henríquez-Ureña, 1977, p. 32.

16. Portuondo, 1977, p. 61.

17. Schlesinger Jr., 1993, pp. 380–381.

18. Ibid., pp. 382, 386.

19. Emery & Emery, 1984, p. 292.

20. Bueno, 1982, p. 403.

21. Schlesinger Jr., 1993, pp. 389, 406; Emery & Emery, 1984, p. 293.

22. Bueno, 1982, pp. 229–230.

23. Ibid., p. 361.

24. In a letter to Federico Henríquez y Carvajal in Bueno, 1982, p. 309.

25. Williford, 1980.

26. Ibid., p. 87.
27. LaFeber, 1978, p. 12; Flores-Jaramillo, 1976, p. 38.
28. Otero, 1946, pp. 367–368.
29. Mesa, 1984, pp. 93–94.
30. Ibid., pp. 85, 97.
31. See *El Nuevo Tiempo*, in Villegas & Yunis, 1978, p. 307.
32. Ibid., pp. 121–122.
33. Mesa, 1984, p. 91.
34. LaFeber, 1978, pp. 13–16.
35. Villegas & Yunis, 1978, p. 251.
36. Ibid., pp. 117, 298.
37. LaFeber, 1978, p. 16.
38. Ibid.
39. Villegas & Yunis, 1978, pp. 49, 51.
40. Ibid., p. 125.
41. Mesa, 1984, pp. 85, 87.
42. Villegas & Yunis, 1978, pp. 273, 298.
43. Mesa, 1984, pp. 137.
44. LaFeber, 1978, p. 14.
45. Ibid.
46. Mesa, 1984, p. 137.
47. Martínez-Fortún y Foyo, 1986, pp. 313–314.
48. Ibid., pp. 148, 152.
49. Ibid., p. 156.
50. Ibid, pp. 156, 159–160.
51. A *Batolome Mitre*, December 19, 1882, in Bueno, 1982, p. 210.
52. Henríquez-Ureña, 1977, p. 27.
53. Avila, 1949, p. 9.
54. Henríquez-Ureña, 1977, p. 25.
55. Fonnegra, 1984.
56. Mesa, 1984, pp. 96–97.
57. Quoted in *El Forjista* (2006), Los silencios y las voces en América Latina: Notas sobre el pensamiento nacional y popular. Retrieved July 7, 2006, from: http://www.elforjista.unlugar.com/lossilencios.htm. Also, read *Latidos de América* (2001, June). La tenaz lucha del pueblo latinoamericano (interview with A. Argumedo). Retrieved July 7, 2006, from: http://www.diariocasual.com.ar/america/alcira.html.
58. *Foreign Policy* creates terrorism index, *Talk of the Nation*, NPR, July 6, 2006. Retrieved July 6, 2006, from: http://www.npr.org/templates/story/story.php?storyId=5538494.
59. *Latidos de América* (2001, June), as cited in fn. 57.

CHAPTER 6. HOT AND COLD WARS, WARM PRESSES

1. Goldstein, 1983, p. 1.
2. Ibid., p. 2.
3. Ibid., pp. 3–5.
4. Rogers, 1997, p. 34.

5. Read Chaffee, Gómez-Palacio, & Rogers, 1990, p. 1020. Also, Rogers, 1997, p. 56.

6. Ibid., p. 102.

7. Romano, 1983, p. 9.

8. Ibid., p. 33. This collaboration ended with the civil war in March 1862.

9. News History Gazette, 1997, p. 11.

10. News History Gazette, 1997, p. 12.

11. Fraleigh & Tuman, 1997, p. 83.

12. Barnett, 2003, p. 170.

13. Fernandina and Amelia, Florida, are the historic islands over which the *Correo del Orinoco* complained about to the U.S. government back in 1821. Read the José Martí Timeline, *Historyofcuba.com*, sec. 3, p. 3. Retrieved June 12, 2006, from: http://www.historyofcuba.com/history/marti/jmtime-3.htm.

14. Romano, 1987, p. 15.

15. Ibid., p. 15. Also read, pp. 16–17.

16. Read Journalism school opens its doors, published in *The New York Times*, 1912 and available in Columbia University Graduate School of Journalism's School History. Retrieved April 2, 2006, from: http://www.jrn.columbia.edu/alumni/history/documents Also, A brief history of the Missouri School of Journalism. Retrieved April 2, 2006, from: http://journalism.missouri.edu/about/history.html

17. See Columbia University's *Class Photos* and Famous Puerto Ricans, p. 2. Retrieved June 1, 2006, from: http://www.topuertorico.org/culture/famousprA-C.shtml

18. The Spanish American War, Historical Museum Exhibition, Miami, Florida, June 1998.

19. Williams, 1929, p. 6. Also, Rogers & Chaffee, 1994, pp. 12–14.

20. Lepidus, 1928, p. 75.

21. Samper Pizano, 1983, p. 33.

22. *Diario El Comercio: 80 Años (1906–1986)*, Quito, Ecuador: Editorial C. A. El Comercio, 1986, preface.

23. Schlesinger Jr., 1993, p. 288.

24. Fountain, 1973, p. 187.

25. Ibid., p. 185. See also Fountain, 2003.

26. Schlesinger Jr., 1993, pp. 408–409, 412.

27. See *Abrams v. United States*, 250 U.S. 616, summarized in Fraleigh & Tuman, 1997, p. 98.

28. See *Schenck v. United States*, 249 U.S. 47, summarized in Fraleigh & Tuman, 1997, p. 98.

29. 249 U.S. 204 [1919].

30. 249 U.S. 211 [1919].

31. Lanao, 1999, pp. 401–402.

32. Ibid., p. 402.

33. Ibid., p. 424.

34. Rives-Sánchez, 2000, pp. 32–33.

35. Ibid., p. 111.

36. Fernández & Paxman, 2000, p. 54.

37. Ibid.

38. Rives-Sánchez, 2000, pp. 111–112, 188.

39. Lanao, 1999.

40. Fonnegra, 1984, p. 22.

41. Germán Arciniegas in Fonnegra, 1984, p. 29.

42. Fonnegra, 1984, pp. 22–23.

43. Ibid., p. 23.

44. Ibid., p. 21.

45. Mesa, 1984, p. 135.

46. Colombia: ante la Llegada del Ferrocarril, 1908, p. 1.

47. El Ferrocarril de Quito, 1908, p. 1.

48. El Ferrocarril del Sur, 1907, p. 1.

49. En el Nuevo Régimen, 1907, p. 1.

50. La Dimisión de la Presidencia, 1911, p. 1.

51. Szászdi, 1974, pp. 17–18.

52. Fonnegra, 1984, p. 31.

53. La cultura mexicana en el siglo XX, *México siglo XX*, no. 6, encounters, *Centro Cultural Español de Cooperación Iberoamericana*, Miami, Florida, 2000, pp. 17–18.

54. Ross, 1965, p. 24.

55. Alvarez & Martínez-Riaza, 1992, p. 214.

56. Ibid.; Ross, 1965.

57. Ibid., pp. 26–27.

58. Alvarez & Martínez-Riaza, 1992, p. 215.

59. Ibid.

60. Art. 7, in Rives-Sánchez, 2000, p. 154.

61. Carpizo & Madrazo, 1992.

62. Lanao, 1999, pp. 400–406.

63. Alvarez & Martínez-Riaza, 1992, pp. 218–219.

64. Mejía-Barquera, 2000, p. 1.

65. Read Head, Sterling, & Schofield (1984). *Broadcasting in America*. Boston, MA: Houghton Mifflin Company, pp. 27, 31, & 265.

66. Téllez, 1974, pp. 14–15.

67. Gálvez, Felipe (1998). Voice and rider of the air, *México en el Tiempo*, no. 23, México Desconocido Online, April, p. 1. Retrieved July 15, 2006, from: http://www.mexicodesconocido.com.mx/english/historia/siglo_xx/imprimir.cfm?idsec=4&...

68. Ibid., p. 2.

69. Ibid., pp. 2–3.

70. Ibid., p. 4.

71. Ibid., p. 5.

72. Noam, 1998, pp. 170–171.

73. Hayes, 2000, p. 7.

74. Mejía-Barquera, 2000, pp. 5–6.

75. Hayes, 2000, p. 6.

76. Ibid., pp. 7–8.

77. Ibid., p. 19.

78. Katz & Wedell, 1977, p. 70.

79. Salwen, 1997, pp. 69, 76–77.

80. Fejes, 1983.

81. Salwen, Garrison, & Buckman, 1991, p. 293.

82. Sesenta años con la misma frecuencia (Sixty years with the same frequency), *El Tiempo*, February 1, 2006, p. 2. Retrieved February 2, 2000, from: http://www.eltiempo.com/hoy/vih_a000tn0.html Erroneously, the Iberian American Organization.

83. *9 de Abril 1948* (2001). A film by María Valencia Gaitán, Instituto Colombiano de la Participación Jorge Eliécer Gaitán, Bogotá, Colombia/New York, NY: Distributed by Latin American Video Archives.

84. Téllez, 1974.

85. Ferreira & Straubhaar, 1988, p. 135.

86. Ibid. Read also, Pareja, 1984.

87. Fox, 1997. Other important works to review are Fox (1988) and Fox & Waisbord (2002). Incidentally, Fox's academic evolution is puzzling to many Latin American observers. After emerging as an articulate proponent of the critical dependency school (with leading communication researchers like Luis Ramiro Beltrán), she accepted to work as a manager of strategic planning at the USIA Bureau of Broadcasting, an entity of questionable roles in the Western Hemisphere. Although it is wise to revisit Professor Mary A. Gardner's view on potential conflicts between both independent media and government investigations, historians should also analyze how pragmatic communication researchers have been over the years, with scholars moving back and forth and with remarkable ease from information federal agencies, to national and international consulting, to the private sector. On February 1, 1994, Dr. Fox discussed before the same congressional Advisory Panel an internal assessment report on *Radio and TV Martí* along with late Cuban-exile leader Jorge mas Canosa and Carlos Alberto Montaner, president of the Union Liberal Cubana. Read Broadcasting to Cuba: Radio Marti & C.A.N.F: 1990–1994, pt. 2, *Cuban Information Archives*. Retrieved July 12, 2006, from: http://cache.zoominfo.com/CachedPage/CachedPageMain.aspx?archive_id=0&page_id=8...

88. Read Johnston, 2003, vol. 1, p. 37.

89. Ibid., p. 38.

90. Ibid, p. 133.

91. Ibid., p. 133.

92. Cámara Venezolana de Industria Radiodifusión (CVIR) (2006). Historia de la Radiodifusión en Venezuela, p. 7.

93. Ibid., p. 10.

94. Mateo, Andrés L. (2001, July 18). El miedo en la era de Trujillo, Listín Digital, pp. 1, 2. Retrieved July 18, 2001 from: http://www.listin.com.do/opinion/opi1.html

95. *9 de Abril 1948*, 2001, a film by María Valencia Gaitán.

96. Castro reveals role in 9 April 1948. (1982, April 11). *El Siglo*, interview with journalist and writer Arturo Alape, Bogota, Colombia, pp. 6–7. Retrieved July 18, 2006, from: http://lanic.utexas.edu/la/cb/cuba/castro/1982/19820411 This interviewed was also broadcasted in the *Caracol* network, April 9, 1982.

97. 9 de Abril 1948, 2001.

98. 9 de Abril 1948, 2001.

99. White, 1993, p. 300.

100. Read Johnston, 2003, vol. 4, p. 221. Professor Straubhaar, first with Michigan State University, then with Bringham Young University, and now with UT–Texas, experienced exactly the opposite of Dr. Fox. Coming from the USIA to join academia, he gradually distanced himself from government consulting, especially federal information agencies.

101. Read Johnston, 2003, vol. 4, p. 221.

102. Soruco, 1988, p. 24.

103. Miralles, 2000, pp. 25–35.

104. Paleologo, 1960, pp. 14, 29.

105. Netto, 1998.

106. Read Johnston, 2003, vol. 4, p. 222.

107. Ibid., vol. 1, pp. 134, 222.

108. Read Johnston, 2003, vol. 1, p. 134.

109. Rodríguez-Revollar, 2004, p. 3.

110. Ferreira & Straubhaar, 1988, p. 133.

111. Mejía-Barquera, 2000, pp. 4–6.

112. Ibid, p. 9. Read also Gutiérrez & Reina-Schement, 1984, pp. 242–246; Hayes, 2000, p. 19.

113. Salwen, 1994, p. 18.

114. Reyes, 2003, pp. 59–60.

115. Hayes, 2000, p. 7.

116. Ibid., p. 21.

117. Téllez, 1974, pp. 19–20, 39.

118. Beltrán and Fox de Cardona, 1979, p. 35. Visit also *Radio Cooperativa* at http://www.cooperativa.cl/p2_icorp/stat/lacompania/html

119. Ibid., p. 47.

120. Ibid., 99–100.

121. Read *Historia* in AIR/IAB, Central office at http://airiab.com/historia.htm

122. Unesco, 1996, p. 15.

123. Ferreira & Straubhaar, p. 140. AED stands for Academy for Educational Development, Washington D.C.

124. Ibid., pp. 140–141.

125. Read Lerner, Daniel. (1958). *The passing of traditional society: modernizing the Middle East*. Glencoe, Ill: Free Press, & Rogers, Everett (1962). *Diffusion of innovations*. New York, NY: Free Press.

126. Maddison, 1971, pp. 9–13.

127. Misión de HCJB, retrieved July 28, 2006, from: http://www.vozandes.org/

128. Johnston, vol. 1, p. 134.

129. Making waves: Stories of participatory communication for social change: Radio Sutatenza. Retrieved July 27, 2006, from: http://www.comminit.com/strategicthinking/pdsmakingwaves/sld-1856.html

130. Making waves: Stories of participatory communication for social change: Miner's Radio Stations. Retrieved July 27, 2006, from: http://www.comminit.com/strategicthinking/pdsmakingwaves/sld-1857.html

131. Bolivian communication research pioneer Luis Ramiro Beltrán refers to Wilbur Schramm (then with Stanford University), as the author of a "universal bible" of development in 1964, along with believers preaching the faith of a "social engineering," such as Lucien Pye, Ithiel De Sola Pool, and Everett

M. Rogers. Read Beltrán, Luis R. (n.d.). Comunicación para el desarollo en Latinoamérica: Una evaluación sucinta al cabo de cuarenta años. Santiago, Chile: Universidad de Chile/Departamento de Pregrado. Read also, Hoy en las historia: un 18 de Junio de, *Los Tiempos.com*. Retrieved July 3, 2006, from: http://www.lostiempos.com/noticias/18_06_05trag.8/php

132. Ferreira, 1999.
133. Paleologo, 1960, p. 12.
134. Otero, 1946, p. 224.
135. Straubhaar, 1998, p. 74.
136. Do Nascimento, 1968, p. 51.
137. Fox, 1997, p. 54.
138. Ibid.
139. Skidmore & Smith, 1992, p. 169.
140. Otero, 1946, p. 226.
141. Fox, 1997, p. 55.
142. Skidmore & Smith, 1992, p. 178.
143. Amaral & Guimaraes, 1994; Straubhaar, 1998, pp. 69–70.
144. Beltrán, 1943.
145. Iriarte, 1996.
146. Knudson, 1987.
147. Marques de Melo, 1976.
148. Knudson, 1987.
149. Ibarra de Anda, 1934a, 1934b.
150. Hernández, 1999, pp. 9–11, 16.
151. Marques de Melo, 1993, p. 182.
152. Knudson, 1987.
153. Ibid.
154. Carty, 1964.
155. Lent, 1977.
156. Alisky, 1990.
157. Ibid., p. 202.
158. Knudson, 1997.
159. Gardner, 1987.
160. Knudson, 1997.
161. Lanao, 1999.
162. Art. 19, no. 15, cl. 3 in Lanao, 1999.
163. Ibid., pp. 208–209.
164. Ibid.
165. International Center for Journalists, 2003, p. 25.
166. Former president Juan Velasco-Alvarado in Beltrán & Fox de Cadona, 1979, p. 53.
167. Pareja, 1984, p. 141.
168. Ibid., p. 84.
169. Fox, 1997, p. 39.
170. Fernández & Paxman, 2000, p. 53.
171. Fox, 1997, p. 37.
172. Pasquali & Vargas-Araya, 1990, p. 27.
173. Pasquali, 1991.

174. Fox, 1997, p. 118.

175. Ibid., p. 119.

176. Ibid.

177. Pasquali & Vargas-Araya, 1990, p. 35.

178. Orozco, pp. 16–18.

179. Ibid., p. 17 & p. 59.

180. Ibid, p. 29.

181. Ibid., p. 52.

182. Ibid., p. 19.

183. In Sinclair, 1999, p. 10.

184. Di Franco, 2001, pp. 5–6.

185. Reyes, p. 261.

186. Orozco, p. 163.

187. Cosas del día, 1957, p. 5.

188. Schmucler, 1983.

189. OEA, 1967, p. 231.

190. Ibid., pp. 218, 233.

191. Ibid., pp. 236, 240.

192. Bloomfield, 1962, p. 114 f.n.

193. OEA, 1967, p. 63.

194. Ibid., p. 226.

195. Hudson, 1990, p. 18; ITU, 1965, p. 292.

196. Amorim, 1984, p. 156.

197. Fadul, 1984, p. 32.

198. Schmucler, 1983, p. 60.

199. Fadul, Fernández, & Schmucler, 1985, p. 8.

200. Satellite to relay Olympic games, 1968, p. 28.

201. U.S. aides in Argentina believe, 1969, p. 52.

202. Schmucler, 1983, pp. 59–61.

203. Fadul, 1984, p. 33.

204. Schmucler, 1983, p. 26.

205. AID, 1981, p. 52.

206. Real, 1990, p. 59.

207. Fregoso, 1990, p. 79.

208. De la Torre, 1982, pp. 15–16.

209. Niño, 1982, p. 153.

210. Fregoso, 1990, p. 70.

211. Read *Report on the Situation of Human Rights in Chile*, Doc. 17, OEA/Ser.L/5/II.66, September 9, 1985. Retrieved August 25, 2006, from: http://www.cidh.org/countryrep/Chile85eng/chap.3b.htm Read also, Chile, Habla Contreras, *BBC Mundo.com*, May 14, 2005, pp. 1–3. Retrieved July 1, 2006, from: http://news.bbc.co.uk./hi/spanish/latin_america/newsid_4545000/4545829.stm

212. September 11, 30 Years After, *Poynteronline*. Retrieved August 23, 2006, from: http://www.poynter.org/dg.1ts/id/31/aid.46811/column.htm

213. Kornbluth, Peter. (September/October 2003). *The El Mercurio File*, Columbia Journalism Review. Retrieved August 22, 2006 from: http://www.cjr.org/issues/2003/5/chile-kornbluth.asp

214. Read Cabot Award Winner Verdugo, Patricia. (2001). *Chile, Pinochet, and the Caravan of Death*. Coral Gables, FL: North-South Center Press/The University of Miami.

CHAPTER 7. DREAMING A FAIR WORLD

1. ASETA, 1985, p. 50.
2. Fox, 1997, p. 27.
3. Herman & McChesney, 1997, p. 80.
4. Montcreiff-Arrarte, 1993, p. 1-K.
5. Davis, 1998, p. 1998.
6. Golden, 1993, p. 3-K.
7. Borrego & Mody, 1989, p. 268.
8. Fadul, Fernández-Christlieb, & Schmucler, 1985, p. 10.
9. Gutiérrez & Schement, 1984, p. 250.
10. Read Altshuler. (1995). *Chapter 18, From Shortwave and Scatter to Satellite: Cuba's International Communications*. Retrieved August 23, 2006, from: http://history.nasa.gov/SP-4217/ch18.htm
11. Santos, 1986, p. 135.
12. Fernández & Paxman, 2000, pp. 102–105.
13. Fadul, Fernandez-Christlieb, & Schmucler, 1985, p. 10.
14. Nettleton & McAnany, 1989, p. 161.
15. Ibid., p. 160.
16. Fox, 1997, p. 58; Straubhaar, 1998, p. 77.
17. Davis, 1998, pp. 54–55.
18. Montcreiff-Arrarte, 1993, pp. 1-K, 3-K.
19. Waisbord, 1998, p. 91.
20. Dunn, 1988, p. 39.
21. Souki-Oliveira, 1992, pp. 14, 21.
22. Ibid., pp. 13, 21.
23. Marques de Melo, 1988, pp. 414–415.
24. Jiménez, 1982, pp. 8, 35.
25. Powell, 1985, pp. 119–120.
26. *The Journal*, ITU, 1992, p. 10
27. Satellite communications, 1992, pp. 62–63.
28. *Rede Glogo de Televisão*, 1985, p. 4.
29. Souki-Oliveira, 1992, p. 4.
30. Fuentes, 1988, p. 129.
31. SELA, 1987, pp. 22–23.
32. Simpson-Grinberg, 1989, p. 34.
33. CELAM, 1986.
34. Gonzáles-Manet, 1988, p. xiv.
35. Arriaga, 1985, p. 271.
36. Argumedo, 1982, p. 280.
37. Arriaga, 1985, p. 294.
38. Argumedo, 1982, p. 280.
39. Martín-Barbero, 1985, p. 171.

40. García-Canclini, 1988.
41. Borge, 1986.
42. Esteinou-Madrid, 1988, p. 420.
43. García-Canclini, 1989, p. 42.
44. Capriles, 1979; Martín-Barbero, 1989.
45. Esteinou-Madrid, 1988, p. 444.
46. Ibid., p. 443.
47. García-Canclini, 1988.
48. Esteinou-Madrid, 1984, pp. 98–107.
49. Schwarz & Jaramillo, 1986, pp. 63–64.
50. Martín-Barbero, 1985.
51. Moragas-Spa, 1988.
52. Pasquali, 1980, p. 95.
53. Quezada, 1988, p. 15.
54. Ballón, 1986.
55. Gallardo & Sánchez, 1986.
56. Finol, 1983, pp. 45, 122–123.
57. Moragas-Spa, 1985.
58. Quezada, 1988.
59. Silva, 1988, pp. 32–33.
60. Blanco & Bendezu, 1988, pp. 52–53.
61. Vilches, 1988, p. 41.
62. Ibid., p. 45.
63. Salinas, n.d.
64. Brown & Sanatan, 1987, pp. 6, 19.
65. Marques de Melo, 1988.
66. CIESPAL, 1977.
67. Osorio, 1985.
68. Capriles, 1979; Gonzáles-Manet, 1988.
69. Mahan, 1987.
70. Osorio, 1985.
71. Tello, 1989.
72. White, 1989.
73. Fernández-Areal, 1977, p. 42.
74. Martín-Barbero, 1989, p. 48.
75. Forero, 1987.
76. Aguilera, 1985, pp. 13–14.

CHAPTER 8. ONE STEP FORWARD, DOZEN BACKWARD

1. Bussey, 2000a, p. 5E.
2. Ibid., p. 1L.
3. Oppenheimer, 2000, p. 3L.
4. Soruco & Ferreira, 1995, pp. 337–338.
5. Matus, 1999.
6. Adams, 2000, p. 3.
7. Ibid., p. 1.

8. *The Americas: Attacks on the Press*, 2004. Go the Americas region in http://www.cpj.org/index.html.

9. See CPJ's 2004 Overview and 2001–2003 annual reports summarizing *Attacks on the Press*. Ibid, 2005.

10. Brown & Sanatan, 1987.

11. Ulibarri, 1988.

12. Gallimore, 1992.

13. Soruco & Ferreira, 1995, p. 339.

14. Ibid.

15. Flanz, 1998.

16. PDBA, 1999a.

17. Carpizo & Madrazo, 1992.

18. PDBA, 1999b. Emphasis added.

19. Buitrago-López, 1998, p. 185.

20. Carlyle, 1989 [1837], p. 229.

21. Uribe-Vargas, 1977, p. 307. Emphasis added.

22. IAPA, 1999a.

23. PDBA, 1999c.

24. Ibid., 1999d.

25. Ortega-Torres, 1983.

26. CPJ, 2005.

27. PDBA, 1999e.

28. Verzura, 1985.

29. IAPA, 1999a, p. 11.

30. Human Rights Watch, 1999.

31. Ibid., p. 1.

32. IAPA, 1999a.

33. Salwen & Garrison, 1991, pp. 15, 22–24.

34. Waisbord, 1998.

35. Soruco & Ferreira, 1995.

36. Ancarola, 1998, p. 615.

37. IAPA, 1999b, pp. 2–3.

38. Cervantes-Angulo, 1980.

39. Gómez, 1991.

40. Duzán, 1993.

41. Castillo, 1986.

42. García Márquez, 1996.

43. Ortega & Romero, 1976.

44. Gargurevich, 1986.

45. Chepesiuk, 1990.

46. Lee III, 1992.

47. IAPA, 1992.

48. Ibid., 1995.

49. *Stop This Inquisition*, 1995, p. 23A.

50. La indagatoria de Santiago Medina, 1995, p. 9A.

51. Los nombres del narco-casete, 1994, pp. 18–19.

52. Arrestan colaborador de Pastrana, 1996, pp. 1A, 6A.

53. Caballero, 1995, p. 14.

54. *The Miami Herald*, 1995, p. 18A.

55. Cocaine, Pot Use Soars Among Young, August 21, 1996, pp. 1A, 10A.

56. Se destapan los candidatos, 1995, p. 39.

57. Ex-sargento del ejército dueño, 1996.

58. El discurso de Samper, 1995.

59. IAPA, 1995, p. 22.

60. *El Nuevo Herald*, 1995, p. 3B.

61. Duzán, 1993, p. 350.

62. Busey, 1995, p. 78.

63. Ibid.

64. Restrepo, 1990, p. 112.

65. Human Rights Watch, 1994, pp. 1, 13.

66. Soruco & Ferreira, 1995, p. 345.

67. Eastman, 1992, p. 260.

68. Las sinrazones del coro anti-samperista, 1995, p. 20.

69. Pasquali, 1996, p. 13.

70. *Clinton anuncia énfasis*, 1996, p. 8A. See also Talk of U.S. troops near Colombia stirs tensions, *The Miami Herald*, May 16, 1996, p. 22A.

71. Smith, 1996.

72. Cocaine, Pot Use Soars, 1996, pp. 1A–10A.

73. Colombia, NPR, 1996.

74. Leave Colombia in peace, 1996, pp. 18A, 22A.

75. Samper-Pizano, 1996, p. 5.

Bibliography

Adams, Jerome R. (1991). *Latin American Heroes: Liberators and Patriots, from 1500 to the Present*. New York: Ballantine Books.

Aguilar, Agustin. (1992, August 12). La comunicación entre los mayas, Ediciones Especiales. *Excelsior*, Mexico DF, pp. 1–5. Retrieved June 1, 2005, from: http://muweb.millersville.edu?~columbus/data/art/AGUILAR1.ART.

Aguilera, Jaime. (1986). Las Telecomunicaciones en el Pacto Andino. In *Integración y Comunicación*. Quito, Ecuador: CIESPAL.

Aguirre-Quezada, Juan P. & González-Oropeza, Brenda A. (2004). El Partido Comunista Mexicano (1919–1982). *Razón Cínica*, Universidad Nacional Autónoma de México, Mexico DF, pp. 1–8. Retrieved November 3, 2004, from: http://www.politicas.unam.mx/publi/publicp/razoncinica/RC121.htm

AID (Agency for International Development) (1981, June). *AID Rural Satellite Program*. Washington DC: AID/Academy for Educational Development, Inc.

Alberro, Solange. (1996[1988]). *Inquisición y sociedad en México 1571–1700*. Mexico DF: Fondo de Cultura Económica.

Alisky, Marvin. (1990). Mass media in the dominican republic. In Stuart H. Surlin & Walter C. Soderlund (eds.), *Mass Media and the Caribbean*. New York: Gordon & Breach, pp. 177–189.

Almgren, Bertil. (1991). *The Viking*. Gothenburg, Sweden: Nordbok.

Altamirano, Liliana. (2000, June). Homenaje al hombre que, sin haber conocido físicamente el mundo maya, descubrió las claves de su escritura y gramática, Centro Nacional para la Cultura y las Artes (CONACULTA), Mexico City, pp. 1–2. Retrieved March 3, 2004, from: http://www.cnca.gob.mx/cnca/nuevo/diarias/1606000/compendi.html

Alvarez, Jesús T. & Martínez-Riaza, Ascensión. (1992). *Historia de la Prensa Hispanoamericana*. Madrid, Spain: Colecciones MAPFRE.

Alvarez-Lejarza, Emilio. (1958). *Las Constituciones de Nicaragua.* Madrid, Spain: Ediciones Cultura Hispánica.

Amaral, Roberto & Guimarães, Cesar. (1994, Autumn). Media monopoly in Brazil. *Journal of Communication*, vol. 44, no. 4, pp. 26–38.

Amorim, J. S. D. (1984). La radiodifusión en Brazil (1974–1981). In *Comunicación y Cultura*, no. 9. Mexico DF: Universidad Autónoma Metropolitana-Unidad Xochimilco.

Ancarola, Gerardo. (1998). Libertad de prensa: todo un retroceso [Freedom of the press: A complete reversing]. In *Revista Jurídica La Ley*, vol. F. Buenos Aires, Argentina: La Ley.

AncientScripts.com. (1997). *Epi-Olmec, Zapotec: Quick Facts.* Webmaster Lawrence K. Lo. Retrieved July 20, 2005, from: http://www.ancientscripts.com/ ws.html

Angulo, Jorge. (1995, November/December). La pictografía en Teotihuacan. *Arqueología Mexicana*, vol. 3, no. 16, pp. 24–29.

Angulo, Jorge. (2001). *Teotihuacan: Ciudad de los dioses.* Mexico DF: Monclem Ediciones.

Archivo del General Miranda, Viajes/Diarios: 1750–1783. (1929). Volume I–XXIV. Caracas, Venezuela: Editorial Sur-America.

Arciniegas, Germán. (1986). *America in Europe: A History of the New World in Reverse.* New York: Harcourt Brace Jovanovich, Publishers.

Argumedo, Alcira. (1982). Comunicación y Democracia: Una Perspectiva Ter-cermundista. In Elizabeth Fox & Héctor Schmucler (eds.), *Comunicación y Democracia en América Latina.* Lima, Peru: DESCO/CLACSO.

Arrestan a colaborador de Pastrana [Pastrana's aide is arrested]. (1996, June 8). *El Nuevo Herald*, pp. 1A, 6A.

Arriaga, P. (1985). Toward a critique of the information economy. *Media, Culture, and Society*, vol. 7, no. 3, pp. 271–296.

ASETA (Asociación de Empresas Estatales de Telecomunicaciones del Acuerdo Subregional Andino/Association of State Telecommunication Enterprises of the Andean Subregional Agreement). (1985, April). *Acta de la XVII Reunión de la Junta Directiva [Minutes of the XVII Meeting of the Board of Directors]*, Quito, Ecuador.

Atwood, Rita. (1986). *Communication and Latin American Society: Trends in Critical Research (1960–1985).* Madison, WI: University of Wisconsin Press, pp. 60–70.

Audiffred, Miryam. (2000, June 16). Lo creado por una mente humana puede ser resuelto por otra, decía Knorosov. *La Jornada*, UNAM, Mexico City, pp. 1–2. Retrieved April 12, 2005, from: http://www.jornada.unam.mx/ 2000/jun00/000616/cul2.html

Avendaño-Amaya, Ismael. (2004). Esbozo histórico del periodismo guatemalteco. *Sala de Prensa*, vol. 3, no. 74, year VI, Diciembre, pp. 1–4. Retrieved January 27, 2006, from: http://www.saladeprensa.org/art575.htm

Avila, Francisco J. (1941, November). La "Gazeta de Caracas," primer periódico de Venezuela. *Revista Nacional de Cultura*, no. 30, Caracas, Venezuela, pp. 1–7. Retrieved February 23, 2006, from: http://www.ucab.edu.ve/ucabnuevo/ svi/recursos/avila_f1.pdfAvila,

Avila, Francisco J. (1949). *Martí en el Periodismo Venezolano*. Caracas, Venezuela: Escuela de Periodismo/Universidad Central de Venezuela.

Ayala, Manuel J. de. (1990). *Diccionario de Gobierno y Legislación de Indias*. Madrid, Spain: Ediciones de Cultura Hispánica.

Bakken, William. (1998, December 28). L'Anse aux Meadows, the Kensington rune stone, and miscellaneous Viking artifacts. *Viking Homepage*. Retrieved February 19, 2000, from: http://www.anthro.mankato.msus.edu/prehistory/vikings/viknfl.html

Ballón, Enrique. (1986). Semiotics in Peru. In T. A. Sebeok & J. Umiker-Sebeok (eds.), *The Semiotic Sphere*. New York: Plenum Press.

Ballón, Enrique. (1990). Semiotics in Peru (1980–1988). In Thomas A. Sebeok & Jean Umiker-Sebeok (eds), *The Semiotic Web 1989*. New York: Mouton de Gruyter, pp. 195–219.

Barba, Arturo. (2002, December 7). Hallan escritura más antigua de América. *Reforma.com*, Mexico City, pp. 1–2. Retrieved May 2, 2005, from: http://busquedas.gruporeforma.com/utilerias/imdservicios3W.DLL?JsearchformatSP&file=...

Barnett, Alex. (2003). *Words That Changed America*. Guilford, CT: The Lyons Press.

Barthel, Thomas S. (1958). Die geganwartige situation in der erforschung der Mayaschrift. *Proceedings of the 32nd International Congress of Americanists* (1956), Copenhagen, Denmark, pp. 476–484.

Baudez, Claude-François. (2002, May/June). Venus y el Códice Grolier. *Arqueología Mexicana*, vol. 10, no. 55, pp. 2–18.

Bauer, Karl J. (1974). *The Mexican War: 1846–1848*. New York: Macmillan Publishing Co., Inc.

Baur, Cynthia. (1994, Autumn). The foundations of telegraphy and telephony in Latin America. *Journal of Communication*, vol. 44, no. 4, pp. 9–25.

Beltrán, Luis R. & de Cardona, E. Fox. (1979). Latin America and the United States: Flaws in the free flow of information. In Kaarle Nordenstreng & Herbert I. Schiller (eds.), *National Sovereignty and International Communication*. Norwood, NJ: Ablex Publishing Corp., pp. 33–64.

Beltrán, Luis R. (2001). *El Gran Comunicador: Simón Bolívar*. Second edition. La Paz, Bolivia: Plural Editores.

Beltrán, Oscar R. (1943). *Historia del Periodismo Argentino*. Buenos Aires, Argentina: Editorial Sopena Argentina, SLR.

Benítez, Fernando. (1993, August/September). La Tumba 7, Monte Albán. *Arqueología Mexicana*, vol. 1, no. 3, pp. 28–34.

Berdan, Frances F. & Rieff-Anawalt, Patricia. (1997). *The essential Codex Mendoza*. Berkeley, CA: University of California Press.

Berry, Charles R. (1974). Díaz, Porfirio (1830–1915); positivism (Mexico). In H. Delpar (ed.), *Encyclopedia of Latin America*. New York: McGraw-Hill, Inc., pp. 192–193, 495–496.

Blanco, Desiderio & Bendezú, Raúl. (1988, November). Semiótica y Comunicación: Correlaciones. *Diálogos*, no. 22.

Blegen, Theodore C. (1968). *The Kensington Rune Stone; New Light on an Old Riddle*. St. Paul, MN: Minnesota Historical Society.

Bloomfield, L. P. (1962). *Outer Space*. Englewood Cliffs, NJ: Prentice Hall, Inc.

Bode, Carl. (1982 [1947]). *The Portable Thoreau*. New York: Penguin Books.

Bolívar, Simón. (1815, September 6). Carta de Jamaica. In *Obras Completas*, vol. 1. La Habana, Cuba: Editorial Lex, pp. 159–175.

Bolívar, Simón. (1947[1826]). Discurso del Libertador al Congreso Constituyente de Bolivia. In *Obras Completas*, vol. 2. La Habana, Cuba: Editorial Lex, pp. 1220–1229.

Bolívar, Simón. (1947[1829]). Una Mirada sobre la América Española. In *Obras Completas*, vol. 2. La Habana, Cuba: Editorial Lex, pp. 1299–1305.

Bolívar, Simón. (1947[1799–1826]). *Obras Completas*, vol. 1. La Habana, Cuba: Editorial Lex.

Bonilla, J. (1983). *Perú Pre-Hispánico*. Lima, Perú: Ediciones Kuntur.

Boone, Elizabeth H. (2000). *Stories in Red and Black*. Austin, TX: The University of Texas Press.

Boone, Elizabeth H. & Mignolo, Walter D. (eds.). (1994). *Writing without Words*. Durham, NC: Duke University Press.

Boorstin, D. J. (1983). *The Discoverers*. New York: Random House, Inc.

Borge, Tomás. (1986). Marginal notes on the propaganda of the FSLN. In Armand Mattelart (ed.), *Communicating in Popular Nicaragua*. New York: International General.

Borrego, Jorge & Mody, Bella. (1989, September). Contextual analysis of the adoption of a communication technology. *Telecommunication Policy*, vol. 13, no. 3, pp. 265–276.

Bracker, Milton. (1954, March 2). Arbenz attacks foreign critics. *The New York Times*, ProQuest Historical Newspapers database (1857–current file), pp. 2, 10.

Brewer, Sam P. (1954, March 2). Unity plea opens Caracas meeting. *The New York Times*, ProQuest Historical Newspapers database (1857–current file), pp. 1, 9.

Brotherston, Gordon. (1995). *Painted Books from Mexico*. London: British Museum Press.

Brown, Aggrey & Sanatan, Roger. (1987). *Talking with Whom? A Report on the State of the Media in the Caribbean*. Mona, Jamaica: UWI/CARIMAC/CARICOM.

Bucich, Antonio J. (1951). *Sarmiento, Periodista*. conferencia pronunciada el 11 de septiembre de 1949, Monografías y Disertaciones Históricas, no. 22. Buenos Aires, Argentina: Museo Histórico Sarmiento.

Bueno, Salvador. (1982). *Martí Por Martí*. Mexico DF: Presencia Latinoamericana, SA.

Buitrago-López, Elker. (1980). *Manual del Derecho de las Comunicaciones en Colombia*. Bogotá, Colombia: Edicolda.

Buitrago-López, Elker. (1998). *Manual del derecho de las comunicaciones en Colombia*. Third edition. Bogotá, Colombia: Ediciones Librería Professional.

Burton, Traci. (2004, January 23). Mary Gardner, longtime MSU journalism prof, dies at age 84. *Lansing State Journal*, Lansing, MI. Retrieved September 10, 2005, from: http://www.lsj.com/news/local/040123_msuobit_2b.html

Busey, James L. (1995). *The Latin American Political Guide*. Twentieth edition. Manitou Springs, Colorado: Juniper Editions.

Bushnell, David. (1974). Miranda, Francisco De (1750–1816). In Helen Delpar (ed.), *Encyclopedia of Latin America*. New York: McGraw-Hill, Inc., pp. 378–379.

Bussey, Jane. (2000a). Fox inherits improving Mexican economy. *The Miami Herald* Business section, pp. 1E, 5E.

Bussey, Jane. (2000b). A grass roots revolution. *The Miami Herald*, pp. 1L–2L.

Cacua Prada, A. (1983). *Historia del periodismo colombiano*. Bogotá, Colombia: Ediciones Sua.

Cahn, Robert & Winter, Marcus. (1993). The San José Mogote Danzante. *Indiana*, vol. 13, pp. 39–64.

Calif. may force schools to drop Indian mascots. (2002, May 16). *CNN.com, education*, pp. 1–2.

Capriles, Oswaldo. (1979). Acciones y Reacciones in San José: El Debate de las Comunicaciones en la UNESCO. In A. Ruiz (ed.), *El Desafío Jurídico de la Comunicación*. Mexico DF: Editorial Nueva Imágen, pp. 79–124.

Carlyle, Thomas. (1989[1837]). *The French Revolution*. New York: Oxford University Press.

Carpizo, Jorge & Madrazo, J. (1992). El Sistema Constitucional Mexicano [The Mexican Constitutional System]. In D. García-Belaúnde, F. Fernández Segado, & R. Hernández-Valle (eds.), *Los Sistemas Constitucionales Iberoamericanos*. Madrid, Spain: Editorial Dykinson, pp. 559–611.

Carrasco, David. (ed.). (2001). *The Oxford Encyclopedia of Mesoamerican Cultures: The Civilizations of Mexico and Central America*, 3 vols. New York: Oxford University Press.

Carrasco, Ricardo. (1951). *Francisco de Miranda: precursor de la independencia hispanoamericana, 1750–1792*. Buenos Aires, Argentina: Editorial Bell.

Carty, James, Jr. (1964). Journalism education in Nicaragua. *Journalism Educator*, vol. 19, no. 1, pp. 40–43.

Carty, James, Jr. (1978). Communist ideology basic to J-education in Cuba. *Journalism Educator*, vol. 33, no. 3, pp. 40–43.

Castañeda-Delgado, Paulino. (1974). Los métodos misionales en América: Evangelización Pura o Coacción? In *Estudios sobre Bartolomé de las Casas*. Sevilla, Spain: Universidad de Sevilla, pp. 123–190.

Castillo, Fabio. (1986). *Los Jinetes de la Cocaína*. Bogota, Colombia: Editorial Norma.

Castro-Caycedo, G. (1991). *El Hurakán*. Bogota, Colombia: Editorial Planeta Colombiana, SA.

Cervantes-Angulo, José. (1980). *La noche de las luciérnagas*. Bogota, Colombia: Plaza & Janés.

Chaffee, Steven H., Gómez-Palacio, Carlos, & Rogers, Everett M. (1990, Winter). Mass communication research in Latin America: Views from here and there. *Journalism Quarterly*, vol. 67, no. 4, pp. 1025–1024.

Chaffee, Steven H. & Rogers, Everett. M. (1997). *The Beginnings of Communication Study in America*. Thousand Oaks, CA: Sage Publications, Inc.

Checa-Godoy, Antonio. (1993). *Historia de la Prensa en Iberoamericana*. Sevilla, España: Ediciones Alfar.

Chepesiuk, Ron. (1990, April 30). Drug lords vs. the press in Latin America. *The New Leader*, vol. 73, no. 7, New York.

Chipp, Herschel B. (1988). *Picasso's Guernica*. Berkeley, CA: University of California Press.

Chivelet, Mercedes. (2001). *Historia de la prensa cotidiana en España*. Madrid, Spain: Acento Editorial.

CIESPAL (Centro Internacional de Estudios Superiores de Comunicación para América Latina/International Center of Higher Studies in Communication for Latin America). (1977). *Comunicación y Desarrollo*, vols. 1–2. Quito, Ecuador: Don Bosco.

Clark, Joan. (1994). *Eiriksdottir*. New York: Penguin Books.

Clinton Anuncia Enfasis en la Lucha Contra las Drogas [Clinton announces emphasis in the war against drugs]. (1996, March 29). *El Nuevo Herald*, p. 8A.

CMC (Canadian Museum of Civilization). (1999). *Writing and hieroglyphics*, Maya Civilization Website Ottawa, Canada, pp. 1–4. Retrieved June 13, 2000, from: http//:www.civilization.ca/civil//maya/mmco4eng.html

Cobean, Robert H. (1993, April/May). El último de los Olmecas: Miguel Covarrubias o la pasión por la arqueología. *Arqueología Mexicana*, vol. 1, no. 1, pp. 64–69.

Códices Prehispánicos. (1997). *Arqueología Mexicana*, vol. 4, no. 23, pp. 14–15.

Coe, Michael D. (1973). *The Maya Scribe and His World*. New York: The Grolier Club.

Coe, Michael D. (1992). *Breaking the Maya Code*. New York: The Grolier Club.

Coe, Michael D. (1991, September/October). A triumph of spirit. *Archaeology*, pp. 39–44. Retrieved August 3, 2004, from: http://muweb.millersville.edu/~columbus/data/art/COE-01.ART

Coe, Michael D. (1994). *Mexico: From the Olmecs to the Aztecs*. Second edition. New York: Thames & Hudson.

Coe, Michel D. (1999[1992]). *Breaking the Maya code*. Revised edition. New York: Thames & Hudson.

Coe, Michel D. & Kerr, Justin. (1998). *The Art of the Maya Scribe*. New York: Thames & Hudson.

Coe, Michel D. & Stone, Mark Van. (2001). *Reading the Maya Glyphs*. New York: Thames & Hudson.

Collier, Simon. (1974a). War of the Pacific (1879–1883). In Helen Delpar (ed.), *Encyclopedia of Latin America*. New York: Barnes & Noble Books, pp. 628–629.

Collier, Simon. (1974b). Rosas, Juan Manuel de (1793–1877). In Helen Delpar (ed.), *Encyclopedia of Latin America*. New York: Barnes & Noble Books, pp. 540–542.

Collier, Simon. (1985). The non-Spanish Caribbean islands (1750–1816). In Simon. Collier, Harold Blakemore, & Thomas E. Skidmore (eds.), *The Cambridge Encyclopedia of Latin America*. Cambridge, Great Britain: University of Cambridge, pp. 201–205.

Colombia: Ante la Llegada del Ferrocarril a Quito [Colombia, before the arrival of the railroad to Quito]. (1908, July 1). *El Comercio*, vol. 3, no. 701, p. 1.

Colombia's search for truth. (1995, December 12). *The Miami Herald*, p. 18A.

Conrad, Robert. (1974). Magalhaes, Benjamin Constant Botelho De (1836–1891); positivism (Brazil). In H. Delpar (ed.), *Encyclopedia of Latin America*. New York: McGraw-Hill, Inc., pp. 352–353, 495.

Consejo Episcopal Latinoamericano (CELAM). (1986). *Comunicación, misión y desafío: manual pastoral de comunicación social*. Bogota, Colombia: DECOS.

Corzo-Gamboa, Arturo. (2002). Knorosov y la escritura maya. *Revista Xictli*, Universidad Pedagógica Nacional, Mexico DF, pp. 1–5. Retrieved February 10, 2005, from: http://www.unidad094.upn.mx/revista/48/arturo.htm

Cosas del Día [Things of the day]. (1957, October 6). *El Tiempo*, Bogotá, Colombia, p. 5.

Moreno, Gerardo Rivas. (ed.) (1998[1818–1822]). *Correo del Orinoco*. Bucaramanga, Colombia: Selene Impresores/Fundación FICA.

CPJ (Committee to Protect Journalists). (2005). *Journalists Killed in the Line of Duty during the Last Ten Years*, CPJ, New Nork. Retrieved October 1, 2005, from: http://www.cpj.org/killed/Ten_Year_Killed/Intro.html

Craine, Eugene R. & Reindorp, Reginald C. (1979). *The Codex Pérez and the Book of Chilam Balam of Maní*. Norman, OK: University of Oklahoma.

Cristina, María T. (1984). La Literatura en la Cosquista y la Colonia. In *Manual de Historia de Colombia*, vol. 1. Bogotá, Colombia: Procultura SA/Instituto Colombiano de Cultura, pp. 495–592.

Cristobal, Ramiro. (1989, March). Los indios americanos dan la espalda al V Centenario. *Cambio 16*, Madrid, Spain, pp. 100–102. Retrieved August 3, 2004, from: http://muweb.millersville.edu/~columbus/data/art/COE-01.ART

Crow, John A. (1992[1946]). *The Epic of Latin America*. Fourth edition. Berkeley, CA: University of California Press.

Cummins, Tom. (1994). Representation in the sixteenth century and the colonial image of the Inca. In Elizabeth H. Boone & Walter D. Mignolo (eds.), *Writing without Words*. Durham, NC: Duke University Press, pp. 188–219.

Cunliffe, Marcus. (1993). Testing a union. In A. M. Scheleesinger Jr. (ed.), *The Almanac of American History*. New York: Barnes & Noble Books, pp. 146–150.

Curtain in Guatemala. (1954, February 9). *The Washington Post*, p. 10.

Davis, Charles N. (1998). Mexico. In Alan B. Albarran & Silvia M. Chan-Olmstead (eds.), *Global Media Economics: Commercialization, Concentration, and Integration of World Media Markets*. Ames, IA: Iowa State University, pp. 51–62.

Davis, Clarence B. & Wilburn, Kenneth E., Jr. (eds.). (1991). *Railway Imperialism*. Wesport, CT: Greenwood Press.

Davis, Mike. (1992). *Magical Urbanism: Latinos Reinvent the U.S. Big City*. New York: Verso.

De la Fuente, Beatriz. (1995, November/December). La pintura mural prehispánica en México. *Arqueología Mexicana*, vol. 3, no. 16, pp. 4–15.

De la Torre, Cristina. (1982). Que pasó con el mundial? In *Las cinco maravillas millonarias de Colombia*. Bogota, Colombia: Editorial Oveja Negra/FESCOL, pp. 11–64.

Demarest, Arthur A. (1976). A critical analysis of Yuri Knorosov's decipherment of the Maya hieroglyphics. In *Studies in Middle American Anthropology*, vol. 22. New Orleans, LA: Tulane University, Middle American Research Institute, pp. 63–73.

Di Franco, Carlos A. (2001). Informe Nacional de Brazil. *Chasqui*, no. 73, Quito, Ecuador, pp. 1–6. Retrieved August 16, 2006, from: http://chasqui.comunica.org/difranco73.htm

Díaz-Callejas, Apolinar. (1997). *Mi Universidad y la Ciudad*. A speech given on December 18, Cartagena de Indias, Universidad de Cartagena, Colombia. Retrieved May 30, 2006, from: http://www.apolinardiaz.org/verdocumento.php?id_tema=7&id_documento=27

Discurso de Samper [Samper's speech]. (1995, May 7). CARACOL-Miami, Noticiero del Mediodía (News at Noon), 1260 AM, Miami, Florida.

Do Nascimento, Luiz do. (1968). *Historia da Imprensa de Pernambuco*. Recife, Brazil: Universidade Federal de Pernambuco.

Doyle, Kate & Kornbluh, Peter. (1997). CIA and assassinations: The Guatemala 1954 documents. *In The National Security Archive: Guatemala Documentation Project*, The Gelman Library, George Washington University, Washington DC, pp. 1–3. Retrieved November 3, 2004, from: http://www2.gwu.edu/~nsarchiv/latin_america/guatemala.html

Dr. Mary Gardner dies at 84. (n.d.). *Communicator*, Communications Arts and Sciences Building, Michigan State University, East Lansing, MI. Retrieved September 9, 2005, from: http://communicator.cas.msu.edu/show/58

Dunn, Hopeton S. (1988). Broadcasting flow in the Caribbean. *Intermedia*, vol. 16, no. 3, pp. 39–41.

Duzán, Maria J. (1993). *Crónicas que Matan*. Third edition. Santafé de Bogotá: Tercer Mundo Editores.

East, Louise. (1999, April 24). Myths of the Maya: Why have modern myths turned a fascinating ancient civilization into a land of time travelers and latter-day soccer enthusiasts? *The Irish Times*, City edition, Weekend section, Belfast, Ireland, p. 66 [Online]. Retrieved March 15, 2004, from: http://web.lexis-nexis.com/univers...5=ccd1b9eeaf451b7b74fd60ff057fl05f

Eastman, Jorge Mario. (1992). *Constituciones Políticas Comparadas de América del Sur*. Second edition. Santafé de Bogotá, Colombia: Tercer Mundo Editores.

Egea-López, Antonio. (1983). *El pensamiento filosófico y político de Francisco de Miranda*. Caracas, Venezuela: Biblioteca de la Academia Nacional de la Historia.

El Ferrocarril de Quito [The Quito Railroad]. (1908, June 25). *El Comercio*, vol. 3, no. 699, p. 1.

El ferrocarril del sur y los derechos del Ecuador [the Southern railroad and the rights of Ecuador]. (1907, April 11). *El Comercio*, vol. 2, no. 357, p. 1.

Elish, Jill. (2002, December). Dig uncovers earliest writing in New World. *FSU Press Release*. Tallahassee, FL: Florida State University.

Emery, Edwin & Emery, Michael. (1984[1954]). *The Press and America: An Interpretative History of the Mass Media*. Fifth edition. Englewood Cliffs, NJ: Prentice Hall, Inc.

Emery, Michael, Emery, Edwin, & Roberts, Nancy L. (2000). *The Press and America: An interpretative History of the Mass Media*. Ninth edition. Boston, MA: Allyn & Bacon.

En el Nuevo Régimen [In the New Regime]. (1907, January 27). *El Comercio*, vol. 2, no. 298, p. 1.

English summary: The Dresden Codex (2001, June 15). *Sachsische Landesbibliothek, Staats und Universitatsbibliothek*, Dresden, Germany. Retrieved November 10, 2001, from: http://www.tu-dresden.de/slub/proj/maya/maya.html

Esteinou-Madrid, Javier. (1984, January). Las Tecnologías de Información y la Confección del Estado Ampliado.In *Cuadernos del Ticom*, no. 30. Mexico DF: Universidad Autónoma Metropolitana-Xochimilco, pp. 1–133.

Esteinou-Madrid, Javier. (1988). The Morelos satellite system. *Media, Culture, and Society*, vol. 10, no. 4, pp. 419–446.

Estudios sobre Fray Bartolomé de las Casas. (1974). Universidad de Sevilla, Sevilla, Spain: Dirección General de Relaciones Culturales.

Evans, Susan T. & Webster, David L. (eds.). (2001). *Archeology of Ancient Mexico and Central America: An Encyclopedia.* New York: Garland Publishers.

Ex-Sargento del Ejército Dueño de Propiedades por 426 Millones de Dólares [Former army sargent owner of property valued at $426 million]. (1996). *El Tiempo,* editorial, May 2.

Fadul, Ligia M. (1984, February). Las Comunicaciones Vía-Satélite en América Latina. In *Cuadernos del Ticom,* no. 31. Mexico DF: Universidad Autónoma Metropolitana-Xochimilco.

Fadul, Ligia M., Fernández, Fátima, & Schmucler, Héctor. (1985, March). Satélite de Comunicación en México. In *Comunicación y Cultura,* no. 13. Mexico DF: Universidad Autónoma Metropolitana-Xochimilco.

Fahmel-Beyer, Bernard. (1993, August/September). Monte Albán: Historia de una ciudad. *Arqueología Mexicana,* vol. 1, no. 3, pp. 24–27.

Fahmel-Beyer, Bernard. (1995, November/December). La pintura mural Zapoteca. *Arqueología Mexicana,* vol. 3, no. 16, pp. 36–41.

Fallece uno de los artífices de la antropología mexicana: Román Piña-Chan (2001, April 12). *Sala de Prensa, Cultura.* Retrieved August 4, 2005, from: http://www.cnca.gob.mx/cnca/nuevo/2001/diarias/abr/120401/rpinacha.html

Farrar, Ronald T. (1999). *A Creed for My Profession: Walter Williams, Journalist to the World.* Columbia, MO: University of Missouri Press.

Fash, William L. (1991). *Scribes, Warriors, and Kings: The City of Copán and the Ancient Maya.* Paperback edition. London: Thames & Hudson.

Febres-Cordero, Julio. (1974). *Historia de la imprenta y del periodismo en Venezuela.* Caracas, Venezuela: Banco Central de Venezuela.

Fejes, Fred. (1983). The U.S. in third world communications: Latin America 1900–1945. *Journalism Monographs,* no. 86, pp. 1–29.

Fernández-Areal, M. (1977). *Introducción al Derecho de la Información.* Barcelona, Spain: ATE.

Fernández, Claudia & Paxman, Andrew. (2000). *El Tigre: Emilio Azcárraga y su Imperio Televisa.* Mexico DF: Editorial Grijalbo, SA de CV.

Ferreira, Leonardo & Straubhaar, Joseph. (1988, Summer). Radio and the new Colombia. *Journal of Popular Culture,* vol. 22, no. 1, pp. 131–144.

Ferreira, Leonardo. (1989). Project Condor: Reasons and Conditions for the Adoption of a Communications Satellite for the Andean Subregion. Unpublished M.A. Thesis. East Lansing, MI: Michigan State University.

Ferreira, Leonardo. (1997). Back to basics. In *Hemisphere,* vol. 7, no. 3. Miami, Florida: Latin American and Caribbean Center (LACC)/Florida International University.

Ferreira, Leonardo. (1999). Antimonopolio y telecomunicaciones en estados Unidos. *Revista Colombiana de Telecomunicaciones (RCT).* Bogotá, Colombia: CINTEL, pp. 53–56.

Ferreira, Leonardo. (2001). Drug-trafficking: Colombia and Peru. In Derek Jones (ed.), *Censorship: A World Encyclopedia,* vol. 1. London: Fitzroy Dearborn Publishers, pp. 692–695.

Ferreira, Leonardo. (2003). Colombia, Ecuador, and Venezuela, status of media. In Donald H. Johnston (ed.), *Encyclopedia of International Media and Communications*, vol. 1. New York: Academic Press, pp. 235–246.

Finol, José E. (1983). *Semiótica, Comunicación, y Cultura*. Maracaibo, Venezuela: Heuriskein.

First vestiges of writing in Americas found. (2002, December 6). *Discovery Channel*, p. 1.

Flanz, Gisbert H. (1998). Constitución Argentina [Argentine Constitution]. In A. P. Blaustein & G. H. Flanz (eds.), *Constitutions of the Countries of the World*. Dobbs Ferry, NY: Oceana Publications, pp. 51–96.

Flores-Jaramillo, Renán (1976). *La prensa en hispanoamérica*. Madrid, Spain: Editorial Magisterio Español y Editorial Prensa Española.

Florida Department of State (1993). *Gold of El Dorado: A Florida Tour*. Tallahassee, FL: Department of State.

Foner, Philip S. (1972). *The Spanish Cuban American War and the Birth of American Imperialism*. New York: Monthly Review Press.

Fonnegra, Gabriel. (1984) *La prensa en Colombia: Cómo informa? De quién es? A quién le sirve?* Bogotá, Colombia: El Ancora Editores.

Forero, C. (1987). *Información e Integración Económica*. Bogotá, Colombia: Tercer Mundo Editores.

Fountain, Anne O. (1973). *José Martí and North American Authors*. Doctoral Dissertation. New York: Columbia University.

Fountain, Anne O. (2003). *José Martí and U.S. Writers*. Doctoral Dissertation. New York: Columbia University.

Fox, Elizabeth. (1988). *Media and Politics in Latin America: The Struggle for Democracy*. Newbury, CA: Sage Publications.

Fox, Elizabeth. (1997). *Latin American Broadcasting: From Tango to Telenovela*. Bedfordshire, UK: University of Luton Press.

Fox, Elizabeth & Waisbord, Silvio. (eds.). (2002). *Latin Politics, Global Media*. Austin, TX: University of Texas Press.

Fraleigh, Douglas M. & Tuman, Joseph S. (1997). *Freedom of Speech*. New York: St. Martin's Press.

Francois, William E. (1994). *Mass Media Law and Regulation*. Prospect Heights, IL: Waveland Press.

Frederick, Howard H. (1993). *Global Communication and International Relations*. Belmont, CA: Wadsworth Publishing Co.

Fregoso, Gilberto. (1990, April/June). Fútbol México-86: Así se Hizo el Mundial [Soccer Mexico-86: This how the World Cup was made]. *Chasqui*, no. 34, pp. 70–79.

Fuentes, Raúl. (1988). *La Investigación de Comunicación en México*. Mexico DF: Ediciones de Comunicación, SA de CV.

Furlong, Ray. (2005, February 12). Dresden raid still a raw nerve. *BBC News*, London. Retrieved September 5, 2005, from: http://news.bbc.co.uk/2/hi/europe/4257827.stm

Furst, Jill L. & Furst, Peter T. (1980). *Precolumbian Art of Mexico*. Albany, NY: State University of New York/Abbeville Publishers.

Galarza, Joaquín. (1997, January/February). Los códices mexicanos. *Arqueología Mexicana*, vol. 4, no. 23, pp. 6–15.

Galich, Manuel. (1974). *El libro precolombino: Comentarios y testimonios*. La Habana, Cuba: Casa de las Américas.

Gallardo, A. & Sánchez, J. (1986). Semiotics in Chile. In T. A. Sebeok & J. Umiker-Sebeok (eds.), *The Semiotic Sphere*. New York: Plenum Press.

Gallimore, Tim. (1992, May). Radio and television broadcasting to Cuba: U.S. Communication Policy and the quest for an International First Amendment. *Proceedings Ninth Annual Intercultural and International Communication Conference (ICC-9)*, Miami, Florida, pp. 159–162.

Gans, Herbert J. (1994). Reopening the black box: Toward a limited effects theory. In *Defining Media Studies: Reflections on the Future of the Field*. New York: Oxford University Press, pp. 271–277.

García-Canclini, N. (1988). Culture and power: The state of research. *Media, Culture, and Society*, vol. 10, no. 4, pp. 467–497.

García-Canclini, N. (1989, October/November). La Experiencia Mexicana. In *Gaceta*, no. 4. Bogotá, Colombia: Colcultura, pp. 42–46.

García Márquez, Gabriel. (1996). *Noticia de un Secuestro*. Santafé de Bogotá, Colombia: The Grupo editorial Norma.

García-Mora, Carlos. (1997, January/February). Mesoamérica: concepto prescindible. In *Actualidades Arqueológicas [Revista de Estuadiantes de Arqueología de México]*, no. 10. México DF: UNAM, pp. 1–3.

Gardner, Mary A. (1971, February). The press of Guatemala. In *Journalism Monograph*. Minneapolis, MN: University of Minnesota, pp. 1–48, 18.

Gardner, Mary A. (1987). Trend toward colegiación of journalists in Latin America and its impact on freedom of the press. *Studies in Latin American Popular Culture*, vol. 6, pp. 235–243.

Gargurevich, Juan. (1986). *Introducción a la Historia de los Medios de Comunicación en el Perú*. Lima, Peru: Editorial Horizonte.

Gilbert, Adrian G. & Cotterell, Maurice M. (1996). *Las profecías Mayas*. Mexico DF: Editorial Grijalbo.

Glick, Thomas F. (1985). Science in Latin America. In *The Cambridge encyclopedia of Latin America and the Caribbean*. Cambridge, Great Britain: University of Cambridge, pp. 421–427.

Golden, Tim. (1993, June 13). Mexico to sell off state-owned TV to create a rival for giant televisa. *The Miami Herald*, p. 3-K.

Goldstein, Robert J. (1983, February). Freedom of the press in Europe (1815–1914). *Journalism & Communication Monograhs*, no. 80, pp. 1–23.

Gómez, Leonidas O. (1991). *Cartel, historia de la droga*. Bogota, Colombia: Grupo Editorial Investigación y Concepto.

Gonzáles-Manet, Enrique. (1988). *The Hidden War of Information*. Norwood, NJ: Ablex.

González-Prieto, Alejandro. (n.d.). Bibliohemerografía de Hernán Laborde. *Sociedad y Cultura*, Mexico DF, pp. 1–5. Retrieved June 5, 2005, from: http://www.memoria.com.mx/156/Gprieto.htm

Gotland University College. (1998, February 13). Chronological table. *Viking Heritage Server & Database*, Visby, Sweden. Retrieved June 6, 2000, from: http://www.viking.hgo.se

Grases, Pedro. (1967). *Historia de la imprenta en Venezuela*. Caracas, Venezuela: Ediciones de la Presidencia de la República.

Grases, Pedro. (1981). *La Imprenta en Venezuela*. Barcelona, Spain: Seix Barral.

Gray, Richard B. (1974). Martí [y Pérez], José [Julián] (1853–1895). In H. Delpar (ed.), *Encyclopedia of Latin America*. New York: McGraw-Hill, Inc., pp. 358–360.

Griffith, Kathleen A. (1998). Mexico. In E. M. Noam (ed.), *Telecommunications in Latin America*. New York: Oxford University Press, pp. 166–191.

Grooscors, G. (1986). *Comunicación e Integración. In Integración y Comunicación.* Quito, Ecuador: CIESPAL/FES/CEE.

Gruson, Sydney. (1953, February 23). Guatemalan reds seek full power. *The New York Times*, p. 4.

Guatemala facing peril of dictator, leftist labor leaders and opportunists form core of powerful movement. (1950, February 21). *The New York Times*, p. 16.

Guerra contra Drogas Deja 3,400 Muertos [War against drugs causes 3,400 deaths]. (1995, November 25). *El Nuevo Herald*, p. 3B.

Gutiérrez, Félix & Schement, Jorge R. (1984). Spanish International Network: The flow of television from Mexico to the United States. *Communication Research*, vol. 11, no. 2, pp. 241–258.

Habermann, Peter. (1985). Development in the Caribbean and media coverage of Grenada: A theoretic view. In S. H. Surlin & W. C. Soderlund (eds.), *Media in Latin America and the Caribbean: Domestic and International Perspectives*. Windsor, Canada: Ontario Cooperative Program in Latin and Caribbean Studies, pp. 208–231.

Habermann, Peter. (1990). Mass media in Haiti. In Stuart H. Surlin & Walter C. Soderlund (eds.), *Mass Media and the Caribbean*. New York: Gordon & Breach, pp. 193–207.

Hall, Robert A. (1982). *The Kensington Stone is Genuine: Linguistic, Practical Methodological Considerations*. Columbia, SC: Hornbeam Press.

Hall, Robert A. (1994). *The Kensington Rune-Stone: Authentic and Important, a Critical Edition*. Lake Bluff, IL: Jupiter Press.

Hamill, Hugh M., Jr. (1974). Hidalgo y Costilla. In Helen Delpar (ed.), *Encyclopedia of Latin America*. New York: McGraw-Hill, Inc.

Hammond, Norman. (1999). Yuri Valentinovich Knorosov (1922–1999). *Antiquity*, vol. 73, pp. 485–492. Retrieved March 11, 2004, from: http://intarch.ac.uk/antiquity/73-281editorial.html

Harrison, M. & Gilbert, S. (eds.). (1993). *Thomas Jefferson: In His Own Words*. New York: Barnes & Noble Books.

Haw, Dora L. (2005, May 2). Censuran expertos labor del Conaculta. *Reforma.com*, Mexico City, pp. 1–5. Retrieved May 2, 2005, from: http://www.reforma.com/cultura/articulo/520422/

Hayes, J. E. (2000, March). Broadcasting the Revolution: Government Radio Policy and Nation Formation(1920–1940). Paper presented at the Annual Meeting of the Latin American Studies Association (LASA), Miami, Florida, pp. 1–26.

Henestrosa, Andrés. (1990). *Periódicos y periodistas*. Mexico DF: Publicaciones Mexicanas, SCL.

Henestrosa, Andrés & Fernández de Castro, José A. (1947). *Periodismo y periodistas de hispanoamérica*. Mexico DF: Secretaría de Educación Pública.

Henríquez-Ureña, Camila, Portuondo, José, A., García del Cueto, Mario, & Alvarez-García, Imeldo. (1977). *El Periodismo en José Martí*. La Habana, Cuba: Editorial Orbe.

Herman, Edward S. & McChesney, Robert W. (1997). *The Global Media: The New Missionaries of Global Capitalism.* London: Cassell.

Hernández, Alejandro. (1999). *El Parlamento de los Pueblos: Edición Conmemorativa del 50 aniversario de la Escuela de Periodismo Carlos Septién García.* Mexico DF: Fotofilia.

Historia de la Inquisición en el Perú. (2003). *Museo de la Inquisición y del Congreso,* Lima, Peru. Retrieved January 23, 2006, from: http://www.congreso.gob.pe/museo/right03-1b.htm

Historiska Museet. (2003). *The Runes of the Kensington Runestone,* Stockholm, Sweden. Retrieved September 26, 2005, from: http://www.historiska.se/exhibitions/kensington/

Hola! (1992). Hola! 1492–1992. Special magazine issue. Madrid, Spain: Hauser & Menet, SA.

Holand, Hjalmar R. (1909, October). An explorers' stone record which antedates Columbus. *Harper's Weekly,* vol. 53, p. 15.

Holand, Hjalmar R. (1910, April). First authoritative investigation of oldest native document in America. *Journal of American History,* vol. 4, pp. 165–184.

Holand, Hjalmar R. (1919a, December). The Kensington rune stone, is it the oldest native document of American history? *Wisconsin Magazine of History,* vol. 3, pp. 153–183.

Holand, Hjalmar R. (1919b). *The Kensington Rune-Stone: The Oldest Native Document of American History.* Ephraim, WS: Private printing.

Holand, Hjalmar R. (1932). *The Kensington Stone: A Study in Pre-Columbian American History.* Ephraim, WS: Private printing.

Holand, Hjalmar R. (1940a). *Westward from Vinland: An Account of Norse Discoveries and Explorations in America, 982–1362.* New York: Duell, Sloan & Pearce.

Holand, Hjalmar R. (1940b). *Norse Discoveries and Explorations in America (982–1362): Leif Eriksson to the Kensington Stone.* New York: Dover Publications.

Houston, Stephen. (1994). Literacy among the pre-Columbian Maya: A comparative perspective. In Elizabeth Boone & Walter D. Mignolo. (eds.), *Writing without Words: Alternative Literacies in Mesoamerica and the Andes.* Durham, NC: Duke University Press, pp. 27–49.

Hudson, Heather E. (1990). *Communication Satellites.* New York: The Free Press.

Human Rights Watch. (1994). Generation under fire: Children and violence in Colombia. *Human Rights Watch Homepage.* Retrieved January 13, 2000, from: http://www.hrw.org/reports/1994/genertoc.htm

Human Rights Watch. (1999). Torture, "disappearance," and extrajudicial execution in Mexico. Library of Congress Catalog Card Number 90-83148. Online Report. Retrieved October 10, 2001, from: http://www.hrw.org/reports/1999/Mexico.

Huyghe, Patrick. (1992). *Columbus was Last.* New York: Hyperion.

IAPA (Inter American Press Association). (1992, October). *Spread of Freedom Remains a "Dreamed Deferred" for Some.* 48th General Assembly in Madrid, Spain. Miami, Florida: SIP.

IAPA. (1995). *Press Freedom in the Americas: Peru.* Annual Report, Miami, Florida.

IAPA. (1996). *Press Freedom in the Americas: Peru.* Annual Report, Miami, Florida.

IAPA. (1999a, March 23). *Conclusions, Country-by-Country Report and Resolutions.* Montego Bay, Jamaica: IAPA Mid-Year Meeting.

IAPA. (1999b, April/May). Mission to Colombia winds up on note of optimism. *IAPA News*, no. 392, pp. 2–3.

Ibarra de Anda, Fortino. (1934a). *El periodismo en México*. Mexico DF: Imprenta Mundial.

Ibarra de Anda, Fortino. (1934b). *Las mujeres periodistas en México*. Mexico DF: Imprenta Mundial.

In Colombia, all things considered. (1996). *National Public Radio* (NPR), WLRN, Miami, Florida, February 13.

Ingstad, Anne S. (1977). *The Discovery of a Norse Settlement in America: Excavations at L'Anse aux Meadows, Newfoundland, 1961–1968*. New York: Columbia University Press.

Instrumentos de torura y pena capital. (2003, May). Exhihition Guide, Museo de la Inquisición, Palacio de la Minería, Centro Histórico, Mexico DF, pp. 1–51.

International Center for Journalists (ICJ). (2003). *Medios y Libertad de Expresión en las Américas*. Washington DC: McCormick Tribune Foundation.

Interview: Gabriel García Márquez. (1983, February). *Playboy Magazine*, Interview, pp. 65–77, 172–178.

Iriarte, Gregorio. (1996, June). La Iglesia y los Medios de Comunicación. *Chasqui*, no. 54, pp. 86–87.

ITU (International Telecommunication Union). (1965). *From Semaphore to Satellite*. Geneva: ITU.

Jackson, Margaret A. (2000). *Notation and Narrative in Moche Iconography*, Cerro Mayal, Perú. Ph.D. Dissertation. Los Angeles, CA: Department of Art History, University of California Los Angeles.

Jackson, Margaret A. (2002). Proto-writing in Moche pottery at Cerro Mayal, Perú. In Helaine Silverman & William H. Isbell (eds.), *Andean Archaeology II*. New York: Plenum Publishers.

Jansen, Maarten. (1997, January/February). Un viaje a la Casa del Sol. *Arqueología Mexicana*, vol. 4, no. 23, pp. 44–49.

Jansen, Sue C. (1991). *The Knot That Binds Power and Knowledge*. New York: Oxford University Press.

Jimenez, Jesús H. (1982). La Ciencia de la Comunicación en América Latina: Un Caso de Dependencia Científica, *Cuadernos del Ticom*, no. 13, Mexico D.F. Mahan, E. (1987). *Broadcasting-State Relations in Latin America: Are Generalizations Valid? Studies in Latin American Popular Culture*, vol. 6, pp. 135–147.

Johnston, Donald H. (ed.). (2003). *Encyclopedia of International Media and Communications*, vols. 1–4. New York: Academic Press.

Jones, Derek. (2001). *Censorship: A World Encyclopedia*, 4 vols. London: Fitzroy Dearborn Publishers.

Jones, R. L. (1996, August 21). Cocaine, pot use soars among young. *The Miami Herald*, pp. 1A, 10A.

Justeson, John S. & Kaufman, Terrence. (1997, July 11). A newly discovered column in the hieroglyph text on La Mojarra Stela 1: A test of the epi-Olmec decipherment. *Science Magazine*, vol. 227, no. 5323, pp. 1–14. Retrieved June 30, 2002, from: www.sciencemag.org/feature/data/justeson.shl

Katz, Elihu & Wedell, George. (1977). *Broadcasting in the Third World: Promise and Performance*. Cambridge, MA: Harvard University Press.

Kaufman, Terrence & Justeson, John. (2001). Epi-Olmec Hieroglyphic Writing and Texts. Paper cited and linked at AncientScripts.com. Retrieved July 20, 2005, from: http://www.ancientscripts.com/epiolmec.html

Kensington Runestone. *Wikipedia*. Retrieved September 26, 2005, from: http://en.wikipedia.org/wiki/Kensington_Runestone

Kettunen, Harri J. (1998, February 7). Relación de las cosas de San Petersburgo: An interview with Dr. Yuri Valentinovich Knorozov. *Revista Xaman*, March, Part I, pp. 1–4 & May, Part II, pp. 1–4. Retrieved April 1, 2004, from: http://www.helsinki.fi/hum/ibero/xaman/articulos/9803/9803_hk.html

Kjaer, Iver. (1994, July). Runes and immigrants in America: The Kensington stone, the World's Columbian Exposition in Chicago and Nordic identity. In *The Nordic Roundtable Papers*, vol. 17. Minneapolis, MN: Center for Nordic Studies, University of Minnesota, pp. 1–37.

Knudson, Jerry W. (1983). Freedom of the press in Latin America: Another view. *Studies in Latin American Popular Culture*, vol. 2, pp. 239–243.

Knudson, Jerry W. (1987). Journalism education's roots in Latin America are traced. *Journalism Educator*, vol. 41, no. 4, pp. 22–24, 33.

Knudson, Jerry W. (1997). Licensing journalists in Latin America: An appraisal. *Journalism & Mass Communication Quarterly*, vol. 73, pp. 878–889.

Knudson, Jerry W. (1998, July). Rebellion in Chiapas: Insurrection by Internet and public relations. *Media, culture, and society*, vol. 20, no. 3, pp. 507–518.

La dimisión de la presidencia [The resignation of the presidency]. (1911, August 14). *El Comercio*, vol. 6, no. 1705, p. 1.

Lafaye, Jacques. (2002). Albores de la Imprenta. In *El libro en España y Portugal y sus posesiones de ultramar (siglos XV y XVI)*. Mexico DF: Fondo de Cultura Económica.

LaFeber, Walter. (1978). *The Panama Canal*. New York: Oxford University Press.

La indagatoria de Santiago Medina [Santiago Medina's questioning]. (1995, August 3). *El Tiempo*, Santafé de Bogotá, Colombia, pp. 8A–10A.

Lanao, Jairo E. (1999). *La Libertad de Prensa y La Ley*. Miami, Florida: Sociedad Interamericana de Prensa.

Landa, Diego De. (1978[1566]). *Yucatan before and after the Conquest [Relación de las Cosas de Yucatan]*. Translated with notes by William Gates. New York: Dover Publications.

Landsverk, Ole G. (1961). *The Kensington Rune-Stone: A Reappraisal of the Circumstances under Which the Stone was Discovered*. Glendale, CA: Church Press.

Landsverk, Ole G. (1969). *Ancient Norse Messages on American Stones*. Glendale, CA: Norseman Press.

Las Sinrazones del Coro Antisamperista [The baseless anti-Samper criticism]. (1995, December 11). *Revista Cromos*, pp. 20–22.

Lavine, T. Z. (1984). *From Socrates to Sartre: The Philosophic Quest*. New York: Bantam Books.

Lavretski, José G. (1991[1974]). *Miranda*. Translated by A. Olivares. Caracas, Venezuela: Biblioteca de la Academia Nacional de la Historia.

Lavrin, Asunción. (1974). Espejo, Francisco Javier Eugenio de Santa Cruz Y (1747–1795). In H. Delpar (ed.), *Encyclopedia of Latin America*. New York: McGraw-Hill, Inc., p. 221.

Leave Colombia in Peace. (1996, June 7). *The Miami Herald*, pp. 22A, 30A.

Lee III, Rensselaer W. (1992). *El Laberinto Blanco: Cocaína y Poder Político [The White Labyrinth: Cocaine and Political Power]*. Bogotá, Colombia: CEREC.

Lent, John. (1977). Formal training program under way in West Indies. *Journalism Educator*, vol. 32, no. 3, pp. 47–49.

León-Portilla, Miguel. (1962). *The Broken Spears: Aztec Accounts of the Conquest of Mexico*. Boston, MA: Beacon Press.

León-Portilla, Miguel. (1986). *Pre-Columbian Literatures of Mexico*. Paperback edition. Norman, OK: University of Oklahoma Press.

León-Portilla, Miguel. (1988). *Mesoamerica 1492, and on the Eve of 1992*. Working Papers no. 1, 1992 Lecture Series. College Park, MD: Department of Spanish and Portuguese, University of Maryland.

León-Portilla, Miguel. (1993, October/November). Los libros de los Mexicas. *Arqueología Mexicana*, vol. 1, no. 4, pp. 37–40.

León-Portilla, Miguel. (1997, January/February). Grandes momentos en la historia de los códices. *Arqueología Mexicana*, vol. 4, no. 23, pp. 16–23.

León-Portilla, Miguel. (2000). *Visión de los vencidos*. Mexico DF: Universidad Nacional Autónoma de México: Coordinación de Humanidades, Programa Editorial.

León-Portilla, Miguel. (2001). *In the Language of Kings: An Anthology of Mesoamerican Literature, Pre-Columbian to the Present*. Paperback edition. New York: W. W. Norton & Co.

León-Portilla, Miguel. (2002). Fray Bernardino de Sahagún y la invención de la antropología. In *Bernardino de Sahagún: Quinientos años de presencia*. Mexico DF: UNAM, pp. 9–27.

Lepidus, Henry. (1928). *The History of Mexican Journalism*. Columbia, MO: University of Missouri, School of Journalism.

Livraga, Jorge A. (n.d.). El códice Porrúa. *Nueva Acrópolis*, Buenos Aires, Argentina. Retrieved September 9, 2005, from: http://www.nueva-acropolis.org.ar/codice_porrua.htm

Lombardi, John H. (1974). Venezuela since 1830. In H. Delpar (ed.), *Encyclopedia of Latin America*. New York: Barnes & Noble Books, pp. 616–619.

Los nombres del narco-casete [The names of the narco-cassette]. (1994, June 27–July 4). *Cambio 16*, no. 55. Santafé de Bogota, Colombia: Espacio de Información General SA, Madrid, Spain, pp. 18–19.

Los nudos de los incas cuentan historias de su mundo. (2005, August 11). Washington DC: Associated Press (AP), p. 1.

Love, Bruce. (1994). *The Paris Codex: Handbook for the Maya Priest*, with introduction by George E. Stuart. Austin, Texas: University of Texas Press.

Luvín-Guzmán, David. (2003). *La Inquisición: El Tribunal del Santo Oficio de la Inquisición en México, Siglos XVI–XIX*. Mexico DF: Muestra del Tribunal del Santo Oficio de la Inquisición.

Lynch, John. (1986). *The Spanish American Revolutions 1808–1826*. Second edition. New York: W. W. Norton & Co.

Maddison, John. (1971). Radio and television in literacy. *Reports & Papers on Mass Communication*, no. 62. Paris: UNESCO, pp. 1–82.

Malvido, Adriana. (1999, April 1). Murió Knorosov, artífice de la clave para descifar glifos mayas. *La Jornada*, UNAM, Mexico City, pp. 1–2. Retrieved March 31, 2005, from: http://www.jornada.unam.mx/1999/abr99/990401/culyuri.html

Mann, Charles C. (2005). *1491: New Revelations of the Americas before Columbus*. New York: Knopf.

Marcos Perez Jimenez dies at 87; General, Venezuelan Dictator. (2001, September 22). *The Washington Post*, based on an AP news wire, p. B06.

MARI (Middle American Research Institute). (2001). *Maya: The Grolier Codex*, 6 images, Tulane University, New Orleans, LA, pp. 1–12. Retrieved March 3, 2002, from: http://www.tulane.edu/~mari/maya.html

Marques de Melo, José. (1976). Brazilian interest grows in communication studies. *Journalism Educator*, vol. 31, no. 1, pp. 46–48.

Marques de Melo, José. (1988). Communication theory and research in Latin America: A preliminary balance of the past twenty-five years. *Media, Culture, and Society*, vol. 10, pp. 405–418.

Marques de Melo, José. (1993, January). La Atracción Fatal de la Universidad y la Industria. *Chasqui*, no. 44, pp. 36–42.

Márquez-Rodiles, Ignacio. (1974). Los libros del México antiguo. In M. Galich (ed.), *El libro precolombino*. La Habana, Cuba: Instituto Cubano del Libro/Casa de las Américas, pp. 17–39.

Martí, José. (1984[1877]). *Las Ruinas Indias*. La Habana, Cuba: Instituto Cubano del Libro.

Martín-Barbero, Jesús. (1985). Comunicación, Pueblo, y Cultura en el Tiempo de las Transnacionales. In M. de Maragas-Spa (ed.), *Sociología de la Comunicación de Masas*. Barcelona, Spain: Editorial Gustavo Gili.

Martín-Barbero, Jesús. (1989, October/November). La Desterritorialización Cultura, Gaceta, no. 4. Bogota, Colombia.

Martínez-Fortún y Foyo, Carlos A. (1986). *Código Martiano, o de ética nacional*. Miami, Florida: Editorial Sibi.

Martínez-Williams, Jaime. (1987/1988). La Prensa en el marco de las leyes. *Cuadernos de la Información*, nos. 4 & 5. Santiago, Chile: Facultad de Comunicaciones/Universidad Católica.

Martos, Luis A. & Camacho, Vicente. (1997, March/April). Acerca del sensacionalismo o el hallazgo en la arqueología. *Actualidades Arqueológicas* (Revista de Estuadiantes de Arqueología de México), no. 11. México DF: UNAM, pp. 1–3.

Mastache, Alba G. (1993, April/May). El México antiguo: Mundo enigmático y complejo. *Arqueología Mexicana*, vol. 1, no. 1, pp. 5–13.

Matus, Alejandra. (1999). *El Libro Negro de la Justicia Chilena [The Black Book of the Chilean Justice]*. Buenos Aires, Argentina: Editorial Planeta Argentina.

Maya-Restrepo, Luz Adriana. (n.d.). *Brujería y reconstrucción étnica de los esclavos del nuevo reino de granada, siglo XVII* and *Magia y resistencia en el nuevo reino de Granada, siglo XVII*. Bogota, Colombia: Biblioteca Luis Angel Arango/Instituto Colombiano de Antropología e Historia (ICANH).

McDowell, Stephen D. (2003). Theory and research in international communication: An historical and institutional account. In Bella Mody (ed.), *International and Development Communication: A 21st Century Perspective*. Thousand Oaks, CA: Sage Publications, pp. 5–18.

Meeren, Marie Vander. (1997). El papel amate: orígen y supervivencia. *Arqueología Mexicana*, vol. 4, no. 23, pp. 70–73.

Mejía-Barquera, Fernando. (2000). Historia Mínima de la Radio Mexicana (1920–1996) [Minimal history of the Mexican radio (1920–1996)]. *Revista Mexicana de la Comunicación*, pp. 1–50. Retrieved August 9, 2001, from: http://www.fundacionbuendia.org.mx.

Memory of the World Register. (1997). Collection of Mexican Codices. *UNESCO*, Webworld, Communication and Information. Retrieved December 10, 2004 from: http://www.unesco.org/webworld/mdm/1997/eng/mexico/mexico_codices.html

Mesa, Darío. (1984). La Vida Política después de Panamá. In *Manual de Historia de Colombia*, vol. 3. Bogotá, Colombia: Instituto Colombiano de Cultura, pp. 83–176.

Mesoamerican Codices in the University Libraries. (2001, January 20). *University at Albany Libraries*. Retrieved February 2, 2001, from: http://library.albany.edu/subject/codices.htm

Mesoamerican relic provides new clues to mysterious ancient writing system. (2004, January 9). *BYU News*, Bringham Young University, UT. Retrieved July 20, 2005, from: http://byunews.byu.edu/release.aspx?story=archive04/Jan/Isthmian

Mexicans for Guatemala. (1954, February 23). *The New York Times*, ProQuest Historical Newspapers database (1857-current file), p. 4.

Mier, Fray Servando Teresa de. (1998[1795–1822]). *The Memoirs of Fray Servando Teresa de Mier*. Translated by Helen Lane. New York: Oxford.

Miller, Mary & Taube, Karle. (1993). *The Gods and Symbols of Ancient Mexico and the Maya*. London: Thames & Hudson.

Miller, Robert R. (ed.). (1975). *Chronicle of Colonial Lima: The Diary of Josephe and Francisco Mugaburu (1640–1697)*. Norman, OK: University of Oklahoma Press.

Mills, Timothy. (1997). *Debunking the Kensington Stone Mystery*, University of Iowa, Ames, IA. Retrieved December 30, 2000, from: http://www.uiowa.edu/~anthro/webcourse/lost/projects97/ken1.htm

Miralles, Ana María. (2000). *Voces Ciudadanas: Una aldea de Periodismo Público*. Medellín, Colombia: Universidad Pontificia Bolivariana.

Mody, Bella & Borrego, Jorge. (1991). Mexicos's Morelos Satellite: Reaching for Autonomy? In Gerald Sussman & John A. Lent (eds.), *Transnational Communications: Wiring the Third World*. Newbury Park, CA: Sage Publications, pp. 150–164.

Montaner, Carlos Alberto. (2001). *Las raíces torcidas de América Latina*. Barcelona, Spain: Plaza & Janés.

Montcreiff-Arrarte, A. (1993, June 13). The cable wave hits Latin America. *The Miami Herald*, p. 1-K.

Montell, Jaime. (2003). *La caída de México-Tenochtitlán*. Mexico DF: Editorial Planeta Mexicana.

Moragas-Spa, Miquel de. (1988). *Semiótica y Comunicación de Masas*. Barcelona, Spain: Ediciones Península.

Moreno, Francisco M. (2004). *Mexico Mutilado: La Raza Maldita*. Mexico DF: Alfaguara.

Muñoz-Fernández, Carmen. (2005, July). Rodriguez Juliá: La formación nacional y las mentiras de la historia. *Ciberletras: Revista de Crítica Literaria y de*

Cultura/Journal of Literary Criticism and Culture, no. 13, Lehman College, CUNY, pp. 1–9. Retrieved September 2, 2005, from: http://www.lehman. cuny.edu/ciberletras/v13/munozfernandez.htm

Musacchio, Humberto. (2005, February 21). Fallece Patricia Rodríguez Ochoa. *Reforma.com*, Mexico City, pp. 1–3. Retrieved May 2, 2005, from: http:// busquedas.gruporeforma.com/utilerias/imdservicios3W.DLL? JsearchformatSP&file=

Myers, Kathleen Ann. (2003). *Neither Saints Nor Sinners: Writing the Lives of Women in Spanish America*. Paperback edition. New York: Oxford University Press.

Nabokov, Peter. (1981). *Indian Running: Native American History and Tradition*. Santa Fe, NM: Ancient City Press.

NCAA puts ban on Indian mascots. (2005, August 5). *SI.com*, *CNN*, pp. 1–3. Retrieved September 20, 2005, from: http://sportsillustrated.cnn.com/2005/ more/08/05/bc.ncaa.indiannicknames.ap/?cnn=yes

Nettleton, G. S. & McAnany, Emile G. (1989, June). Brazil's satellite system. *Telecommunication Policy*, vol. 13, no. 2, pp. 159–166.

Netto, Accioly. (1998). *O Imperio de Papel: Os Bastidores de O Cruzeiro*. Porto Alegre, Brazil: Editora Suliya.

News History Gazette: Extra, Extra. (1997). *The History of News: Exclusive Newseum Report*, vol. 1, no. 1, Arlington, VA, pp. 1–34.

Niño, Jaime. (1982). El satélite SATCOL o el precio de la soberanía sobre la órbita geoestacionaria. In *Las cinco maravillas millonarias de Colombia*. Bogota, Colombia: Editorial Oveja Negra/FESCOL.

Noam, Eli M. (ed.). (1998). *Telecommunications in Latin America*. New York: Oxford University Press.

Northwestern University Library. (2001). *The Paris Codex, a Complete Digital Reproduction*, images 1–22. Retrieved February 1, 2003, from: http://digital. library.northwestern.edu/codex/background.html

Nucete-Sardi, José. (1950[1974]). *Historia del Intento de Don Francisco de Miranda para Efectuar una Revolución en Sur América*. Caracas, Venezuela: Academia Nacional de Historia.

Núñez Cabeza de Vaca, Alvar. (2001[1542]). *Naufragios, Comentarios*. Mexico DF: Editorial Oceáno de México.

Ocampo-López, Javier. (1984). El Proceso Político, Militar, y Social de la Independencia. In *Manual de Historia de Colombia*, vol. 2. Bogota, Colombia: Procultura SA/Instituto Colombianos de Cultura, pp. 495–592.

OEA (OAS, Organización de Estados Americanos). (1967). *Derecho del Espacio*. Second edition. Washington DC: OEA/serv. 1/VIICIJ/89.

Ojeda-Díaz, María de los Angeles. (1997). Los códices del Grupo Borgia. *Arqueología Mexicana*, vol. 4, no. 23, pp. 50–55.

Orozco, Guillermo. (2002). *Historias de la Televisión en América Latina*. Barcelona, Spain: Gedisa Editorial.

Oppenheimer, Andrés. (2000). Fox to give foreign policy a new look. *The Miami Herald*, pp. 1L–2L.

Oppenheimer, Andrés. (2004, July 4). Latin America: Independence heroes revisited in a harsher light. *The Miami Herald*, pp. 1–2. Retrieved July 20, 2005, from: http://www.keepmedia.com/pubs/miamiherald/2004/ 07/04/501443/print/

Oppenheimer, Andrés. (2005, January 23). Bush's crusade to spread democracy could back fire. *The Miami Herald*, p. 14A.

Ortega, Carlos & Romero, Carlos. (1976). *Las Políticas de Comunicación en el Perú*. Paris: Editorial de la Unesco.

Ortega-Torres, Jorge. (1984). *Constitución Política de Colombia [Political Constitution of Colombia]*. Bogotá, DE: Editorial Temis.

Osorio, R. (1985). Propuesta para un Nuevo Orden de la Comunicación en Latinoamérica. In *Nuevo Orden Mundial de la Información*. Bogotá, Colombia: CPB/Editorial Prag.

Otero, Gustavo A. (1946). *El Periodismo en América*. Lima, Perú: Empresa Editora Peruana, SA.

Oudijk, Michel R. (2004, November/December). La escritura zapoteca. *Arqueología Mexicana*, vol. 12, no. 70, pp. 32–35.

Oviedo y Pérez de Tudela, Rocío. (n.d.). *Periodismo Hispanoamericano de Independencia y sus Antecedentes*, Universidad Complutense, Madrid, Spain. Retrieved May 22, 2006, from: http://www.ucm.es/BUCM/revistas/fll/02104547/articulos/ALHI808011067A.pdf

Paleologo, Constantino. (1960). *Brazil en América Latina: una experiencia en periodismo internacional*. Translated by U. S. Gelsi. Rio de Janeiro: Ediçoes O Cruzeiro.

Paredes-Cruz, Joaquín. (1984). *Colombia al Día*. Third edition. Bogotá, Colombia: Plaza y Janés Editores.

Pareja, Reynaldo. (1984). *Historia de la Radio en Colombia*. Bogotá, Colombia: Servicio Colombiano de Comunicación Social.

Parker, D. S. (2000). Parallel Codes: Criminal Law and the "Laws of Honor" in Uruguay and Argentina. Paper presented at the Latin American Studies Association, Law and Justice Panel, Miami, Florida, pp. 1–18.

Parks Canada. (2000, May 12). *L'Anse aux Meadows National Historic Site*. Retrieved January 25, 2002, from: www.parcscanada.gc.ca/parks/newfoundland/anse%5Fmeadows/english/sagas_e.htm

Parry, J. H. (1990[1966]). *The Spanish Seaborne Empire*. Berkeley, CA: University of California Press.

Pasquali, Antonio. (1980). *Comunicación y Cultura de Masas*. Caracas, Venezuela: Monte Avila Editores.

Pasquali, Antonio. (1991). *El Orden Reina: Escritos sobre Comunicaciones*. Caracas, Venezuela: Monte Avila Editores.

Pasquali, Antonio. (1996, March). Comunicación para Cuál Desarollo? *Chasqui*, no. 53, Quito, Ecuador: CIESPAL, pp. 12–15.

Pasquali, Antonio & Vargas-Araya, Armando. (1990). *De la Marginalidad al Rescate: Los Servicios Públicos de Radiodifusión en la América Latina*. San José, Costa Rica: Editorial Universidad Estatal a Distancia.

PDBA (Public Data Base of the Americas). (1999a[1994]). *Constitución de la Nación Argentina*, Georgetown University, Washington DC. Retrieved September 21, 2000, from: http://pdba.georgetown.edu/Constitutions/Argentina/argentina.html

PDBA. (1999b). *Constitución Política de los Estados Unidos Mexicanos* [1917, as amended through 2004], Georgetown University, Washington DC. Retrieved September 21, 2000, from: http://pdba.georgetown.edu/Constitutions/Mexico/mexico.html

PDBA. (1999c). *Constituição da República Federativa do Brasil* [1988, as amended through 2005], Georgetown University, Washington DC. Retrieved July 19, 2003, from: http://pdba.georgetown.edu/Constitutions/Brazil/brazil.html

PDBA. (1999d). *Constitución Política de Colombia* [1991, as amended through 2005], Georgetown University, Washington DC. Retrieved July 19, 2003, from: http://pdba.georgetown.edu/Constitutions/Colombia/colombia.html

PDBA. (1999e). *Constitución Política de Nicaragua* [1987, as amended in 1995 and 2000], Georgetown University, Washington DC. Retrieved July 19, 2003, from: http://pdba.georgetown.edu/Constitutions/Nica/nica.html

Peabody Museum of Archaeology and Ethnography. (1999). *Against the Winds: American Indian Running Traditions.* Cambridge, MA: Harvard University.

Pérez, Joseph. (2005). *The Spanish Inquisition: A History.* New Haven, CT: Yale University Press.

Pierce, Robert N. (1979). *Keeping the Flame: Media and the Government in Latin America.* New York: Hastings House.

Piña-Chan, Román. (1993). *El lenguaje de las piedras: Glífica Olmeca y Zapoteca.* Mexico DF: Fondo de Cultura Económica.

Pinzón, Silvia & Auxillou, Ray. (1998). *The Early History of Belize.* Ambergriscaye, Belize. Retrieved June 1, 2004, from: http://www.ambergriscaye.com/earlyhistory/ Also available in Latin American Network Information Center (LANIC) at http://www.lanic.utexas.edu/la/ca/belize/

Pohl, Mary E. D., Pope, Kevin O., & von Nagy, Christopher. (2002, December 6). Olmec origins of Mesoamerican writing. *Science Magazine*, vol. 298, pp. 1984–1987.

Pombo, Manuel A. & Guerra, José J. (1986[1892]). *Constituciones de Colombia.* Fourth edition, with introduction by Carlos Restrepo-Piedrahita. Bogotá, Colombia: Banco Popular.

Popkin, Richard H. (1999). Bentham, Jeremy. In *Encarta Encyclopedia 99.* Seattle, WA: Microsoft Corporation.

Portuondo, José Antonio. (1977). El Compañero José Martí. In C. Henríquez-Ureña, et al. (eds.), *El Periodismo en José Martí.* La Habana, Cuba: Editorial Orbe, pp. 39–71.

Powell, Jon T. (1985). *International Broadcasting by Satellite.* Westport, CT: Quorum Books.

Powers, Lenita. (2002, December 15). Reno anthropologist is on "earliest writing" find. *Reno Gazette-Journal*, Reno, NV, pp. 1–3. Retrieved December 21, 2002, from: http://www.rgj.com/news/stories/html/2002/12/15/30043.php?sp1=&sp2=&sp3=

Quezada, Oscar. (1988, November). Semiótica y Comunicación Social en el Perú. *Diálogos*, no. 22, pp. 14–27.

Racine, Karen. (2003). *Francisco de Miranda: A Transatlantic Life in the Age of Revolution.* Wilimngton, DE: SR Books.

Ramírez-Almaráz, Jesús G. (1997, January/February). Mesoamérica, Mesoamérica y el norte qué? In *Actualidades Arqueológicas (Revista de Estuadiantes de Arqueología de México)*, no. 10. México DF: UNAM, pp. 1–4.

Real, Michael. (1990, April/June). Comunicación, Publicidad y Deportes. *Chasqui*, no. 34, pp. 57–65.

Red cell in Guatemala. (1952, March 4). *The Washington Post*, p. 12.

Rede Globo de Televisão. (1985, October). No espaço, Un Sinal Bem Brasileiro. In *A Rede Globo Aos 20 anos: Uma História de Suceso*, no. 134. Sao Paulo, Brazil: Globo TV.

Redmond, Jeffery R. (1979). *Viking Hoaxes in North America*. New York: Carlton Press.

Reds in Guatemala honors party paper. (1951, June 23). *The New York Times*, Historical Newspapers database (1857–current file), p. 4.

Reese, L. (1995). Sor Juana Ines de la Cruz. In Ruth Ashby & Deborah Gore-Ohrn (eds.), *Her Story: Women Who Changed the World*. New York: Penguin Books.

Requejo, J. V. (1986). *El periodismo en el Perú*. First edition. Lima, Peru: Centro de Documentación e Información Andina.

Restrepo, Javier D. (1990). Reporteros en un País en crisis [reporters in a country on crisis]. In *Primer Seminario Internacional de Periodismo*. Medellín, Colombia: Imprenta Municipal.

Restrepo-Piedrahita, C. (1986). Constituyentes y Constitucionalistas Colombianos. In M. A. Pombo & J. J. Guerra (eds.), *Constituciones de Colombia*, vol. 1. Bogotá, Colombia: Banco Popular, pp. 9–191.

Reyes, Gerardo. (2003). *Los Dueños de América Latina*. Mexico DF: Ediciones B/Grupo Zeta.

Riding, Alan. (1982, August 28). A stolen relic is a problem for Mexicans. *The New York Times*, Sunday, Late City Final edition, pp. 1–2. In Lexis-Nexis expanded academic universe, document 32 of 40. Retrieved September 3, 1999, from: http://web.lexis-lexis.com/univers...5=d8c21d0ce89a5f62bbb6d0ae83191a76

Riding, Alan. (1995, March 12). Museums and the spoils of war. *The New York Times*, Sunday, sec. 4, p. 3.

Rives-Sánchez, Roberto. (2000). *La constitución mexicana hacia el siglo XXI*. Mexico DF: Plaza y Valdés Editores SA de CV.

Robertson, William S. (1909). *Francisco de Miranda and the Revolutionizing of Spanish America*. Washington DC: Government Printing Office.

Robinson, Andrew. (2002). *Lost Languages: The Enigma of the World's Undeciphered Scripts*. New York: McGraw-Hill, Inc.

Roca, O. (1976, January/February). El Sesquicentenario de la Independencia de Bolivia. *Revista Casa de las Américas*, vol. 16, no. 94, pp. 92–103.

Rock, David. (1987). *Argentina 1516-1987: From Spanish Colonization to Alfonsin*. Berkeley, CA: University of California Press.

Rodríguez-Castelo, Hernán. (1996, June). Espejo, Periodista Esencial. *Chasqui: Revista Latinoamericana de la Comunicación*, no. 54, pp. 83–85.

Rodríguez de Alonso, Josefina. (1982). *Miranda y sus Circunstancias*. Caracas, Venezuela: Biblioteca de la Academia Nacional de Historia.

Rodríguez-Díaz, María del Rosario. (1997). *El Destino Manifiesto en el Discurso Político Norteamericano (1776–1849)*. Michoacán, Morelia, México: Universidad Michoacana de San Nicolás de Hidalgo.

Rodríguez-Ochoa, Patricia, Marín, Edgar G., & Cerda-González, Miriam. (eds.). (1999). *Compendio Xcaret de la escritura jeroglífica maya decifrada por Yuri V. Knorosov*. Chetumal, Mexico: Universidad de Quintan Roo, Promotora Xcaret-Vía Láctea-Sextante.

Rodríguez-Revollar, Richard. (2004, July). *De la imprenta a Internet: Una mirada rápida a la aparición de los noticieros, Sala de Prensa*, vol. 3, no. 69, year 6. Retrieved May 21, 2006, from: http://www.saladeprensa.org/art554.htm

Rogers, Everett M. (1997). *A History of Communication Study*. New York: The Free Press.

Rogers, Everett M. & Chaffee, Steven H. (1994, December). Communication and journalism from "Daddy" Bleyer to Wilbur Schramm: A palimpsest. *Journalism Monographs*, no. 148.

Romano, Vicente. (1987). *Sobre Prensa, Periodismo y Comunicación*. Madrid, Spain: Alfaguara.

Rosny, Léon de. (1887). *Codex Peresianus: Manuscrit hiératique des anciens Indiens de l'Amerique Centrale conservé à la Biblothèque Nationale de Paris*. Paris: Société Americaine.

Ross, Stanley R. (ed.). (1965). *Fuentes de la Historia Contemporánea de México: Periódicos y Revistas*. Mexico DF: Unión Gráfica SA.

Roth, Cecil. (1996[1964]). *The Spanish Inquisition*. New York: W. W. Norton & Co.

Ruge, Tiahoga & Herrera, Eduardo. (2000). *El desciframiento de la escritura Maya [The decipherment of the Maya script]*, with a script by Olaga Cáceres. Mexico City: Conaculta.

Salas de León, Elia. (2001). *Historiografía de Tlaxcala*, Universidad Abierta, San Luis Potosí, SLP. Retrieved December 23, 2005, from: http://www.universidadabierta.edu.mx/Biblio/SalasElia_HistoriografiaTlaxcala.htm

Salcedo-Bastardo, José L. (1981). *Crucible of Americanism*. Caracas, Venezuela: Cuadernos Lagoven.

Salinas, Raquel. (1989, June). No es fácil romper la dependencia: El caso de las noticias. *Diálogos de la Comunicación*, no. 24, Lima, Perú.

Salwen, Michael B. (1994). *Radio and Television in Cuba: The Pre-Castro Era*. Ames, IA: Iowa State University.

Salwen, Michael B. (1997). Broadcasting to Latin America: Reconciling industry–government functions in the pre-voice of America Era. *Historical Journal of Film, Radio, and Television*, vol. 17, no. 1, pp. 67–89.

Salwen, Michael B. & Garrison, Bruce. (1991). *Latin American Journalism*. Hillsdale, NJ: Lawrence Erlbaum Associates, Publishers.

Salwen, Michael B., Garrison, Bruce, & Buckman, Robert T. (1991). Latin American and the Caribbean. In John C. Merrill (ed.), *Global Journalism*. Second edition. New York: Longman, pp. 267–310.

Samper-Pizano, Daniel. (1983). *Llévate Esos Payasos*. Bogotá, Colombia: Editorial Pluma.

Samper-Pizano, Daniel. (1996). The mote in thy brother's eye.... *Hemisphere*, vol. 7, no. 1, pp. 4–5.

Sánchez i Cervelló, Josep. (1995). *La revolución portuguesa y su influencia en la transición española (1961–1976)*. Madrid, Spain: Editorial Nerea.

Santos, Enrique. (1986). Tecnología, Imperialismo, y Educación. In *Comunicación y Cultura*, no. 3. Mexico DF: Universidad Autónoma Metropolitana-Xochimilco.

Sarmiento, Domingo F. (1951[1847]). In A. P. Castro (ed.), *Discurso sobre San Martín y Bolívar*, Series no. 4, no. 3. Buenos Aires, Argentina: Museo Histórico Sarmiento/Instituto Histórico de Francia.

Satellite Communications. (1992, September). *The Journal of ITU*, Secretaria de Transportes y Comunicaciones (SCT), El Sistema de Comunicaciones por Satélite Morelos, Geneva, Switzerland.

Satellite to Relay Olympic Games, Exploded (1968, September 19). *New York Times*, p. 28.

Saunders, Nicholas J. (2005, March/April). El jaguar en el México prehispánico. *Arqueología Mexicana*, vol. 12, no. 72, pp. 18–27.

Saxon State and University Library Dresden [Sachsische Landesbibliothek – Staats und Universitatsbibliothek Dresden]. (2001). *Dresden Codex, Commentary in English*, pp. 1–2. Retrieved December 9, 2001, from: http://www.tu-dresden.de/slub/proj/maya/mayaeng.html

Schele, Linda & Freidel, David. (1990). *A Forest of Kings: The Untold Story of the Ancient Maya*. New York: William Morrow.

Schelesinger, Arthur. M., Jr. (ed.). (1993). *The Almanac of American History*. New York: Barnes & Noble Books.

Schmucler, H. (1983). *Los satélites en la expansión tranasnacional: el caso de América Latina*. Mexico DF: ILET.

Schmucler, H. (1993). Veinticinco Años de Satélites Artificiales. In *Chasqui*, no. 9. Mexico DF, pp. 1–60.

Schuster, Angela M. H. (1997, July 29). Epi-Olmec decipherment. *Archaeology* (online news), Archeological Institute of America, p. 1.

Schuster, Angela M. H. (1999, January/February). Redating the Madrid Codex. *Archaeology* (newsbriefs), vol. 52, no. 1, pp. 1–2.

SDSU President Stephen Weber announces decision on use of Aztecs and Montezuma. (2000, November 16). *Marketing and Communications*, San Diego State University, San Diego, CA. Retrieved September 2, 2002, from: http://advancement.sdsu.edu/marcomm/Spring2002News/ReleasesONLY/mascotdec.html

Se Destapan los Candidatos [Candidates in the open]. (1995, October 31–November 7). *Semana*. Santafé de Bogotá, Colombia: Publicaciones Semana SA, pp. 39–44.

Seigenthaler, John. (1991, February). The first amendment: The first 200 years. *Presstime*, pp. 24–30.

SELA (Sistema Económino Latinoamericano). (1987). *El Reto Informático y sus Implicaciones sobre América Latina*, compiled by Edson Fregni. Buenos Aires, Argentina: Ediciones La Flor.

Severin, Werner J. & Tankard, James W., Jr. (2001). *Communication Theories*. New York: Longman, pp. 329–354.

Sharer, Robert J. (1996). *Daily Life in Maya Civilization*. Westport, CT: Greenwood Press.

SIDBOL (Servicio de Información y Documentación de Bolivia). (1987, June). *Cronología Económico-Política*. La Paz, Bolivia/Bogotá, Colombia: Medin-formática, pp. 1–15.

Siebert, Detlef. (2002, September 18). British bombing strategy in World War Two. *BBC News*, London. Retrieved December 3, 2004, from: http://www.bbc.co.uk/history/war/wwtwo/area_bombing_05.shtml

Silva, Armando. (1988, November). La Semiótica y la Comunicación Social Colombia. *Diálogos*, no. 22, pp. 28–37.

Silva, Luis E. (1987/1988). Libertad de expresión periodística y desinformación, *Cuadernos de Información*, nos. 4 & 5, Facultad de Comunicación/ Universidad Católica de Chile, pp. 1–14.

Silva, Renán. (2002). *Los Ilustrados de Nueva Granada (1760-1808)*. Medellín, Colombia: Fondo Editorial/Universidad EAFIT.

Simpson-Grinberg, Máximo. (1989). *Comunicación Alternativa y Cambio Social*. Second edition. Tlahuapan, Mexico: Premia Editores.

Sinclair, John. (1999). *Latin American Television: A Global View*. New York: Oxford University Press.

Singletary, Otis A. (1960). *The Mexican War*. Chicago, IL: The University of Chicago Press.

Skidmore, Thomas E. & Smith, Peter H. (1992). *Modern Latin America*. New York: Oxford University Press.

Smith, Peter H. (1996). *Talons of the Eagle: Dynamics of U.S.-Latin American Relations*. New York: Oxford Press.

Smithsonian Institution. (2000). *Vikings: The North Atlantic Saga*. Exhibition, April 29–August 13, National Museum of Natural History, Washington DC. Retrieved December 15, 2001, from: http://www.mnh.si.edu/vikings/start.html

Socolow, Susan M. (2000). *The Women of Colonial Latin America: New Approaches to the Americas*. Cambridge, UK: Cambridge University Press.

Solanes-Carraro, María del Carmen. (1993, April/May). El mundo teotihuacano. *Arqueología Mexicana*, vol. 1, no. 1, pp. 49–52.

Soruco, Gonzalo. (1988). The cocaine paranoia: Another peril to freedom of the press in Bolivia. In Andrew MacFarlane & Robert Henderson (eds.), *Encounter'88*. London, Ontario: University of Western Ontario.

Soruco, Gonzalo & Ferreira, Leonardo. (1995). Latin America and the Caribbean. In J. C. Merrill (ed.), *Global Journalism*. Third edition. New York: Longman, pp. 329–354.

Sotelo-Santos, Laura E. (1997, January/February). Los códices Mayas. *Arqueología Mexicana*, vol. 4, no. 23, pp. 34–43.

Souki-Oliveira, Omar. (1992, May 21–25). New Media and Information Technologies: For Freedom or Dependency? Paper presented at the International Communication Association (ICA) Conference, Miami, Florida.

Staines-Cicero, Leticia. (1995, November/December). Los murales Mayas del Posclásico. *Arqueología Mexicana*, vol. 3, no. 16, pp. 56–61.

Stannard, David E. (1992a, October 19). *The Nation*, pp. 430–434. Retrieved April 1, 2004, from: *Columbus and the Age of Discovery*, CIRS, Helen A. Ganser Library, Millersville, PA. http://muweb.millersvile,edu/~columbus/data/art/STANN-01.ART

Stannard, David E. (1992b). *American Holocaust: Columbus and the Conquest of the New World*. New York: Oxford University Press.

Stapley, Monica. (2000). Fragments of thought: The Olmec script. *Origins of Writing*, pp. 1–9. Retrieved August 31, 2002, from: http://www.usu.edu/anthro/origins_of_writing/main.html

Stop this Inquisition. (1995, November 14). *The Miami Herald*, p. 23A.

Straubhaar, Joseph D. (1984, April). Brazilian television: The decline of American influence. *Communication Research*, vol. 11, no. 2, pp. 221–240.

Straubhaar, Joseph D. (1998). Brazil. In Alan B. Albarran & Sylvia M. Chan-Olmstead (eds.), *Global Media Economics*. Ames, IA: Iowa State University Press, pp. 65–80.

Stuart, David. (1998, July). "The arrival of strangers": Teotihuacan and Tollan in Classic Maya history. *PARI Newsletter*, no. 25. Retrieved January 4, 2000, from: http://www.mesoweb.com/pari/news/archive/25/strangers/strangers.html

Stuart, David. (1999, November/December). The Maya finally speak. *Discovering Archeology*. Retrieved December 20, 1999, from: www.dicoveringarcheology.com/0699toc/6cover8-maya.shtml

Sullivan, William. (1996). *The Secret of the Incas*. New York: Three Rivers Press.

Su majestad el Rey Don Juan Carlos habla para Hola! con ocasión del año 1992. (1992, January). *Revista Hola! Special edition: 1492–1992*. Madrid, Spain: Hauser y Menet, pp. 8–14.

Szászdi, A. (1974). Alfaro, [José] Eloy (1842–1912). In H. Delpar (ed.), *Encyclopedia of Latin America*. New York: McGraw-Hill, Inc., pp. 17–18.

Tamayo-Herrera, José. (1985). *Nuevo Compendio de Historia del Perú*. Lima, Peru: Editorial Lumen.

Tarragó, Rafael E. (1996, November/December). The presses roll in colonial times. In *Americas*, vol. 48, no. 6. Washington DC: Organization of American States, pp. 22–27.

Taube, Karl A. (2001, March/April). La escritura teotihuacana. *Arqueología Mexicana*, vol. 8, no. 48, pp. 58–63.

Téllez, Hernando. (1974). *Cincuenta Años de Radiodifusión en Colombia*. Bogotá, Colombia: Editorial Bedout.

Tello, M. (1989). La Historia Efectiva de una Utopia: Políticas y Planificación de la Comunicación en América Latina. *Diálogos*, no. 24, pp. 1–13. Retrieved from: http://www.felafacs.org/dialogos-24?PHPSESSID=06324e6ace24555ec35e78c2e69cbf9

The Sagas of Icelanders: A Selection. (2000). With a preface by Jane Smiley. New York: Penguin Books.

The United Fruit Historical Society. (2001). *Biographies: Jacobo Arbenz (1913–1971)*, The UFCO, Inc., California, pp. 1–3. Retrieved November 3, 2004, from: http://unitedfruit.org/arbenz.html

Thomas, David H. (1999). *Exploring Ancient Native America: An Archaeological Guide*. New York: Routledge.

Thompson, John E. (1975). The Grolier Codex. In John A. Graham (ed.), *Studies in Ancient America II*, no. 27. Berkeley, CA: University of California, pp. 1–9.

Timeline: Guatemala, a chronology of key events. (2004, September 23). *BBC News*, World edition, pp. 1–4. Retrieved November 5, 2004, from: http://news.bbc.co.uk/2/hi/americas/country_profiles/1215811.stm

Timmons, Wilbert H. (1996). *Morelos: Sacerdote, Soldado y Estadista*. Mexico DF: Fondo de Cultura Económica.

Topical Currents, with Joseph Cooper. (2005, August 31). *Featuring Herald Editorial Contributor Edward Wasserman*, WLRN, Miami, Florida.

Toussaint, Florence. (1988, October). La Prensa y Don Porfirio. *Revista Mexicana de la Comunicación*. Retrieved July 11, 2000, from: http://www.fundacionbuendia.org.mx/seminario/porfirio.html

Tradition of Dr. Linda Schele lives on with Maya meetings. (1999, March 2). *Office of Public Affairs University of Texas*, Autin, Texas. Retrieved November 17, 2004, from: http://www.utexas.edu/opa/news/99newsreleases/nr_199903/nr_maya990302.html

Trenti-Rocamora, José L. (1948). *La Cultura en Buenos Aires hasta 1810*. Buenos Aires, Argentina: Universidad de Buenos Aires.

Tuck, Jim. (2000). The artist as activist: David Alfaro Siqueiros (1896–1974). *Mexico Connect*, Mexico DF, pp. 1–2. Retrieved June 2, 2005, from: http://www.mexconnect.com/mex_/history/Jtuck/Jtsiqueiros.html

Ulibarri, E. (1988). *Periodismo para Nuestro Tiempo [Journalism for Our Times]*. San Jose, Costa Rica: Libro Libre.

Uribe-Vargas, Diego. (1977). *Las Constituciones de Colombia [Constitutions of Colombia]*, vol. 1. Madrid, Spain: Ediciones Cultura Hispánica.

U.S. Aides in Argentina Believe Europeans are best customers. (1969, February 23). *New York Times*, p. 52.

Vaca, Cabeza de. (1992). *A Film Directed by Nicolás Echevarría*. Los Angeles, CA: New Horizons Home Video.

Vela, Enrique. (1993, April/May). Los murales de Teotihuacán. *Arqueología Mexicana*, vol. 1, no. 1, p. 20.

Velázquez-Yebra, Patricia. (1999, October 30). Knorosov, el primero en descifrar la escritura maya. *El Universal*, Mexico DF, pp. 1–2. Retrieved April 2, 2005, from: http://www.eluniversal.com.mx/pls/impreso/noticia_busqueda.html?id_nota=1881&tabla=cult...

Velázquez-Yebra, Patricia. (2000, June 13). Rescatan en video, la obra del linguista ruso Yuri Knórosov. *El Universal*, Mexico DF, pp. 1–2. Retrieved September 11, 2004, from: http://www.eluniversal.com.mx/pls/impreso/noticia_busqueda.html?id_nota=4607&tabla=c...

Velasco-Márquez, Jesús. (1995). Manifest destiny: A Mexican viewpoint in the war with the United States: U.S. Mexican war, a prelude to war. *PBS*, Washington DC, pp. 1–7. Retrieved June 30, 2006, from: http://www.pbs.org/kera/usmexicanwar/prelude/md_a_mexican_viewpoint.html

Vilches, Lorenzo. (1988). Algo Más que Buena Vecindad entre Semiótica y Comunicación de Masas. *Diálogos*, no. 22, pp. 38–46.

Villacorta, Carlos A. & Villacorta, J. Antonio. (1930). *Códices Mayas*. Ciudad de Guatemala, Guatemala: Tipografía Nacional.

Villamarín-Carrascal, José. (2006). Los primeros periódicos y la prensa insurgente en América Latina. *Sala de Prensa*, vol. 3, no. 87, year 6, pp. 1–6. Retrieved January 29, 2006, from: http://www.saladeprensa.org/art655.htm

Villanueva-Castillo, Carlos R. (1991, July 27). Códices indígenas 500 años después. *Por Esto!* Merida, Yucatan, Mexico. Retrieved April 4, 2004, from: http://muweb.millersville.edu/~columbus/data/art/VILLA-25.ART

Villegas, Jorge & Yunis, José. (1978). *La Guerra de los Mil Dias*. Bogota, Colombia: Carlos Valencia Editores.

Verzura, José Abel. (1985[1923]). *Constitución de la Provincia de Córdoba [Constitution of the Cordoba Province]*. Buenos Aires, Argentina: Ediciones DePalma.

Von Hagen, Victor W. (ed.). (1959). *The Incas of Pedro de Cieza de León*. Traducido por Harriet de Onis. Norman, OK: University of Oklahoma Press.

Wade, Richard C. (1993). Expanding resources (1901–1945). In A. M. Schlesinger Jr. (ed.), *The Almanac of American History*. New York: Barnes & Noble Books, pp. 400–405.

Wahlgren, Erik. (1958). *The Kensington Rune-Stone: A Mystery Solved*. Madison, WI: University of Wisconsin Press.

Wahlgren, Erik (1986). *The Vikings and America*. New York: Thames & Hudson.

Waisbord, Silvio. (1998). Argentina. In A. B. Albarran & S. M. Chan-Olmstead (eds.), *Global Media Economics*. Ames, IA: Iowa State University Press, pp. 81–96.

Ward, Matthew. (2004). *Washington Unmakes Guatemala*, The Council on Hemispheric Affairs, Washington DC, pp. 1–10. Retrieved November 5, 2004, from: http://www.coha.org/NEW_PRESS_RELEASES/Matt%20Ward/MW_Appendix_A.htm

White, G. Edward. (1993). *Justice Oliver Wendell Holmes: Law and the Inner Self*. New York: Oxford University Press.

White, R. A. (1989). *The Public Sphere as an Integrating concept for Development Communication*. Rome, Italy: Center for Interdisciplinary Study of Communications, The Gregorian University.

Whitman, Walt. (1997[1855]). *Leaves of Grass: The First Edition, 1855*. New York: Barnes & Noble Books.

Whittaker, Gordon. (2002). The Zapotec writing system. In V. Reifler-Bricker (ed.), *Handbook of Middle American Indians* (Supplement: *Epigraphy*, vol. 5, pp. 5–19). Austin, TX: University of Texas Press.

Williams, Sara L. (1929). *Twenty Years of Education for Journalism*. Columbia, MO: E.W. Stephens Publishing Co.

Williford, Miriam. (1980). *Jeremy Bentham on Spanish America*. Baton Rouge, LA: Louisiana State University Press.

Winn, Peter. (1999). *Americas: The changing Face of Latin American and the Caribbean*. Updated edition. Berkeley, CA: The University of California Press.

Wolfram, Dietrich. (1943). *Belgrano y San Martín: la revolución en Sudamérica*. Translated by E. M. Blanco. Santiago, Chile: Ediciones Ercilla.

Xcaret dictionary of Mayan hieroglyphics. (1997). *Revista Xcaret*, vol. 1, no. 4. Cancún, Mexico: Comercializador Xcaret, pp. 2–3.

Zelizer, Barbie. (2004). *Taking Journalism Seriously*. Thousand Oaks, CA: Sage Publications.

Index

About the Author

LEONARDO FERREIRA is Associate Dean and Director of Graduate Studies at the University of Miami and a consultant to the Inter-American Press Association, the Grupo de Diarios America, and BBC Latin America.